Big Data and Competition Law

Recent studies on competition law and digital markets reveal that accumulating personal information through data collection and acquisition methods benefits consumers considerably. Free of charge, fast and personalised services and products are offered to consumers online. Collected data is now an indispensable part of online businesses to the point that a new economy, a data-driven sector, has emerged. Many markets such as the social network, search engine, online advertising and e-commerce are regarded as data-driven markets in which the utilisation of Big Data is a requisite for the success of operations. However, the accumulation and use of data brings competition law concerns as they contribute to market power in the online world, resulting in a few technology giants gaining unprecedented market power due to the Big Data accumulation, indirect network effects and the creation of online ecosystems. As technology giants have billions of consumers worldwide, data-driven markets are truly global. In these data-driven markets, technology giants abuse their dominant positions, but existing competition law tools seem ineffective in addressing market power and assessing abusive behaviour related to Big Data. This book argues that a novel approach to the data-driven sector must be developed through the application of competition law rules to address this. It argues that current and potential conflicts can be mitigated by extending the competition law assessment beyond the current competition law tools to offer a modernised and unified approach to the Big Data–related competition issues. Promoting new legal tests for addressing the market power of technology giants and assessing abusive behaviour in data-driven markets, this book advocates for cooperation between competition and data protection authorities. It will be of interest to students, academics and practitioners with an interest in competition law and data protection.

Alptekin Koksal is a lecturer in law at Istanbul Medeniyet University School of Law. He studied law at the University of Ankara and holds LL.M. and Ph.D. in law degrees from the University of Exeter.

Routledge Research in Competition Law

The Internationalisation of Competition Rules
Brendan J. Sweeney

Antitrust Federalism in the EU and the US
Firat Cengiz

Competition and Regulation in the Airline Industry
Puppets in Chaos
Steven Truxal

Merger Control in Post-Communist Countries
EC Merger Regulation in Small Market Economies
Jurgita Malinauskaite

Merger Control in Europe
The Gap in the ECMR and National Merger Legislations
Ioannis Kokkoris

Harmonising Regulatory and Antitrust Regimes for International Air Transport
Jan Walulik

Collective Redress and EU Competition Law
Eda Sahin

Competition Policy and Network Industries
Structural Separation in the Telecommunications Sector
Pierluigi Congedo

Competition Laws, National Interests and International Relations
Ko Unoki

For more information about this series, please visit: www.routledge.com

Big Data and Competition Law
Market Power Assessment in the
Data-Driven Economy

Alptekin Koksal

LONDON AND NEW YORK

First published 2024
by Routledge
4 Park Square, Milton Park, Abingdon, Oxon OX14 4RN

and by Routledge
605 Third Avenue, New York, NY 10158

Routledge is an imprint of the Taylor & Francis Group, an informa business

© 2024 Alptekin Koksal

The right of Alptekin Koksal to be identified as author of this work has been asserted in accordance with sections 77 and 78 of the Copyright, Designs and Patents Act 1988.

All rights reserved. No part of this book may be reprinted or reproduced or utilised in any form or by any electronic, mechanical, or other means, now known or hereafter invented, including photocopying and recording, or in any information storage or retrieval system, without permission in writing from the publishers.

Trademark notice: Product or corporate names may be trademarks or registered trademarks, and are used only for identification and explanation without intent to infringe.

British Library Cataloguing-in-Publication Data
A catalogue record for this book is available from the British Library

ISBN: 978-1-032-60143-4 (hbk)
ISBN: 978-1-032-60375-9 (pbk)
ISBN: 978-1-003-45879-1 (ebk)

DOI: 10.4324/9781003458791

Typeset in Times New Roman
by Apex CoVantage, LLC

Contents

Preface   viii

1 A New Data-Driven Economy   1
   1.1 Introduction 1
   1.2 A Market Power Problem 6

2 Big Data Challenges for Competition Law   8
   2.1 Definition of Big Data for Competition Law 8
      2.1.1 Characteristics of Big Data 9
      2.1.2 Creation of the Big Data Value Chain 11
      2.1.3 The Competitive Significance of Big Data 15
   2.2 Major Issues in Data-Driven Markets 21
      2.2.1 Monopolisation in Markets 21
      2.2.2 Assessment of Market Power 26
      2.2.3 Anti-Competitive Conduct 29
   2.3 Concluding Remarks 34

3 Data-Driven Market Structures and Monopolisation   37
   3.1 Data-Driven Markets 37
      3.1.1 Digitalised Traditional Markets 38
      3.1.2 Newly Emerged Markets 39
      3.1.3 Online Advertising as a Market Itself 43
   3.2 Market Characteristics of Data-Driven Markets 45
      3.2.1 Multi-Sided Nature 45
      3.2.2 Indirect Network Externalities 49
      3.2.3 Accumulation of Big Data 54
   3.3 Monopolisation 58
      3.3.1 Winner Takes All 58
      3.3.2 Moligopolists 60
      3.3.3 Concerns over Data-opolies 61

3.4 Data-Driven Acquisitions 65
  3.4.1 Concerns Related to Data-Driven Acquisitions 65
  3.4.2 New Global Value Chains 66
  3.4.3 Conglomerate Effects 68
3.5 Concluding Remarks 73

4 Assessment of Data-Related Market Power in Data-Driven Markets   75
4.1 Market Definition 75
4.2 Relevant Product Market Failure in the Data-Driven Economy 78
  4.2.1 Market Segmentation 80
  4.2.2 Non-horizontal Effects 83
  4.2.3 Functionality Test 90
  4.2.4 Potential Data Merging 92
  4.2.5 Overlaps Between Market Segments 94
4.3 Ineffective Tools to Assess Market Power in the Data-Driven Economy 99
  4.3.1 Substitutability and Zero-Price Problem 100
  4.3.2 Digital Ecosystems and Market Shares Problem 105
4.4 New Tests for Market Power Assessment in the Data-Driven Economy 109
  4.4.1 Dynamic Nature of the New Economy 110
  4.4.2 Innovative Character of the New Economy 111
  4.4.3 Big Data as a Misleading Factor 114
  4.4.4 Creation of Online Ecosystems 118
  4.4.5 Multi-Sided Market Confusion 121
4.5 Concluding Remarks 124

5 Abusive Behaviour in Data-Driven Markets   126
5.1 Abuse Through Leveraging Market Power 126
  5.1.1 Self-Preferencing 128
  5.1.2 Google's Abuse and Theory of Harms 133
  5.1.3 "Frenemy" Situation in Multi-Sided Markets 141
5.2 Abuse Through Access to Data 146
  5.2.1 Refusal to Access and Discriminatory Access 147
  5.2.2 Applicability of Essential Facilities Doctrine 152
  5.2.3 Mandatory Data Sharing as a Remedy 160
  5.2.4 Data Portability as an Alternate Remedy 165

5.3 Abuse Through Data Privacy 169
　5.3.1 A Novel Abuse 169
　5.3.2 The Bundeskartellamt's Facebook Investigation 171
　5.3.3 Discussion of Privacy Policies Under Article 102 of the TFEU 177
　5.3.4 Italian Competition Authority's Facebook Investigation 181
5.4 Applying Article 102 of the TFEU to Big Data–Related Abuses 183

6　The Way Forward　　　　　　　　　　　　　　185
6.1 Ways to Approach the Big Data Issue From a Competition Law Perspective 185
　6.1.1 Non-interventionist Approach 185
　6.1.2 Broadening Competition Law's Goals 190
　6.1.3 Sector-Specific Regulation 196
　6.1.4 Optimising the Current Legal Framework 200
6.2 Benchmarks for Intervention 203
　6.2.1 Necessity 203
　6.2.2 Proportionality 204
　6.2.3 Fostering Innovation 205
6.3 New Legal Tests to Apply 207
　6.3.1 Intermediation-Regulatory Powers 208
　6.3.2 Big Data as a Source of Market Power 211
　6.3.3 Novel Abusive Behaviour Related to Big Data 214
　6.3.4 Application 219
6.4 Concluding Remarks 223

7　Epilogue　　　　　　　　　　　　　　　　　　225

Bibliography　　　　　　　　　　　　　　　　　*228*
Index　　　　　　　　　　　　　　　　　　　　*250*

Preface

Big Data–related competition law infringements are among the most controversial topics in the competition law world. This controversial issue brings considerable trouble to the application of competition law tools in Europe. The accumulation and use of data bring competition law concerns as they contribute to market power in the online world, resulting in a few technology giants gaining unprecedented market power due to the Big Data accumulation, indirect network effects and the creation of online ecosystems. As technology giants have billions of consumers worldwide, data-driven markets are truly global. In these data-driven markets, technology giants abuse their dominant positions, but existing competition law tools seem ineffective in addressing market power and assessing abusive behaviour related to Big Data. Sector-specific regulation seems to be the most favoured step to address the competition law problems in the data-driven sector.

In order to address problems specific to the area of law, this work resulted from a study engaged for the PhD in Law degree at the University of Exeter under the supervision of Professor Andrea Lista, whose invaluable suggestions and kindness helped me mould this book in a more coherent way. As my journey started back at the beginning of 2018, many developments occurred in the area of law. Now in 2023, the scene looks completely different and relatively more established in terms of addressing the problems stemming from Big Data usage in the data-driven sector. The European Commission has already set an approach to tackle the issues pertaining to the data-driven sector. Thus, most studies took shape around the strategy of the EU. However, discussions on alternative approaches have somehow remained weak up to this point.

Therefore, this book argues that a novel approach to the data-driven sector must be developed through the application of competition law rules to address the problem instead of an *ex-ante* regulation. The book argues that current and potential conflicts can be mitigated by extending the competition law assessment beyond the current competition law tools to offer a modernised and unified approach to Big Data–related competition issues. Promoting new legal tests for addressing the market power of technology giants and assessing abusive behaviour in data-driven markets, this book advocates for cooperation between competition and data protection authorities. In this sense, this book expertly introduces all the relevant terms and literature regarding Big Data and competition law, offering postgraduate students, lawyers, courts and those interested in the area of law an accessible and coherent study on this important topic of European competition law. I hope this book will be helpful to anyone who wishes to delve deeper into the area of law, where comprehensive studies are needed for the evolution of competition law. In order words, it will interest students, academics and practitioners interested in competition law and data protection.

I want to express my gratitude to numerous people to whom I am greatly indebted. First, I am grateful to my supervisors, Professors Andrea Lista and Mihail Danov, for their support during my doctorate journey. In the first year, they patiently helped me gain focus and develop ideas for my work. I am indebted to my supervisor, Professor Andrea Lista of the University of Southampton, for all his patience, invaluable intellectual and moral support and all the discussions, advice and expertise during my PhD years that ignited new thoughts to be enshrined in this book. None of this would have been possible without his support and encouragement.

Second, I would like to record my thanks to Professor Mihail Danov of the University of Exeter, a man of vast intellect and talent from whom I have learned much regarding the topic of my study and the science of law. We have had many helpful and thoughtful discussions on my research, including competition law and policy in general. Third, I also would like to thank Dr Matthew Cole of the University of Exeter; he helped me throughout my journey at the University of Exeter. I am really proud to be a part of the University of Exeter Law School. These intellectual academics contributed to my progression and development as a relatively successful academic.

Special thanks go to Recep Gunduz, a former head of the department of the third chamber of the Turkish Competition Authority, from whose expertise in the specific area of law I have learned a lot. His invaluable suggestions, kindness and friendship helped me shape this book in a more coherent way. Also, special thanks to Siobhán Poole of Taylor & Francis, who followed and supported this book from the beginning until the end of its process to fruition, for her patience and courtesy. I also would like to thank Sanjo Joseph Puthumana for his support, work and assistance in publishing this book.

Lastly, I would like to thank my family and friends for their motivation and accompany. My deepest gratitude goes to these lovely people who were with me all the time. I thank my parents, Güzen and Ismail Koksal, for their motivation during the most challenging times. Finally, and most importantly, I thank my wife, Seda, for her boundless support, encouragement and love from the first day to the very last. I cannot imagine this work without her; I would not have written this book without her. She was always next to me when I failed and needed a shoulder to lean on. She is my strength. I have no words to express my gratitude to them; I would not be at this point without them.

Dr Alptekin Koksal
Istanbul, 20 May 2023

1 A New Data-Driven Economy

1.1 Introduction

The fourth industrial revolution is underway, and the global economy is now in the process of transformation. Transformation in business life and the commercial landscape is inevitable through rapid technological development. Technological development and digitalisation are currently shaping a new economy. In this new economy, data holds critical importance for undertakings in every sector. Rapid technological developments have led to new technologies such as data collection and mining, data processing (analytics) and storage.[1] However, this new environment fuelled by data technologies contains many competition issues which need immediate attention from competition authorities and regulators. Rapid digitalisation leads to novel anti-competitive strategies such as rising entry barriers, creating network effects to limit market access and high concentration in the online ecosystem.[2]

As Ioannis Lianos expresses: "[T]he development of digital capitalism . . . has led to an important information overload".[3] Also, in one of her speeches, the European Commission Commissioner Margrethe Vestager expressed:

> We need all the help we can get to stop climate change getting out of hand. So, if Big Data can help us to get more electricity from our wind farms, and help us to use less fossil fuels, that is a pretty important contribution.[4]

Technological development undeniably affects the types of transactions and decision-making processes, including strategic decisions and business structures.

---

1 Daniel L Rubinfeld and Michal S Gal, 'Access Barriers to Big Data' (2017) 59 Arizona Law Review 339, 341.
2 Ariel Ezrachi and Maurice Stucke, 'Emerging Antitrust Threats and Enforcement Actions in the Online World' (2017) 13(2) Competition Law International 125–36, 136.
3 Ioannis Lianos, 'Competition Law for the Digital Era: A Complex Systems' Perspective' (2019) CLES Research Paper Series 6/2019, 7.
4 Margrethe Vestager, 'Check Against Delivery' Big Data and Competition EDPS-BEUC Conference on Big Data, Brussels, 29 September 2016.

DOI: 10.4324/9781003458791-1

2 A New Data-Driven Economy

Due to digital technology, reaching information, services and products has become simple and fast.[5] Since the ability to reach relevant information is simple and fast today, the value of data has inevitably risen.

However, the importance of digital technology is not about quickly and easily reaching products or services from the consumer's perspective. In the context of competition law, data means more. According to Schönberger and Cukier, there are far fewer limitations on how much data can be managed by businesses.[6] Over time, a highly technical environment has been developed, and it is now possible to assess nearly all available data at once.[7] Contrary to the way it is now, the tools to collect and analyse data were quite limited in the past; thus, it was only possible to work with minimal data.[8] However, rapid technological development has enabled new data collection, mining, analytics, synthesising and storage techniques.[9]

As a result of data collection and analytics, waves of innovation and efficiencies have occurred in digitalised markets worldwide, which has benefited consumers.[10] Increased transparency, low to zero prices and a greater selection of choices in e-commerce and data-driven economy might seem to bring the ideals of perfect competition at first glance.[11] However, an initial analysis reveals that the new environment has many problems from a competition law perspective. New market structures – in this case, digitalisation and the efficient use of user data – bring many anti-competitive strategies, including barriers to market access and high concentration in online markets.[12] Contrary to the non-interventionist approach to dynamic markets and new technologies, which argues that a passive approach is needed to foster economic growth and innovation, intervention seems necessary if the effects of the abuse of market power, exclusionary practices and market foreclosing are present in the new economy.[13] In this situation, the main focus should be on super online platforms – technology giants – that gain market power and undercut the competition in data-driven markets.

The main point which needs to be identified is the role of Big Data in the new economy. In the data-driven economy, technology giants have recently gained unprecedented market power. Truthfully, the market power of dominant undertakings in data-driven markets stems from the effective use of Big Data. Big Data

---

5 Viktor Mayor-Schonberger and Kenneth Cukier, *Big Data: A Revolution That Will Transform How We Live, Work and Think* (1st edn, John Murray Publishers 2013) 19.
6 ibid 20.
7 ibid.
8 For example, Amazon has the ability to make nearly 2,500,000 price changes in a day. On the other hand, Walmart, which has been one of the biggest brick-and-mortar stores in the world, has the ability to make only 50,000 price changes by hand in the course of an entire month. Salil Mehra, 'Antitrust and the Robo-Seller: Competition in Time of Algorithms' (2015) 100 Minnesota Law Review 1323, 1334–35.
9 Rubinfeld and Gal (n 1) 341.
10 Ezrachi and Stucke (n 2) 125.
11 ibid.
12 ibid 136.
13 ibid.

technology is increasingly used in undertakings to gain market power and ample competitive advantage in data-driven markets. After explaining the technology itself, the second point that needs to be underlined is the relationship between Big Data and competition law. In other words, the main gap in competition law is the relationship between data and market power. This relationship did not seem to be an issue of competition to the competition authorities and the courts for a long time, to the extent that authorities did not relate competition in markets to the market power generated by the utilisation of Big Data. The truth is that new economy markets are a reality today, and the role of Big Data is quite crucial in establishing market power. Moreover, there are many concerns that bigger online platforms' efficiencies and immense success will soon turn them into monopolists implementing anti-competitive behaviour.[14] Inevitably, monopoly positions and the accumulation of vast amounts of personal data bring various market problems. As a result, an inclusive debate around anti-competitive conduct, data-driven markets and competition law must be conducted.

Considering the increasing relevance of Big Data to competition law, a thorough study of Big Data–driven markets should be conducted to understand the current structure and dynamics. Therefore, the primary motivation for this book is that Big Data must be regarded as a source of market power which eventually affects commercial life and market competition. Thus, competition law needs appropriate tools and a rationale to deal with this newly emerging issue. In this regard, this research focuses on data-driven markets and Big Data to identify new market structures and substantial challenges while assessing market power and identifying the anti-competitive behaviour of dominant undertakings. These challenges must be identified, and remedies should fit the objectives of competition law in the EU. To be more precise, the main discussion in this analysis is on the structures of data-driven markets and the anti-competitive conduct generated through the utilisation of Big Data. In this manner, the EU competition law provisions on the assessment of the market power and its effects on today's abuse cases in data-driven markets are criticised.

However, curiously, why are monopolies and dominant positions more dangerous in the Big Data era? Several implications can be derived from the current market structures. The first consideration is the super-dominant positions of technology giants, thanks to excessive indirect network effects.[15] Indirect network effects are among the main characteristics of data-driven markets, strengthening the dominant positions of technology giants unprecedentedly. In these markets, the accumulation of behavioural data and locking consumers into a specific ecosystem are the primary fuels of market power, thanks to data processing and analytics methods. These techniques extract the actual value of data, which already comprises characteristics such as volume, velocity and variety. As a result of the distinctive

---

14 Sebastian Felix Janka and Severin Benedict Uhsler, 'Antitrust 4.0 – The Rise of Artificial Intelligence and Emerging Challenges to Antitrust Law' (2018) 39(3) European Competition Law Review 113.
15 See Chapter 4.

characteristics of Big Data, especially velocity, dominant positions held by technology giants and related abuses are more dangerous than traditional dominant position abuses today.[16]

In ecosystems where technology giants control all available data, a huge problem occurs as available data becomes a potential tool to distort competition.[17] Therefore, the second consideration is the velocity of data itself: in other words, the simultaneous monitoring and prediction power of undertakings. It is called 'nowcasting', which brings a substantial competitive advantage to undertakings in data-driven markets.[18] Undertakings use massive and rich databases to adjust their market strategies instantly due to near-perfect consumer behaviour analysis.[19] On top of that, the freshness of data – velocity – creates a situation in which these massive datasets could only be relevant – valuable – for a short period. Therefore, a competitor with access to Google's or Amazon's couple-of-days-old data as a mitigative remedy after a competition investigation might not positively affect the competition in that market.[20]

Third consideration of why data-driven dominance is more dangerous than traditional dominance is the fast-changing nature of data-driven markets. The fast pace of technological development has brought many tools to make people's lives easier, along with numerous efficiencies. Digital markets are constantly evolving, and they all become data driven, thus becoming a part of the online ecosystem. In the wake of the millennia, the growth of algorithms and their effects on commercial life were not noticeable or predictable. Thus, the unprecedented growth of search engines such as Google and e-commerce web pages such as Amazon was not anticipated. In this dynamic ecosystem, a winner-takes-all system, many undertakings have dethroned dominant undertakings and acquired immense market power. Neither Google nor Facebook was the first mover in its respective market. However, this does not mean that digital markets are competitive or that the entry barriers in these markets are low. Due to the Big Data–related effects, data acquisitions of start-ups and exclusionary conduct create persistent dominant positions or monopolies in time.

It is believed that an undertaking could dethrone Google in the search engine market as Google did to AltaVista. In academia, the emergence of Google and the dominance of AltaVista in the late 1990s are often given as examples. Google started using algorithms to create organic search results in 2001 and accumulated enormous amounts of data in the following years.[21] However, at that time, AltaVista, Yahoo and other competitors of Google were using a cataloguing method

---

16 See Chapter 2.1.1.
17 Maurice E Stucke and Allen Grunes, *Big Data and Competition Policy* (1st edn, OUP 2016) 286.
18 ibid.
19 The Competition and Markets Authority, The Commercial Use of Consumer Data Report on the CMA's Call for Information (2015) para 2.72.
20 See Chapter 5.2.3.
21 Jens Prüfer and Christoph Schottmüller, 'Competing with Big Data' (2017) Tilburg Law School Research Paper No. 06/2017, TILEC Discussion Paper No. 2017-006, Center Discussion Paper 2017-007, 27.

conducted by staff members.[22] The difference resulted in a huge quality difference between Google and its competitors. Inevitably, Google's growth continued exponentially. Today, it seems quite impossible for an entrant to dethrone Google in normal market conditions without having access to massive datasets, data analytics, algorithms, sufficient scale and network effects.

Turning to the fast-changing character of data-driven markets, the search engine market in the 1990s was not the same as it is in the 2020s. Today, the search engine market is a part of a more extensive digital ecosystem intertwined with online advertising, shopping, vertical search and many others features. All segments of the ecosystem take advantage of the indirect network effects and data utilisation methods. The fast-changing nature of data-driven markets is not about having market shares or entry to markets; instead, it is about the evolution of the new economy and digital markets. Although fast changes in market shares or dominance do not seem to be an issue for competition law, the evolution of ecosystems and persistent dominance lead the way to anti-competitive conduct.

Big Data effects, including competitive advantage, data protection concerns, indirect network effects and the fast-changing dynamic nature of new economy markets, reveal the question about data-related abuses. What should be the approach of competition law and policy in data-driven markets? Some commentators argue that competition intervention would have chilling effects on innovation, and possible remedies could be detrimental to consumer welfare.[23] Therefore, a passive approach must be taken for markets to self-correct in time. On the other hand, some argue that markets do not necessarily self-correct, abuses are real, and intervention is necessary.[24] Thus, lasting anti-competitive conduct would harm consumers and the innovation process.[25] Additionally, some commentators believe that those current tools are sufficient when an intervention is necessary.[26] Lastly, there is an

---

22 ibid.
23 Pinar Akman, 'The Theory of Abuse in Google Search: A Positive and Normative Assessment Under EU Competition Law' (2017) 2 Journal of Law, Technology and Policy 301; Daniel F Spulber, 'Unlocking Technology: Antitrust and Innovation' (2008) 4(4) Journal of Competition Law and Economics 915; Daniel Crane, 'Search Neutrality and Referral Dominance' (2012) 8(3) Journal of Competition Law and Economics 459–68; Robert H Bork and J Gregory Sidak, 'What Does theChicago School Teach About Internet Search and the Antitrust Treatment of Google?' (2012) 8(4) Journal of Competition Law and Economics 663–700; Geoffrey A Manne and William Rinehart, 'The Market Realities That Undermined the FTC's Antitrust Case Against Google' (2013) Harvard Journal of Law and Technology Occasional Paper Series 12; Spencer Weber Waller and Matthew Sag, 'Promoting Innovation' (2015) 100 Iowa Law Review 2223–47, 2226.
24 Nathan Newman, 'Search, Antitrust, and the Economics of the Control of User Data' (2014) 31(2) Yale Journal on Regulation; Joaquín Almunia, Vice President of the European Commission responsible for Competition Policy, 'Competition in the Online World, LSE Public Lecture, London' (11 November 2013).
25 Carl Shapiro, 'Exclusivity in Network Industries' (1999) 7 George Mason Law Review 673.
26 Evelin Hlina, 'Dominant Undertakings in the Digital Era: A Call for Evolution of the Competition Policy Towards Article 102 TFEU?' (2016) 9 ICC Global Antitrust Review.

argument that competition intervention and possible remedies are not sufficient since the new economy evolves extremely fast.[27]

For these reasons, the appropriate approach of competition law to data-driven markets should be an interventionist one to some extent. Thus, the identification of data-driven abusive conduct is a main regulatory challenge for competition law and policy in the EU. Unlike in other jurisdictions, the stance of the European Commission has always been more interventionist against unilateral conduct. Cornerstone cases against Microsoft and Intel in the 80s and 90s verify the aggressive approach of the Commission towards innovative high-technology markets in the wake of the digital age. However, identifying abuses is crucial if an interventionist approach is taken. Although technology giants such as Google and Microsoft have already faced various abuses of dominant cases before the EU authorities more recently,[28] identification of abuse and intervention to data-driven markets remains as significant challenges for competition law.

1.2 A Market Power Problem

The current situation brings the verdict on whether the new structures of data-driven markets serve healthy and efficient competition or foster anti-competitive conduct and monopolisation. The question is, "Do super online platforms that have control over specific relevant markets weaken competition? If so, does this market power cause anti-competitive conduct and facilitate concentration?" The correlation between the data utilisation and assessment of market power, including relevant market definition, points out that the nature of abusive behaviour in the online world is unique, and technology giants use specific data techniques to utilise relevant information to abuse their market powers. Therefore, these novel techniques also significantly impact adjudicators' and regulators' assessments regarding the nature of the abusive behaviour. Therefore, how should the objectives of competition law be pursued in these data-driven markets: through case law or regulatory actions? What are the substantial challenges in ensuring healthy competition in data-driven markets? Ultimately, can the objectives of competition be met? This flow of ideas ignites the spark of debate in this research and helps identify the gaps in this area of law.

Therefore, the main questions are: "Is current competition regulation effectively dealing with these issues in the EU? Is there a case for reform in the approach of EU competition law?" The main problem in the law is applying competition tools to Big Data–related market power. However, to achieve a systematic analysis, several

---

27 William H Page, 'Mandatory Contracting Remedies in the American and European Microsoft Cases' (2008) 75 Antitrust Law Journal 787; William H Page and Seldon J Childers, 'Measuring Compliance with Compulsory Licensing Remedies in the American Microsoft Case' (2009) 76 Antitrust Law Journal 239.
28 Case COMP/C-3/37.792 Microsoft; Case COMP/C-3/39.530 Microsoft; Case T-201/4 *Microsoft Corp. v Commission*; Case AT.39740 Google Search (Shopping); Case No COMP/AT.40099, Google Android; Case No COMP/AT.40411 Google AdSense.

questions must be addressed before determining how to intervene in Big Data–related market power in terms of competition law. The starting point of the research is Big Data technology. Therefore, the first objective is to systematically address the Big Data issue in terms of competition law since the application of competition law and the current Big Data findings have seen increasing relevance so far. In this manner, the assessment focuses on Big Data as a competition law issue. By this means, the first question is: "How does Big Data contribute to the market structures of the new economy?" In order to assess what Big Data means for competition purposes, a framework is drawn, and the characteristics of Big Data are explained. Then the competitive significance of Big Data for market power is discussed.

Following that, the second question is: "How could dominant undertakings use Big Data to undermine the process of competition?" In this part of the study, the behaviour of dominant undertakings is scrutinised, together with the structures of data-driven markets. Data acquisitions are also under scrutiny since they are a part of the Big Data value chain and are used to gain competitive advantage and market power. Therefore, this part aims to address the challenges in the assessment of market power and anti-competitive conduct, which are a result of increasing Big Data usage by technology giants in the digital age.

It is followed by the third question, which is the main argument of this book: "Is current competition regulation effectively dealing with these issues in the EU? Is there a case for reform in the approach of EU competition law?" Therefore, the main objective of this book is to evaluate the effectiveness of the EU competition law and its assessment tools, which are currently applied to competition issues in digital markets. The study addresses issues in the context of EU competition law. By this means, the main focus of the study is on European Union legislation and case law in first place. In this context, this research critically assesses how European competition authorities should react to the Big Data issue and newly emerging data-driven markets. In other words, the application of EU competition law rules is criticised throughout the study.

After analysing the strengths and weaknesses of competition law and policy, a roadmap for EU competition policy is drawn. By this means, the need for reform through a lawmaking process can also be identified. Thereby, the final question is: "How should market power be defined for competition law purposes?" Setting an approach for data-driven markets and competition law objectives is crucial. Thus, another objective and contribution of this study is to make recommendations for remedies to mitigate potential future conflicts concerning the effectiveness of the current regulation regarding EU competition law. At this point, the necessity of a single, coherent application of competition law in the EU is also mentioned throughout the analysis.

2 Big Data Challenges for Competition Law

2.1 Definition of Big Data for Competition Law

Consumer data and, more specifically, Big Data and data analytics affect markets in every aspect of the new economy. In order to address competition law challenges in data-driven markets, Big Data should be defined. Big Data refers to a technical aspect of the digital world. The *term Big Data*, which computer scientists first used, is now quite famous and widely used across various disciplines.[1] Therefore, Big Data might mean something slightly different in different contexts. However, this study does not have the objective of "defining" Big Data, which refers to a technological aspect of the digital world. Instead, this section aims to define the boundaries of Big Data technology in the context of competition law and policy. By this means, it will be possible to see Big Data as an infrastructural resource, capital, input, a value-creation mechanism and a source of market power.[2]

Therefore, the assessment of market power must also be addressed in light of the new dynamics of the new economy. If Big Data is found to be a value creation mechanism and a source of market power through the analysis, understanding of market power might also need a change, at least for data-driven markets. To be more specific, narrow product market definitions based on the traditional concept of market definition in data-driven markets are not appropriate for assessing market power.[3] As Big Data becomes a value creation mechanism and a source of market power, the definition of relevant market becomes obsolete since it does not reflect the characteristics of the new economy, businesses strategies such as online ecosystems and the importance of Big Data.[4] Therefore, the following subsections

---

1 OECD, Ania Thiemann and Pedro Gonzaga, "Big Data: Bringing Competition Policy to the Digital Era" (2016) DAF/COMP 14, 5.
2 OECD, *Data-Driven Innovation, Big Data for Growth and Well-Being* (OECD Publishing 2015) 22–28.
3 Vanessa Turner and Agustin Reyna, 'Market Definition in EU Competition Law Enforcement: Need for an Update' BEUC's Response to the Public Consultation (2020) 3.
4 European Commission Notice on the Definition of Relevant Market for the Purposes of Community Competition Law [1997] OJ C 372/5; However, there is also the New Draft Version of Commission Notice on the Definition of Relevant Market for the Purposes of Union Competition Law [2022] 8 November 2022.

DOI: 10.4324/9781003458791-2

explain how Big Data has started to serve as a tool to gain market power and abusive behaviour.

2.1.1 Characteristics of Big Data

What is the difference between ordinary data and Big Data? Big Data has unique characteristics which distinguish it from ordinary data or wastes of information. A few decades ago, all online information was regarded as a waste of information in the public's eyes since it was too big to be sorted and extracted. Not only the amount of data but also the utility of data is important. Relevant information must be collected, extracted, aggregated, and then processed to become relevant data. Only after that can the information found in an endless data sea be valuable. Andrea De Mauro proposes a definition of Big Data as an information asset established by three distinct features (volume, velocity and variety), which also needs technology and analytical methods to make true use of its nature (value).[5] By this means, Big Data can be simplified as the 4Vs, and these 4Vs actually make Big Data both quantitatively and qualitatively different from ordinary data.[6]

Volume: The first distinctive attribute of Big Data is the amount of data collected. Information can be regarded as the fuel of Big Data.[7] The more information collected, the more utilisation of Big Data can be possible. According to the OECD, data collection has been increasing through the digitalisation of media, consumer services and all social and economic activities in the digital world.[8] Today, the amount of data collected from the internet in a second is the same as the amount collected online in a year just twenty years ago.[9] To exemplify this, Walmart gathers data at about 2.5 petabytes (millions of gigabytes) every hour from its consumers.[10] McAfee estimates that the amount of data Walmart collects online in an hour is approximately 50 million bookcases worth of text.[11]

Velocity: Another distinctive attribute of Big Data is the actual speed of data creation. In data-driven markets, the velocity of data is even more critical than the volume of data. Data creation at fast speeds, such as extracting real-time information, has enabled more accurate analytics and improved services. Various autonomous systems, such as traffic and map nowcasting, automated stock trading and

---

5 Andrea De Mauro, Marco Greco and Michele Grimaldi, 'A formal definition of Big Data based on its essential features' (2016) 65 Library Review 3, 122–35, 131.
6 Marc Bourreau, Alexandre de Steel and Inge Graef, 'Big Data and Competition Policy: Market Power, Personalised Pricing and Advertising' [2017] Centre on Regulation in Europe Project Report 11.
7 De Mauro, Greco and Grimaldi (n 5) 124.
8 OECD, Data-Driven Innovation (n 2) 23.
9 Andrew McAfee and Erik Brynjolfsson, 'Big Data: The Management Revolution' (2012) 90 Harvard Business Review 10, 62.
10 ibid.
11 ibid.

many others, could be given as examples here.[12] Rubinfeld and Gal also express that velocity could be regarded as the "freshness" of data.[13] In this regard, they indicate the importance of the dynamic characteristic of data-driven markets, which makes old data obsolete fast, and the speed of processing Big Data in the new economy.[14] For instance, medical nowcasting could be used as a demonstration to indicate the importance of the velocity of data outside the market economy. According to a report from *Science Daily*, data extracted from the Google search engine could derive accurate real-time information on epidemics.[15] Thus, official reports on flu infection rates are presented, with a week delay, based on Google trend information.[16]

Variety: Not only the amount of data and the speed of data creation but also the variation in collected data should be underlined. Through media devices and the Internet of Things (IoT), undertakings can collect different data types, even from a single source. The amount of different socio-economic consumer information available to undertakings is rising exponentially through the digitalisation of data.[17] Today, people rely on mobile devices for various commercial and non-commercial activities. From a single device, such as a mobile phone, undertakings can collect data about shopping, location and nearly every type of information about consumers.[18] Thus, a variety of data is used to better understand consumers' behaviour and preferences. As Stucke and Grunes indicate, Walmart merges various information collected from consumers to create a portfolio of consumers and consumers' behaviour in order to compete against Amazon, which also uses the same technique, called "data fusion".[19]

Value: Veracity is maybe the most critical attribute of Big Data. This characteristic refers to the accuracy and usefulness of processed data. As mentioned earlier in detail, relevant pieces of information can be derived for specific uses through Big Data analytics, which is regarded overall as valued data. In this sense, Prescott draws an analogy between Big Data and archaeology: that is, Big Data can be regarded as a technique for data archaeology.[20] Additionally, Stucke and Grunes argue that the initial 3 Vs of data create the value of data.[21] In the same vein, Peter

---

12 Maurice Stucke and Allen Grunes, *Big Data and Competition Policy* (1st edn, OUP 2016) 19; OECD, Data-Driven Innovation (n 2) 4.
13 Daniel L Rubinfeld and Michal S Gal, 'Access Barriers to Big Data' (2017) 59 Arizona Law Review 339, 346.
14 ibid.
15 University of Warwick, 'Adaptive "Nowcasting" Key to Accurate Flu Data Trends Using Google Search Terms' *Science Daily* (30 October 2014) <www.sciencedaily.com/releases/2014/10/141030114853.htm>
16 ibid.
17 McAfee and Brynjolfsson (n 9) 63.
18 ibid.
19 Stucke and Grunes (n 12) 22.
20 Andrew Prescott, 'Bibliographic Records as Humanities Big Data' [2013] IEEE International Conference on Big Data 57 <https://doi.org/10.1109/BigData.2013.6691670>
21 Stucke and Grunes (n 12) 23.

Norvig from Google expresses that they do not have better algorithms; they simply have better data (in terms of volume, variety and velocity).[22]

In total, with these unique characteristics attributed, Big Data is now an important value creation mechanism. Big Data is now considered an intangible asset for value creation in markets, together with intellectual property rights such as copyrights, patents and even goodwill.[23] Moreover, Big Data is now seen as an indispensable part of the economic process, along with people, resources and other types of capital.[24] It is coming to the point where economic growth and innovation will not be able to occur without the aid of Big Data in the future.[25] In the same vein, it is argued that Big Data is now becoming "the oil" of the 21st century due to its attributed importance.[26] Strictly speaking, this statement is arguable. Creating a correlation between a resource for the economy and a total value creation mechanism is not feasible. However, it is pretty accurate that data is now one of the most valuable resources in today's market economics.

2.1.2 Creation of the Big Data Value Chain

Undertakings now have effective use of people's data in many markets. User data can provide personalised services for consumers both online and offline.[27] Not only pricing mechanisms through online marketplaces, but, for instance, data collected from social networks can also be personalised in order to offer better-fitted products, advertisements and content for consumers. Another example is the location services and geographical data of consumers. Online providers can use real-time location data to customise products or services available to consumers' physical geographical locations.[28] The use of personal data for targeted advertisements, customised shopping and other purposes can be seen in many instances, such as Google's ad services, location services, map services, Facebook advertisements, applications for mobile devices, Yahoo, and many others. According to Lerner,[29] studies have shown that customers acknowledge the situation and are willing to

---

22 McAfee and Brynjolfsson (n 9) 63.
23 Mira Burri, 'Understanding the Implications of Big Data and Big Data Analytics for Competition Law: An Attempt for a Primer' in Klaus Mathias and Avishalom Tor (eds), *New Developments in Competition Behavioural Law and Economics* (1st edn, Springer 2018) 244.
24 ibid.
25 James Manyika and others, *Big Data: The Next Frontier for Innovation, Competition, and Productivity* (2011) McKinsey Global Institute 6.
26 'The World's Most Valuable Resource Is No Longer Oil, but Data – The Data Economy Demands a New Approach to Antitrust Rules' *The Economist* (6 May 2017) <https://www.economist.com/leaders/2017/05/06/the-worlds-most-valuable-resource-is-no-longer-oil-but-data>
27 Andres V Lerner, 'The Role of Big Data in Online Platform Competition' (2014) SSRN Working Paper 12 <http://dx.doi.org/10.2139/ssrn.2482780>
28 ibid.
29 ibid.

give their information in order to benefit from targeted and personalised marketing, services, products and offers.[30]

In order to create a value chain in ecosystems, undertakings use several ways to collect personal information through services. In data-driven markets, data can be collected by undertakings directly from users in the form of their shopping history, abandoned baskets, views, clicks and many more.[31] In other words, information collected online can be collected directly from an undertakings' products or services, such as data collection from transactions on an e-commerce platform. This type of collected data is called first-party data. First-party data is data collected about consumers of a service or product who interact with the business directly. In this case, sale data, search results data, behavioural data and social network data are all considered first-party data, which is the primary source of data collection.[32]

First-party data enables businesses to uncover consumer needs better and contributes to data utilisation through personalised services. None of the technology companies will have access to the same datasets in first-party data, which means all companies are likely to collect different personal and behavioural information and create unique datasets.[33] In this sense, the uniqueness of datasets belonging to different businesses may create a barrier for new entrants in data-driven markets.[34] The need for relevant data to compete is addressed in the following chapters. First-party data collection can be conducted either voluntarily or without the knowledge of consumers. For the latter, the tracked information of consumers – in other words, website cookies – are used.[35] This is a common way to gather data online, in which browser tracking history and cross-device tracking are present.[36]

In addition to first-party data, businesses can acquire data without direct interaction with consumers, called "third-party data".[37] Third-party data comes from outside sources such as other businesses inside an online ecosystem. Like first-party data, third-party data is also data on user behaviour, shopping behaviour or demographic data collected and consolidated from online services or products.[38] User consent is not present in this type of data, and third-party data can be shared across different businesses.[39] The ability to share could also pose risks regarding the data privacy of consumers apart from competition concerns.

---

30 ibid, citing The Study of Nasri, Grace Nasri, 'Why Consumers Are Increasingly Willing to Trade Data for Personalization' *Digital Trends* (10 December 2012).
31 Bourreau, de Steel and Inge Graef (n 6) 11.
32 Srikant Kotapalli, 'First-Party Data for Enriched, Responsible Marketing' *Use Insider* (29 September 2020) <https://useinsider.com/first-party-data-strategy/>
33 Jay Modrall, 'Antitrust Risks and Big Data' (2017) Norton Rose Fulbright Competition World 14, 14.
34 ibid.
35 Bourreau, de Steel and Inge Graef (n 6) 11.
36 ibid 12.
37 Modrall (n 33) 15.
38 ibid.
39 ibid.

One way to collect third-party data is through mergers and acquisitions in the online world.[40] Acquisitions of third-party data create efficiencies of scale and contribute to the accumulation of Big Data, which creates enormous barriers to entry in data-driven markets.[41] As businesses can access a richer data pool, combining different sources such as first-party data and third-party data can create significant synergies. After a merger, a combination of first- and third-party data through data analytics can determine a business's market power, position and ability to access adjacent market segments in an online ecosystem.[42] For instance, an online advertising business that is also prevalent on the social network market can increase its targeting and personalised advertisement value by acquiring a social media network and embedding its online advertising services and consumer data into the acquired social media.[43] The European Commission has noted the importance of combined datasets, which could have an impact on competition in its *Google/DoubleClick* investigation:

> [T]he merged entity would be able to combine DoubleClick's and Google's data collections. Such a combination, using information about users' IP addresses, cookie IDs and connection times to correctly match records from both databases, could result in individual users' search histories being linked to the same users' past surfing behaviour on the internet. . . . The merged entity may know that the same user has searched for terms A, B and C and visited web pages X, Y and Z in the past week. Such information could potentially be used to better target ads to users.[44]

However, last year Google announced that they would cease using third-party cookies and cross-site tracking (through third-party data) for their services, including their ad network, by the end of 2022.[45] This move may indicate the end of third-party data tracking for data-driven markets and the online world as a whole. The CMA's latest ongoing investigation against Google – an investigation into Google's privacy sandbox browser changes – entails assessing third-party cookies' role in online and digital advertising.[46] Google's announced changes that will

---

40 Reuben Binns and Elettra Bietti, 'Dissolving Privacy, One Merger at a Time: Competition, Data, and Third-Party Tracking' (2020) 36 Computer Law and Security Review 1.
41 ibid 14.
42 ibid 22.
43 ibid.
44 Case No COMP/M.4731, Google/DoubleClick C [2008] 927 Final, para 360.
45 Justin Schuh, 'Building a More Private Web: A Path Towards Making Third-Party Cookies Obsolete' *Chromium Blog* (14 January 2020) <https://blog.chromium.org/2020/01/building-more-private-web-path-towards.html>; Michael Shearer, '3rd-Party Is Dead: How to Improve Your First-Party Data Strategy' *Claravine* (29 January 2020) <https://www.claravine.com/2020/01/29/first-party-data-strategy/>
46 Competition and Markets Authority, Press Release, 'CMA to Investigate Google's Privacy Sandbox Browser Changes' (8 January 2021) <https://www.gov.uk/government/news/cma-to-investigate-google-s-privacy-sandbox-browser-changes>

14   *Big Data Challenges for Competition Law*

disable third-party cookies on the Chrome browser and search engine may be an indicator of a competition law problem or even a privacy law problem in the online world. The investigation reveals a legality issue questioning Google's conduct.

However, in this case, where third-party cookie traction is ceased either by companies or regulators, collection and utilisation of first-party data will become much more crucial for data-driven businesses. In this sense, first-party datasets need to be as comprehensive and rich as possible for better utilisation.[47] However, this could also be an indicator of monopolisation of data-driven markets since only a few technology giants have been able to collect vast numbers of datasets and have the ability to process vast amounts of data.[48]

Also, while arguable, another method used to gather third-party data is through data intermediaries. Undertakings may also exchange, buy or sell their data through "data brokers".[49] According to the CERRE report on Big Data, authorities did not fully understand the secondary market for data yet.[50] In addition to that, in its 2014 report on data brokers, the FTC acknowledged the grey structure of data brokers in its findings.[51] According to the study, the data intermediary industry is quite complex. There are multiple layers of the market in which brokers access data collected from various sources by third parties.[52] Another finding is that data brokers can collect and store data regarding every consumer in the US from both online and offline market data.[53] Moreover, this vast amount of data can be analysed and combined by brokers in order to create sensitive assumptions and inferences about consumers.[54] Still, data brokers and data markets do not seem relevant for the functioning of data-driven markets.

Data storage and data analytics also have crucial roles in the Big Data value chain. First, is now possible for even the smallest businesses in markets to collect large datasets. However, storage of these datasets might be troublesome since it requires huge data centres consisting of numerous computers and hard drives connected by local networks and the World Wide Web.[55] Construction of a data storage facility is quite costly, and only a small number of businesses have the ability to store Big Data in facility. However, due to cloud computing technology today, every business now has the opportunity to store its data by renting storage space from clouds (storage providers).[56]

---

47   Shearer (n 45).
48   Bourreau, de Steel and Inge Graef (n 6) 12.
49   ibid.
50   ibid 13.
51   Data Brokers: A Call for Transparency and Accountability, a Report of the Federal Trade Commission (May 2014) <https://www.ftc.gov/reports/data-brokers-call-transparency-accountability-report-federal-trade-commission-may-2014>
52   ibid 46.
53   ibid.
54   ibid.
55   Bourreau, de Steel and Inge Graef (n 6) 13.
56   For more information on cloud computing and competition law, see Sara Gabriella Hoffman, *Regulation of Cloud Services Under US and EU Antitrust, Competition and Privacy Laws* (Peter Lang 2016).

Data utilisation is the most critical link in the Big Data value chain. After collecting data, massive datasets must be analysed and sorted into relevant data and correlation patterns.[57] The vast amount of personal and behavioural data obtained through online and offline activity cannot be sorted and analysed by humans. In other words, hardware and software (both applications and algorithms) are needed to bring the relevant pieces of information to light. The ability to process endless datasets effectively and quickly through artificial intelligence (computer algorithms) has seen rapid development recently. Machine learning and artificial intelligence have led to the utilisation of enormous amounts of real-time information and caused an exponential growth in data analytics.[58]

In total, huge data collections obtained through medical records, governmental records, webpages, e-commerce, social networking and other sources are all called Big Data. As Kenneth Cukier expressed in 2010, "The effect is being felt everywhere, from business to science, from government to arts, the phenomenon: big data".[59] As a revolution in the information technology industry, Big Data has several roles in markets. Today, people's personal and behavioural data, interests, shopping habits, political opinions and all other personal information can be obtained by businesses and used when necessary to improve these services. Innovative marketing strategies such as personalised advertisements and personalised products such as smart homes, live traffic maps, driverless cars, after-sale services and improved processes are all examples of Big Data use in the new economy.[60] All in all, Big Data creates a value chain together with algorithms, and undertakings can derive a crucial competitive advantage from this value chain.

2.1.3 The Competitive Significance of Big Data

As seen earlier, personal data can create significant advantages and might have benefits to the economy and society as a whole. However, businesses could also facilitate their data advantage into an anti-competitive animus under suitable circumstances.[61] For example, collected personal data may contribute to and can be a legitimate source of market power. However, this power could also be abused as a result of anti-competitive conduct.[62] The main concern of competition regulators relates to this idea. Unlike a decade ago, when many data-driven mergers were cleared, and it was believed that Big Data was irrelevant for competition regulation

---

57 Bourreau, de Steel and Inge Graef (n 6) 14.
58 For more information on machine learning and competition law, see Ariel Ezrachi and Maurice Stucke, *Virtual Competition: The Promise and Perils of the Algorithm-Driven Economy* (1st edn, Harvard UP 2016).
59 Kenneth Cukier, 'Data, Data Everywhere' *The Economist* (London, 25 February 2010) <https://www.economist.com/special-report/2010/02/25/data-data-everywhere>
60 Bourreau, de Steel and Inge Graef (n 6) 14.
61 Bruno Lasserre and Andreas Mundt, 'Competition Law and Big Data: The Enforcers' View' (2017) 4 Italian Antitrust Review 90.
62 ibid.

since it was only related to pro-competitiveness in the new economy, regulators now do not dismiss the Big Data issue for competition law purposes.[63] Furthermore, regulators are now highly concerned over anti-competitive conduct in data-driven markets,[64] which may cause irreversible economic, social and democratic damages to society.

The current issues in competition law need to be identified clearly by evaluating how Big Data affects the new economy. In order to identify these problems, using a step-by-step method could be helpful. In one of their early studies, Maurice Stucke and Allen Grunes indicate that the existing literature sets out competition problems stemming from Big Data and summarises them around five main themes.[65] At the first stage, as mentioned earlier, undertakings adapt their operation models based on technology, where businesses mainly try to take control of a massive amount of data. Thus, personal data becomes a key input in these data-driven business models.[66] As a result, both traditional and digitalised businesses tend to rely on their data accumulation more than ever. At the same time, it is important to note that collecting data might not be as valuable as predicted by undertakings. In certain circumstances, old data might lose its usefulness for daily businesses.[67] However, recent technologies in the accumulation of data could quickly negate the adverse outcomes of data-driven business and management.[68]

After the race for data collection and accumulation, some undertakings gain an unprecedented data advantage over others through earlier adaptation to new technologies at the second stage.[69] These undertakings are specifically data-driven businesses. According to an MIT-led study,[70] data-driven businesses perform better on both operational and financial management decisions.[71] Businesses that characterise themselves as data driven and are in the top third of their industries are seen to be more productive (5%) and more profitable (6%) than their competitors.[72] Along with making them more productive, the usage of Big Data could also bring significant financial savings for businesses. As the European Commission noted in 2015, in the next five years, the top 100 manufacturers in Europe could save up to €425 billion with the aid of Big Data, and this could contribute to the

---

63 Akiva A Miller, 'The Dawn of the Big Data Monopolists' (2016) 1 <https://ssrn.com/abstract=2911567>
64 ibid.
65 Maurice E Stucke and Allen P Grunes, 'Debunking the Myths Over Big Data and Antitrust' (2015) Competition Policy International Antitrust Chronicle, University of Tennessee Legal Studies Research Paper No. 276, 2–3.
66 ibid.
67 Miller (n 63) 5.
68 ibid.
69 Stucke and Grunes (n 65) 2–3.
70 330 North American companies were interviewed about management practices and technology by a team at the MIT Centre for Digital Business and McKinsey Business Technology Office.
71 McAfee and Brynjolfsson (n 9) 63–64.
72 ibid 64.

economic growth of the EU at a percentage of 1.9, which means a GDP increase of €206 billion.[73]

Not only is the amount of collected data, financial savings and efficiencies increasing, but the gap between competitors is also. In markets where Big Data is a necessity, the market structure seems to become highly concentrated. This result is achieved by the "snowball effect".[74] The snowball effect occurs through the self-reinforcing nature of data.[75] Incumbents having a more comprehensive range of services and being well versed in Big Data usage can collect vast amounts of relevant data from consumers. This data collection and analytics can help produce personalised services, products and advertisements. As a matter of course, these services bring additional data to incumbents. Ultimately, this value chain leads to efficient feedback loops and network effects. In this case, small competitors obtain less data as they attract fewer consumers.[76] Consequently, smaller competitors lack product, service and feedback. To sum up, the gap between data collection ends in a gap between savings, products, quality, services and many other areas, which forces smaller competitors out of the market and eventually contributes to the monopolisation of data-driven markets.[77]

As Stucke and Grunes express, the "fight" for data does not end there, and it inevitably jumps into a third stage: data acquisitions.[78] Undertakings choose the data acquisition route as a strategic step to enter into new markets or to improve their services in their core markets. It becomes more profitable than collecting data directly from consumers in some instances.[79] By this means, undertakings can create greater efficiencies in their businesses and gain greater data advantage through these acquisitions.[80] A study of the OECD shows that data-driven mergers rose from 55 to 134 in only four years between 2008 and 2012.[81] This sole example demonstrates how Big Data strategies affect data acquisitions.

---

73 The European Commission, 'Why We Need a Digital Single Market, Factsheets on Digital Single Market' (6 May 2015) <https://ec.europa.eu/commission/publications/why-we-need-digital-single-market_en>
74 Lasserre and Mundt (n 61) 91.
75 ibid.
76 ibid.
77 ibid.
78 Maurice E Stucke and Allen P Grunes, 'No Mistake About It: The Important Role of Antitrust in the Era of Big Data' (2015) The Antitrust Source April, University of Tennessee Legal Studies Research Paper No. 269, 3 <https://ssrn.com/abstract=2600051>
79 For instance, even Google collects data through online cookies, internet searches, affiliated websites, and its applications; the company also searches for strategic acquisitions such as the ones with DoubleClick, Waze, Applied Semantics and DeepMind Technologies, all of which involved data-driven goals.
80 Stucke and Grunes (n 78) 3.
81 European Data Protection Supervisor, 'Report of EDPS Workshop on Privacy, Consumers, Competition and Big Data' (2014) <https://edps.europa.eu/data-protection/our-work/publications/reports/report-edps-workshop-privacy-consumers-competition-and_en>; OECD, Data-Driven Innovation (n 2).

As a result, anti-competitive risks also occur. In this context, two different competition law issues arise.[82] First is the intention to breach competition rules by using data power obtained through mergers.[83] In this case, potential harm needs to be evaluated circumspectly – feedback loops and snowball effects on markets gain prominence in this scenario. In the second scenario, which is a more traditional method, some undertakings try to eliminate smaller competitors and new entrants or force them out of markets through strategic data acquisitions.[84] In this scenario, the evaluation of eliminating competitors is more straightforward. There have been instances when crucial anti-competitive results have occurred since these data-driven mergers were cleared in the EU. Although some commentators argue that the Commission's assessments of these mergers were accurate, since it mainly focused on the horizontal overlap and vertical foreclosure effects in markets,[85] it can be presumed that current merger assessments have not been healthy in the EU due to the variety of conglomerate risks created by the accumulation of data in the long term.

Lastly, as literature identifies, undertakings that obtain data power and data-driven competitive advantages tend to maintain their positions and powers and abuse them.[86] As mentioned earlier, the competition authorities' attitudes towards Big Data have.

> If a company's use of data is so bad for competition that it outweighs the benefits, we may have to step in to restore a level playing field.[87]

However, in this scenario, the EU competition law faces challenges from both regulatory and structural aspects of competition. In other words, the assessment of market power might be compelling due to the characteristics of the new economy. Also, the abuse of a dominant position that stems from Big Data might show up in different forms. As a non-exhaustive list, preventing rivals from accessing critical data,[88] preventing competitors from achieving efficient scale,[89] various vertical integration forms[90] and leveraging data power[91] can be listed as different types of abusive behaviour in data-driven markets. Due to these challenges, competition regulators have lately scrutinised the assessment of market power, market definitions,

---

82 Damian Geradin and Monika Kuschewsky, 'Competition Law and Personal Data: Preliminary Thoughts on a Complex Issue' (2013) 2 Concurrences 6.
83 ibid.
84 ibid.
85 Massimiliano Kadar and Mateusz Bogdan, '"Big Data" and EU Merger Control – a Case Review (2017) 8(8) Journal of European Competition Law and Practice 479.
86 Stucke and Grunes (n 78) 3.
87 Margrethe Vestager, 'Competition in a Big Data World' DLD 16, Munich, 17 January 2016.
88 Maurice Stucke and Allen Grunes, *Big Data and Competition Policy* (1st edn, OUP 2016) 288.
89 ibid 289.
90 ibid 293.
91 ibid 290.

theories of anti-competitive effects and possible types of consumer harm.[92] Due to this policy footstep, both Google and Facebook have faced several investigations, and huge fines have already been levied by the European Commission and National Competition Authorities.[93]

However, there is still much debate about competition law's role in the Big Data world.[94] Many academics argue that problems stemming from Big Data in data-driven markets belong to consumer protection and privacy laws in the legal world.[95] According to this idea, any competition policy towards regulating or controlling Big Data in innovative, dynamic markets would be erroneous. Sokol and Comerford explicitly state the practical and legal dangers of antitrust intervention in the Big Data issue. According to them, using antitrust tools would reduce competition and stifle innovation in general.[96] These ideas seem to be quite obsolete today. It must be underlined that the power of Big Data technology affects competition in markets, and data utilisation is now a valuable tool for undertakings. Unlike the widespread idea in the public domain, the Big Data issue does not pertain only to consumer protection rules or privacy protection laws specifically. It consists of a competitive characteristic as a valuable asset, an input, and a value creation mechanism itself, as mentioned earlier. Therefore, competition law and policy need to be

---

92 Miller (n 63) 7.
93 Three European Commission investigations on Google: Case AT.39740 Google Search (Shopping) [2017] 4444 Final; Case AT.40099 Google Android [2018]; Case COMP/AT.40411 Google AdSense C [2019] 2173; Italian Competition Authority, Press Release, 'Facebook Fined 10 Million Euros by the ICA for Unfair Commercial Practices for Using Its Subscribers' Data for Commercial Purposes' (7 December 2018) <http://en.agcm.it/en/media/press-releases/2018/12/Facebook-fined-10-million-Euros-by-the-ICA-for-unfair-commercial-practices-for-using-its-subscribers%E2%80%99-data-for-commercial-purposes>; Bundeskartellamt, Publications, 'Preliminary Opinion on the Investigation of Facebook – Background on the Facebook Proceeding' (19 December 2017) <https://www.bundeskartellamt.de/SharedDocs/Publikation/EN/Diskussions_Hintergrundpapiere/2017/Hintergrundpapier_Facebook.pdf?__blob=publicationFile&v=6>
94 Greg Sivinski, Alex Okuliar and Lars Kjolbye, 'Is Big Data a Big Deal? A Competition Law Approach to Big Data' (2017) 13(2–3) European Competition Journal; OECD, Thiemann and Gonzaga (n 1)14; Simonetta Vezzoso, 'Competition Policy in a World of Big Data' in F Xavier Olleros and Majlinda Zhegu (eds), *Research Handbook on Digital Transformations* (Edward Elgar 2016) SSRN <https://ssrn.com/abstract=2717497>; Jens Prüfer and Christoph Schottmüller, 'Competing with Big Data' (2017) Tilburg Law School Research Paper No. 06/2017, TILEC Discussion Paper No. 2017-006; Robert P Mankhe, 'Big Data as a Barrier to Entry' (2015) 2 Competition Policy International Antitrust Chronicle; Nathan Newman, 'The Costs of Lost Privacy: Consumer Harm and Rising Economic Inequality in the Age of Google (2014) 40 William Mitchell Law Review 849, 54; Ayşem Diker Vanberg and Mehmet Bilal Unver, 'The Right to Data Portability in the GDPR and EU Competition Law: Odd Couple or Dynamic Duo?' (2017) 8 European Journal of Law and Technology 1; Marianna Meriani, 'Digital Platforms and the Spectrum of Data Protection Competition Law Analyses' (2017) 38 European Competition Law Review 2; Stucke and Grunes (n 78).
95 Maureen K Ohlhausen and Alexander P Okuliar, 'Competition, Consumer Protection and the Right (Approach) to Privacy' (2015) 80 Antitrust Law Journal 121, 156; David A Balto and Matthew Lane, 'Monopolizing Water in a Tsunami: Finding Sensible Antitrust Rules for Big Data' (2016) 9 <https://ssrn.com/abstract=2753249>
96 D Daniel Sokol and Roisin Comerford, 'Antitrust and Regulating Big Data' (2016) 23(5) George Mason Law Review 1129, 1160.

at the centre of the discussion of the Big Data issue. The reason behind this is that competition law should protect not only consumers' pockets but also the competitive process, markets and even competitors in markets.

Regarding Big Data as a competition law issue, some academics argue that Big Data benefits markets as a pro-competitive tool and cannot pose any anti-competitive threats to markets in the context of competition law and policy.[97] According to this idea, Big Data can hardly be a part of anti-competitive conduct, and it is just a better tool used to improve products and services for consumers.[98] Moreover, according to this idea, policymakers and the public tend to mischaracterise Big Data due to their misunderstanding of the technology.[99] Therefore, commentators argue that undertakings have several pro-competitive rationales to collect and use Big Data in online and offline markets, which can be listed as improved quality for products and services, enhanced innovation and lower-priced (usually zero-priced) products. To be precise, it is unarguable that this idea remains obsolete today. As mentioned before, policymakers, competition authorities and academics have recently recognised the anti-competitive effects of Big Data.

On the other hand, according to Sokol and Comerford, the argument over the monetisation of free products is the most persuasive benefit of Big Data.[100] They state that low- to zero-priced products are desired by competition policy.[101] To be precise, lower prices will benefit consumers more. Lerner also advocates the monetisation of free services to the extent that they are rational behaviours (economically speaking), a means of profit maximisation and beneficial for competition in total.[102] Also, Big Data allows undertakings to improve their services by utilising personal data to deliver services.[103] This phenomenon is known as "click-and-query" data, enhancing the consumer experience in every section of the online world.[104] For instance, many online shopping websites today use personalised services such as "recommended products" or "frequently bought together products" for consumers. Another example of using "click-and-query" data would be search engines, social media and online businesses. Online businesses use the search histories of individuals for recommendations such as online newspaper journals, summer vacations or even new pairs of shoes.[105] In general, the flow of personal data online allows businesses to operate efficiently and deliver enhanced services and better products to consumers. Big Data, in turn, provides competitive advantages for businesses that successfully utilise it.

---

97 ibid; Lerner (n 27); Darren S Tucker and Hill B Wellford, 'Big Mistakes Regarding Big Data' (2014) 14 Antitrust Source 1.
98 Tucker and Wellford (n 97) 11.
99 ibid.
100 Sokol and Comerford (n 96) 1133.
101 ibid.
102 Lerner (n 27) 13.
103 ibid 11.
104 ibid.
105 Sokol and Comerford (n 96) 1135.

Although there are several opinions on the pro-competitive significance of Big Data in the new economy and commentators have expressed the significance of using Big Data for gaining competitive advantages in markets,[106] that kind of competitive advantage might bring great distortion to markets from a competition law perspective. Therefore, the implications of free products or services, improved quality and enhanced innovation, all of which benefit competition, seem incorrect today. To exemplify, the implication of free products seems to be incorrect. These products are not actually free, but consumer welfare economics fail to identify relevant markets and non–price competition in multi-sided markets since the assessment of an economic-based approach is actually price-centric. The price is the consumers themselves and their information in these markets. Therefore, in the next chapter, it becomes necessary to delve into multi-sided market economics and the economic approach in competition law. Also, the reasons behind these three so-called efficiencies will be discussed in the following sections in detail in order to demonstrate that they are actually distortive for competition law.

2.2 Major Issues in Data-Driven Markets

2.2.1 Monopolisation in Markets

Digital markets have been experiencing oligopolistic tendencies through the power of Big Data lately. In other words, high concentration and even monopolisation in specific markets do not seem unrealistic for the near future. Strong market power is a norm today, and there are only a dwindling number of competitors in data-driven markets. More precisely, current market structures in digital markets clearly show signs of super dominance and monopolisation.[107] Especially in markets where Google (Alphabet), Amazon, Facebook (Meta) and Apple are dominant, this situation can be seen clearly. Dominance contributes to these companies collecting even more data in data-driven markets.

The analysis in Chapter 3 reveals that these undertakings have definitely had an irreversible competitive advantage over their competitors due to Big Data and analytics, and their near-monopoly positions cannot be compared with traditional monopolies.[108] According to some, data-driven markets have low to zero entry barriers.[109] Thus, starting a business in one of these markets would require much less investment than in many other traditional markets. They also argue that Big Data acquisitions and the use of Big Data are not types of anti-competitive practice

---

106 Brad Brown, Michael Chui and James Manyika, 'Are You Ready for the Era of Big Data' *McKinsey Quarterly* (2011) <https://www.mckinsey.com/business-functions/strategy-and-corporate-finance/our-insights/are-you-ready-for-the-era-of-big-data>; McAfee and Brynjolfsson (n 9) 10.
107 Gustavo Grullon, Yelena Larkin and Roni Michaely, 'Are US Industries Becoming More Concentrated?' (2017) <https://ssrn.com/abstract=2612047>; Lina M Khan, Amazon's Antitrust Paradox (2016) 126 Yale Law Journal 3.
108 See Chapter 3.
109 Tucker and Wellford (n 97) 1.

covered by competition law.[110] On the contrary, there is no empirical support for the idea that there are low to zero entry barriers in innovative digital markets.[111] Thus, through a fact-by-fact analysis, entry barriers are found to be very high in these markets, which is explained more deeply in Chapter 3.

Demand-side economies of scale (in other words, network effects) are the most critical point which needs to be identified.[112] There are significant differences between traditional and data-driven monopolies in terms of network effects. For instance, strong indirect network externalities can be explained here as the main difference. Strong indirect network effects trigger lock-in (consumer) effects. In this type of network effect, utilisation of a free online service or product increases the utility of the complimentary service. In the context of data-driven markets, it is online advertising services. To be more precise, indirect network effects occur when there are different consumer groups, such as advertisers and users, in a search engine or another online ecosystem. In this scenario, the utility of a service by one group contributes to the growth of the other consumer group in a market.[113]

Technology giants in the online world, such as Facebook or Google, enjoy the externalised power of network effects created by billions of consumers. For example, creating a mobile chat application might not require high costs or technology and might be relatively easy to launch. However, when a new free mobile chat application hits the markets, it would be quite hard to compete with the existing one(s) since network effects in data-driven markets are much stronger than in traditional markets. The main reason behind this is the indirect network externalities in these markets, which create barriers to new entrants. Due to extensive network externalities, the new chat application would barely compete with the incumbent(s). Not only do new entrants struggle to compete in markets, but incumbents are willing to spend vast amounts of money to strengthen their positions based on their established network effects. Microsoft, for example, would not have spent more than $4.5 billion developing algorithms and enhancing its Big Data storage capacity to operate its free search engine Bing[114] if entry barriers were as low as Tucker and Wellford have argued.

Another example is the case of Google. Google has formed an ecosystem through its applications, such as Google Search, Google+, YouTube, Gmail, Google Drive, and many others, to create strong direct and indirect network effects. Primarily, all these applications are tools for Google to obtain relevant data from consumers.[115] For instance, even though Google was not the first mover and did not have the

---

110 ibid.
111 Maurice E Stucke and Allen P Grunes, 'Data-Opolies' (2017) Concurrences No. 2, University of Tennessee Legal Studies Research Paper No. 316, 3 <https://ssrn.com/abstract=2927018>
112 See Chapter 3.2.2.
113 Andrei Hagiu and David B Yoffie, 'Network Effects' in Mie Augier and David Teece (eds), *The Palgrave Encyclopedia of Strategic Management* (Palgrave Macmillan 2018) 1104–7.
114 Stucke and Grunes (n 111) 5.
115 Nathan Newman, 'Search, Antitrust, and the Economics of the Control of User Data' (2014) 31(2) Yale Journal on Regulation 407.

first mover advantage in terms of collecting user data, Google's expansion into various adjacent markets, such as operating systems (Android), video streaming (YouTube), social networking and many others, and creating an online ecosystem contributed to the accumulation of vast numbers of datasets. This behaviour has strengthened Google's position.[116] Google's control over mass data on individuals and consequent market power explains its expansion to various markets.[117] For instance, YouTube, which Google acquired, attracts more than four billion daily views, and except for Google Search, YouTube's search capacity is much higher than any search engine such as Bing.[118] It means that Google owns not only the most popular search engine in the online world but also the second one: YouTube.

Google's vice president for engineering, Vic Gundotra, emphasised that the actual intention of Google+ is to integrate consumers' data across the Google ecosystem and ultimately serve better ads to its consumers.[119] Also, Matt Rosoff stated:

> The Google+ service is bait. All Google wants you to do is create a profile and link to some friends with it. After that, Google really does not care if you never visit again. As long as you sign in for any other Google service (like Gmail), and then recommend an ad or a Web site once in a while, so Google can put that information in front of your other Google friends, all is well with the world.[120]

Google's business model has a unique characteristic created by consumer data. Data collected from sources such as social networking, search queries, calendar data, location, dietary information, photos, videos, emails and everything else that could be included in this list can be used to create personalised services or targeted advertisements for consumers.[121] Through the creation of personalised advertisements, Google entrenches its position and knowledge to create a monopoly position and entry barriers in the online advertising sector.[122] It can be deduced that competitors struggle to find a place in the online advertising market and adjacent markets in which Google's network of applications operates efficiently.

Unarguably, the ecosystem created by Google poses crucial concerns for competition law and policy, which must be identified and dealt with urgently. Intrinsically,

---

116 ibid 410.
117 ibid 420.
118 ibid 427.
119 ibid 431, citing Nick Bilton, 'Countering the Google Plus Image Problem' *New York Times Bits Blog* (6 March 2012, 3:47 PM) <http://bits.blogs.nytimes.com/2012/03/06/google-defending-google-plus-shares-usage-numbers>
120 ibid, citing Matt Rosoff, 'So That's What Google+ Is Really About: Advertising, Bus' *Insider* (6 March 2012, 5:19 PM) <http://articles.businessinsider.com/2012-03-06/tech/31126307_1vic-gundotra-google-service-google-service>
121 ibid, citing, Sunni Yuen, 'Exporting Trust with Data: Audited Self-Regulation as a Solution to Cross-Border Data Transfer Protection Concerns in the Offshore Outsourcing Industry' (2007) 9 Columbia Science and Technology Law Review 41, 44.
122 ibid 407.

competition authorities have started several investigations. In Europe, Google has already been fined billions of dollars for its anti-competitive conduct. However, on the other side of the Atlantic, many academics, the Department of Justice (DOJ), the Federal Trade Commission (FTC) and many lawyers favoured Google until late 2020.[123] Daniel Crane,[124] David A. Balto,[125] Robert H. Bork and J. Gregory Sidak,[126] Geoffrey A. Manne, and Joshua D. Wright[127] have all expressed that Google's position cannot be regarded as a monopoly, or there would be no legal cases under competition law and policy to follow in the US.[128] In the same vein, in the EU, through a positive and normative assessment, Pinar Akman has argued that there were no cases under Article 102 of the TFEU for the Google Search case back in the day.[129]

The specific problem here is the understanding of competition law and policy in the first place. The aforementioned commentators all pursue *laissez-faire* competition and thus fail to identify structural and behavioural shortcomings in the context of Big Data power. To exemplify, David Balto, a former DOJ and FTC lawyer, argues that modern competition laws are equipped to deal with every issue, including consumers' data, since they aim to maximise consumer welfare.[130] Thus, competition law either handles problems related to consumers and their data, or there is no actual consumer harm caused in the market.[131] Unlike these ideas, there is a great need for a reconsideration of competition law and policy in the age of Big Data.

Consequently, what undertakings such as Microsoft (via Bing) and Google try to achieve today is to create a strong market position by being efficient users and collectors of Big Data. As an inevitable conclusion, data-driven markets are witnessing rapid monopolisation.[132] This kind of monopoly can be called a "data-opoly",[133] bringing a handful of harms to markets.[134] Pricing practices can be explained briefly to demonstrate one of these harms. In the short term, it is unarguable that visible pro-competitive effects such as price decreases might occur in markets. For instance, before the acquisition of WhatsApp by Facebook,

---

123 ibid 408.
124 Daniel Crane, 'Search Neutrality as an Antitrust Principle' (2012) 19 George Mason Law Review 1199, 1203.
125 Balto and Lane (n 95) 6.
126 Robert H Bork and J Gregory Sidak, 'What Does the Chicago School Teach About Internet Search and the Antitrust Treatment of Google?' (2012) 8(4) Journal of Competition Law and Economics 663–700, 700.
127 Geoffrey A Manne and Joshua D Wright, 'Google and the Limits of Antitrust: The Case Against the Antitrust Case against Google' (2011) 34 Harvard Journal of Law and Public Policy 74.
128 Newman (n 115) 408.
129 Pinar Akman, 'The Theory of Abuse in Google Search: A Positive and Normative Assessment Under EU Competition Law' (2017) 2 Journal of Law, Technology and Policy 301, 370.
130 Balto and Lane (n 95) 12.
131 ibid.
132 Maurice E Stucke, 'Should We Be Concerned About Data-Opolies?' (2018) 2 Georgetown Law Technology Review 275.
133 ibid.
134 ibid.

WhatsApp was not free of charge on the mobile application markets in some countries, charging an annual sum of approximately 1$. After the Facebook/WhatsApp acquisition, WhatsApp was made free in every mobile application market.[135] In this scenario, the dominant undertaking did not exercise higher prices, unlike what traditional dominant/monopolies would do. However, lowering prices as a predatory practice is defined by the US court as unlawfully anticompetitive only if there is a "dangerous probability that the firm ... [will] later recoup ... by raising prices to monopoly levels".[136] The Court also indicates that "lower prices improve consumer welfare".[137] For this reason, people even question the monopolistic powers of technology giants[138] due to the classical assessment of competition law in markets where these platforms do not charge monetary prices.

However, this does not mean that new monopolies are not harmful to consumers.[139] Eventually, crucial anti-competitive effects start to occur. These include less innovation, degraded quality, privacy concerns, welfare transfer from consumers to data-opolies and so on.[140] Moreover, commentators argue that harms occurring in digital markets due to the strong market power created by Big Data should not be compared to the activity in traditional monopolies since the negative effects of digital monopolies will likely outrun traditional monopolies.[141] Thus, current market structures, innovative markets, and dynamic competition need to be re-examined to address these concerns and create an understanding.[142] Also, the digital monopoly problem and the difficulty in competition law identifying market structures are scrutinised in the following chapter.

There are exceedingly difficult questions for the regulators that need to be dealt with urgently. The main question scrutinised in Chapter 3 is how these new market structures affect competition law assessment regarding market power and abusive conduct. Therefore, it is quite challenging to identify problems inherent to the structures of data-driven markets. However, the Big Data–related dominance and the creation of monopolies based on Big Data must be addressed before focusing on other issues. In order to do that, a systematic analysis is carried out, followed by an assessment of recent rulings and interim reports in Europe.

However, data-related challenges are not inherent to the structures of new economy markets where Big Data has prominence. In addition, there are several crucial regulatory problems derived from Big Data collection and usage that need to be identified in terms of competition law and policy. For instance, the acquisition of

---

135 Mark Scott, 'WhatsApp, the Internet Messenger, to Become Free Digital Economy' *The New York Times* (18 January 2016) <https://bits.blogs.nytimes.com/2016/01/18/whatsapp-the-internet-messenger-to-become-free/?_r=0>
136 Case *United States v Apple* 791 F. 3d 290, 332 (2d circuit 2015).
137 ibid.
138 Stucke (n 132) 281.
139 ibid 279.
140 ibid.
141 ibid 322.
142 See Chapter 3.

vast numbers of datasets by technology giants is a huge problem. The literature usually refers to these acquisitions as R&D mergers, which are meant to have pro-competitive effects such as efficiency gains for both consumers and businesses. However, these acquisitions might pose anti-competitive threats to the online world.[143] Technology giants are purchasing small online platforms and start-ups with little or no turnover due to their greater value over their collected data. As a result, data-rich undertakings accumulate these new datasets for commercial purposes, which contributes to the creation of online ecosystems through platforms and network effects. Therefore, the question is, how does Big Data restructure global value chains? Global value chains are crucial to identify since data-driven acquisitions are more likely to have strong conglomerate effects in the online world. Thus, price-centric traditional assessments of competition – horizontal and vertical – seem to be ill equipped due to the recent growth in conglomerate effects in data-driven mergers. In the same vein, dominant undertakings also use their data dominance in markets that are not actually data-driven. Together, both situations create enormous negative long-term effects in data-driven markets and in the online world.

2.2.2 Assessment of Market Power

Another major challenge is the traditional assessment of market power. As mentioned earlier, data-driven market structures are entirely different from traditional ones, and problems inevitably arise in assessing the market power of undertakings. As identified in the study on the European Parliament's Directorate-General for Internal Policies regarding the digital economy, competition authorities face various challenges while applying Article 102 of the TFEU to data-driven abusive conduct.[144] According to the European Parliament study, tools and analytical steps are inappropriate for market power assessment.[145] As Article 102 of the TFEU states, the abusive practices of dominant undertakings in the internal market are prohibited.[146] Identifying anti-competitive unilateral conduct has two main pillars: finding dominance in a relevant market and finding abusive practices that cause consumer harm. Thus, the method of market power assessment starts with framing a relevant product market, followed by a market share and market power assessment of the alleged undertaking. Lastly, appropriate anti-competitive behaviour is addressed.[147]

Problems occur at the very first phase of abuse cases, which is defining the relevant market. Competition in data-driven markets is driven by rapid innovation; thus, market boundaries in data-driven markets are continuously redefined.[148] As

---

143 Marixenia Davilla, 'Is Big Data a Different Kind of Animal? The Treatment of Big Data Under the EU Competition Rules' (2017) 8 Journal of European Competition Law and Practice 6, 373.
144 Nikolai Van Gorp and Olga Batura, 'Challenges for Competition Policy in a Digitalised Economy' A Study for the ECON Committee, Directorate General for Internal Policies, European Parliament, July 2015, IP/A/ECON/2014-12 PE 542.235, 70.
145 ibid.
146 Article 102 of the TFEU.
147 Van Gorp and Batura (n 144) 50.
148 ibid.

a result, a traditional step-by-step market power analysis does not work correctly for data-driven markets shaped by innovation.[149] The reason behind this is that the strong feedback effects actually follow the opposite route of the traditional analysis. In the traditional method, a market structure assessment (relevant market, number of sellers-buyers, entry barriers, products) is followed by an anti-competitive conduct analysis (tactics, strategy, pricing), which moves analysis into performance gains in the final step (profits, quality, differentiation).[150]

New economy markets reverse this chain. Contrary to the former, performance gains affect anti-competitive conduct and market structure at the same time.[151] It can be said that gains such as profits, product quality and product differentiation affect the market structure (such as barriers to entry) and anti-competitive behaviours (such as strategies or pricing) to exemplify this paradigm shift.[152] This paradigm shift has carved out a niche in European competition law in the past. In 2001, Alex Jacquemin indicated that the innovative character of new industrial economies has inevitably affected the technical assessment of market power in the EU. Analysis has evolved towards a microeconomic theory approach, including imperfect competition models and the game theory perspective.[153] By this means, Jacquemin has also indicated that new methodological aspects of the assessment of market power have now replaced more static approaches by referring to Schumpeter's theory on innovative markets and competition.[154] Although incorporating new methodological models can affect market power assessment and case law, the step-by-step approach has not fundamentally changed in European competition law assessment.[155] Consequently, and due to Big Data's influence nowadays, strong network effects and feedback loops in data-driven markets are highly likely to create a misleading assessment of market power in cases of the abuse of a dominant position.

In the same vein, according to the OECD report on Big Data and Competition Policy:[156]

> Many of the current instruments of competition analysis, such as market definition, may be insufficient to fully account for the features of digital markets. . . . [T]ools such as the SSNIP test, as well as the most consensual measures of market concentration, fall short of capturing the specific features of these markets.[157]

---

149 ibid.
150 ibid.
151 ibid.
152 ibid.
153 Alexis Jacquemin, 'Theories of Industrial Organisation and Competition Policy: What Are the Links?' (2000) European Commission Forward Studies Unit, Working Paper 11.
154 ibid.
155 Van Gorp and Batura (n 144) 50.
156 OECD, Thiemann and Gonzaga (n 1) 15.
157 ibid.

In a traditional market, an undertaking charges prices to consumers and advertisers, such as a car manufacturer or media organ.[158] Thus, tests such as the small but significant and non-transitory increase in price (SSNIP) test or hypothetical monopoly test fit assessment since they both rely on pricing in markets.[159] However, in data-driven markets, undertakings have both monetary and non-monetary transactions in the exchange of data markets. Eventually, near zero-to-zero prices in data-driven markets make it challenging to implement tests based on pricing mechanisms.

Additionally, undertakings usually operate in various markets and have multiple roles.[160] For instance, undertakings such as Google or Apple are simultaneously developers, manufacturers, content providers, advertisement sellers and buyers, clearly indicating multiple roles. The multiple roles of undertakings are another reason the definition of a relevant market is a troublesome issue in these cases. In other words, the dynamic and innovative character, along with the multi-sided structure in data-driven markets, make it a challenging task to define a relevant market for nearly every data-driven abuse in an abuse of a dominant position case.

For another example, market share assessment also seems to be an issue with the current competition tools. As the guidance from the European Commission on Enforcement Priorities, in applying Article 102, states, the assessment of market share is a useful tool for assessing market power.[161] According to the guidance, there will likely be dominance if an undertaking's market share is over 40% in a relevant product market.[162] However, this type of market share assessment does not seem relevant in data-driven markets. The reason behind it is the irrelevancy of market share in digital dominance since data-driven markets have a dynamic character and tend to change very quickly.[163] To exemplify, Myspace had a market share of 76.35% of all visits in the US, and Facebook only had 12.57% in December 2007.[164] In only one and a half years, Myspace lost its share to Facebook in the social networking market[165] and then disappeared from the market in subsequent years. The buy-out power of incumbents in data-driven markets or new entrants

---

158 ibid.
159 ibid.
160 ibid.
161 Communication from the European Commission, Guidance on the Commission's Enforcement Priorities in applying Article 82 of the EC Treaty to abusive exclusionary conduct by dominant undertakings (Text with EEA relevance) [2009] OJ C45/9, para 13.
162 ibid para 14.
163 Daniel Mandrescu, 'Applying EU Competition Law to Online Platforms: The Road Ahead – Part 2 (2017) 38 European Competition Law Review 9, 410–22, 413.
164 Marketing Charts, 'Myspace Got 76% of US Social Network Traffic in 07, Facebook's Grew 51%' (18 January 2008) <https://www.marketingcharts.com/demographics-and-audiences/youth-and-gen-x-3075>
165 Chloe Albanesius, 'More Americans Go to Facebook Than Myspace' *The PC Mag* (16 June 2009) <https://www.pcmag.com/article2/0,2817,2348822,00.asp>

that leverage their power stemming from collected datasets from third markets definitely affect market share analysis overall.[166]

In conclusion, the dynamic character of data-driven markets and the "winner-takes-all" structure leads data-driven market players to operate in multiple markets intertwined with each other, such as online search, online advertising or social networking. Thus, assessing an undertaking's market power in an abuse case becomes quite challenging whether or not it has a dominant position.[167] The real difficulty lies in the power comparison that needs to be determined together with its competitors, both individually and cumulatively. According to Daniel Mandrescu, material addressing the diversity across interrelated markets is currently vague, and clarification is needed to determine market power and dominance to legitimise the intervention and remedies.[168] Even if a given market share were relevant for an undertaking in the online world, without the innovative character of the market, the importance of market shares would stay insignificant.[169] As in the Myspace-Facebook example, an established market share might change drastically in a short period and distort the market power analysis in the abuse case.[170] Not only the speed of change but also the thresholds for dominance in a given market might become quite challenging to detect.[171]

In light of this information, it is apparent that competition law and policy need to reconsider the current tools and existing policy frameworks together with a structural analysis. In order to achieve that and to develop an argument, several issues need to be addressed in Chapter 4. First, the definition of relevant markets for data-driven acquisitions and market power must be analysed in order to determine the criteria by which to assess Big Data and market power. Second, the importance of innovation, ecosystems and the multi-sidedness of data-driven markets are discussed in the context of this study. The analysis is engaged to find market power assessment failures in data-driven markets. Overall, the crucial misevaluations on assessing market power in Big Data–related cases in data-driven markets are enunciated, and solutions are sought in Chapter 4.

2.2.3 Anti-Competitive Conduct

Another major competition law challenge in the online world is the anti-competitive conduct of dominant undertakings. Technology giants such as Google, Apple, Amazon, Microsoft and Facebook have recently faced various abuse of dominant position cases before the European competition authorities. Microsoft

---

166 Bundeskartellamt and Autorité de la Concurrence, 'Competition Law and Data' (2016) 30 <https://www.bundeskartellamt.de/SharedDocs/Publikation/DE/Berichte/Big%20Data%20Papier.html;jsessionid=FCE1A15B6F85CD160925E13F58EE7524.1_cid378?nn=3600108>
167 Mandrescu (n 163) 413.
168 ibid.
169 ibid.
170 ibid.
171 ibid 414.

has received fines totalling nearly €2 billion for several abuse of dominant position cases brought by the European Commission.[172] Google also has three important abuse of dominant position cases before the Commission. In the first case, the *Google Shopping* case, the Commission fined Google a total of €2.4 billion for abusing its dominant position in the comparative online shopping and online advertisement market, which was a record fine at the time.[173] Although Google brought case before the CJEU, the General Court dismissed Google's action almost in its entirety, upholding the fine of € 2.4 billion.[174] In the second case involving Android, the Commission fined Google €4.3 billion over its Android operating system for abusing its dominant position.[175] The third case involving Google, also in the advertising sector, the *Google AdSense* case, the Commission fined Google €1.49 billion.[176] Although there are various cases in data-driven markets, possibly the most debated behavioural challenge for competition authorities in the age of Big Data is the identification of anti-competitive conduct.

In data-driven markets, exclusionary and predatory conduct seem to be quite common. On top of that, due to the insufficiency of the current competition tools to assess market power, as mentioned earlier, the identification of anti-competitive conduct and assessing the potential harms of alleged abuses are also quite misleading. To note, the dynamic context of data-driven markets leads undertakings to anti-competitive conduct, and these markets make collusion quite unlikely, according to the ECON report.[177] Data-driven markets are now at the centre of most commercial activities, and undertakings use their powers stemming from their mass collection of data in digitalised markets. Thus, control over mass personal data leads to exclusionary and discriminatory conduct, and challenges faced in abuse of dominant position cases must be discussed cautiously.

Tying is an example of exclusionary conduct and an important concern in data-driven markets. Through tying, dominant undertakings leverage their market powers in other markets.[178] Leveraging is done by tying or bundling new or little-used products to their main competitive products or services to gain an advantage over rivals in adjacent markets.[179] Not only does this result in gaining market share or market power, but smaller competitors are also driven out of the markets since they cannot compete with the undertaking, which uses its data power and externalises network effects. One example is Microsoft and its old web browser, Microsoft

---

172 Case COMP/C-3/37.792 Microsoft; Case COMP/C-3/39.530 Microsoft; Case T-201/4 *Microsoft Corp. v Commission* [2007] ECLI:EU:T:2007:289; 2008.
173 Case AT.39740 *Google Search (Shopping)* [2017] 4444 Final.
174 Case T-612/17 *Google and Alphabet v Commission (Google Shopping)* [2021] ECLI:EU:T:2021:763.
175 Case No COMP/AT.40099, *Google Android* [2018] Commission Decision of 18 July 2018, C(2018) 4761 Final.
176 Case No COMP/AT.40411 *Google AdSense* [2019] C(2019) 2173 Final.
177 ibid.
178 Maurice Stucke and Allen Grunes, *Big Data and Competition Policy* (1st edn, OUP 2016) 290.
179 Konstantinos Stylianou, 'Exclusion in Digital Markets' (2018) 24 Michigan Telecommunications and Technology Law Review 2, 190.

Explorer. Back in the 90s and early 2000s, Microsoft offered the Explorer web browser along with its main product, Windows, which enjoyed a near-monopoly position in the operating systems market.[180] To be more precise, Explorer was the default web browser of Windows OS, and 90% of consumers ended up using Explorer as their computer's web browser. Through this conduct, Microsoft gained power in the web browser market by leveraging its almost monopolistic control of the operating systems market into the browser market in order to eliminate rivals in the web browser application market and drive them out of the Windows ecosystem.

In addition to tying, leveraging data advantage can be an abusive behaviour that leads to the exclusion of rivals. For example, the Belgian Competition Authority fined the National Lottery €1.2 million in September 2015 after the Belgian National Lottery launched a new betting product called "Scooore!"[181] According to the Investigation and Prosecution Service, the National Lottery used its data advantage in favour of its new sports betting service "Scooore!"[182] This is an abuse of dominant position case in which the National Lottery used its legal monopoly position to leverage its market power. To be more precise, the National Lottery used its datasets, Big Data, collected from the National Lottery Service, where they enjoy a monopoly position to leverage their power into the sports betting market. The data was not collected following the competition on merit by the National Lottery; thus, it was not possible for competitors to obtain data such as the contact details or preferences of consumers within a reasonable period.[183] This example shows that through exclusionary practices, the data power of undertakings can be used as leverage in other markets, and Big Data, data collection and data advantage all contain huge risks for markets from a competition law perspective.

Another exclusionary practice in data-driven markets is the refusal to supply or provide access to data. As mentioned earlier, personal data has a prominent role in the operation of businesses in data-driven markets; thus, there have been discussions on how denial of access to data might affect competition in these markets and whether it is an abuse of a dominant position.[184] There are arguments about the characteristics of Big Data in digital markets. On one side, commentators argue that processed data does not have the qualifications to be regarded as an essential facility.[185] They advocate the non-rivalrous and non-exclusive nature of data as evidence of it not being an essential facility.[186] On the other side, commentators argue that data might be an essential facility in specific markets. Thus, established case law should be referred to in these instances in which data should be regarded

---

180 ibid.
181 Stucke and Grunes (n 178) 291; Belgian Competition Authority Press Release, The Belgian Competition Authority Imposes a Fine of 1.190.000 EUR on the National Lottery N°15/2015 (23 September 2015) <https://www.belgiancompetition.be/en/about-us/actualities/press-release-nr-15-2015>
182 ibid.
183 ibid.
184 Mandrescu (n 163) 418.
185 Lerner (n 27) 20.
186 ibid 20–21.

as an essential facility.[187] According to the essential facilities doctrine, if there are no other ways for competitors to operate in a market without having access to data a dominant undertaking has, then cooperation should be expected from the data controller. In order to apply this doctrine, there must be a product or service which is indispensable for an activity in the market,[188] and refusal to supply this product or service must have an effect on competition. It must also affect further developments or services since competitors cannot have access to that input. Lastly, there should not be any justifications for the refusal to supply situation.[189] The CJEU has established these conditions in the rulings of the *Bronner*,[190] *Microsoft*[191] and *IMS Health*[192] cases.[193]

Anti-competitive conduct in data-driven markets using Big Data as a tool is not limited to the aforementioned instances. There are several more abuse types that can occur in data-driven markets. The aforementioned lock-in effects created by network effects, increasing switching costs for consumers, vertical integration in the form of abuse, exclusionary agreements for access to data and even price discrimination have distorting effects in data-driven markets. These actions raise high barriers to entry for new entrants and even force incumbents to leave markets. However, there might also be completely novel types of abuses.[194] The most important example is the investigation of Facebook by the *Bundeskartellamt* (the German Federal Cartel Office). According to the *Bundeskartellamt*, Facebook abuses its dominant position in the social networking market by collecting and generating data through third-party services such as Instagram, WhatsApp, websites, embedded games and application programming interfaces (APIs).[195] In other words, Facebook breaches competition rules by violating its data protection rules to the disadvantage of consumers.[196] According to Maximilian Volmar and Katharina Helmdach, this investigation tightens the relationship between competition law and data protection law, and this novel type of abuse might lead to a rethinking

---

187 Inge Graef, Sih Yuliana Wahyuningtyas and Peggy Vackle, 'Assessing Data Access Issues in Online Platforms' (2015) 39 Telecommunications Policy 5, 375–87.
188 Inge Graef, *EU Competition Law, Data Protection and Online Platforms: Data as Essential Facility* (Wolters Kluwer 2016) 214.
189 ibid.
190 Case C-7/97 *Oscar Bronner GmbH & Co. KG v Mediaprint Zeitungs- und Zeitschriftenverlag GmbH & Co. KG and Others* [1998] ECLI:EU:C:1998:569.
191 Case T-201/4 *Microsoft Corp. v Commission of the European Communities* [2007] ECLI:EU:T:2007:289.
192 Case C-418/01 *IMS Health GmbH & Co. OHG v NDC Health GmbH & Co. KG.* [2004] ECLI:EU:C: 2004:257.
193 Bundeskartellamt and Autorité de la Concurrence (n 166) 18.
194 See Chapter 5.3.1.
195 *Bundeskartellamt*, Press Release, 'Preliminary Assessment in Facebook Proceeding: Facebook's Collection and Use of Data from Third-Party Sources Is Abusive' (19 December 2017) <https://www.bundeskartellamt.de/SharedDocs/Meldung/EN/Pressemitteilungen/2017/19_12_2017_Facebook.html>
196 ibid.

of abuse of dominant position cases and the application of Article 102 of the TFEU in data-driven markets.[197]

As seen earlier, European authorities have endeavoured to assess the dominance of technology giants and Big Data's relevance to market power. For the approach of European authorities, the head of the US DOJ's Antitrust Division, Makan Delrahim, mentions that even the aim of competition laws and policy are quite similar in the EU and US (referring to the consumer welfare approach and the commitments of EU Commissioners Mario Monti, Neelie Kroes, Joaquin Almunia and Margrethe Vestager regarding the prominence of consumer welfare standards in EU law), but there are also sizeable differences between their laws.[198] Therefore, he adds that competition laws enforce special duties upon market players with dominant positions in Europe, unlike US law.[199] Although he admits there are concerns about data-driven markets, he expresses that the US authorities would not impose special duties upon dominant market players when there is no proven harm in competition law.[200] He justifies this idea through the flexibility of an evidence-based approach to consumer welfare economics by applying data-driven abuse of dominant position cases.[201] Another justification is the non-interventionist stance of competition law not to stifle innovation in these dynamic and competitive markets. The concern here is consumer benefit. However, the approach of the US authorities could well change from 2023 onwards.[202]

Furthermore, some commentators in Europe also hold the aforementioned non-interventionist ideas. According to Evelin Hlina, Article 102 of the TFEU is theoretically sufficient to deal with abuse in digitalised markets.[203] Thus, the Commission has attempted to adopt a more evidence-based approach through reviews[204] and guidance papers.[205] According to Hlina, if the CJEU and competition authorities in Europe continue to follow a formalistic approach, it might create problems

---

197 Maximilian N Volmar and Katharina O Helmdach, 'Protecting Consumers and Their Data Through Competition Law? Rethinking Abuse of Dominance in Light of the Federal Cartel Office's Facebook Investigation' (2018) 14 European Competition Journal 2, 200–1.
198 Makan Delrahim, 'Good Times, Trust Will Take Us Far: Competition Enforcement and the Relationship Between Washington and Brussels' SPEECH in Brussels, 21 February 2018 <https://www.justice.gov/opa/speech/assistant-attorney-general-makan-delrahim-delivers-remarks-college-europe-brussels>
199 ibid.
200 ibid.
201 ibid.
202 See Chapter 6.1.2.
203 Evelin Hlina, 'Dominant Undertakings in the Digital Era: A Call for Evolution of the Competition Policy Towards Article 102 TFEU? (2016) 9 ICC Global Antitrust Review 154.
204 European Commission, 'DG Competition Discussion Paper of December 2005 on the Application of Article 82 of the Treaty to Exclusionary Abuses' <http://ec.europa.eu/competition/antitrust/art82/discpaper2005.pdf>
205 European Commission, 'Communication from the European Commission, Guidance on the Commission's Enforcement Priorities in Applying Article 82 of the EC Treaty to Abusive Exclusionary Conduct by Dominant Undertakings (Text with EEA Relevance)' [2009] OJ C45/9.

in data-driven markets and eventually be detrimental to consumers and innovation.[206] In contrast to Hlina's arguments, the current competition policy might not be as effective as anticipated.[207]

In conclusion, all these issues are scrutinised in Chapters 5 and 6, along with the competition cases of prominent market players such as Google, Facebook, Amazon and Apple, and outcomes of the current structures of data-driven markets specified in Chapter 3. In this part, particular emphasis is also given to theories and discussions on implementing the essential facilities doctrine while examining discriminatory access to data as anti-competitive conduct in data-driven markets.

2.3 Concluding Remarks

The analysis in this chapter has revealed the relevance between Big Data and digitalised markets by creating a framework for Big Data and analytics in the context of competition law. Therefore, Big Data is found to be a value-creation mechanism in digitalised markets. Collected data and computer algorithms have increasing roles in business management, decisions, and behaviour. Therefore, digitalised markets evolved into "data-driven markets", where data is the key to these markets' functioning, as this research proposes. Due to the significant impact of Big Data on commercial life and markets, Big Data is not only a market-defining value-creation mechanism but also a significant tool for gaining market power. Undertakings utilising Big Data technology create significant efficiencies in data-driven markets. Thus, they also gain ample competitive advantage over rivals. Therefore, the analysis has moved on to the Big Data-related anti-competitive effects in data-driven markets since the main objective of this chapter is to identify the challenges in terms of competition law and policy.

As a result, three main challenges are found for consideration. It has been identified that Big Data is not only a tool to create efficiencies, produce better products and enhance quality. Undertakings utilise Big Data for anti-competitive practices to distort competition. In data-driven markets where competitive advantage deriving from Big Data is visible, manipulation, discrimination or any abuse driven by the data power of undertakings (as in the example of giant online platforms) is likely to occur. However, the identification of abusive conduct is also misleading due to the current assessment of market power in competition law. Misevaluation in this area creates various problems eventually. Moreover, relentless data collection and data-driven acquisitions might lead to strong monopolies in data-driven markets and could have distortive conglomerate effects on markets. In total, these concerns are grounds for an urgent intervention of competition law in data-driven markets.

The identification of challenges has enabled the discussion to reveal the strengths and weaknesses of the current structure. In the following chapters, this discussion is held in order to demonstrate the need to propose soft or hard laws to

---

206 Hlina (n 203) 154.
207 See Chapter 6.1.4.

deal with the Big Data issue. As a result, it can be clarified that various challenges await the competition authorities and lawmakers to respond immediately regarding competition law and policy. Hence, this study aims to provide adequate guidance on resolving current and probable legal uncertainties in this newly emerged area. That being said, the analysis focuses on the market structures in the new economy in the following chapter. In order to do that, the critical relationship between innovation and competition policy is underlined in the first place. Following that, an understanding of the characteristics of dynamic markets over the decades is discussed, and the situation today is examined. Only then will it be possible to delve deeper into the data-driven economy to reveal the driving force behind using data technology. Following that, the issue of monopolisation in digitalised markets is examined thoroughly.

It is unarguable that competition law needs to stand against Big Data–related concerns. Not only academics but also competition authorities and governments are all aware of it. As seen earlier, current investigations and arguments covered by academics and officials point out the significance of competition concerns in data-driven markets for the future. The intervention of competition law in anti-competitive practices related to Big Data and competition law itself in the EU could also be scrutinised with novel types of conduct in the dawn of the digital era of services.

There are several ideas for approaching competition law in the digital age. As an option, a non-interventionist approach to data-driven markets in terms of competition law is unlikely to mitigate the current and future competition problems in these markets. Another option is intervention. Legal intervention should be the core feature of data-driven markets.[208] Consequently, technological developments and new business types challenge the law in the first place.[209] Thus, technology and new market dynamics will likely override current regulations.

Moreover, technology giants such as Google, Amazon, Facebook and Apple are experts at legal engineering, bringing efficiency claims as merger defences or minimising their tax burdens.[210] Apple's case relating to tax benefits in Ireland[211] and Google's attempt to avoid the application of laws outside the US[212] are relevant examples of their conduct.[213] For instance, in the case of territoriality of competition rules, Big Data, online markets and the global ecosystem of technology giants have made the current rules outdated. What competition law cannot capture today will

---

208 Alain Strowel and Wouter Vergote, 'Responses to the Public Consultation on the Regulatory Environment for Platforms, Online Intermediaries, Data and Cloud Computing and the Collaborative Economy' (2016) 9 <http://ec.europa.eu/information_society/newsroom/image/document/2016-7/uclouvain_et_universit_saint_louis_14044.pdf>
209 ibid.
210 ibid.
211 Case No. COMP/SA.38373 Commission Decision of 30.8.2016 on State Aid (2014/C) (ex 2014/NN) (ex 2014/CP) implemented by Ireland to Apple Brussels, 30 August 2016 C (2016) 5605 final.
212 Case C-131/12 *Google Spain SL and Google Inc. v Agencia Española de Protección de Datos (AEPD) and Mario Costeja González* [2014] ECLI:EU:C:2014:317.
213 Strowel and Vergote (n 208) 9.

be the most significant problem for consumers in the future. Thus, developments in the online world necessarily affect the legal landscape and will trigger developments in the context of competition law.

In conclusion, the necessity of a modern approach in the EU is the main claim of this research. This examination has been carried out by scrutinising the effectiveness of competition law, reforms for EU competition law to apply new legal tests to markets in the context of Big Data and its effects proposed. This conclusion seems inevitable in the wake of Big Data and e-commerce. Therefore, the EU needs the necessary tools and legal tests to apply and enforce competition law in data-driven markets. Above all, it should not be forgotten that technology does not follow regulations, and regulatory actions should not stifle innovation. However, along with the development of technology and digital markets, the legal landscape also needs urgent change and development in the context of EU law.

3 Data-Driven Market Structures and Monopolisation

3.1 Data-Driven Markets

The industrialisation and commercialisation of personal computers and the internet have led to the creation of online ecosystems for business and daily life. All forms of data were collected and easily stored for various economic and social transactions online and offline through these decades.[1] Data collection increased the amount of available data for governments and private businesses.[2] Due to the introduction of Big Data and data analytics in the last couple of decades, commercial markets are under the influence of Big Data more than ever today. There are two main types of commercial markets in the new economy. The first type is the digitalised markets which were at one time traditional. Most already-known commercial activities can be included in this category. The utility of Big Data in online and offline activities opens the way to the transformation of economic and social activities. Even the most fundamental transactions are done online today. For instance, banking[3] and grocery shopping have moved to the online world lately. In these activities, data is effectively used, kept and analysed for future transactions aimed at various efficiencies on all sides of these markets.

The second type of data-driven market is much newer to commercial and social life: online platforms or intermediaries. In the memorandum of a regulation proposal regarding fairness and transparency for online businesses, the European Commission stated that:

> Online platforms are key enablers of digital trade.... More than a million EU enterprises trade through online platforms in order to reach their customers, and it is estimated that around 60% of private consumption ... of goods

---

1 Jens Prüfer and Christoph Schottmüller, 'Competing with Big Data' (2017) Tilburg Law School Research Paper No. 06/2017, TILEC Discussion Paper No. 2017-006, Center Discussion Paper 2017-007, 1.
2 ibid.
3 As mentioned earlier.

DOI: 10.4324/9781003458791-3

and services related to the total digital economy are transacted via online intermediaries.[4]

Most of these markets have just emerged through recent technological developments. They mainly profit from offering free products or services on one side of the market and bring different buyer and seller groups together. Thus, they tend to attract consumers and generate huge advantages through data collection and network effects.[5] For instance, Google, Amazon and many others act as online intermediaries. The main revenue of these undertakings is online advertising. Search engines, social media, online video sharing, games and messaging markets offer free services to end users and get an advantage from the other side of the market, which is the online advertisement side aiming to attract more consumers. Many players in these markets try to catch consumers' attention; thus, they frequently add new features to their products or services.[6] These two types of markets, digitalised and newly emerged, are further explained next.

3.1.1 Digitalised Traditional Markets

A digitalised market is a market in which products or services are moved onto web-based operations. The online environment gave rise to transaction platforms in the wake of the 21st century, when Amazon and eBay launched their first online services.[7] Transaction platforms act as both an online intermediary that connects individual buyers and sellers and a seller in that market. For instance, eBay provides a safe ecosystem through PayPal technology, where many buyers and sellers trade safely.[8] This ecosystem reduces the costs of reaching buyers from the businesses' side and sellers from the consumers' side. Eventually, the online intermediary gains revenues through transaction fees and targeted advertisements. Some platforms, like Amazon, have started businesses that sell merchandise directly from their warehouses. Amazon provides merchandise under its own trading name and acts as a retailer in addition to numerous small retailers on amazon.com,[9] where it provides a platform to gather sellers and buyers.[10] Today, most smaller online

---

4 European Commission, Proposal for a regulation of the European Parliament and of the Council on Promoting Fairness and Transparency for Business Users of Online Intermediation Services, COM(2018)238, later: PE/56/2019/REV/1 OJ L 186, 11 July 2019 (P2B Regulation).
5 David S Evans, 'Attention Rivalry Among Online Platforms' (2013) 9 Journal of Competition Law and Economics 2, 313.
6 ibid.
7 Inge Graef, 'Data as Essential Facility: Competition and Innovation on Online Platforms' (PhD Thesis, KU Leuven Faculty of Law 2016) 28.
8 David S Evans, 'Antitrust Issues Raised by the Emerging Global Internet Economy' (2008) 102 Northwestern University Law Review 291.
9 amazon.co.uk/amazon.de/amazon.it/amazon.ru/amazon.cn and many others.
10 Evans (n 8) 291.

retailers depend on transaction platforms such as Alibaba, eBay and Amazon to gain revenue and sales.[11]

Additionally, transaction platforms can be found on many other web-based platforms. Global web-based platforms like Google and Facebook also act as transaction platforms as part of their businesses. These global giants provide web-based services to other businesses by making their software services available to them.[12] For example, various games and music services of third-party businesses are available via Facebook for social media users.[13] Various popular applications are accessible through Facebook, and they raise the value of Facebook as a whole by attracting more consumers.[14] To give another example, Google provides its mapping service not only for its users but also for third-party application creators and other web-based businesses.[15] By this means, Google allows developers to write applications based on their map service, making Google popular and increasing its value overall. Even Apple used the Google Maps service for iOS by default until recently.[16] These are examples of multi-sided platforms where many intermediary or retailer businesses enjoy revenues through transaction costs, online advertisement fees and software licensing agreements based on the digitalised economy. Smaller businesses and retailers in the online world now rely on these transaction platforms to reach their target audiences.[17] Through the traffic created by retailers and consumers, the value of the transaction platforms rises, attracting even more consumers and creating strong feedback loops.

3.1.2 Newly Emerged Markets

Like digitalised markets, newly emerged markets act as online transaction platforms and intermediary market participants. That being said, their business model is mainly based on online advertising-supported models. The search engine and social media (network) markets are the most recognised markets where this model is put into practice effectively. Both markets need substantial advertising for their functioning.[18] The common characteristic of both digitalised and newly emerged markets is the business model of utilising the Big Data technique, which enables platforms to function on more than one side of a market. Most data-driven markets are multi-sided.

The search engine market, for instance, is an online platform where users can conduct searches through the internet to access needed information, services or products. The business model of search engines is basically to connect users, content

---

11 ibid 292.
12 ibid.
13 ibid.
14 ibid.
15 ibid.
16 Default between 2007 and 2012, until Apple released its own mapping software and service.
17 Evans (n 8) 292.
18 Graef (n 7) 21.

providers and advertisers looking for each other on that platform.[19] Accordingly, Google expresses its objective as: "Our mission is to organise the world's information and make it universally accessible and useful" on its web page.[20] When Google started its operations as a search engine, it did not collect or store users' data.[21] It took until around 2001 for Google to utilise consumer data for further searches and transactions.[22] While competitors like AltaVista, AOL and Yahoo were trying to catalogue search results for consumers with actual staff members working, Google started using algorithms to create organic search results.[23] Google's "learning-by-doing" or "trial-and-error" method was the key to its success.[24] The most relevant results are generated and shown to users through algorithms in the Google search engine.[25]

In this method, according to users' search terms, algorithms determine results that the user would likely be searching for by mathematical calculations.[26] Results are ranked based on the algorithm due to previous and similar searchers.[27] The search engine judges each result to generate what the user might have sought by typing the search terms.[28] More people using search engines means more data to utilise and more trials for the trial-and-error method.[29] Thus, the Google search engine would likely learn by doing while storing more data with every search done by mapping users' personal preferences.[30] This would result in better search results, eventually attracting even more users to engage with the search engine. As Google became increasingly popular due to accurate and relevant results, more room opened for more tests on Google's side.[31] Eventually, the popularity of Google increased even more.[32] It is important to note that this method requires a robust infrastructure to collect, store and analyse data to subtract value from it, which many of Google's rivals are incapable of doing.

Due to its success in utilising Big Data for its search engine service, Google has surpassed its competitors in the search engine market and has become a leading company in just a couple of decades. Today, Google receives 63,000 searches

---

19 Ioannis Lianos and Evgeniya Motchenkova, 'Market Dominance and Search Quality in the Search Engine Market (2012) 9 Journal of Competition Law and Economics 2, 419–55, 421.
20 <https://about.google/>
21 Around 1998.
22 Prüfer and Schottmüller (n 1) 27.
23 ibid.
24 Maurice Stucke and Allen Grunes, *Big Data and Competition Policy* (1st edn, OUP 2016) 173.
25 ibid.
26 Testimony of Eric Schmidt, Executive Chairman, Google Inc. Before the Senate Committee on the Judiciary Subcommittee on Antitrust, Competition Policy, and Consumer Rights, 112th Congress (21 September 2011) 2.
27 ibid.
28 ibid.
29 Stucke and Grunes (n 24) 175.
30 ibid.
31 Pamela Jones Harbour and Tara Isa Koslov, 'Section 2 in a Web 2.0: An Expanded Vision of Relevant Product Markers' (2010) 76 Antirust Law Journal 777.
32 Stucke and Grunes (n 24) 178.

per second on average.[33] The success of Google in the learning-by-doing method entrenched its dominance.[34] In recent years, Google has widened its business to many sectors. Connecting markets is one of Google's key accomplishments. Through acquisitions and investments, Google channelled its Big Data accumulation to various web-based and traditional sectors.[35] Starting only as a web-based search engine provider, Google now focuses on other sectors like autonomous car manufacturing, video sharing, cinema-music sectors, map and navigation sectors and many others.[36] As a giant in the search engine and online advertisement markets, it is only a matter of time before Google becomes a giant in another sector. For this reason, Google's success is much more related to its ability to connect markets today. Google has seven products or services with more than a billion users in total.[37]

The social network market is another example of a newly emerged market. Although they emerged in the 1990s, the first successful social networks were Friendster and Myspace in the early 2000s.[38] Facebook initially followed them and attained immense success in later years. Following the closure of Google+ in April 2019, there are three primary social networking services: Facebook, Instagram (which is also owned by Meta) and Twitter. Also, various social networks aim to attract specific consumers, like LinkedIn, ResearchGate and Tinder, but their scope is much more limited than that of Facebook or Instagram. The most significant distinction between social networks and other web-based services is that social networks do not offer any content provided by the service itself.[39] Unlike other markets mentioned here, the social network does not create content for users themselves in its business model and requires users to provide their content.[40] In this business model, businesses mainly offer their services for free[41] and let users create content by posting ideas, sharing photos and videos and interacting with each other.[42]

Although the business model is slightly different, the revenue sources of social networks are more or less the same as those of other web-based services. The main revenue item for social networks is online advertising. While providing free access to users, the social network relies on advertising to operate.[43] For instance, Facebook provides space to advertisers on people's profiles, and newsfeeds to

---

33 'Google Search Statistics' *Seotribunal.com* (26 September 2018) <https://seotribunal.com/blog/google-stats-and-facts>
34 Stucke and Grunes (n 24) 183.
35 Prüfer and Schottmüller (n 1) 30.
36 ibid.
37 Anita Balakrishnan, 'Here's How Billions of People Use Google Products' *CNBC* (18 May 2017) <https://www.cnbc.com/2017/05/18/google-user-numbers-youtube-android-drive-photos.html>
38 Graef (n 7) 24.
39 ibid 25.
40 ibid.
41 Social networks like LinkedIn and Tinder also have paid premium memberships.
42 Graef (n 7) 25.
43 ibid.

display to Facebook, Facebook Messenger and Instagram users.[44] Like Google, Facebook's algorithms aim to match users with advertisers as relevant as possible. Facebook uses algorithms to deliver relevant ads to users by their interests, based on their profiles, geographic locations and many other factors determined by automated systems.[45] In 2018, 98.5% of Facebook's total revenue was generated from algorithm-delivered advertisements.[46] It is expected that Facebook will generate 99% of total revenue from online advertising only.

Additionally, Facebook generates revenue from other payments from application developers and the Oculus business. Various third-party application developers use Facebook's web-based services to reach consumers for their games and other kinds of applications. Facebook then receives payment for each application developed and presented to users on the social network service. Recently, it has been reported that Facebook is also working on a blockchain-based payment system for the near future.[47] Similar to Google, Facebook now has over one billion users due to its acquisition of the messaging application WhatsApp.[48]

In summary, collecting personal data combined with data analytics is a vital resource for a functioning online advertising-supported business model and online intermediary markets. As mentioned in the previous chapter, the high amount,[49] speed[50] and variation[51] of data collected from consumers by online transaction platforms amplify the total value of web-based services and enable new techniques to process and use data for consumer services and products. The unique feature of digital markets is the utility of Big Data and the implementation of data analytics technologies. Big Data technologies are the reason today's technology giants are giants, and Big Data has a significant impact on commercial and social life.

This analysis reveals that digitalised economies are not characterised only by their web-based functionalities. The contribution and infrastructure provided by the internet are not meant to be negated here. The recent technologies have forced businesses to move their operations to the online world and eventually led to the creation of digitalised markets. However, it is unarguable that Big Data determines the bone structure of digitalised economies today. In this structure, data is used as a source for online advertising. Therefore, in addition to digitalised and newly emerged markets, the existence of the online advertising market is another critical discussion in this sense.

---

44 What Is Facebook's Revenue Breakdown? *Nasdaq.com* (28 March 2019) <https://www.nasdaq.com/articles/what-facebooks-revenue-breakdown-2019-03-28-0>
45 ibid.
46 ibid.
47 ibid.
48 Stucke and Grunes (n 24) 182.
49 *Volume*; Section 2.1.1.
50 *Velocity*; Section 2.1.1.
51 *Variety*; Section 2.1.1.

3.1.3 Online Advertising as a Market Itself

In data-driven markets, businesses implement the classic method of advertising-media model for various services and products.[52] In this model, web-based content is used to attract consumers in order to create traffic.[53] Then, access to this nascence is provided to businesses that prepare advertisements through this traffic to attract consumers for their products or services.[54] Today, businesses like Google, Facebook, Amazon, eBay and Alibaba effectively use online advertising–supported business models, and these models are regarded as the most significant developments in recent history.[55] For instance, most online newsletters and blogs, even well-known ones, rely on Google advertisement services for revenue.[56] These web-based businesses sell space on their web pages to advertisers and their advertisements to third-party web pages by Google Ad, an intermediary provider.[57] By this means, businesses enjoy ad revenues together with Google itself as the online traffic occurs through web pages. Inge Graef stresses the importance of Big Data and data analytics in the advertising-supported media model in data-driven markets. Hereunder, the two most important characteristics of this business model are explained.

First, the advertisements provided on various online platforms are not random at all. Businesses in the online world use targeted advertisements quite efficiently. For instance, Amazon,[58] eBay,[59] Google[60] and Facebook[61] collect their users' preferences via data on product views, previous purchases, virtual shopping baskets, behavioural factors, geographic location and even demographic information like age.[62] Then, these personal preferences are used to generate possible results, which are recommendations of various products to consumers. For instance, on amazon.com, advertisements are displayed both on product pages and in search results.[63] Advertisers determine keywords for their products, and together with product-category and product-page contents, advertisements are filtered automatically and shown to relevant consumers.

Similarly, the Google Ad service, which many web-based businesses use today, runs audience- and content-targeting advertisements. Google lets advertisers design

---

52 David S Evans, 'Antitrust Issues Raised by the Emerging Global Internet Economy' (2008) 102 Northwestern University Law Review 290.
53 ibid.
54 ibid.
55 ibid 291.
56 ibid 292.
57 ibid.
58 Amazon Advertising Preferences <https://www.amazon.co.uk/adprefs>
59 eBay AdChoice Service <https://www.ebay.co.uk/help/account/adchoice/adchoice?id=4648>
60 Google Ads <https://support.google.com/google-ads/answer/1704368?hl=en>
61 What Are My Ad Preferences and How Can I Adjust Them on Facebook? <https://en-gb.facebook.com/help/247395082112892?helpref=uf_permalink>
62 Graef (n 7) 28.
63 ibid.

a profile for their ads to reach a wider and more relevant audience. For instance, Google explains that if a San Francisco–based dog day-care centre adds the keywords "dog", "day care", and "San Francisco" to its advertisement, consumers who search "dog" or "day-care centre" through Google are shown these advertisers' ads.[64] Similarly, when a business designs advertisements for special event costumes, consumers who visit web pages related to Halloween or other special occasions are shown the advertisers' ads by the display network of Google Ads.[65]

Moreover, the recommendation system is widely used together with targeted advertisements on e-commerce platforms.[66] Even smaller businesses embed recommendation systems on their platforms today. These systems hold substantial importance for advertisers. Suggestions displayed to consumers subsequently increase sales by reaching relevant customers quickly and easily.[67] These sales are also subject to transaction fees and form the primary revenue source for intermediaries.[68] The personal preferences mentioned earlier, like data on product views, previous purchases, virtual shopping baskets and every other interaction made by consumers in the past, are used by the recommendation system to improve suggestions. The recommendation system of transaction platforms mainly uses "collaborative filtering" algorithms that make automatic estimates through machine learning to deliver the most relevant advertisements for consumers.[69] Consequently, Big Data and data analytics let the ad services of transaction platforms predict appropriate assumptions of what a specific consumer might be interested in. Examples can be seen on websites like Amazon or eBay in the form of "customers who bought this also bought", "frequently bought together", "products related to this item", or "items based on your recent views".[70]

Apart from being a business model as the core part of the online commercial world, the online advertising business can be regarded as a market itself.[71] David Evans proposes the phrase "attention markets" for that newly emerged market.[72] As mentioned earlier, there is a side in data-driven markets where services or products are offered for free to consumers, such as in the search engine and social networking. This is one side of the market. On the other side, businesses enjoy advertising revenues by offering ad spaces to advertisers in their web-based services. Thus, it is widely discussed how these markets can be defined in competition law assessment. There are two options. The first is to define a standalone market for the online

---

64 Google Ads <https://support.google.com/google-ads/answer/1704368?hl=en>
65 David S Evans, 'The Online Advertising Industry: Economics, Evolution, and Privacy (2009) 23 Journal of Economic Perspectives 3, 41.
66 Graef (n 7) 28.
67 ibid.
68 ibid.
69 ibid.
70 ibid.
71 Jan Kupcik and Stanislav Mikes, 'Discussion on Big Data, Online Advertising and Competition Policy' (2018) European Competition Law Review 397.
72 David S Evans, 'The Economics of Attention Markets' (2017) Global Economics Group; University College London <https://papers.ssrn.com/sol3/papers.cfm?abstract_id=3044858>

advertising business.[73] The second is to define a broader market that comprises all sides of a web-based platform.[74] That being said, if there is a separate market, called the "attention market" by academics, how can this market be assessed with other data-driven markets? It still remains unclear how to react to these markets in specific competition law cases, which is discussed throughout Chapter 4.[75] In the next section, the discussion moves to the characteristics of data-driven markets in order to emphasise how they lead to high concentration and monopolisation.

3.2 Market Characteristics of Data-Driven Markets

3.2.1 Multi-Sided Nature

In order to assess Big Data–related competition infringements on markets, the starting point should be an understanding of two-sided platforms.[76] Big Data's effects on online markets have made it necessary to identify a multi-sided platform since the most prominent feature of data-driven markets is their multi-sided nature. Literature on two-sided platforms is relatively comprehensive and dates back to the 1950s.[77] At first, there were industries like traditional advertising-supported media operating in a multi-sided way even before the introduction of new economy industries.[78] Australian economist Warner Max Cordon identified the business method of newspapers back in 1953. He revealed that the newspaper industry has two sides: advertising and non-advertising.[79] Later, in 1963, Brian Reddaway studied the newspaper industry and delved into the issue between advertisers and newspaper

---

73 Kupcik and Mikes (n 71) 397.
74 ibid.
75 See Chapter 4.
76 Daniel Sokol and Roisin Comerford, 'Antitrust and Regulating Big Data' (2016) 23 George Mason Law Review 5, 1141.
77 Julian Wright, 'One-Sided Logic in Two-Sided Markets' (2004) 3 Review of Network Economics 1; Mark Armstrong, 'Competition in Two-sided Markets' (2006) 37 The RAND Journal of Economics 3, 668–91; Bernard Caillaud and Bruno Jullien, 'Chicken and Egg: Competition Among Intermediation Service Providers' (2003) 34 The RAND Journal of Economics 2, 309–28; David S Evans, 'The Antitrust Economics of Multi-Sided Platform Markets' (2003) 20 Yale Journal on Regulation 2; David S Evans, 'Some Empirical Aspects of Multi-Sided Platform Industries (2003) 2 Review of Network Economics 3; Jean-Charles Rochet and Jean Tirole, 'Cooperation Among Competitors: Some Economics of Payment Card Associations' (2002) 33 The RAND Journal of Economics 4, 549–70; Jean-Charles Rochet and Jean Tirole, 'Platform Competition in Two-Sided Markets' (2003) 1 Journal of the European Economic Association 4, 990–1029; Jean-Charles Rochet and Jean Tirole, 'An Economic Analysis of the Determination of Interchange Fees in Payment Card Systems' (2003) 2 Review of Network Economics 2; Jean-Charles Rochet and Jean Tirole, 'Defining Two-Sided Markets' (2004) <https://web.mit.edu/14.271/www/rochet_tirole.pdf>; Thomas Höppner, 'Defining Markets for Multi-Sided Platforms: The Case of Search Engines' (2015) 38 World Competition 3, 349–66.
78 David S Evans and Richard Schmalensee, 'The Industrial Organization of Markets with Two-Sided Platforms' (2007) 3 Competition Policy International 152.
79 WM Corden, 'The Maximisation of Profit by a Newspaper' (1953) 20 The Review of Economic Studies 3, 181–86.

companies while acknowledging the two sides of the market: sales and advertising.[80] In other words, the idea of multi-sided markets was not new to competition law. However, traditional media outlets like radio, television and newspaper cannot use algorithms to match users and advertisements in the offline world. Thus, there is a clear difference in how advertising models are developed due to Big Data and data analytics.

Since the emergence of new economy industries, the importance of identifying relevant markets regarding two-sided platforms for competition authorities and courts has become more apparent.[81] Thus, many different definitions have been proposed for advertising-supported web-based industries.[82] Jean-Charles Rochet and Jean Tirole have been discussing a proper definition for two-sided platforms.[83] One of their earlier studies identified strong network effects in two-sided markets, and these markets are characterised by network effects.[84] Thus, two-sided markets can be defined as markets having internal and external network effects together. Armstrong, Caillaud and Julian underlined the importance of indirect network externalities between two or more customer groups.[85] In addition to that, in 2006, Rochet and Tirole proposed another definition. According to their study,

> [A] market is two-sided if the platform can affect the volume of transactions by charging more to one side of the market and reducing the price paid by the other side by an equal amount; in other words, the price structure matters, and platforms must design it so as to bring both sides on board.[86]

Moreover, they made a distinction between one-sided and two-sided markets by narrowing down the definition.[87] According to the distinction, a market

> is one-sided if the end-users negotiate away the actual allocation of the burden (i.e., the Coase theorem applies); it is also one-sided in the presence of

---

80 WB Reddaway, 'The Economics of Newspapers' (1963) 73 The Economic Journal 290, 204.
81 Evans and Schmalensee (n 78) 152.
82 Lapo Filistrucchi, Damien Geradin and Eric van Damme, 'Identifying Two-Sided Markets' (2012) TILEC Discussion Paper No. 2012-008; M Rysman, 'The Economics of Two-Sided Markets' (2009) 23(3) Journal of Economic Perspectives 125; David S Evans, 'The Antitrust Economics of Multi-Sided Platform Markets' (2003) 20 Yale Journal on Regulation 2.
83 Jean-Charles Rochet and Jean Tirole, 'Two-Sided Markets: A Progress Report' (2006) 37 The RAND Journal of Economics 3, 645–67; Also (Rochet and Tirole 2002, 2003, 2006).
84 Jean-Charles Rochet and Jean Tirole, 'Platform Competition in Two-Sided Markets' (2003) 1 Journal of the European Economic Association 4, 990–1029, 1017–18.
85 Mark Armstrong, 'Competition in Two-Sided Markets' (2006) 37 The RAND Journal of Economics 3, 668–91, 668; Bernard Caillaud and Bruno Jullien, 'Chicken and Egg: Competition Among Intermediation Service Providers' (2003) 34 The RAND Journal of Economics 2, 309–28, 309.
86 Rochet and Tirole (n 83) 665.
87 Gönenç Gürkaynak and others, 'Multi-Sided Markets and the Challenge of Incorporating Multi-Sided Considerations into Competition Law Analysis (2017) Journal of Antitrust Enforcement 5, 103.

asymmetric information between buyer and seller if the transaction between buyer and seller involves a price determined through bargaining or monopoly price-setting, provided that there are no membership externalities.[88]

The definition proposed by Rochet and Tirole relies solely on the pricing structures on both sides of the market. This is a result of a study on the payment systems market, a two-sided market. There are two sides to the payment systems market where pricing structures affect the demand on the other side of the market. This situation creates a functional deficit in identifying two-sided markets through Rochet and Tirole's definition. Today, there are many multi-sided platforms where "price" is not a parameter on one side of the market due to the fact that prices for products or services are mostly non-existent.[89] As a result, this approach is not fully applicable to many web-based platforms.[90] Gürkaynak et al. argue that in markets such as social media or search engines, transactions on one side of the market cannot be identified (especially on the end users' and platform providers' side), and it would be hard to assess whether pricing structures affect the other side of the market.[91]

On the other hand, David Evans proposes a different approach for multi-sided platforms. He argues that standard market definitions, pricing strategies, restraints and other effects must be redefined for multi-sided markets.[92] According to Evans, there are three important conditions for identifying a market, whether multi-sided or not. First, there must be more than one distinct group of consumers like software developers and software users or credit merchants and debit card users in a given platform.[93] Second, there must be network externalities in a given platform.[94] For instance, credit card merchants benefit when more users use credit cards, and cardholders benefit when they enjoy smooth transactions worldwide. The same applies to all web-based services. Third, there must be an intermediary in the platform. In multi-sided markets, intermediaries internalise the externalities created by both sides of the market.[95] In light of these conditions, Evans and Schmalensee propose the definition of multi-sided platforms as

> [B]usinesses [serving] distinct groups of customers who need each other in some way. . . . The core business is to provide a common (real or virtual) meeting place and to facilitate interactions between members of the two distinct customer groups.[96]

---

88 Rochet and Tirole (n 83) 665.
89 Gürkaynak and others (n 87) 103.
90 ibid.
91 ibid 104.
92 Evans (n 82) 331.
93 ibid.
94 ibid 332.
95 ibid.
96 Evans and Schmalensee (n 78) 152.

Furthermore, Andre Hagiu and Julian Wright proposed another definition regarding multi-sided platforms. According to them, the definitions mentioned earlier have limitations.[97] Thus, multi-sided platforms have two fundamental requirements as their key features are independent of other parameters like network effects. First, a multi-sided platform enables direct "interactions" between two or more distinct consumer groups, and second, all sides of the market are "affiliated" with the platform itself.[98] Hagiu and Wright focus on the "interaction" and "affiliation" terms. According to the context, interaction means any pricing, bundling, marketing and transaction between two different sides of the market.[99] However, affiliation means users of a platform consciously make a specific expenditure to interact directly with the other side of the market. For instance, any access fees (like buying a video game console), spending resources other than money (like time spent while using or developing mobile phone applications) or fees for any opportunities (like participating in the loyalty scheme of a business) can be regarded as affiliation.[100]

Gürkaynak et al. argue that the new definition of Hagiu and Wright seems to have limitations also.[101] While criticising that network effects should not be the main parameter in multi-sided platforms, the authors' new definition does not seem to be fit for data-driven markets like search engines and social media.[102] In these markets, users of a given platform do not make any specific investments to go online through web-based platforms and do not need to have any particular "affiliations". Thus, the definition does not seem to catch the structure of quintessential web-based multi-sided platforms.[103] In addition to that, pricing interactions proposed by Hagiu and Wright focus on pricing as a key parameter for these interactions. Along the same line, in multi-sided platforms where pricing is not a parameter at all, "interactions" cannot be identified clearly to demonstrate the multi-sided characteristic.

Accordingly, the European Commission has also discussed a definition for the "ad network" and "ad exchange" markets to identify and assess competition in these web-based platforms. In 2008, the Commission cleared the Google/DoubleClick merger, in which Google acquired an intermediation platform for ad exchange that sells advertisement services.[104] DoubleClick's intermediation services are offered through "ad exchanges" and "ad networks", and they were identified as two-sided markets.[105] In order to identify the relevant market for the merger analysis, the Commission found it necessary to define multi-sided platforms. According to the

97 Andrei Hagiu and Julian Wright, 'Multi-Sided Platforms' (2015) 43 International Journal of Industrial Organization 5.
98 ibid.
99 ibid.
100 ibid.
101 Gürkaynak and others (n 87) 104.
102 ibid.
103 ibid.
104 Case No COMP/M.4731, Google/DoubleClick C [2008] 927 Final, para 5.
105 ibid para 20.

ruling, "an ad network is a two-sided platform serving (on the one side of the market) publishers that want to host advertisements, and (on the other side of the market) advertisers that want to run ads on those sites".[106] Similarly, as a two-sided platform, "an ad exchange provides a marketplace where advertisers and publishers buy and sell ad space on a real-time basis".[107] Although there are significant differences between these two markets, they provide a closed system and an open (virtual) marketplace for various buyers to sellers who can access and execute transactions. In other words, both businesses act as intermediary service providers.[108]

To sum up, it can be deduced that these distinct definitions underline specific characteristics of multi-sided platforms. Examining the literature on multi-sided platforms reveals that definitions through pricing structures or affiliations may not be fully applicable since the emergence of free products and services on different sides of these businesses. However, they all apply to some extent to multi-sidedness discussions, which have greatly extended in the last couple of decades. Therefore, the debate is definitely moving on, and broader definitions, including other features of multi-sided platforms, are all to be welcomed in the future. Along the same line, Filistrucchi et al. underline the contribution from the literature regarding multi-sided platforms and the value of each of them.[109]

3.2.2 Indirect Network Externalities

Economies of scale are common in data-driven markets, and it occurs as a result of indirect network effects. First-mover undertakings especially tend to become dominant on all sides of a multi-sided platform where the innovation leads to a new product or service. In new economy industries where indirect network externalities are internalised, undertakings can cut high fixed costs to operate the platform and focus on more R&D investments due to the scale effects. Therefore, web-based platforms offer a variety of products with almost the same fixed costs due to network effects.[110] In other words, offering more than one service on a platform costs much less than to offer each of them separately.

Then how are network effects important in data-driven markets? Traditional network effects have always been important for specific products. For instance, two-way communication systems create a direct network effect on users of the system. For instance, when users of a telephone or messaging application increase, the value created by the telephone network or the messaging application also increases. If many people have iPhones, they derive more value from the iMessage application. This is the simplistic example of direct network effects, where the total value

---

106 ibid para 20.
107 ibid para 21.
108 ibid.
109 Filistrucchi, Geradin and van Damme (n 82) 9.
110 Cento Veljanovski, 'Network Effects and Multi-Sided Markets' (2007) 7 <https://papers.ssrn.com/sol3/papers.cfm?abstract_id=1003447&download=yes>

of the system or service increases with the increasing number of users.[111] However, indirect network effects can also be observed in data-driven markets aside from direct network effects to the point that indirect network effects characterise data-driven markets. A simple example of indirect network effects is the use of web-based platforms.

It is then important to distinguish the main groups and the linkage of network effects between them in data-driven markets. For instance, the search engine market has three main user groups: search engine users, content providers and advertisers.[112] There are low to zero direct network effects for all consumer groups in the search engine market. For instance, advertisers do not benefit from having more advertisers in the ecosystem since their advertisements become less attractive, and they need to pay more for them. Also, search engine users do not have any positive direct interaction with advertisements, and consumers' view of advertisements are usually negative. Similarly, content providers do not benefit from having more content providers on the search engine results page since their chances to appear on the search results page are significantly lower when more websites are listed by the search engine.[113] In brief, there are low direct network effects (positive) between the main groups in the search engine market.[114]

However, the situation with indirect network effects is dissimilar. Positive indirect network effects are quite high in data-driven markets, such as the search engine market.[115] Indirect network effects can be observable when consumers derive value from additional products or services with the increasing number of consumers and services offered by third parties through an intermediary in a platform. In other words, more content attracts more consumers since they are able to search and find relevant content for their desires. Thus, more search queries/more consumers make search engines more attractive for advertisers at the same time.[116] For advertisers, more search queries/consumers mean a larger target audience, and a popular search engine where they can advertise much more effectively becomes crucial to more advertisers.

Another example of the same value derived is in the software programs or operating systems market. If fewer people owned an iPhone, third-party application developers would likely develop fewer applications and products specific to iPhones and iOS. The limited use of Apple products limits the direct network effects inside the Apple ecosystem and any indirect effects received from third-party businesses. Thus, when more people use iPhone and more developers offer products for the iPhone, the value created on each side of the market affects the other. Thus, network externalities on both sides of the market can be internalised

---

111 ibid.
112 Barbara Engels, 'Data Portability Among Online Platforms' (2016) 5 Internet Policy Review 2, 11.
113 German Monopolies Commission (*Monopolkommission*), 'Competition Policy: The Challenge of Digital Markets' (2015) Special Report No. 68, p. 56.
114 Engels (n 112) 11.
115 ibid.
116 ibid.

by the platform's operator. Eventually, developers develop more applications and offer sales in the ecosystem, becoming far more valuable for content providers, advertisers and consumers alike.

In many cases, network effects are beneficial for users, especially in the short term.[117] Strong network effects create valuable products or services for consumer use. Consequently, the value of a product increases its utility.[118] However, network effects and feedback loops on data-driven markets also bring crucial negatives. Extensive network externalities seem to create barriers to entry for new entrants and allow dominant undertakings to monopolise data-driven markets. On this side of the coin, the accumulation of Big Data, tipping effects, lock-in effects, and increasing switching costs are negative results of indirect network effects regarding healthy competition in data-driven markets.

The accumulation of Big Data and feedback loops in data-driven markets increase returns to scale due to strong indirect network effects. By this means, the technology giants monetise their data supplies. More data attract advertisers to the platform, which can deliver better-targeted advertisements on the market's other side (user side). The loop enables the platform owner to create newer and better products or services when the platform is fed from both sides of the market. Additional data means additional sources of better services and products by third parties and platform owners. The positive feedback loop which brings more data, more users and more revenues to the platform is due to complex indirect network effects in data-driven markets. The multi-sidedness and utilisation of Big Data are the specific features for the feedback and monetisation loops for the platform owners.

The importance of indirect network effects is more visible in data-driven markets than in any other market. Stucke and Grunes give the example of toothpaste and search engine.[119] Unlike traditional product markets, in data-driven markets, network effects amplify the gain and loss of users.[120] For instance, when someone purchases one toothpaste, the other toothpaste will not lose its quality. The effect occurs on the sales and profits grounds, which means the rival toothpaste company will definitely lose extra profits in this circumstance. However, in data-driven markets like the search engine market, every single search query is important since it leads to the accumulation of Big Data. The winner in data-driven markets gains extra profits, search queries increase the quality of service, and the winner takes more control of the market.[121] Stucke and Ezrachi claim that undertakings' ability to utilise and monetise Big Data significantly increases through better quality and more relevant search results.[122] At the same time, it significantly decreases the

---

117 Inge Graef, 'Data as Essential Facility: Competition and Innovation on Online Platforms' (PhD Thesis, KU Leuven Faculty of Law 2016) 44.
118 ibid.
119 Stucke and Grunes (n 24) 201.
120 ibid.
121 ibid 202.
122 Maurice E Stucke and Ariel Ezrachi, 'When Competition Fails to Optimize Quality: A Look at Search Engines' (2016) 18 Yale Journal of Law and Technology 70, 90–91.

quality of the rival search engine providers' service. Potential degradation of quality means more consumer loss for the rival undertakings.

The main reason behind it is the inequality in access to data.[123] When a rival loses search queries to Google, they also lose consumers, and the gap widens between the two undertakings. When Google controls most consumer data and practices more learning-by-doing trials to offer better services, the rival companies lose all these potential data, and the quality of their products eventually lowers. In contrast to the toothpaste market, every loss is a profit loss and a quality loss for competitors in the search engine market. At this point, Stucke and Ezrachi underline the gap between the dominant undertaking and its rivals, which widens significantly to the point that rivals cannot compete in the market at all.[124] The reason behind this is that the dominant search engine can use advantages in scale and scope to intentionally lower the quality of its products to increase its revenues and manipulate search results in its favour.[125] In the toothpaste market, rivals can lower their quality to offer cheaper products to obtain market share and profits. However, in the search engine market, the dominant undertaking can better utilise the mass amounts of data and algorithm results to offer better services than its rivals, which cannot collect and utilise enough data. Thus, smaller rivals in the search engine market cannot lower their quality to compete with the dominant rival and struggle to offer services to users due to insufficient data.[126] Consequently, indirect network effects and positive feedback loops on these platforms create irrevocable barriers in the market in favour of the dominant undertaking.

Indirect network effects create rather large minimum efficient scales in data-driven markets. In contrast to what some academics argue,[127] entry barriers to data-driven markets are not low. Investments necessary to enter data-driven markets and the minimum scales necessary to operate multi-sided platforms are huge. In its Microsoft/Yahoo merger decision, the European Commission underlined that Google's rivals could not achieve sufficient scales in the search engine market. According to the Commission, Google is a strong player in the search engine market.[128] On the other hand, its rival, Yahoo, despite having been in the business for over a decade, could not make sufficient investments to reach the minimum scale to compete effectively with Google.[129] In the same vein, Microsoft (Bing) invests

---

123 ibid 103.
124 ibid 96.
125 ibid 96–97.
126 ibid 97.
127 Andres Lerner, 'The Role of Big Data in Online Platform Competition' (2014) SSRN Working Paper <http://dx.doi.org/10.2139/ssrn.2482780>
128 Case No COMP/M.5727, Microsoft/Yahoo! Search Business C [2010] 1077 Final, para 159.
129 ibid.

heavily in search engines and algorithms but cannot achieve sufficient scale to compete effectively with Google.[130] Also, the Commission adds that:

> Additionally, the market investigation has revealed that currently Google enjoys a large competitive advantage compared to other search engines and is perceived as a "must-have" for users. Therefore, it is possible that if the transaction, through the scale effects, leads to a stronger competitor more able to innovate, Google will also have an incentive to keep, or even accelerate, its innovation efforts in the market.[131]

At the time of the decision, Google had a 94% market share, and Bing and Yahoo had 1.5% market shares separately; today, none of their market shares has changed at all.[132]

Moreover, the European Commission explicitly states in its guidelines for abusive exclusionary conduct by dominant undertakings that economies of scale and scope and network effects can be barriers to market entry and anti-competitive conduct there may create entry barriers. Paragraph 17 states that:

> Barriers to expansion . . . may take the form of advantages specifically enjoyed by the dominant undertaking, such as economies of scale and scope. They may also include costs and other impediments, for instance, resulting from network effects. . . . The dominant undertakings own conduct may also create barriers to entry. . . . Persistently high market shares may be indicative of the existence of barriers to entry and expansion.[133]

Are all the features mentioned here leading to entry barriers and anti-competitive conduct in data-driven markets? The view of the European Commission in the noteworthy merger decisions in recent history seems to be somewhat neutral on network effects. In its *Facebook/WhatsApp* decision, the Commission ruled that the mere existence of network effects does not reflect any market competition problems.[134] Thus, competition problems may arise if undertakings controlling network effects foreclose competitors and prevent them from expanding their customer base.[135] Therefore, network effects must be examined on a case-by-case basis.[136] Accordingly, in the *Google/DoubleClick* decision, the Commission acknowledges

---

130 ibid.
131 Case No COMP/M.5727, Microsoft/Yahoo! Search Business C [2010] 1077 Final, para 219.
132 Search Engine Market Share Europe 2019 <https://gs.statcounter.com/search-engine-market-share/all/europe/2019>
133 Communication from the European Commission, Guidance on the Commission's Enforcement Priorities in Applying Article 82 of the EC Treaty to Abusive Exclusionary Conduct by Dominant Undertakings (Text with EEA Relevance) [2009] OJ C45/9, para 17.
134 Case No COMP/M.7217, Facebook/WhatsApp C [2014] 7239 Final, para 130.
135 ibid.
136 ibid.

that network effects are primary to achieving success and sufficient scale and could be subject to various foreclosure strategies.[137] However, the Commission did not find network effects themselves as a cause of and evidence for anti-competitive behaviour.[138] Moreover, their investigation suggests that network effects would not lead to tipping effects in data-driven markets. (This actually seems to be an inaccurate implication.)[139] Even more, the Commission stresses in its *Microsoft/Skype* decision that:

> Respondents to the market investigation also stress the existence of network effects . . . as a barrier to expansion. They consider that the more users a provider of communications has, the better its chance to expand the user base. However, the network effects are mitigated by the fact that most consumers of communications services make the majority of their voice and video calls to the small number of family and friends that make up their so called "inner circle". . . Moreover, the Commission observes that consumers multi-home to a certain degree among various providers of consumer communications services.[140]

In the *Microsoft/Skype* decision, the Commission clearly underlines multi-homing as a factor that diminishes the potential anti-competitive effects of network externalities in data-driven markets. Some academics also argue that multi-homing is an important feature in most data-driven markets since services and products are mostly free on one side of the data-driven market. It is quite an easy task for users to switch services as they are only one click away.[141] However, in data-driven markets like the search engine, online advertising or social network markets, the effects of network externalities and scale economies seem to exceed the implications of the Commission. Thus, the Commission's outcomes do not reflect the real potential of scale economies and indirect network effects in these markets. Proof of competition problems can be found in tipping and lock-in effects, which eventually monopolise data-driven markets after these mergers.[142] The phenomenon of "multi-homing" does not seem to relieve the competition concerns and excessive network effects in new economy industries.

3.2.3 Accumulation of Big Data

In many new economy industries, network effects and the accumulation of Big Data lead to snowballing and tipping effects. In the Google/Waze merger, the UK

---

137 Case No COMP/M.4731, Google/DoubleClick C [2008] 927 Final, para 304.
138 ibid.
139 ibid.
140 Case No COMP/M.6281, Microsoft/Skype C [2011] 7239 Final, paras 91–92.
141 Konstantinos Stylianou, 'Exclusion in Digital Markets' (2018) 24 Michigan Telecommunications and Technology Law Review 2, 223–26; Lerner (n 127).
142 See Chapter 3.3.

Competition Authority explicitly stated that an undertaking could accelerate its growth based on network effects.[143] According to the authority, when more consumers use a network, the network becomes more valuable to those users.[144] More importantly, where these network effects exist, "there is the potential for the market to 'tip', so whilst there may still be competition from other suppliers, there is one leading supplier, although it is not clear the extent to which this may occur here".[145] Dominance is the key to tipping effects in markets. In markets where no undertaking is dominant, rivals try to prevent each other from tipping the market. However, network and scale effects lead to dominance. As mentioned earlier, a considerable amount of quality difference occurs due to network effects, and the market would likely tip in one undertaking's favour.[146]

When dominance is established in a market and the market has tipped, smaller rivals cannot acquire stable market access[147] or even a sufficient scale to operate their services or offer products. For instance, at the time of the Microsoft (Bing) and Yahoo merger, Google had more than 90% of the search engine market; years after (in 2019), its strongest rival, Bing, only had 2.25% of the search engine market in the EU.[148] The reason behind this is the quality of Bing's service. Bing has fewer consumers and thus has lower-quality search results than Google. Bing's algorithms cannot predict and create better search results than Google's since the algorithm works with much less data. As a result, Google attracts more users and liquidates search results with paid services like advertisements or paid search results. Moreover, Prüfer and Schottmüller stress that dominant undertakings can make continuous small investments in innovation to raise their services' quality, resulting in tipping.[149] According to them, this is a feature of dynamic competition and data-driven markets thereof.

Competition problems are not limited to dominance and tipping effects in data-driven markets. Prüfer and Schottmüller identify that the first movers in data-driven markets can create monopolies due to the aforementioned effects.[150] The reason behind this is the inherent feature of data-driven markets. In these markets, there are meagre incentives for smaller rivals to innovate, which leaves the dominants alone in the market and contributes to the creation of monopolies.[151] Likewise, Stucke and Grunes argue that although the data-driven network effects do not automatically reward the first mover undertakings, first movers have strong advantages

---

143 UK Office of Fair Trade, Google/Waze ME/6167/13, para 44.
144 ibid footnote 28.
145 ibid.
146 Prüfer and Schottmüller (n 1) 2.
147 ibid.
148 Search Engine Market Share Europe 2019 <https://gs.statcounter.com/search-engine-market-share/all/europe/2019>
149 Prüfer and Schottmüller (n 1) 2.
150 ibid.
151 ibid.

to gain dominance in markets.[152] As a result, anti-competitive or pro-competitive incentives of the first mover firms would likely increase in this scenario. In other words, dominant undertakings would likely exercise anti-competitive behaviour to tip the market in their favour.[153] Consequently, dominant undertakings may use network effects and feedback loops to prevent their rivals from competing and become monopolies. It is a data race, first gaining control over mass data, innovating, becoming a first mover, becoming dominant and ultimately creating a monopoly position.

Prüfer and Schottmüller studied those dominant undertakings that also use their inherent data advantage and Big Data feedback loops to dominate other markets. Undertakings aware of the power of Big Data utilisation as a key input for services and products in data-driven markets tend to map potential markets where they can extend their powers.[154] Consequently, with the utilisation of mass datasets, they move their business to adjacent markets where Big Data can be effectively used. To be more precise, dominant undertakings leverage their market power into other markets. Through the utilisation of Big Data, this situation creates a domino effect. Prüfer and Schottmüller express that "a first mover in market A can leverage its dominant position, which comes with an advantage on user information, to let connected market B tip, too, even if market B is already served by traditional incumbent firms".[155] Google is the pioneer firm in connecting markets through Big Data utilisation.[156]

The argument of the existence of low switching costs in data-driven markets might be a remedy for excessive network effects and tipping of the markets.[157] However, data-driven markets experience lock-in effects affecting users even though consumers use free products on one side of the market. According to the European Commission, "The vast majority of social networking services are provided free of monetary charges".[158] Along the same line, most data-driven markets provide free-of-charge services. Therefore, these free services and products are monetised through other mechanisms, such as advertising or charges for premium services.[159] On this basis, multi-sided platforms are generally characterised by free products or services on one side of the platform. At that point, it may be assumed that switching costs in data-driven markets are quite low. Any user could change to a different search engine or social media platform since the services are offered for free. One click would be enough in the online world.

However, this is not the reality. In data-driven markets, competition is not one click away, and consumers are usually locked into services they choose in the first

---

152 Stucke and Grunes (n 24) 204.
153 ibid.
154 Prüfer and Schottmüller (n 146) 3.
155 ibid.
156 See Chapter 4.2.4.
157 Case No COMP/AT.39740, Google Search (Shopping) [2017] 4444 Final, para 270.
158 Case No COMP/M.7217, Facebook/WhatsApp C [2014] 7239 Final, para 47.
159 ibid.

place. In theory, consumers can easily change the services and products they use in the online world. However, the data advantage and network effects that some platforms enjoy make it partially invalid. For instance, although ordinary users may leave the Google search engine, they cannot expect to find better search results for their preferences elsewhere.[160] Their personal preferences have been accumulated and tailored by Google's algorithms to adopt higher-quality search results for individuals.[161] Smaller rivals of Google are not capable of adapting search results to the consumers' expectations.[162] In time, this situation starts to lock consumers to the Google search engine.

Another example is Facebook. Most social media users in the world use Facebook. People have contacts, family, friends, acquaintances, photos, memories and other personal information on Facebook. Thus, when users consider switching to another social media platform, these established connections would likely dissuade them. Therefore, smaller rivals of Facebook do not have as many users as Facebook; thus, users would not be likely to find their connections in Facebook alternatives.[163] As a result, users face lock-in effects and considerably high switching costs in the social media market. This argument excludes markets like China, where Facebook versus rival competition is not present.

In their study, Whittington and Hoofnagle underline high switching costs in data-driven markets. According to them, consumers invest by providing their personal information using a platform. Those investments are specific to the platform being used. This means that consumers may feel locked into the platform where they have made investments.[164] To sum up, switching costs occur when users choose to change a product or service they have been using. In order to do so in data-driven markets, consumers need to make the same investments to move onto a different provider in the online world. At this point, many would realise that they are already locked in or need to cope with high switching costs to the specific service or product due to the limited portability of data, including network and scale effects.

Overall, characteristics of data-driven markets such as indirect network externalities, accumulation of Big Data and tipping effects reveal an important concern about data-driven markets: the increasing concentration in data-driven markets. A few quite successful undertakings have created their own business ecosystems around specific markets in the online world.[165] In these markets, oligopolistic tendencies can be traced, and this is the first sign of a greater problem: monopolisation

---

160 Graef (n 117) 52.
161 ibid.
162 ibid.
163 Instagram can be regarded as a strong rival to Facebook in social media today. However, Facebook owns 100% of Instagram. The author does not think there is a real rivalry between these platforms since they share same data pool: e.g., When someone posts something on their Facebook page, it can automatically appear on their Instagram page also, and vice versa.
164 Jan Whittington and Chris Jay Hoofnagle, 'Unpacking Privacy's Price' (2012) 90 North Carolina Law Review 1327, 1354.
165 See Chapter 4.4.4.

in the online world. This oligopoly structure can hamper innovation and competition and create entry barriers in data-driven markets to a great extent.

3.3 Monopolisation

The situation reveals that there are dominant undertakings in the online world, and they are in near-monopoly positions in various data-driven markets. The main concern here is how dangerous the increasing concentration of online platforms is for consumers in the EU. The fierce competition in the online world through innovations is good for a functioning market. Innovation and first-mover advantage are inherent in dynamic competition. In the same vein, these do not pose any competitive threats themselves. These are the characteristic features of data-driven markets. However, newly emerging monopolies and high concentration differentiate notably from the traditional monopoly concept; thus, it is hard to determine anti-competitive behaviour in data-driven markets since the current competition tools are designed to engage with anti-competitive actions towards the traditional competition concept.

3.3.1 Winner Takes All

According to the EU law, dominance in a market can be observed if an undertaking has a 40 to 50% share of the relevant market. In the Commission's guidance paper regarding abuse of dominant position, it is indicated that dominance would not likely occur if an undertaking's share were below 40% in the relevant market.[166] An exception to the rule can be found in the *British Airways* case before the CJEU. The General Court ruled that British Airways has a dominant position in the UK market for air travel agency services with only 39.7% market share.[167] In brief, undertakings have dominant positions if they have approximately half of the relevant market. However, in most data-driven markets, dominance is established by over 85–90% of market share. Accordingly, the market positions of Microsoft, Google and Facebook must be regarded as "super-dominance". Super-dominance is an indication of a near-monopoly position in a market. Thus, near-monopoly digital markets must be under different scrutiny than traditional abuse cases.

Super-dominance is a result of the aforementioned effects in markets where competitors fight over the control of the market. In data-driven markets, the winner takes all. Therefore, technology giants are able to create impregnable monopolies.[168] Google has been the dominant undertaking in the global search engine market for

---

166 European Commission, Communication from the Commission, Guidance on the Commission's enforcement priorities in applying Article 82 of the EC Treaty to abusive exclusionary conduct by dominant undertakings (Text with EEA relevance) (2009/C 45/02) para 14.
167 Case T-219/99 *British Airways v Commission* [2003] ECLI:EU:T:2003:343, para 195–225.
168 David S Evans, 'Antitrust Issues Raised by the Emerging Global Internet Economy' (2008) 102 Northwestern University Law Review 302.

a couple of decades,[169] and Facebook has established a strong dominance worldwide.[170] Numbers reveal that the super-dominance of online platforms is not fragile at all. Neither of them was a first mover. Google surpassed Yahoo, and Facebook surpassed Myspace back in the 2000s. However, the establishing situation and evolution of data-driven markets reveal that the accumulation and utility of Big Data surpassed the point at which rivals dethrone incumbents through an innovation cycle. In other words, today, it is nearly impossible to dethrone super-dominant undertakings for smaller rivals without controlling and utilising Big Data.

In addition to that, a handful of undertakings having near-monopoly positions are now connecting markets together and controlling specific segments of the online world since their positions are protected by the scale effects and Big Data advantage.[171] Super-dominant undertakings can combine subtracted data from other market segments.[172] Therefore, to compete in winner-takes-all markets, rivals need to enter multiple platforms simultaneously with further innovations to attract consumers. However, it is quite hard to achieve since there are many distinct services. Rivals need to attract advertisers on one side and users on the other. Therefore, investments on both sides of the market without having a data advantage would be quite troublesome for rivals.[173] Undertakings that desire to compete with technology giants today need to invest in more than one area at once.[174]

Technology giants such as Google and Facebook and the rise of data-driven markets have created a paradox.[175] Today, many online start-ups that might well be competitors for technology giants in the future rely on Google or Facebook advertising in the first place. The reason behind this is that the only revenue channel for start-ups is online advertising in the new economy. The online advertising industry is a highly concentrated market with very few players. Without using an online advertising revenue channel, start-ups cannot reach the audience for their services or products, like message applications, navigation or social media. Rivals must compete with the services of technology giants by using their online advertising services. However, these players are also inherent rivals for start-ups. Thus, it is quite challenging for start-ups to offer high-quality products that equal competitors' product quality. The out-of-balance data advantage between start-ups and established technology giants creates a relationship called "frenemy" in data-driven markets.[176]

---

169 Jason Furman, *Unlocking Digital Competition: Report of the Digital Competition Expert Panel* (HM Treasury 2019) <https://www.gov.uk/government/publications/unlocking-digital-competition-report-of-the-digital-competition-expert-panel>
170 For instance, over 70% of page views of all social media sites came from Facebook and Instagram in December 2018 in the UK. Furman (n 169) 25.
171 Evans (n 168) 302.
172 Kupcik and Mikes (n 71) 399.
173 ibid.
174 ibid.
175 ibid.
176 See Chapter 5.1.3.

3.3.2 Moligopolists

Maurer et al. underline the current situation in data-driven markets dramatically. They express that "Google has become the main interface for our whole reality".[177] Along the same line, in his comments towards Google's investigation by the European Commission, Cade Metz states that:

> Google . . . is not just a search engine. It is a multi-billion-dollar company that offers countless other internet services involving everything from news search and image search to video hosting, maps, finance, and even price-comparison shopping. . . . Now controlling as much as 85 per cent of the search market, this de facto internet gateway is also a place where Google can deliver its own services to netizens across the globe. YouTube, Google Maps, Google Product Search, and any other Google service – as well as any service Google might build in future years – all have an obvious advantage over competitors.[178]

Another main point here is the quasi-rivalry between online platforms. In traditional markets like manufacturing or retail, competition among firms is based on similar services or products.[179] However, rivals in the online world are super dominant in their markets and do not only compete in their core markets.[180] For instance, Apple is primarily in the software and hardware business (personal computers and mobile phones), Google is mainly a search engine, Facebook is a social media platform, and Amazon is primarily an e-commerce platform.[181] They are all near monopolies in their respective markets, but they also form oligopolies together in wider-connected markets.[182] These undertakings may be coming from divergent online markets, yet they are top competitors for each other in most data-driven markets.[183]

In his study, Nicolas Petit mentions a concept called "moligopoly" for data-driven markets. He underlines the theory of competition between technology giants as a "three-dimensional competitive process".[184] According to the findings,

---

177 Hermann Maurer and others, *Report on Dangers and Opportunities Posed by Large Search Engines, Particularly Google 16* (Institute for Information Systems and Computer Media, Graz University of Technology 2007) <http://citeseerx.ist.psu.edu/viewdoc/download?doi=10.1.1.94.5633&rep=rep1&type=pdf>
178 Cade Metz, 'We Probe the Google Antitrust Probe: Vigorously' *Register* (1 December 2010) <http://www.theregister.co.uk/2010/12/01/google_eu_investigation_comment>
179 David S Evans, 'Attention Rivalry Among Online Platforms' (2013) 9 Journal of Competition Law and Economics 2, 330.
180 Konstantinos Stylianou, 'Exclusion in Digital Markets' (2018) 24 Michigan Telecommunications and Technology Law Review 2, 249.
181 Evans (n 179) 330.
182 Furman (n 169) 31.
183 Stylianou (n 180) 249.
184 Nicolas Petit, 'Technology Giants, the Moligopoly Hypothesis and Holistic Competition: A Primer' (2016) SSRN 46 <https://ssrn.com/abstract=2856502>

the degree of competition in data-driven markets is not linear.[185] These undertakings offer substitute products or services outside their core markets. For instance, Google, Facebook, Apple and Microsoft are all in rivalry in the personal communication application market through their products like Hangouts, iMessage, Skype and Facebook Messenger. The same applies to mail services and many more. In addition to rivalry in linked markets, they also compete against each other by creating new market segments and obtaining the first-mover advantage. This is done to gather information and create a data advantage or to monetise their advantage in new markets and establish dominance. In other words, the rivalry among online platforms has three pillars: substitute product competition in the same market, escape competition in order to create new market segments and capitalise on data and other entrepreneurial assets. While they have super-dominant positions in their own core markets and compete against each other in various other markets, they tend not to compete in their core markets. Petit explains that "those firms follow each other outside of the core, to keep iron in the fire".[186]

In other words, when competition exists in data-driven markets, five technology giants are frequently in that competition.[187] These are Google (dominates online search), Facebook (dominates social media), Google and Apple (duopoly in mobile app services), Microsoft (dominates PC operating systems and software) and Amazon (dominates e-commerce). All these undertakings have control over separate online ecosystems which they own. This trend shows how a few technology giants have become prominent in the online world. Also, the Furman Report states that:

> Many stakeholders also submitted evidence to the Panel arguing that such a trend can be harmful to competition. . . . This strategy can create barriers to entry, as new firms need to offer an entire ecosystem by competing across a range of related markets to survive.[188]

As discussed in detail earlier, the increasing concentration in data-driven markets is a direct result of the indirect network effects, accumulation of Big Data, feedback loops, tipping and lock-in effects.

3.3.3 Concerns over Data-opolies

As mentioned earlier, digital monopolies have novel features and need urgent attention from a competition law perspective. Problems arise when tools for the assessment regarding abuse of dominant position cases and data-driven mergers are used. The situation is visible in the decisions of the Commission and also the Competition Authorities in Europe. Also, rules for dynamic competition and innovation

---

185 ibid.
186 ibid.
187 Furman (n 169) 31.
188 ibid.

are not vis-à-vis applicable to data-driven markets since the market participants compete on three fronts. Technology giants do not compete to dethrone each other in specific markets but compete on a wider basis to establish connected markets. By this means, undertakings hoard a mass amount of data that even governments do not have.

For example, the persistence of high concentration and super dominance is a crucial concern regarding data-driven markets. Super-dominant Google has control over the largest search engine globally, and the Google search engine can be identified as the gateway to the internet. It is not erroneous to state that Google has become the internet itself for many people. It is the first step when people go online and connect to the internet nowadays. In such a situation, Google integrates maps, video, images, shopping, news, books, flights, restaurants and finance-related searches into its search engine with other online services such as mail, cloud storage, YouTube and numerous others. In this structure, Google makes peoples' lives easier if they use Google's services exclusively. As a result, Google has become not only the largest search engine but also the largest map service, video streaming service and email service. Competitively speaking, Google's rivals, which compete with Google in one or more segments of this ecosystem, have a significant competitive disadvantage in servicing comprehensive, high-quality online services due to a lack of data and Google's strong indirect network externalities.

Similarly, to exemplify the persistence of high concentration, the situation in the mobile operating system market where Google and Apple have become a worldwide duopoly can be given. Millions of mobile applications are produced for either Apple's iOS or Google's Android, which allows both operating systems to offer competitive and attractive products.[189] Even once-huge competitors in the mobile software and hardware industry, such as Nokia and BlackBerry, cannot succeed due to the prominence of iOS and Android in the market. When these companies were dethroned by Samsung (Android) and Apple (iOS) phones back in the day, there was no such thing as software, and applications were more important than the device itself to becoming competitive and offering attractive products. However, today, new entrants do not have a chance to offer competitive and attractive products if millions of mobile applications do not swarm their mobile operating systems. Thus, Microsoft ceased its mobile operating system in 2017 and moved to Android for their mobile phones, just like BlackBerry did in 2016.[190] Microsoft reported that "one factor behind the lack of success had been app developers' reluctance to develop apps for the Windows operating system (mobile) because they were already making apps for two larger operating systems".[191] As Geoffrey Parker et al. stress:

> In the complexity of the governance issues they face, today's biggest platform businesses resemble nation-states. With more than 1.5 billion users,

---

189 ibid 40.
190 ibid.
191 ibid.

Facebook oversees a 'population' larger than China's. Google handles 64 per cent of the online searches in the U.S. and 90 per cent of those in Europe, while Alibaba handles more than 1 trillion yuan (162 billion US dollars) worth of transactions a year and accounts for 70 per cent of all commercial shipments in China. Platform businesses at this scale control economic systems that are bigger than all but the biggest national economies.[192]

Another concern related to super-dominant undertakings is the wider consumer harm outside commercial transactions, such as political processes. For instance, the Chinese government collaborates with one of the biggest technology giants in China, Tencent Holdings, owner of the WeChat mobile communication service, to monitor its citizens. The Chinese state news agency published information on a pilot system in which Tencent Holdings cooperates with the Chinese Ministry of Public Security to create a digital identification system in Guangzhou.[193] According to the report, it is clear that the Chinese government relies on the Big Data power and digital capabilities of technology giants to monitor its population.[194] Although collaboration between firms and governments to execute services is not novel, the extent to which the Chinese government uses information extracted from the WeChat application for the private commutation of Tencent Holdings brings the situation to another level. Similar executions of this idea will create huge risks for people, their privacy, and their democracy in the Western world and worldwide.

Along the same line, the *New York Times* claims that Russia manipulated US political elections by using social media platforms such as Google's YouTube media, Facebook's social network and Instagram.[195] Google, Facebook and Twitter reported that most US citizens saw some Russian-backed propaganda online.[196] Therefore, it is claimed that Russia affected the outcome of the election in the US considerably. Similarly, the Russian government claimed that Google and Facebook circulated "interfered adverts" to manipulate elections in Russia recently.[197] Facebook responded that Russia must talk to advertisers that are responsible for complying with laws in Russia.[198] Also, Google expressed that they only supported "responsible advertising", which complied with Russian laws. No matter what the

---

192 Geoffrey G Parker, Marshall W Van Alstyne and Sangeet Paul Choudary, *Platform Revolution: How Networked Markets Are Transforming the Economy – and How to Make Them Work for You* (WW Norton & Company 2016) 159.
193 Alyssa Abkowitz, 'The Internet Tightens: Popular Chinese WeChat App to Become Official ID' *The Wall Street Journal* (31 December 2017) <https://www.wsj.com/articles/internet-tightens-popular-chinese-wechat-app-to-become-official-id-1514541980>
194 ibid.
195 Mike Isaac and Daisuke Wakabayashi, 'Russian Influence Reached 126 Million Through Facebook Alone' *The New York Times* (30 October 2017) <https://www.nytimes.com/2017/10/30/technology/facebook-google-russia.html>
196 126 million Facebook users saw posts, 131.000 tweet was sent and over 1000 YouTube videos uploaded.
197 Russia Complains About Facebook and Google Election Ads, *BBC News* (9 September 2019) <https://www.bbc.co.uk/news/technology-49634688>
198 ibid.

claims and outcomes are, if people, groups or governments can manipulate elections in these countries through social media, it is quite hard to imagine the power limits of super-dominant undertakings.

Not only the data-driven sector but also markets that are not data-driven are affected. Digital super dominance and monopolies influence other industries and spread their dominance by leveraging their power. The Big Data power of technology giants may well contribute to creating higher-quality products for consumers. However, eliminating competitors and exploiting and manipulating market power will pose quality, privacy, welfare, social, and even moral concerns. Recent abuse of dominant position investigation for the online markets acknowledges these concerns. However, to put a finer point on it, it should be noted that competition regulations and authorities could not have anticipated three-dimensional competition in data-driven markets in the past. Digitalisation and the creation of new economy markets generate a situation that the competition law of the 1970s may not be able to cope with. Therefore, tools to assess market power, dominance, and merger control should be reconsidered in light of data-driven markets.

In order to address persistent high concentration, dominance, monopolies, and concerns over peoples' free will and choice, it is important to acknowledge that data-driven markets do not have a self-corrective nature; thus, intervention should not be seen as detrimental. According to the conservative claim, markets self-correct upon new entries and the emergence of new competitors.[199] However, this claim is relevant only if market entry is relatively easy. When there are entry barriers, strong oligopolies, and super-dominant platforms, market dynamics characterise the conduct of dominant undertakings. In this situation, the super-dominant technology giants also set the online world's rules and eventually become *de facto* regulators.[200] In other words, huge barriers are created in data-driven markets. With the accumulation of Big Data and other characteristics of data-driven markets, new market entries and effective competition become almost non-existent.

In brief, high concentration in the online world does not seem to contribute to competition positively. Market structures in data-driven markets are not healthy for the functioning of the market in the long run at all. However, the problem is not limited to market structures. Business practices also harm competition, such as abusive conduct and data acquisitions. Data acquisition is not a result but a method to gain market power through the power of data. How data acquisitions lead to monopolies is discussed next.

---

199 Frank H Easterbrook, 'The Limits of Antitrust' (1984) 63 Texas Law Review 2–3; Jonathan B Baker, 'Taking the Error Out of "Error Cost" Analysis (2015) 80 Antitrust Law Journal 1, 1–38, 8–9.
200 See Chapter 6.3.1.

3.4 Data-Driven Acquisitions

3.4.1 Concerns Related to Data-Driven Acquisitions

The acquisition of vast numbers of datasets by technology giants is a real concern. The literature usually refers to these kinds of acquisitions as R&D mergers, which are meant to have pro-competitive effects such as efficiency gains for both consumers and businesses. R&D mergers could have pro-competitive outcomes in terms of providing high-quality and innovative products or services.[201] For instance, the accumulation of consumer data in the hands of an undertaking through data acquisitions might lead to significant improvements in the quality of products since undertakings can obtain increased feedback, thus providing more personalised services to consumers.[202]

Another example would be the initialisation of free-to-use services online. Through the power of Big Data, it is now possible for undertakings to operate using a multi-sided business model.[203] On the one side, there is a market where undertakings operate free services such as online newspapers and use social networking to gather data.[204] On the other side, they sell the gathered data to generate revenue in the form of online advertisements.[205] By this means, they can offer free services on the market while monetising them through advertisers.[206] In the end, high-quality, free-of-charge services inherently benefit consumers.

Various issues threaten markets from a competition law perspective, which may occur after a data-driven merger. First, a merged entity could take control of a massive amount of data through a horizontal merger to increase its market power and create barriers to entry for its competitors to reduce competition in the market.[207] According to paragraph 36 of the Horizontal Merger Guidelines, through mergers that restrict competitors' ability to compete, merged undertakings may have control over important entities such as the supply of inputs, patents or other types of intellectual property (IP) rights.[208] In this case, the argument should be whether Big Data is such input for businesses. Additionally, these undertakings may raise costs or degrade the quality of services in general.[209]

Second, threats may occur through vertical and conglomerate mergers. Undertakings may choose not to acquire data through competitors but instead merge

---

201 Ben Holles de Peyer, 'EU Merger Control and Big Data' (2017) 13 Journal of Competition Law and Economics 4, 767–90, 776.
202 ibid 777.
203 ibid.
204 Damian Geradin and Monika Kuschewsky, 'Competition Law and Personal Data: Preliminary Thoughts on a Complex Issue' (2013) 2 Concurrences 3.
205 ibid.
206 Holles de Peyer (n 201) 777.
207 ibid 769.
208 European Commission, Guidelines on the Assessment of Horizontal Mergers Under the Council Regulation on the Control of Concentrations Between Undertakings [2004] OJ C31/03, para 36.
209 ibid.

66 *Data-Driven Market Structures and Monopolisation*

vertically downstream or upstream.[210] According to the Non-Horizontal Merger Guidelines, a merged undertaking might limit access to important inputs for downstream or upstream rivals.[211] In this scenario, after a merger, an undertaking that has acquired datasets from upstream or downstream markets might foreclose input or restrict the access of other market players to these datasets, which might be essential for businesses.[212] Additionally, this foreclosure might eventually result in raised prices, degraded quality of products and services, or the elimination of competitors ultimately.

In the conglomerate scenario, undertakings might tie their own services to acquired datasets or services.[213] By this means, undertakings try to leverage their market power in related markets. According to a study by the CMA, businesses gain market power from datasets in their own markets and then enter into other markets for data analytics with the aid of tying their products to datasets.[214] Then they use the gathered information for further data analytics.[215] Although the identification of conglomerate effects might be more complicated in these scenarios, the analysis of broader anti-competitive effects should not be excluded from merger control tools. The broader effects of data-driven acquisitions are explained next.

3.4.2 New Global Value Chains

Online platforms take over innovation-centric firms to gain competitive advantage through the accumulation of Big Data. In other words, M&As have become instruments to collect data under the name of R&D mergers. Acquisitions aiming to obtain data from smaller businesses might pose anti-competitive threats in the internal market.[216] This is called the acquisition of nascent rivals,[217] and through these kinds of acquisitions, technology giants obtain data, preserve concentration or even monopolise the online world.[218] Prime examples of this action are Google's, Facebook's, Apple's and Microsoft's recent acquisitions.[219] There have been more

---

210 Holles de Peyer (n 201) 774.
211 European Commission, Guidelines on the Assessment of Non-Horizontal Mergers Under the Council Regulation on the Control of Concentrations Between Undertakings [2008] OJ C265/7, para 36.
212 Holles de Peyer (n 201) 775.
213 ibid.
214 The Competition and Markets Authority, 'The Commercial Use of Consumer Data Report on the CMA's Call for Information (2015) 90 <https://www.gov.uk/cma-cases/commercial-use-of-consumer-data>
215 ibid.
216 Marixenia Davilla, 'Is Big Data a Different Kind of Animal? The Treatment of Big Data Under the EU Competition Rules' (2017) 8 Journal of European Competition Law and Practice 6, 373.
217 Keith Hylton, 'Digital Platforms and Antitrust Law' (2019) Boston University School of Law, Law and Economics Research Paper No. 19-8, 10–11.
218 Bundeskartellamt and Autorité de la Concurrence, 'Competition Law and Data' (2016) 16–17 <https://www.bundeskartellamt.de/SharedDocs/Publikation/DE/Berichte/Big%20Data%20Papier.html;jsessionid=FCE1A15B6F85CD160925E13F58EE7524.1_cid378?nn=3600108>
219 See Chapter 4.

than 400 acquisitions in the last decade.[220] Most of these acquisitions were not harmful to competition or at least were deemed to have future pro-competitive benefits according to the EUMR rules. However, the aforementioned acquisitions raised the issue of whether risks are contained in vertical and conglomerate mergers in the online world since there is a boom in conglomerate mergers, and the traditional assessment tools for mergers and abusive conduct could be ill-equipped to address the market characteristics and structures. Conglomerate mergers do contain competitive risks, and these important acquisitions are dealt with in detail in the following chapter.

That being said, there is a growing pace of data acquisitions in the online world in general. Technology giants create value chains based on Big Data through data acquisitions and the collection of consumer data directly from users. The question is, how do data acquisitions create or restructure global value chains? Furthermore, how do businesses create data-related dominance in online platforms through data-driven mergers?

The answer is similar to data collection. Due to the network effects, accumulation of Big Data and data analytics, the value of data is derived, and better products and services are offered to consumers. However, in addition to the sheer accumulation of data, high concentration is created way faster due to data acquisitions. As mentioned in the previous sections, competition for the market is the main type of competition, and data acquisitions also impede competition for the market. Acquisition of nascent rivals is a way for technology giants to swallow new entrants and their research and developments in addition to their data related to consumers of that service or technology. Therefore, the acquisition of innovations and start-ups to pre-empt smaller businesses from becoming their competitors in the online world.[221] As barriers to entry rise, competition weakens, and even new waves of competition for the market are prevented; high concentration occurs in data-driven markets and the online world.[222]

The presence of a few technology giants in the online world is a risk since they establish and entrench market power in different industries quite easily due to their huge data advantage. In other words, data-driven acquisitions become the very first step to leveraging market power in data-driven markets. It is the most common way exercised by technology giants. Through data-driven acquisitions, businesses such as Google and Apple have extended their reach beyond core markets like social media or search engines into a wide ecosystem, including wearable devices (smartwatches and AR/VR glasses), autonomous vehicle technologies, online broadcasting services, even the energy sector.[223] Data-driven acquisitions demonstrate how they can easily embody conglomerate effects but can also be overlooked by

---

220 Furman (n 169) 91.
221 Inge Graef, 'Rethinking the Essential Facilities Doctrine for the EU Digital Economy' (2019) 53(1) Revue juridique Thémis de l'Université de Montréal 33–72, 39.
222 ibid.
223 ibid 39–40.

competition authorities. The prime examples would be Google's DoubleClick acquisition in 2010[224] and the Fitbit acquisition in 2020.[225] In 2010, the European Commission cleared the Google/DoubleClick acquisition on the basis that there would not be any conglomerate effects between the search engine market and the online advertising sector, which was a huge error. In time, the search engine market and online advertising were welded into one bigger ecosystem of Google, and Google has immense control over online advertising today. In a similar vein, Google notified the European Commission regarding the Google/Fitbit acquisition ten years after the DoubleClick decision. However, this time, the Commission's first response was the concerns over conglomerate effects that could occur between wearable devices and online advertising.[226] Departure from old ideas and the realisation of the new global value chains through data-driven acquisitions are important in applying competition in the digital age. However, the overlooked points in previous acquisitions will be discussed in detail in the following chapter.

3.4.3 Conglomerate Effects

Conglomerate effects: Data-driven acquisitions contain conglomerate strategies, and they are used to create new global chains. Although such conglomerate strategies cannot be deemed anti-competitive *per se*[227] or problematic, it is an important aspect of data-driven acquisitions, and competition authorities should assess them in every case related to data-driven markets and online ecosystems. The reason behind this is that the pattern of data-driven acquisitions containing conglomerate strategies to exploit data advantage is hard to assess compared to traditional markets. As mentioned earlier, data acquisitions affect not only the related markets of the parties in the acquisition but also adjacent online markets, digitalised traditional markets, future innovation and ultimately, the method of competition there: competition *for* the market. Thus, these acquisitions need a comprehensive understanding and analysis of how the acquirer could utilise data. However, it is important to mention that these data-driven acquisitions do not have to pose threats to competition even if they contain conglomerate strategies.[228]

The first problem faced by the competition authorities is addressing conglomerate effects in an acquisition of a start-up by a technology giant where huge sums of money are paid for small businesses. As a matter of course, the record takeover bids for small R&D businesses that do not have high capital stocks have aroused the competition authorities' interest in Europe. Technology giants have been purchasing small online platforms with little or no turnover. For instance, in 2014,

---

224 Case No COMP/M.4731, Google/DoubleClick C [2008] 927 Final.
225 Case No COMP/M.9660, Google/Fitbit [2020] Prior Notification of a Concentration OJ 2020/C 210/09.
226 ibid.
227 Graef (n 221) 39–40.
228 Furman (n 169) 93.

when Facebook acquired WhatsApp for almost $20 billion;[229] WhatsApp's had only $10 million in revenue and a net loss of $138 million. Facebook broke down the money it spent for the acquisition as $450 million for the WhatsApp brand, $288 million for tech, $2 billion for the user base, and the rest (more than $15 billion) for something that competition authorities overlooked.[230] It is said that the huge difference was spent on "future growth", "potential monetisation opportunities", and "strategic advantages provided in the digital mobile ecosystem".[231]

The point is these smaller companies, such as WhatsApp, hold great value due to their databases, which have already been collected and classified and are waiting for utilisation for better products, but also the creation of ecosystems, lock-in effects, abusive behaviour and monopolisation. However, this potential significance of the consumer data was not acknowledged in the merger transactions in the near past. Therefore, the question remains: Will consumer data become prominent and competitive? If so, do undertakings that do not have data fall behind in data-driven markets in the future?[232] As Margrethe Vestager states, controlling relevant data could make it impossible to compete with these data controller undertakings.[233] Thus, data or, more specifically, Big Data (containing 4Vs) is already becoming essential in businesses operating in both the digital and traditional economies, where businesses can also engage in more successful marketing and more profitable decisions.[234]

In light of these concerns, European and American authorities have investigated a considerable number of mergers.[235] In 2008, the Google/DoubleClick merger was approved by the European Commission and the Federal Trade Commission of the US. The main justification was that the collected data was non-rivalrous, and competitors (such as Microsoft) had easy access to the data.[236] It was one of the earliest decisions regarding Big Data and its effects on competition, and it has been proven that the assessment of this acquisition was quite erroneous. Another highly debated acquisition, the Facebook/WhatsApp merger, was approved by both Commissions

---

229 Case No COMP/M.7217, Facebook/WhatsApp C [2014] 7239 Final.
230 Josh Constine, 'WhatsApp's First Half of 2014 Revenue Was $15M, Net Loss of $232.5M Was Mostly Issuing Stock' *Techcrunch* (29 October 2014) <https://techcrunch.com/2014/10/28/whatsapp-revenue>
231 ibid.
232 Davilla (n 216) 371.
233 Dafydd Nelson, 'Microsoft, LinkedIn Should Heed Vestager's Warning About "Unique" Data' *MLex Market Insight* (9 September 2016) <https://mlexmarketinsight.com/insights-center/editors-picks/mergers/europe/microsoft-linkedin-should-heed-vestagers-warning-about-unique-data>
234 Davilla (n 216) 371.
235 Case No COMP/M.4731 *Google/DoubleClick* C[2008] 927 final; Case No COMP/M.5727 *Microsoft/Yahoo! Search Business* C[2010] 1077 final; Case No COMP/M.6314 *Telefónica UK/Vodafone UK/Everything Everywhere/JV* C[2012] 6063 final; Case No COMP/M.6281 *Microsoft/Skype* C[2011] 7239 final; Case No COMP/M.7217 *Facebook/WhatsApp* C [2014] 7239 final; Case No COMP/M.8124 *Microsoft/LinkedIn* C [2016] 8404 final; Case No COMP/M.8228 *Facebook/WhatsApp* C [2017] 3192 final.
236 Case No COMP/M.4731 *Google/DoubleClick* C [2008] 927 final, para 344.

70 Data-Driven Market Structures and Monopolisation

in 2014. The main justification was the irrelevancy between WhatsApp's consumer data and Facebook's targeted advertising services.[237] However, both Facebook's data-driven efficiency claims and the Commission's assessment were inaccurate. Consequently, in 2017, the Commission fined Facebook €110 million for providing misleading information about the WhatsApp merger.[238]

In academia, some commentators argue that the EU Merger Regulation is sufficient to deal with the Big Data issue.[239] According to Kadar and Bogdan, these recent merger approvals clearly show a degree of consistency in their approach.[240] Thus, the established theories of harm, including conglomerate effects, could be sufficiently flexible to be applied to Big Data mergers.[241] However, some commentators argue that merger control in the EU has proved its insufficiency in assessing mergers involving Big Data.[242] According to this idea, substantive analysis is not adequate for the new economy market structures, and the tools used to assess mergers are misleading.[243]

Thresholds: As a precursor/preliminary policy response, an issue has emerged regarding the effectiveness of turnover-based thresholds in data-driven mergers since merger control tools might not capture every transaction that contains serious anti-competitive threats for data-driven markets.[244] According to a European Commission public consultation, in which stakeholders' views were sought on the effectiveness of the turnover-based jurisdictional thresholds of merger control in the EU, the effects of controlling valuable data might be quite significant, especially in the digital and pharmaceutical industries.[245] In Germany, lawmakers have identified a problem with such an assessment: the ineffectiveness of the current *ex-ante* merger control measures. For this reason, an amendment in the German Competition Act (ARC) came into force back in 2017. The ninth amendment to the German Competition Act brought a major change to merger control, and an additional threshold was added to merger transactions. According to the amendment, mergers must be announced when the transaction value is more than €400 million in total, where the target has little or no turnover (less than €5 million) in

---

237 Case No COMP/M.7217 *Facebook/WhatsApp* C [2014] 7239 final, paras 179–89.
238 European Commission Press Release, 'Mergers: Commission Fines Facebook €110 Million for Providing Misleading Information About WhatsApp Takeover' Brussels, 18 May 2017 <http://europa.eu/rapid/press-release_IP-17-1369_en.htm>
239 Massimiliano Kadar and Mateusz Bogdan, ' "Big Data" and EU Merger Control – A Case Review (2017) 8 Journal of European Competition Law and Practice 8; Holles de Peyer (n 201) 767–90.
240 Kadar and Bogdan (n 239) 486.
241 ibid.
242 Hanna Stakheyeva and Fevzi Toksoy, 'Merger Control in the Big Data World: To Be or Not to Be Revisited?' (2017) 38 European Competition Law Review 6, 265–71, 270.
243 ibid 270–71.
244 European Commission, 'Consultation on Evaluation of Procedural and Jurisdictional Aspects of EU Merger Control' (2016) <http://ec.europa.eu/competition/consultations/2016_merger_control/index_en.html>
245 ibid.

Germany.²⁴⁶ Discussion spread over Europe. For instance, France has opted against an amendment related to value-based transactions and turnover thresholds but considered *ex-post* control mechanisms over data-driven acquisitions for mitigation.²⁴⁷ It can be predicted that merger control mechanisms, either *ex-ante* or *ex-post*, are also subject to change in light of these situations on the EU level.

On the other hand, Jacques Crémer et al. argue in their report for the European Commission regarding competition policy in the digital era that the thresholds of the EU Merger Regulation should not be changed as was done in Germany.²⁴⁸ According to the idea, although there are competitive concerns over the acquisition of start-ups with no significant thresholds, it is still early for an EU-wide regulatory amendment. Thus, they consider waiting to see how the new transaction thresholds affect merger control in Germany before introducing the new EUMR thresholds for data-driven markets.²⁴⁹ To put it a different way, the authors advocate for more detailed monitoring regarding threshold issues and emphasise the importance of the wider effects of a merger in data-driven markets. Therefore, for a substantive assessment of acquisitions, possible new theories of harm are needed to capture the wider effects of acquisitions on competition in the online world.²⁵⁰ Thus, they argue that merger analysis must include a discussion on how undertakings create online ecosystems through mergers, entrench their positions and shield these ecosystems from competitive pressure.²⁵¹ In this sense, if strong indirect network effects and economies of scale are already present in a market, acquisitions could likely lead to high concentration and leveraging market power.²⁵² For this reason, competition assessment for the acquisitions of start-ups must be conducted carefully to analyse the ecosystem structure and conglomerate effects correctly.

Fortunately, the approach to data-driven mergers seems to be changing, for example, in the case of data-driven efficiencies, the new market structures and especially Big Data's role in the competition.²⁵³ This can be seen in the latest investigations of the European Commission.²⁵⁴ Contrary to earlier merger decisions, the European competition authorities are now focusing their methods on assessing Big Data and data-driven markets and the wider effects of data utilisation in the cases of technology giants and online platform owners. New investigations will hopefully bring more clarification to the area of law.

---

246 Germany, Act Against Restraints of Competition (Competition Act – GWB) s(35)1.2.
247 Jacques Crémer, Yves-Alexandre de Montjoye and Heike Schweitzer, *Competition Policy for the Digital Era: Final Report* (Publications Office of the European Union 2019) 114.
248 ibid 115–16.
249 ibid 115.
250 ibid 124.
251 ibid.
252 ibid.
253 Akiva Miller, 'The Dawn of the Big Data Monopolists' (2016) 7 <https://ssrn.com/abstract=2911567>
254 Case No COMP/M.9660, Google/Fitbit [2020] Prior Notification of a Concentration OJ 2020/C 210/09.

72 Data-Driven Market Structures and Monopolisation

Data privacy dimension: In addition to the discussion of conglomerate effects and possibly ineffective *ex-ante* merger control tools, another challenge is the non-price dimension of competition law related to Big Data: privacy. Do the competition authorities analyse the effects of a merger in the non-price dimension of competition law? Although the privacy as a quality (non-price) parameter was discussed in the EU in mergers such as Facebook/WhatsApp, Microsoft/Yahoo! and Microsoft/LinkedIn and was found to be a quality parameter of non-price competition,[255] the European Commission also ruled in the Facebook/WhatsApp merger that

> Any privacy-related concerns flowing from the increased concentration of data within the control of Facebook as a result of the Transaction do not fall within the scope of the EU competition law rules but within the scope of the EU data protection rules.[256]

Similarly, scholars advocate that privacy concerns stemming from data should be addressed by data protection laws solely.[257] However, competition law becomes relevant whenever a violation of the data protection rules also violates the competition rules, such as Article 102 TFEU.[258]

As competition policy is concerned with a healthy and functioning market and consumer welfare, if privacy becomes a fundamental parameter to be assessed for competition in data-driven markets, it must be addressed within competition law since data protection laws definitely have different aims than competition law.[259] However, it also does not mean that there cannot be a case in which both competition and data protection laws are relevant.[260] Discussion on competition assessment through the quality-innovation-privacy triangle in Chapter 5 demonstrates that privacy should be incorporated into competition law and become a non-price dimension of competition law assessment in the EU.

To sum up, it seems that data-driven mergers should be analysed in light of new market dynamics.[261] Even the assessment method might need to change, as in the example of the amendment of the competition act of Germany, since Big Data

---

255 Case No COMP/M.5727, Microsoft/Yahoo! Search Business C [2010] 1077 Final, para 101–223; Case No COMP/M.7217, Facebook/WhatsApp C [2014] 7239 Final, para 87.
256 Case No COMP/M.7217, Facebook/WhatsApp C [2014] 7239 Final, para 164.
257 Davilla (n 216) 380.
258 *Bundeskartellamt*'s Facebook investigation. See Chapter 5.3.2.
259 Giuseppe Colangelo and Mariateresa Maggiolino, 'Data Protection in Attention Markets: Protecting Privacy Through Competition?' (2017) 8 Journal of European Competition Law and Practice 363, 367; Thorsten Mager and Philipp Otto Neideck, 'European Union: Data-Related Abuse of Dominance' (2018) Global Competition Review <https://globalcompetitionreview.com/insight/e-commerce-competition-enforcement-guide/1177726/european-union-%E2%80%93-data-related-abuse-of-dominance>
260 Nils-Peter Schepp and Achim Wambach, 'On Big Data and Its Relevance for Market Power Assessment' (2016) 7 Journal of European Competition Law and Practice 2, 120–24, 123.
261 See Chapter 4.

changes the structure of economic transactions in the digital age. In order to find the appropriate remedy, the first point which needs to be addressed is the global value chains created by Big Data since data-driven mergers are more likely to have strong conglomerate effects on markets, as discussed. Therefore, price-centric traditional assessments – horizontal and vertical – for markets seem ill equipped due to the growth in data-driven conglomerate mergers. In the same vein, dominant undertakings use their data dominance in adjacent markets for anti-competitive purposes. Together, these two situations create enormous negative long-term effects in terms of competition, which is the main finding of this book. In the following chapters, both issues are discussed in detail.

3.5 Concluding Remarks

Data-driven markets are the new economy markets created by the commercialisation of the internet and the utilisation of Big Data through algorithms and artificial intelligence. Innovation is the predominant characteristic of data-driven markets, and competition for the market is the main type of competition. Competition for the market creates innovation cycles, leading to first-mover advantage and dominance in data-driven markets. In the online world, the Big Data user undertakings tip markets in their favour, which creates barriers by the strong indirect network effects. Therefore, the accumulation of Big Data creates irreversible damage to markets regarding competition, and markets tip in favour of dominant undertakings. Having an inherent advantage by having and using Big Data, these undertakings achieve efficient scales. Thus, smaller rivals cannot dethrone or even compete with dominant undertakings. Even though the monopolisation of markets and tipping effects cannot be deemed anti-competitive itself by looking at the current structure of a market in the new economy, the accumulation of Big Data and contributory effects create barriers to entry in data-driven markets and do not contribute to healthy competition positively. Thus, there are no low-entry barriers in data-driven markets, and it is impossible for markets to self-correct, as *laissez-faire* competition claims suggest.

The utilisation of Big Data affects the structures of newly emerged markets and changes the structures in traditional markets considerably. Due to the creation of the online advertising market, many firms which may want to be rivals of technology giants in commercial life actually depend on revenues and consumers stemming from the online advertising services of super-dominants. However, the online advertising industry is in the hands of a few firms that hoard massive amounts of user data. These undertakings and their services have millions and even billions of users worldwide. These undertakings enjoy the externalised power of indirect network effects created by billions of consumers. However, this network effect develops differently than in traditional markets of manufacturing or the telecom sector. In addition to the direct network effects in traditional markets, there are indirect network effects on both sides of the markets in multi-sided platforms where the platform owner can internalise both sides for benefits. Only a handful of businesses can compete in markets in which strong indirect network effects and returns to scale are present.[262] As a result, near monopolies are established.

These near monopolies are not ephemeral in data-driven markets due to the inherent advantages given by Big Data to undertakings. In the last decade, the evolution of data-driven markets has shown signs that digital monopolies will be the norm in the near future. Three-dimensional competition between "moligopolists" and near monopolies of super-dominant undertakings poses several concerns. The structure in data-driven markets is not temporary, and data-driven markets do not seem self-corrective. Tipping the markets and sophisticated relationship between technology giants proves that the existent and potential rivals of technology giants in the online world cannot revert the situation since they all rely on the services of technology giants. Digital monopolies are a problem for healthy competition and new markets. However, the current structure and behaviour of dominant undertakings also bring up further issues regarding the abuse of dominant position, data acquisitions and assessment of market power. Upcoming chapters delve deeper into many of the highlighted issues in recent cases and investigations. However, case law is quite far from mitigating the current problems.

---

262 Crémer (n 247) 36.

4 Assessment of Data-Related Market Power in Data-Driven Markets

4.1 Market Definition

Competition law consists of various legal norms and rules. Many concepts, either legal or economic, are utilised in this framework. The definition of the relevant market is one of these concepts.[1] Primarily, it is not a legal norm for competition law purposes. Instead, it is an interpretation of an economic concept in the legal context. Today, market power assessment, including relevant market definitions, is economically based in most jurisdictions in terms of competition law. In other words, economic analysis is used by the competition authorities, and market definition serves as an analytical tool for competition law purposes.[2] The so-called hypothetical monopolist test (HMT), small but significant non-transitory increase in price test (SSNIP) and demand-supply side substitutability assessment can be mentioned as examples. However, only after the initial economic analysis are the legal concepts created. Therefore, concepts such as "dominant position" or "relevant market" find a place in the legal context.

In the traditional assessment of market power, in order to measure concentration, defining a relevant market is a must.[3] According to the European Commission, market definition is a tool to define the boundaries of competition between firms.[4] Thus, the main purpose of defining a relevant market is to engage a systemic analysis regarding how undertakings are involved in anti-competitive conduct.[5] The conventional inquiry of defining the relevant market is an empirical method in which the undertaking's market shares are calculated to determine whether it

---

1 Viktoria HSE Robertson, 'The Relevant Market in Competition Law: A Legal Concept' (2019) 7 Journal of Antitrust Enforcement 158–76, 167.
2 ibid 175.
3 Jason Furman, *Unlocking Digital Competition: Report of the Digital Competition Expert Panel* (HM Treasury 2019) 24, 33 <https://www.gov.uk/government/publications/unlocking-digital-competition-report-of-the-digital-competition-expert-panel>
4 European Commission Notice on the Definition of Relevant Market for the Purposes of Community Competition Law (Text with EEA Relevance) [1997] OJ C 372/5, para 2.
5 ibid.

DOI: 10.4324/9781003458791-4

is large enough for possible abusive behaviour.[6] Milton Friedman expresses the main underlying reason for the relevant market analysis by referring to the hypothesis of Alfred Marshall.[7] According to the idea, undertakings can be separated into different industries based on the similarities between them and their products.[8] These specific industries can be identified through similar problems that arise in that industry. For many problems, similarities between undertakings in each industry are more important than their differences.[9] For instance, small changes in the demand for a product or an effect on the supply would affect all undertakings in the same industry to a larger extent than players in other industries.[10] However, it is also important to note that not every undertaking in a specific industry is affected at the same level: for instance, in case of a change in demand. Detrimental effects can differ.

In order to assess the abusive behaviour of dominant undertakings, case law in the EU established a two-stage procedure to identify relevant markets and then examine the alleged undertakings' position in the relevant market.[11] After this two-stage procedure, the abusive behaviour of the alleged undertaking is addressed. According to the Court of Justice (CJEU), the identification of a relevant market holds an essential significance for the purposes of competition law.[12] Identification of relevant markets is engaged for defining the boundaries of competition between undertakings.[13] Identification of the relevant market and boundaries of competition would reveal any kind of competitive constraints in which undertakings might have been involved.[14]

Technically speaking, reaching a relevant market for a product or service has two dimensions. First, the market needs to be defined on a product basis. Friedman defines a product as

> a collection of units that are perfect substitutes to purchasers, so the elasticity of demand for the output of one firm with respect to the price of another firm in the same industry is infinite for some price and some outputs.[15]

---

6 William Landes and Richard Posner, 'Market Power in Antitrust Cases' (1980) 94 Harvard Law Review 937–38.
7 Milton Friedman, 'The Methodology of Positive Economics' in *Essays in Positive Economics* (Chicago UP 1966) 3–16, 30–43, 35; Alfred Marshall, 'The Present Position of Economics' (1885), reprinted in AC Pigou (ed), *Memorials of Alfred Marshall* (Macmillan & Co. 1925); John Stuart Mill, *Principles of Political Economy* (Ashley ed.; Longmans, Green & Co. 1929).
8 ibid.
9 ibid.
10 ibid.
11 Alison Jones and Brenda Sufrin, *EU Competition Law* (5th edn, OUP 2014) 304.
12 Case 6–72 *Europemballage Corporation and Continental Can Company Inc. v Commission of the European Communities* [1973] ECR 1973–00215, p 217 (para 14).
13 Commission Notice (n 2) para 2.
14 ibid.
15 Friedman (n 7) 35.

Assessment of Data-Related Market Power in Data-Driven Markets 77

The second dimension is geographical. The main purpose of defining markets on both product and geographical dimensions is to reveal the actual and potential competitors for an undertaking, which could restrict the behaviour of that undertaking and could also prevent them from acting independently through competitive pressure.[16] In this respect, defining a relevant market also enables the identification of the market shares, which can provide useful information about market power, assess dominance and apply Article 102 TFEU.[17]

The method of defining a relevant market is relatively straightforward. Identifying related buyers and sellers for a specific product, including substitute products, is necessary, along with the purchasing and output decisions.[18] In its "Notice on the Definition of Relevant Market", the European Commission defines "relevant product markets" as markets created by interchangeable or substitutable products or services based on their processes, intended use and characteristics.[19] In order to identify the relevant market and assess competition within it, the elasticity and interchangeability of a specific product must be determined first.[20] Then, whether the specific product and its substitutes constitute a separate market must be identified. The relevant market concept refers to the effective competition between undertakings.[21] When there is a sufficient degree of substitutability between similar products or services which constitute a separate market, then it can be presumed that there is competition between these products or services in that specific market.[22] Along the same line, regarding data-driven markets, the Commission expresses in the *Google Search (Shopping)* decision:

> For the purposes of investigating the possible dominant position of an undertaking on a given product market, the possibilities of competition must be judged in the context of the market comprising the totality of the products or services which, with respect to their characteristics, are particularly suitable for satisfying constant needs and are only to a limited extent interchangeable with other products or services.[23]

Additionally, according to the CJEU, products must be classified not only by their packaging or other sale similarities but also by the specific characteristics of

---

16 Commission Notice (n 2) para 2.
17 ibid.
18 Gönenç Gürkaynak, Büşra Aktüre and Sıla Coşkunoğlu, 'Challenges of the Digital Age: The Relevant Product Market Definition in Online and Offline Sales' in Gönenç Gürkaynak (ed), *The Second Academic Gift Book of ELIG Gürkaynak Attorneys-at-Law on Selected Contemporary Competition Law Matters* (Legal Yayincilik 2019) 219.
19 Commission Notice (n 2) para 7.
20 Case 6–72 *Europemballage Corporation and Continental Can Company Inc. v Commission of the European Communities* [1973] ECR 1973-00215, p 217 (para 14).
21 Case 85–76 *Hoffmann-La Roche & Co. AG v Commission of the European Communities* (1979) ECLI:EU:C:1979:36, para 28.
22 ibid.
23 Case No COMP/AT.39740, *Google Search (Shopping)* C[2017] 4444 Final, para 145.

the production process that make them similarly suitable for their purposes.[24] That being said, relevant product market analysis is not limited to interchangeability. It also covers the objective characteristics of products or services.[25] This is called the functionality test. The CJEU repeatedly underlines the importance of competitive structure in identifying the relevant market. According to the Court, "the competitive conditions and the structure of supply and demand on the market must also be taken into consideration".[26] Therefore, in the relevant market analysis, undertakings are subject to three sources of competitive constraints: demand substitutability, supply substitutability and potential competition.[27] Demand substitutability is the most prominent and reliable way of considering and defining a relevant market. However, supply substitutability can also be referred to when it is found as effective as demand substitutability.

Along with the relevant product market, the identification of relevant geographical markets is also important. The Commission defines "relevant geographical market" as a market in which undertakings are involved in the supply and demand of relevant products where conditions are more or less uniform.[28] In other words, the geographical market is a territory where competition is homogeneous between rival undertakings. Therefore, these markets can become distinguishable from other markets since the competition occurring in that market is specifically different from others.[29] Identifying the geographical market together with the product market seems necessary to assess the market power of undertakings and the competition in a given case. Regarding data-driven markets, identifying a relevant geographical market is not practical since all players in data-driven markets operate on a global scale; thus, examinations and investigations of the CJEU and the Commission would reveal that the relevant geographical market is the EEA in every single case.[30] There are no physical or geographical boundaries in the online world. It is effectively an unprecedented global sector.

4.2 Relevant Product Market Failure in the Data-Driven Economy

The main problem of relevant market definition in data-driven markets is finding a relevant "product" market for the competition law analysis. As data-driven markets have such unique characteristics,[31] defining a relevant product market as

---

24 Case 6–72 *Europemballage Corporation and Continental Can Company Inc. v Commission of the European Communities* [1973] ECR 1973-00215, p 217 (para 14).
25 Case 322–81 *NV Nederlandsche Banden Industrie Michelin v Commission of the European Communities* (1983) ECLI:EU:C:1983:313, para 37.
26 ibid; Case No COMP/AT.39740, *Google Search (Shopping)* C[2017] 4444 Final, para 146.
27 ibid para 149.
28 European Commission Notice on the definition of relevant market for the purposes of Community competition law (Text with EEA relevance) [1997] OJ C 372/5, para 8.
29 ibid.
30 For instance, Case No COMP/M.4731 *Google/DoubleClick* C[2008] 927 final, paras 82–84.
31 See Chapter 3.2.

the first stage of conducting market power analysis might not be relevant today. Although there is a new draft that replaces the previous Commission Notice from 1997 to provide guidance on how to define the relevant market and focus on the analysis of digital markets, it seems to be far from resolving issues pertaining to relevant market definition.[32] The draft notice acknowledges that data-driven markets may have different characteristics than traditional markets, such as network effects, multi-sided platforms and economies of scale, which make it more difficult to define the relevant market, as the same product or service may have different substitutes in different parts of the market. The draft notice proposes some changes to provide additional information on various key market definition issues, such as explanations of the principles of market definition; greater emphasis on non-price elements such as innovation and quality of products and services; clarifications regarding the forward-looking application of market definition, such as technological or regulatory changes; new guidance regarding multi-sided markets and digital ecosystems; and new principles on innovation-intensive markets.[33] In other words, the notice highlights the importance of Big Data in data-driven markets, as data can be a crucial input for many services, such as targeted advertising, personalisation of services and artificial intelligence.

However, a weakness of the new draft notice is that it does not provide clear guidance on how to assess the market power of undertakings in dynamic industries since data-driven markets are characterised by rapid technological innovation, short product life cycles and fast-changing consumer preferences. In these markets, it can be difficult to determine whether a company has a dominant position, as its position may be quickly overtaken by new entrants or innovative products. Another potential weakness of the draft Commission Notice is its limited discussion of the role of Big Data in relevant market definitions. While the notice acknowledges the importance of data in digital markets, it does not provide clear guidance on how to define data-driven markets or assess the market power of undertakings. This is a significant gap, as data-driven markets are becoming increasingly important and may have significant impacts on competition and consumers.

To sum up, the definition of the relevant market is a crucial step in the assessment of competition law cases, and the new Commission Notice provides useful guidance on how to define the relevant digital market. However, it is important to recognise that the market definition must be assessed in considering the specific facts of each case separately. Therefore, the Commission's conduct in defining relevant markets in data-driven markets is discussed in the following section. In this sense, the analysis is divided into separate discussions regarding the definition of relevant product markets, the interchangeability of products and how narrow product markets are defined in competition law analysis regarding data-driven markets;

---

32 Draft Revised Market Definition Notice; European Commission, Press Release, 'Competition: Commission Seeks Feedback on Draft Revised Market Definition Notice' (Brussels, 8 November 2022) <https://ec.europa.eu/commission/presscorner/detail/en/ip_22_6528>
33 ibid.

why narrower product market definitions are irrelevant is discussed next. To note, geographical relevant market analysis is left out of this discussion since there are no geographical limits for the functioning of most data-driven markets.

4.2.1 Market Segmentation

The European Commission received a notification about a merger between Google Inc. and DoubleClick Inc. in 2007. The investigation was about one newly emerged market: online advertising,[34] where Google had already established worldwide dominance. The investigation found that both Google and DoubleClick are parts of the "online advertising industry".[35] The online advertising market is regarded as separate from the offline advertising market[36] and has become a whole sector.[37] After the second phase of the merger investigation, the Commission concluded that the merger would not have detrimental effects on competition in the internal market, and the merger was cleared.

The Commission segmented the online advertising market into several fragments in its investigation. Three main types of ads – search ads, non-search or display ads and classified ads – are found in the investigation.[38] The Commission

---

34 Online advertising started as a business model for undertakings operating in the online world. The online advertising industry has three main players: advertisers who buy space to show their ads, web publishers who sell that space to advertisers to gain revenue and the intermediaries who provide ad services and bring advertisers and publishers together. Although it started in 1998, Google's first online advertising service was launched in 2000 (AdWords). AdWords was the first service which placed advertisements on Google search results pages. Later, in 2002, Google launched an updated version of its AdWords service, which was based on cost-per-click pricing. Following investments, in a short period of time, Google reached 100,000 advertisers on its online ad services. At that time, Google's daily search count was about 200 million worldwide. Shortly after, in 2003, Google expanded its online advertisement business and started to offer click-through rate-based targeted advertisements to users (AdSense). This was a significant breakthrough in the online advertisement sector. In 2005, Google launched another service, site targeting. This service enabled advertisers to reach specific websites to show their ads in order to narrow their audience and generate more relevant advertisements. James Ratliff and Daniel Rubinfeld, 'Online Advertising: Defining Relevant Markets' (2010) 6 Journal of Competition Law and Economics 3, 658; Google, Press Release, 'Google Builds World's Largest Advertising and Search Monetization Program' (4 March 2003) <http://www.google.com/press/pressrel/advertising.html>
35 Case No COMP/M.4731 *Google/DoubleClick* C[2008] 927 final, para 8.
36 Case No COMP/M.4731 *Google/DoubleClick* C[2008] 927 final, paras 45–51; Case No COMP/M.5727 *Microsoft/Yahoo! Search Business* C[2010] 1077 final, para 61; Case No COMP/M.7217 *Facebook/WhatsApp* C [2014] 7239 final, paras 75–79; Case No COMP/M.8124 *Microsoft/LinkedIn* C [2016] 8404 final, para 159; Ratliff and Rubinfeld (n 34) 653–86.
37 It is important to point out that offline advertising in print media like newspapers and magazines has experienced sharp decreases since the emergence of the online advertising business model. Thomas Höppner, 'Defining Markets for Multi-Sided Platforms: The Case of Search Engines' (2015) 38 World Competition 3, 359; Florence Thépot, 'Market Power in Online Search and Social Networking: A Matter of Two-sided Markets' (2013) 36 World Competition 2, 211–12; Avi Goldfarb and Catherine Tucker, 'Substitution Between Offline and Online Advertising Markets' (2011) 7 Journal of Competition Law and Economics 37, 39; Ratliff and Rubinfeld (n 34) 665–70.
38 Case No COMP/M.4731 *Google/DoubleClick* C[2008] 927 final, para 11.

argued that the main difference between these fragments is the way of targeting and reaching the audience.[39] The argument is that the non-search ads are more general and non-specific for users, meaning they are less targeted than others.[40] However, search ads are more relevant to users since these ads can actually be shown after a search query; users have to type some keywords to search in the engine. These ads target consumers since users reveal their interests, geographic locations and more by conducting search queries. In this way, advertisements appear to be more relevant for users.

Nonetheless, the Commission found a narrower product market definition unnecessary by defining separate display or search advertisement markets since there was no relevant distinction between the fragments of online advertising for the investigation.[41] The reason behind this is the method used to distinguish these services: the demand-side substitutability of mentioned segments of online advertising. A demand-side substitutability test was performed for search and display ads from the advertisers' point of view.[42] The Commission investigated the technical part of the online advertising market and concluded that the differences between them are actually diminishing.[43] They argued that the ability of non-search/display ads to target consumers is improving significantly.[44]

The decision not to define a separate narrow online advertising market seems to have been the correct move. This decision is nuanced in the investigations of Microsoft/Yahoo!,[45] Facebook/WhatsApp, Telefonica/Vodafone/EE and Microsoft/LinkedIn.[46] It has been more than a decade since the decision in 2008; today, the online advertising market functions slightly differently. Today, non-search/display advertising can target consumers and be 100% relevant to them. Today, algorithms not only use the online history of users and user profiling systems through efficient use of Big Data, but their respective algorithms also use personal assistants like Siri, Alexa, Cortana and Google Assistant for improved services, which also include all types of advertising. Therefore, it can be assumed that there is no need for a search query to make an ad more relevant to the end user today.

On the other hand, the French Competition Authority distinguished search and display advertising. In its opinion in 2018, the aspects of online advertising were discussed, and two issues were found: social network online advertising and the

---

39 ibid para 50.
40 Höppner (n 37) 360.
41 Case No COMP/M.4731 *Google/DoubleClick* C[2008] 927 final, para 48.
42 ibid para 53.
43 ibid para 52.
44 ibid para 52.
45 Case No COMP/M.5727 *Microsoft/Yahoo! Search Business* C[2010] 1077 final, para 75; Case No COMP/M.7217 *Facebook/WhatsApp* C [2014] 7239 final, para 76; Case No COMP/M.6314 *Telefónica UK/Vodafone UK/Everything Everywhere/JV* C[2012] 6063 final 151; Case No COMP/M.8124 *Microsoft/LinkedIn* C[2016] 8404 final, para 161.
46 Case No COMP/M.4731 *Google/DoubleClick* C[2008] 927 final, para 56.

level of substitutability between display and search advertising.[47] According to the discussion, users were still experiencing the difference in targeting. The discussion was actually based on a study carried out through consultation with stakeholders. The authority found that search ads are better at targeting than social media ads or display ads in their results.[48] Also, the search ads market structure seemed to be different from that of the display ad market.[49] The number of suppliers in the search ad market is significantly less than in the display ad market due to the established barriers to entry and the expansion of Google and its subsidiaries.[50] The key to eliminating that barrier is creating a powerful search engine and an intermediary platform for online advertising, which is quite difficult. Along the same line, the Federal Trade Commission (FTC) concluded that search and non-search/display advertising segments are not substitutes; thus, they must be regarded as different markets.[51]

Another important issue in the Google/DoubleClick investigation is that the Commission defined a separate market for the ad intermediation and ad servicing markets.[52] In data-driven markets, publishers may sell ad spaces directly to ad providers. In this method, publishers can charge higher prices for ad spaces.[53] However, the existence of an intermediary/ad server service creates another method for selling ad space. This way, publishers and ad providers come together via an intermediary or an exchange service. In other words, there is always a third player in the market. However, it is argued that this market is not a relevant market. Segmentation of the intermediary services market as ad intermediation and ad services/exchanges is a widely discussed issue. The French Competition Authority makes a clear distinction between these markets.[54] Along the same line, Geradin and Katsifis argue that not only ad intermediation and ad servicing but also further segmentation of these two markets is desirable.[55] Further possible segmentation is not within the scope of this analysis. However, the segmentation of ad intermediation/ad servicing seems to be the main reason the Commission found the merger not to be detrimental to competition within the EEA.

---

47 Autorité de la Concurrence, French Competition Authority, Opinion 18-A-03 on Data Processing in the Online Advertising Sector (6 March 2018) para 176.
48 ibid para 179.
49 ibid para 182.
50 ibid.
51 Federal Trade Commission, 'Statement of Federal Trade Commission Concerning Google/DoubleClick' FTC File No. 071-0170, 3 <https://www.ftc.gov/system/files/documents/public_statements/418081/071220googledc-commstmt.pdf>
52 Case No COMP/M.4731 *Google/DoubleClick* C[2008] 927 final, para 68.
53 Damien Geradin and Dimitrios Katsifis, 'An EU Competition Law Analysis of Online Display Advertising in the Programmatic Age' (2018) 15 European Competition Journal 55–96, 68.
54 Autorité de la Concurrence, French Competition Authority, Opinion 18-A-03 on Data Processing in the Online Advertising Sector (6 March 2018) para 185 <https://www.autoritedelaconcurrence.fr/sites/default/files/integral_texts/2019-10/avis18a03_en_.pdf>
55 Geradin and Katsifis (n 53) 68.

Assessment of Data-Related Market Power in Data-Driven Markets 83

In Google/DoubleClick, the Commission defined a separate market for online display ad services, distinguishing them from other ad services, including ad intermediation.[56] Therefore, the Commission decided that, as a search engine and a player in the online advertising industry, Google is the dominant undertaking (through AdSense) in the ad intermediary segment of the online advertising industry.[57] Therefore, its main competitors in the ad intermediation market are Yahoo! (around 5% market share) and Microsoft (around 5% market share).[58] On the other hand, DoubleClick is found to be the dominant undertaking in the display ad servicing segment of the online advertising market.[59] As a result, its main competitors are identified as aQuantive/Atlas, Real Media/Open AdStream and ADTECH/AOL.[60] Market analysis shows that dominance and competition are parallel in the EEA and worldwide for both Google and DoubleClick. Consequently, it was decided that Google and DoubleClick are not main competitors to each other, there would be a sufficient number of competitors left in both markets after the merger, and the elimination of DoubleClick from competition would not impede competition within the EEA.

4.2.2 Non-horizontal Effects

The Google/DoubleClick investigation missed an important discussion on the value chain created by Google in the online advertising sector and a comprehensive analysis regarding the non-horizontal effects in the segments of the online advertising sector. First, the segmentation of the online advertising market made it difficult to see the wider effects in the value chain. Google operates in every segment of the online advertising market, and Google's presence in these segments enables a dual-channel data analytics service.[61] Moreover, the latest of Google's technologies allow the processing of all data across the online advertising sector (display, search and others).[62] The new analytic systems integrate third-party data for advertisers by combining data from sources like websites, audiences and CRMs[63] to make ads more relevant for users.[64] Also, the new analytics systems integrate Google's ad services AdSense, Ad Mob, AdWords and all others.[65]

---

56 Case No COMP/M.4731 *Google/DoubleClick* C[2008] 927 final, paras 74–81.
57 ibid para 92.
58 ibid para 110.
59 ibid para 113.
60 ibid para 115.
61 Autorité de la Concurrence (n 54) para 147.
62 Google Analytics Suite 360: Analytics 360 (formerly known as GA Premium), Attribution 360 (formerly known as Adometry), Data Studio 360(new), Tag Manager 360(new), Optimize 360(new), Audience Center 360(new) <https://www.blog.google/products/marketingplatform/360/introducing-google-analytics-360-suite>
63 Consumer Data.
64 Paul Muret, 'Introducing the Google Analytics 360 Suite: An Enterprise-Class Solution for a Multi-Screen World' (15 March 2016) <https://www.blog.google/products/marketingplatform/360/introducing-google-analytics-360-suite>
65 Autorité de la Concurrence (n 54) para 147.

It is crucial to point out that Google is a unique company that operates on both display and search advertising segments, including ad intermediation and advertisement serving.[66] Google's competitors like Microsoft or Yahoo! also offer display and search ads via their search engines, but they have never had an ad intermediation service like Google. Under its unique operation, Google used several algorithm-based analytics services to develop a relationship between its online ad services' display and search advertising segments.[67] In other words, Google created a mechanism to derive value from the cross-correlation of available data. This affected the way advertisements are served and targeted to users. Everything else aside, newer data analytic systems of Google to generate relevant data by emerging all available data to them across the online platforms (Google's wider ecosystem) would have been quite challenging to be predicted by competition authorities during the investigation.

Nevertheless, the role of Big Data in the value chain, algorithms and possible data analytics has not been included in the analysis. Instead, datasets were mentioned only as an asset. The discussion was on the probability of what would happen if Google utilised DoubleClick's datasets. Google's investigation on the other side of the Atlantic was no different. The Federal Trade Commission concluded that a data combination created by Google and DoubleClick would not harm competition for reasons similar to those mentioned earlier. In this regard, Google already had an enormous amount of user data prior to the merger, and the data which DoubleClick was collecting belonged to publishers.[68] As a result, any info would be protected due to foreclosure restrictions since Google had already committed to the sanctity of these agreements.

Moreover, there was no evidence found even if Google managed to use this data for competitive advantage in the online ad intermediation services.[69] However, trade commissioner Pamela Jones Harbour gave a dissenting statement for the FTC's decision regarding Google and DoubleClick. In her comments, Harbour underlined the importance of data for these kinds of mergers in which network effects are prominent, but the FTC overlooked the issue of data-driven efficiencies. Harbour argued that excessive network effects would be generated due to this merger, and this would likely affect the development of online advertising services in its entirety.[70] Also, she added that the merger would create additional network effects which were non-existent beforehand.[71] As mentioned in Chapter 3, Big Data creates network effects and a value chain that gives access to a vast advertising data inventory.

---

66 ibid para 144.
67 ibid para 145.
68 Federal Trade Commission (n 51).
69 ibid.
70 Federal Trade Commission, Dissenting Statement of Commissioner Pamela Jones Harbour, in the Matter of Google/DoubleClick F.T.C. File No. 071-0170 (2007) 4 <https://www.ftc.gov/sites/default/files/documents/public_statements/statement-matter-google/doubleclick/071220harbour_0.pdf>
71 ibid.

A couple of years after the Google/DoubleClick merger, the European Commission received a notification of a merger between Microsoft Corporation and Yahoo! Inc. The Microsoft/Yahoo! investigation is noteworthy since it identifies the online search market for the first time. A definition was given for online search engines: tools consisting of search boxes where users enter their queries to search for information on the web.[72] In regard to defining a relevant market for online advertising, the investigation nuanced its previous decision in Google/DoubleClick. In line with the Google decision, the Commission stated that the online advertising market constitutes the relevant market of the merger.[73] Hereunder, a distinction was made between offline and online advertising markets, and a segment called the ad intermediation services market in the online advertising market was found.[74] The situation was slightly different for the search and non-search (display) advertising markets.[75] Microsoft argued that search advertising should be separated as a product market for the investigation since its characteristics are unique and different from those of the display advertising market. The results of the market investigation carried out by the Commission for a larger number of market respondents also gave relatively similar results.[76] However, the Commission found it unnecessary to define separate search and display markets and open the exact product market definition.[77] As for intermediation services, since the Commission identified them as a separate segment, they did not find it necessary to define a narrower market and left this definition open also.[78]

In its decision, the Commission found the relevant market to be the online advertising market and not the online search engine market, which could also be determined as the relevant market for this specific investigation.[79] According to the ruling, the Microsoft (Bing) and Yahoo! merger must be successful in the online search market to affect the online advertising market in the first place. For this reason, the notifying party argued that Google is the dominant undertaking in the online search and online advertising markets; thus, Microsoft lacks scale, and Yahoo has

---

72 Case No COMP/M.5727 *Microsoft/Yahoo! Search Business* C[2010] 1077 final, para 30; The search results which rely on algorithms to generate most relevant information may be in the form of text (links), images, videos, news, shopping and even maps. Furthermore, there are distinct types of search engines; horizontal and vertical. General, or horizontal, search engines are targeted to users for searching through a vast available online index. On the other hand, vertical search engines are for more specialised uses like travel, library, medical or academic search. Vertical search engines use a smaller portion of the index available online which focuses on the type of the search engine. However, the commission left open the issue of defining a relevant separate market for vertical internet searches. As a result, the differentiation between the segments of the internet search market, vertical and horizontal, and whether they are separate markets was not discussed further.
73 ibid para 87.
74 ibid paras 61, 82–83.
75 ibid para 62.
76 ibid paras 71–74.
77 ibid para 75.
78 ibid para 87.
79 ibid para 86.

a declining performance in the online advertising market.[80] Notifying parties also acknowledged that data is an important ingredient to achieve scale and become a successful search engine. However, at the same time, it approved Google's argument that the value of the incremental data loses its importance when the amount of collected and analysed data increases.[81] On the Commission's part, the decision led to an analysis of the legality of the transaction regarding the online advertising market while merging discussions on the internet search engine.[82] Thus, the Commission assessed any potential pro-competitive and anti-competitive effects of the merger on the relevance of internet search, the multi-homing issue, achieving scale, algorithms, variety of choice and innovation.[83]

As a result, the Commission did not find Microsoft and Yahoo to be competitors in the online advertising markets except in the UK and France within the EEA.[84] Initial analysis of advertisers, publishers and distributers drew the conclusion for the online advertising market.[85] However, Microsoft (through Bing) and Yahoo! were long-time competitors in the online search market within the EEA and the world. The Microsoft/Yahoo! merger was a missed opportunity for an in-depth analysis of the online search market and its conglomerate links with market segments such as online or mobile advertising. Additionally, for internet search and search advertising, both parties' activities were found to be quite limited, with a combined share below 10% within the EEA, leading to the situation in which Microsoft and Yahoo! cannot compete with Google.[86] For these reasons, the merger was found to be pro-competitive, and the Commission declared it compatible with the internal market and competition law.

In another Microsoft merger, Microsoft/Skype, as for the potential competition, the Commission discussed the structure of the communication services market. In this sense, the focus was on internet communication services – the first time the internet communication services market was studied from a demand-side substitutability point of view.[87] Later, a similar assessment would also be made in the Facebook/WhatsApp merger. The decision made a distinction between consumer communications and enterprise communication services, declaring them two distinct markets.[88] For consumer communications, any communication across platforms between individuals falls into this category: instant messaging, voice calls and video calls. WhatsApp Messenger, Telegram, Viber, Facebook Messenger, Skype, Hangouts (Google Messaging), FaceTime, iMessage and many others can

---

80 ibid paras 136–49.
81 ibid para 174.
82 Inge Graef, 'Data as Essential Facility: Competition and Innovation on Online Platforms' (PhD Thesis, KU Leuven Faculty of Law 2016) 93.
83 ibid; Case No COMP/M.5727 *Microsoft/Yahoo! Search Business* C[2010] 1077 final, paras 220–26.
84 ibid para 132.
85 ibid para 255.
86 ibid paras 252–54.
87 Case No COMP/M.6281 *Microsoft/Skype* C[2011] 7239 final, para 20.
88 ibid para 17.

be listed as consumer communication services. However, the Commission opened the discussion of whether consumer communication services should be separated into different markets based on platform or operating system differences.[89] On par, the Commission did not further segment the enterprise communication services on the basis of OS, platform or functionality.[90] The Commission defined enterprise communication services in the *Cisco/Tandberg* decision,[91] which stated these services are used by business customers in order to improve collaborative communications, thus providing a consistent but simple user experience.

The Microsoft/Skype merger also has non-horizontal links. In its assessment, the Commission widely discussed possible foreclosure effects, incentives to foreclosure and overall impact on competition for the consumer communications market.[92] The ability to foreclose was studied through three practices in the investigation: tying, bundling and degradation of interoperability. Foreseeable effects of all three practices were found to be limited to non-existent in the present case. Thus, the Commission considered the merger compatible with the internal market regarding consumer communication services. For enterprise communication services, conglomerate effects were found to be irrelevant.[93] The course taken by the Commission lacks an assessment of data effects for the conglomerate structure. The necessity of an argument around Big Data analytics, capabilities, and non-horizontal effects on several markets is inarguable by the investigation. This is not an assumption that the Microsoft/Skype merger led to anti-competitive incentives through connecting several online markets. However, before the conclusion, an analysis should at least be undertaken on how Microsoft could use Skype, Bing or any of its services to channelise available datasets for foreclosure purposes or tipping effects. As revealed in the previous case, Microsoft and Yahoo were identified as participants in the online advertising market. Although both lacked scale and struggled to compete with Google, the initial Microsoft/Yahoo merger would have changed the situation. A retrospective analysis of the capabilities of Microsoft in the online advertising market and possible conglomerate effects was skipped in the investigation.

In the most recent Microsoft merger, Microsoft/LinkedIn, the online advertising market was again studied by the Commission. In the investigation, eight separate relevant markets were determined. In seven of them – namely, the PC operating systems, productivity software, CRM[94] software, sales intelligence, online communications services, social network services and online recruitment services – the Commission concluded that Microsoft and LinkedIn are not competitors since they were not operating at the same time in any of these digital markets.[95] In other

---

89 ibid paras 10–43.
90 ibid paras 44–63.
91 ibid para 9.
92 ibid paras 133–70.
93 ibid para 203.
94 Customer Relationship Management Software Solutions.
95 Case No COMP/M.8124 *Microsoft/LinkedIn* C[2016] 8404 final, paras 8–151.

words, the parties both offer services only in the online advertising market; Microsoft offers search and non-search (display) ads, and LinkedIn provides non-search ads.[96] Following its previous decisions,[97] the Commission distinguished offline and online advertising markets but left further market segmentation questions open and did not assess search and non-search advertising markets separately.[98]

Although cross-market influence was found in the Microsoft/LinkedIn merger, along the same line as the Yahoo! and Skype mergers, the data issue was not seen by the Commission as a source to create non-horizontal links with close markets in the ecosystem. Instead, arguments on data were focused on data merging. According to the decision, the proposed transaction would not raise concerns about competition due to the data combination in the possession of the parties, especially for online advertising purposes.[99] The Commission underlines that merged entities must comply with the applicable data protection rules of the EU, which is the General Data Protection Regulation (GDPR) of 2016.[100] Therefore, such data combination would significantly limit the merged entity's ability to exercise foreclosure effects, and possible anti-competitive effects would be limited to non-existent.

The Commission then identified a couple of possible horizontal effects in the assumption that the data protection rules allow such data merging. First, combining datasets of two previously independent undertakings can hypothetically increase the merged entity's market power.[101] In this scenario, a merged entity can increase barriers to entry due to the supply of data by forcing competitors to hold and analyse more datasets. However, these barriers can be created intrinsically without a merger; every competitor would collect more data to compete effectively in the online advertising market. Second, before the merger, there might be effective competition between merging entities based on data-collection and ad services, and the transaction would eliminate competition between these undertakings. However, these possible effects are for the assumption that data protection rules allow data merging without limitations.

The proposed merger would not raise any competition concerns regarding data use and online advertising since these entities are tiny players in the online advertising market and its arguable sub-segments, according to the Commission.[102] Although both Microsoft and LinkedIn provide online advertising services as part of their businesses, the parties' post-merger market share of online advertising revenues is estimated to be less than 5%.[103] Thus, there will be a vast amount of data out of Microsoft's control for online advertising after the transaction. Other

---

96 ibid paras 8–152.
97 Case No COMP/M.5727 *Microsoft/Yahoo! Search Business* C[2010] 1077 final, para 61; Case No COMP/M.4731 *Google/DoubleClick* C[2008] 927 final, paras 45–46, 56.
98 Case No COMP/M.8124 *Microsoft/LinkedIn* C[2016] 8404 final, para 159.
99 ibid para 176.
100 General Data Protection Regulation (GDPR), Entry into force 25 May 2018.
101 Case No COMP/M.8124 *Microsoft/LinkedIn* C[2016] 8404 final, para 179.
102 ibid para 180.
103 ibid para 169.

competitors in the online advertising market, especially Google, control most user data collected online. Data issues were left in the hands of the EU data protection rules, and the examination of Big Data's effect on competition was shallow. If this ruling were for Google, it could create significant barriers to entry, as it did after the DoubleClick decision. Therefore, it is inarguable that the conclusion of the Commission regarding the conglomerate effects related to the accumulation of data was erroneous in the Microsoft/LinkedIn merger,[104] just like Google/DoubleClick, and the change in how the Commission interprets the situation regarding the conglomerate effects can be seen in the preliminary assessment of the Google/Fitbit merger in 2020.[105]

Just recently, the European Commission opened an in-depth investigation into the acquisition of Fitbit by Google on 25 June 2020, following the notification of Google. Fitbit is a US-based company that manufactures and develops smartwatches and fitness trackers, which are spectacularly efficient in consumer data collection. Therefore, the Commission is highly concerned that the acquisition will contribute to and strengthen the already-established dominance of Google in the online advertising market by allowing Google to use additional consumer data extracted from Fitbit for personalised advertising and other linked services.[106] It is a welcomed investigation after the failed analysis of the Google/DoubleClick merger. It demonstrates that the European Commission acknowledges strong conglomerate data-related effects in the online world. Margrethe Vestager states that:

> The use of wearable devices by European consumers is expected to grow significantly in the coming years. This will go hand in hand with an exponential growth of data generated through these devices. This data provides key insights about the life and the health situation of the users of these devices. Our investigation aims to ensure that control by Google over data collected through wearable devices as a result of the transaction does not distort competition.[107]

After the first-phase investigation of Google/Fitbit, the Commission concluded that collecting consumer data through wearable mobile devices such as fitness trackers would entrench Google's market power since it increases the data advantage of dominant Google in the online world.[108] By acquiring Fitbit, Google would also acquire the database of Fitbit users' health and fitness and the technology that could allow the development of an extensive database based on Fitbit's data. The

---

104 ibid paras 185–86.
105 Case No COMP/M.9660, Google/Fitbit [2020] Prior Notification of a Concentration OJ 2020/C 210/09.
106 European Commission, Press Release, 'Merger: Commission Opens in-Depth Investigation into the Proposed Acquisition of Fitbit by Google' (Brussels, 4 August 2020) <https://ec.europa.eu/commission/presscorner/detail/en/ip_20_1446>
107 ibid.
108 ibid.

Commission expresses that Google's data analytics capabilities would allow more ad personalisation via their search engine and other internet pages, making it harder for rivals to compete with Google in the online advertising market and raising higher barriers to entry for new entrants.[109] Google's expansion may initially result in the monopolisation of the online advertising market of the online world. The competition world will welcome the decision.

Although the European Commission realised the conglomerate effects in data-driven acquisitions by accumulating and utilising data in 2020, this was not realised in the 2008–2010 era. Thus, for the aforementioned reasons, the relevant market analysis in the Google/DoubleClick merger seems to have been unsuccessful in identifying the competitive structure of the online advertising market and the market power of Google, DoubleClick and Google's rivals such as Microsoft and Yahoo!

4.2.3 Functionality Test

In 2014, Facebook submitted a notification to the Commission for the acquisition of WhatsApp wholly into Facebook Inc. Facebook is a provider of applications and websites, operates in the social network market and offers consumers communications services, including photo- and video- sharing features. The other party, WhatsApp, also offers consumer communications services but not a full social network service. In the first stage of the market power assessment, the social networking market, consumer communications market and online advertising were found to be possible relevant markets regarding the transaction.

This decision is important since it was the first time the Commission had identified a market for social networks beyond data-driven markets.[110] Although the social network market is potentially relevant for the transaction, the decision underlines a functionality difference between social networks and consumer communications. Social networks provide features such as newsfeeds, timelines and user profiles.[111] The idea was that social networking services provide a wider and richer experience than consumer communication services.[112] Therefore, the conclusion was that WhatsApp and Facebook Messenger were not social networking services. During the initial investigation, further sub-segmentation of social network services was also considered since these social network services are offered on different devices (PCs, smartphones) and platforms (iOS, Android, Windows, Mac). No functional differences were found in the services of an undertaking between devices or platforms, and the question was ultimately left open.[113] However, it is important to note that today, WhatsApp and Facebook Messenger offer a "status" sharing service in text, photo and video formats, which was initially offered on Facebook and

---

109 ibid.
110 Graef (n 82) 96.
111 Case No COMP/M.7217 *Facebook/WhatsApp* C [2014] 7239 final, para 48.
112 Graef (n 82) 96.
113 Case No COMP/M.7217 *Facebook/WhatsApp* C [2014] 7239 final, paras 57–59.

Instagram by Facebook. Today, WhatsApp's and Facebook Messenger's status services should be regarded as a novel type of newsfeed. This instance is a good indication of how online services/markets may evolve further in future.

Back to the Facebook/WhatsApp transaction regarding relevant markets: the Commission expressed that only Facebook is active in the online advertising market. Although both offer consumer communication services, WhatsApp and Facebook do not provide advertising space in their consumer communications applications. However, Facebook offers advertising space in non-search (display) ads in its social network service.[114] Facebook collects user data from its social network service and executes data analytics through algorithms to serve "targeted" advertisements on behalf of various advertisers who are actually customers of Facebook ad services.[115] Another point is that Facebook neither provides its data analytics services to customers who provide advertisements nor offers any datasets collected from social network users as separate services selling space for display advertising purposes.[116]

Therefore, merging parties were considered competitors in the consumer communications services market but not in the social network market or in the online advertising market. As mentioned earlier, WhatsApp offers a mobile communication application for a nominal fee,[117] and Facebook's consumer communication service, Facebook Messenger, is offered free of charge. In other words, they both offer consumer communication applications; thus, the market power assessment should be engaged in this relevant market. However, curiously enough, Facebook Messenger and WhatsApp are not considered close competitors. In other words, although they compete with each other on the market, the Commission did not regard them as close competitors, which initially gave way to clear the transaction. The Commission makes two implications problematic for the transaction: misevaluation of market power due to erroneous market definition and misunderstanding of Big Data issues at the stage of market power assessment from a conglomerate point of view.

In Facebook/WhatsApp, the Commission expressed that merging parties' consumer communications services are quite different in certain aspects. Even though the applications have similar consumer audiences and networks, there are many functionality differences between them which significantly decrease competition.[118] One example would be the way to join the service and the source of contacts (Facebook ID and friend list for Messenger, phone number and address book for WhatsApp).[119] Today, there are no differences between applications from this aspect since these functional differences are diminished. Today, Facebook Messenger also uses phone numbers and address books if consent is given, just

---

114 ibid para 69.
115 ibid para 70.
116 ibid para 70.
117 WhatsApp became free of charge after the transaction.
118 Case No COMP/M.7217 *Facebook/WhatsApp* C [2014] 7239 final, para 103.
119 ibid para 102.

92 Assessment of Data-Related Market Power in Data-Driven Markets

like WhatsApp. Another difference identified by the Commission was the user experience and the features offered by the products. Today, there are no functional differences, as both applications offer group chats, voice calls, video calls, emojis and other functions. The Commission also underlined that the privacy policies of these applications were remarkably distinct. Unlike WhatsApp, Facebook's application allows data to be collected from users for the purpose of online advertising.[120] This aspect assumed that, in case of a successful merger, the merged entity would not benefit from any data from WhatsApp since they were not collected prior to the merger.[121]

4.2.4 Potential Data Merging

Another vital point in Facebook/WhatsApp was the misevaluation of data accumulation regarding its relevance to competition law and policy. The Commission acknowledged a potential data concentration after the transaction even though WhatsApp does not collect user data regarding age, gender, habits or other characteristics for online advertising purposes.[122] Moreover, WhatsApp does not categorise and store the data of its users but only associates data sent and received with mobile numbers.[123] Nonetheless, many concerns were raised about data collection and privacy at that time.[124] The reason is the privacy policy of Facebook. Just after its acquisition of Instagram in 2012, Facebook changed its privacy policy.[125] The policy change was especially crucial since users perceived WhatsApp as a valuable source for close, private and accurate sharing and communication due to its strict data protection policy.[126] Therefore, a similar policy change might occur after the merger.[127] In Facebook/WhatsApp, the Commission strictly defined the borders for competition law and policy in terms of data collection and privacy matters that might occur after the merger.[128] According to the ruling, any privacy-related concerns must be referred to the EU data protection rules. The EU competition law rules must not address any privacy concerns related to the increased concentration due to a merger.[129] As a consequence, possible data concentration was discussed from the perspective of Facebook's online advertising services.[130]

---

120 ibid.
121 Maurice E Stucke and Allen Grunes, *Big Data and Competition Policy* (1st edn, OUP 2016) 76.
122 Case No COMP/M.7217 *Facebook/WhatsApp* C [2014] 7239 final, para 166.
123 ibid.
124 Nikolai Van Gorp and Olga Batura, 'Challenges for Competition Policy in a Digitalised Economy' A Study for the ECON Committee, Directorate General for Internal Policies, European Parliament, July 2015, IP/A/ECON/2014-12 PE 542.235, 43.
125 ibid.
126 ibid.
127 Stucke and Grunes (n 121) 76.
128 Van Gorp and Batura (n 124) 43.
129 Case No COMP/M.7217 *Facebook/WhatsApp* C [2014] 7239 final, para 164.
130 ibid paras 165–90.

In terms of online advertising, two possible theories of harm were identified for the proposed transaction: Facebook might introduce advertising services on WhatsApp or use WhatsApp as a source for Big Data accumulation, contributing to its advertising services.[131] The relatively low market shares of Facebook in the online advertising market in the EU (around 20% to 30% at that time) and the slim chance of a change in the privacy policy of WhatsApp meant that the first theory of harm was not a concern in the assessment of the Commission. Even if Facebook introduced advertising on WhatsApp, it would not raise any competition concerns in the EU since there are many competitors where advertisers can purchase online advertising space.[132] In this regard, Google, Microsoft and some other local providers were mentioned as online advertising space providers. The same reasoning applied to the second theory of harm. Even though it was not believed that Facebook would be able to collect data from WhatsApp after the merger due to the existing data protection scheme, the possible data accumulation would not raise any competition concerns due to the existence of competitors.[133] As a result, the merger was cleared and declared to be compatible with the internal market.

In brief, the assessment of the competition in the consumer communications market was inaccurate and led to an erroneous implication that WhatsApp and Facebook were not close competitors. In addition, even though data was assumed to be a source of market power, concerns regarding data collection were decided to be a matter primarily for the EU data protection scheme. However, in the summer of 2016, Facebook announced that it would change "the terms of service and privacy policy" of WhatsApp. According to the policy change, Facebook could now acquire user data on WhatsApp through user matching technology and transfer it to its data analytics to improve advertisement services. This resulted in an action in which the parent company could obtain information like phone numbers, photos and statuses for targeted online advertisements. The Commission considered this an infringement based on intentionally supplying incorrect information during the merger in 2014.[134] By then, Facebook stated that cross-platform data sharing was impossible unless a substantial re-engineering was made to Facebook and WhatsApp.[135] In other words, Facebook argued that data sharing between WhatsApp and Facebook was technologically impossible in 2014. However, it is now possible to transfer and process data, and Facebook's action was found intentional back then. The Commission considered this an infringement of supplying incorrect and misleading information, at least negligently. As a result, the Commission decided to impose penalties under Article 14 of the current Merger Regulation, which was a total of €110 million for the infringements falling within Article 14(1)(a) and 14(1)(b) of the Merger Regulation. One can see that the Authority considers

---

131 ibid para 167.
132 ibid para 176.
133 ibid para 188.
134 ibid para 56.
135 ibid para 61.

matters arising from the data accumulation of the merged entity as a competition concern by their having imposed penalties under the Merger Regulation. If the Commission were to follow the implication that any privacy-related issue should be referred to data protection rules, the privacy change of WhatsApp should not have been dealt with in the Merger Regulation. That being said, Facebook also announced in January 2021 that it would change the privacy policy of WhatsApp on 8 February 2021 but delayed it until 15 May 2021 due to the extensive criticism about privacy and competition around the world.[136]

Nevertheless, another event in the aftermath of the merger clearly shows problems related to merger assessment in the EU.[137] The Commission's post-merger investigation into supplying inaccurate information regarding data collection and data merging was not enough to reflect the concerns in the market. In February 2019, the *Bundeskartellamt* (the German Competition Authority) concluded its investigation of Facebook, alleging that the company abuses its dominant position in the social media market by collecting data from third-party sources such as WhatsApp and Instagram[138] and merging it with relevant Facebook data.[139] In order to address this investigation, a retrospective analysis of the Facebook/WhatsApp investigation is a must since the theory of harm was not accurately addressed in the investigation. This led to the abuse of dominance case before the German Competition Authority. Irreversible competitive damage has likely been done to the social media market already. If the EU merger regulation and market power assessment were effective enough, problems could have been prevented at an earlier stage: during the initial merger investigation.[140]

4.2.5 Overlaps Between Market Segments

The most important case concerning Big Data–related infringements in data-driven markets is the *Google Search (Shopping)* case, followed by the *Google Android* and *Google AdSense* cases.[141] The ground-breaking decision that changed perspectives on Big Data and data-driven markets in terms of competition policy was

---

136 Katie Canales, 'WhatsApp Is Delaying a New Policy Change After Critics Claimed the Update Would Have Turned Over' *Business Insider* (15 January 2021) <https://www.businessinsider.com/whatsapp-privacy-policy-delay-three-months-2021-1?r=US&IR=T#:~:text=WhatsApp%20is%20delaying%20its%20privacy,company%20blog%20post%20published%20Friday.&text=WhatsApp%20also%20said%20no%20one's,scheduled%20to%20go%20into%20effect>
137 Hedvig K Schmidt, 'Taming the Shrew: Is There a Need for a New Market Power Definition for the Digital Economy?' in Björn Lundqvist and Michal S Gal (eds), *Competition Law for the Digital Economy* (1st edn, Edward Elgar Publishing 2019) 39.
138 *Bundeskartellamt*, Press Release, 'Preliminary Assessment in Facebook Proceeding: Facebook's Collection and Use of Data from Third-Party Sources Is Abusive' (19 December 2017) <https://www.bundeskartellamt.de/SharedDocs/Meldung/EN/Pressemitteilungen/2017/19_12_2017_Facebook.html>
139 ibid.
140 Schmidt (n 137) 39.
141 These three separate investigations are also known as *European Union v Google*.

started in 2010. A small, UK-based vertical search company called Infederation Ltd. (Foundem) filed a complaint against Google before the Commission regarding allegations that Google manipulated search results and eventually harmed competition. Additional complaints were made by competitors who were also somewhat active in the online advertising sector.[142] Later during the investigation, cases that were started by others' complaints were merged under a single case: COMP/C-3/39740.[143] The Commission concluded that two relevant markets need to be examined: the general search engine market and the online comparison-shopping market.[144] This indicates that the Commission approached the issue from a traditional approach by looking at the demand/supply-side substitutability of the products.[145]

Discussions on the search engine market were particularly important. Unlike in the *Microsoft/Yahoo!* decision, the Commission found it relevant to assess the differences between vertical and general (horizontal) search engines. That being said, numerous distinctive characteristics were found. The first finding was the nature of horizontal and vertical searches. Horizontal and vertical search engines are quite different from each other, and their substitutability is extremely limited.[146] Vertical search engines do not show results from all over the internet. Instead, their services specialise in specific topics, and results are often monetisable. Therefore, their scope and consumer audience are considerably limited compared to those of a general search engine. For this reason, sources of horizontal and vertical search engines also differ. On one side, horizontal search engines such as Google and Bing use all available data online. Thus, they generate relevant results using data analytics services. On the other side, a vertical search engine's main input is not readily available data through the internet. Instead, it provides results supplied by third parties relevant to the search engine. For instance, hotel search web pages like booking.com do not originate results from any hotel/accommodation data available on the internet. Instead, they provide relevant information about specific businesses participating in the vertical search engine.

According to the Commission, the creation of vertical and horizontal search engines followed different evolutionary routes.[147] Vertical search engines have always been separate from horizontal search engines and have existed as standalone products in the online world. Shopping, hotel, flight and insurance search services are examples of vertical search engines that do not require any specific link to horizontal search engines to function. Therefore, substitutability between

---

142 These include eJustice.fr, Ciao GmbH, VfT, VDZ, BDZV, nntp.it, AEDE, Euro-Cities, Hotmap, Streetmap EU, Elfvoetbal, Twenga, Yelp, Expedia, TripAdvisor, Nextag, Odigeo, Visual Meta GmbH and BEUC, Deutsche Telekom, HolidayCheck, Trivago and many others. Case No COMP/AT.39740, *Google Search (Shopping)* C[2017] 4444 Final, paras 38–106.
143 Case No COMP/AT.39740, *Google Search (Shopping)* C[2017] 4444 Final, para 55.
144 ibid para 154.
145 Schmidt (n 137) 48.
146 Case No COMP/AT.39740, *Google Search (Shopping)* C[2017] 4444 Final, paras 166–67.
147 ibid paras 169–71.

general search engines and specialised ones is nearly non-existent on the demand side. Likewise, the Commission regards Google's shopping service as a standalone product from its search engine service. The decision refers to Google's own categorisation of its products.[148] In this context, Google offers its shopping service under the "specialised search" category, whereas Google Search is categorised as a "web search".

The Commission also refers to the study of *Monopolkommission* (Monopolies Commission of Germany) regarding market definition in the search engine market. The *Monopolkommission* underlines the interdependencies between types of search engines and expresses that vertical search engines do not act as substitutes but rather as complements to horizontal search engines.[149] However, the *Monopolkommission* stresses that the relationship between vertical and horizontal services is increasingly more interrelated than in the past. Horizontal search engines such as Google have started to include more specific and specialised services in their general services for consumers.[150] In other words, today, general search engines also provide specialised searches in the forms of maps, news, videos and others, including restaurant and hotel searches. Incorporating vertical results into horizontal search platforms illustrates that general search engines can be substituted for specialised search engines. Not only general search engines but also specialised vertical services are putting competitive pressure on general search engines.[151] For instance, even platforms like Amazon, Facebook and Twitter today offer comprehensive search results, including products, news, information, and videos. Facebook specifically incorporated a marketplace into its social network platform, and Amazon offers online services wider than just e-commerce-specific products. In the near future, it can be expected that other platforms will grow bigger and wider and come closer to what a horizontal search engine offers today. Therefore, the differences between vertical and horizontal search engines are not enough to consider them separate markets. The Commission should have focused more on the interplay between these services and potential overlaps.

The second important discussion was about the comparison shopping and online advertising markets. In its *Google Search (Shopping)* case, the Commission concluded that Google's comparison shopping services must be considered apart from other specialised search services and online search advertising services since the comparison shopping services constitute a separate market.[152] The decision argues that there is very limited substitutability between comparison shopping and online advertising services from the demand side perspective.[153] In order to expand on the

---

148 ibid paras 169–72.
149 German Monopolies Commission (*Monopolkommission*), 'Competition Policy: The Challenge of Digital Markets' (2015) Special Report No. 68, para 183; Case No COMP/AT.39740, *Google Search (Shopping)* C[2017] 4444 Final, para 174.
150 German Monopolies Commission (n 149) para 244.
151 Graef (n 110) 96.
152 Case No COMP/AT.39740, *Google Search (Shopping)* C[2017] 4444 Final, para 193.
153 ibid paras 196–97.

issue, the Commission stressed the divergence between the services. First, users and online retailers are said to perceive such services as dissimilar.[154] Those who use search engines for specific queries for shopping purposes expect to see services related to their searches. The Google comparison shopping service is a result of a search query navigable by users. The Google comparison shopping service is exclusively accessible through Google search results.[155] On the other side, users do not perceive online advertising services as services for them. The Google ad service is not limited to the search engine, and Google displays only a limited number of online display ads (sponsored links) on the search results page. Moreover, users usually try to avoid these types of advertisements, and online advertising is perceived as "compensation for the use of free online services".[156] Nevertheless, online retailers use online advertising services to promote their products or gain additional revenue by selling ad space on their web pages to other advertisers.

In addition to demand-side differences, comparison shopping and online advertising did not seem to be rivals or substitutes for each other from the supply side in the eyes of the Commission.[157] Not every advertiser can bid to be listed on search results pages in comparison shopping services. Online retailers and merchants can only be listed for comparison online shopping services due to the provisions of comparison shopping services. Also, advertisers in the ecosystem must give their structured data access to Google to be listed as sellers.[158] Accordingly, price changes and related information can be reflected in the advertisement without clicking the link itself, and buyers can easily navigate the comparison shopping service.

On the other hand, any service or product can be shown through advertisement spaces in online advertising services. This is not a shopping service specifically. The advertisement might contain links to the actual online shopping service, or it can be a slogan only, and the advertisement might not be linked to a separate online service. For instance, it can be a McDonald's advertisement without McDonald's or Deliveroo's web page link. Inherently, comparison shopping services contain richer online accessibility, navigation and shopping options than the online advertising model.[159]

In brief, the Commission distinguished the search and comparison shopping services from each other in its decision. The search engine market was further sub-segmented into vertical and horizontal search services. According to this idea, both vertical and horizontal search and comparison shopping and online advertising are identified as complementary services rather than rivals. This indicates how the Authority still presumably defines narrower markets for competition concerns regarding data-driven markets. Additionally, the decision left open the argument about how the online advertising market is affected by the abusive behaviour of

154 ibid para 197.
155 ibid para 205.
156 ibid para 198.
157 ibid paras 199–200.
158 ibid para 201.
159 ibid para 202.

Google.[160] This is particularly important for identifying a relevant market since the value chain is created specifically for advertising purposes. Therefore, the value chain around Big Data and related value-creation mechanisms was avoided. However, a narrow product market definition seems highly inaccurate for data-driven markets. Many unaddressed issues have remained regarding the specific characteristics of data-driven markets in the *Google Search (Shopping)* case.

For instance, Sebastien Broos and Jorge Marcos Ramos argue that online search services and comparison shopping services operate in the same relevant market.[161] The argument was discussed from both consumers' and advertisers' perspectives. Although there might be slight differences in the functioning of these services, users and advertisers sometimes consider online advertising and comparison shopping as substitutes. For instance, users often expect to see almost the same results when they click the links of online advertising and comparison-shopping ads. Thus, both services' intended use is to get clicked by the users.[162] For advertisers, the situation is not dissimilar. Although comparison shopping services are for online retailers, online advertising is open to everyone. Therefore, comparison shopping and online advertising could become substitutes for retailer advertisers.[163] Also, a study from Adobe, using US market data, indicates that comparison shopping services are substitutes for most retailers' online advertisements:[164] different business models can co-exist in a market and compete to attract users and advertisers. In this case, a narrower relevant market definition will miss a huge part of the value creation mechanism.[165] Consequently, it can be assumed that these services are highly interrelated with each other and might well be perceived as rivals from both users' and advertisers' perspectives.

To sum up, the fundamental part of the traditional market power assessment – identification of a relevant product market – was quite limited in recent merger investigations and abuse of dominant position cases regarding data-driven markets. There are more than a couple of reasons. First, the non-horizontal effects of data were shallowly examined. The multi-sided nature of data-driven markets was not efficaciously discussed, and analysis stayed limited to the consumers' and advertisers' side of demand substitutability of certain products or services. Additionally, the conglomerate effects deriving from indirect network effects resulting from data

---

160 Konstantina Bania, 'The European Commission's Decision in Google Search: Exploring Old and New Frontiers of Competition Enforcement in the Digital Economy' in Björn Lundqvist and Michal S Gal (eds), *Competition Law for the Digital Economy* (1st edn, Edward Elgar Publishing 2019) 278.
161 Sébastien Broos and Jorge Marcos Ramos, 'Google, Google Shopping and Amazon: The Importance of Competing Business Models and Two-Sided Intermediaries in Defining Relevant Markets' (2017) 62 The Antitrust Bulletin 2, 11.
162 ibid 12.
163 ibid.
164 Adobe, Global Digital Advertising Report Adobe Digital Index Q4 2014, 12–14 <https://offers.adobe.com/en/na/marketing/landings/_64058_q414_digital_advertising_report.html>
165 Even defining a wider relevant market consisting of online advertising and comparison shopping in this case seems to be questionable for the assessment of market power.

collection and processing were not stressed well, and competition in these markets could not be addressed accurately. In these analyses, efforts to establish a specific product market in fast-growing, innovation-driven markets have resulted in a discussion of sub-segmentation of already amorphous markets. As seen from discussions regarding consumer communications, social networks, search engines and online advertising markets, the Commission classified products and services by functionalities.[166] By this means, several separate relevant markets in which companies offer functionally diverse services were identified, and analysis of these individual markets eventually limited the scope of the competition analysis.

4.3 Ineffective Tools to Assess Market Power in the Data-Driven Economy

A persistent problem regarding data-driven markets lies with the tools to assess market power in competition law. Market power assessment is undertaken through various tests and benchmarks, which are all economic in nature.[167] These include market shares, the number of actual and potential competitors, countervailing buyer power and many others.[168] That being said, the identification of market power in competition law cases must be executed within the legal framework. Therefore, competition law and related case law in the EU have created their own tests based on economic indicators. The most prominent way is the undertaking's position on a specific market, market shares and time scale.[169] In addition, the case law has established many other indicators, such as network effects, product differentiation, possession of intellectual property rights, access to essential inputs and vertical integration throughout the history of recent case law.[170]

The market power assessment and its legal basis clearly show that law constantly evolves to determine market competitive structures and needs. In other words, as Hedvig Schmidt stresses, the development of legal definitions of market power and its analysis where different tools are initially used proves that case law adopts in due course to the market's needs.[171] In this manner, it can be assumed that EU competition law and case law should identify the conditions of data-driven markets and adopt its market power assessment in the wake of the Big Data era. In this manner, at least a couple of challenges await competition authorities to shed

---

166 Graef (n 110) 99.
167 Schmidt (n 137) 55.
168 ibid.
169 ibid.
170 Case COMP/C-3/37.792 *Microsoft* C[2004] 900 final, paras 437–47, Case C-27/76 *United Brands Company and United Brands Continentaal BV v Commission of the European Communities* [1978] ECLI:EU:C:1978:22, paras 91–92, Case C-333/94 P *Tetra Pak International SA v Commission of the European Communities* [1996] ECLI:EU:C:1996:436, Cases C-6 and 7/73 *Istituto Chemioterapico Italiano and Commercial Solvents v Commission* [1974] ECLI:EU:C:1974:18, Case C-27/76 *United Brands Company and United Brands Continentaal BV v Commission of the European Communities* [1978] ECLI:EU:C:1978:22, paras 70–81.
171 Schmidt (n 137) 57.

light on them. The first is about defining relevant markets for competition law analysis: How could economic-oriented tools based on price be effective in identifying dominance in data-driven markets where the price is not a prominent parameter? Second, regarding an undertaking's dominance: When is an undertaking regarded as dominant, and how prominent are the market shares in identifying dominance in data-driven markets?

4.3.1 Substitutability and Zero-Price Problem

Many products and services on at least one side of data-driven markets are free of charge. The services mentioned earlier, such as the Google search engine, Facebook Messenger, WhatsApp, Bing, Amazon, YouTube and many other social networks, search engines, dictionaries, video-music streaming services and online storage services, are mostly free consumer goods: in other words, *freemium* goods. Many of these platforms also offer *premium* goods: consumers pay monthly fees to access supplemental services, which are not necessary to use the basic products or services.[172] In the online world, freemium products and services are the primary methods to catch consumers' attention.[173] However, these companies aim to generate revenue since most of their services are essentially commercial. Crémer et al. argue that a platform owner often cannot charge a price because they are willing to subsidise participation among users, and payments for widely used online services would have detrimental effects on increasing consumer numbers.[174] Therefore, monetisation of free services must be done through alternative means, such as advertising.

Although most services are free of charge, companies exchange consumers' personal information instead of a monetary price or exchange consumers' attention for various targeted online advertising purposes.[175] Therefore, it can be deduced that free services are not free and are exchanged at the cost of consumer information. This transaction is also acknowledged as an economic exchange[176] since platform owners monetise personal information through technological developments in Big Data and algorithms. In the *Google Search (Shopping)* case, the Commission ruled

---

172 Michael S Gal and Daniel L Rubinfeld, 'The Hidden Costs of Free Goods: Implication for Antitrust Enforcement' (2016) 80 Antitrust Law Journal 521, 525.
173 Even users of premium services first try freemium versions of these services.
174 Jacques Crémer, Yves-Alexandre de Montjoye and Heike Schweitzer, *Competition Policy for the Digital Era: Final Report* (Publications Office of the European Union 2019) 44.
175 Jason Furman (n 3) 33, 22; Gal and Rubinfeld (n 172) 527; Chris Jay Hoofnagle and Jan Whittington, 'Free: Accounting for the Costs of the Internet's Most Popular Price' (2014) 61 UCLA Law Review 606, 608–26; John Newman, 'Antitrust in Zero-Price Markets foundations' *(2015)* 164 University of Pennsylvania Law Review 165; John Newman, 'Antitrust in Zero-Price Markets: Applications' (2016) 94 Washington University Law Review 1, 54; Magali Eben, 'Market Definition and Free Online Services: The Prospect of Personal Data as Price' (2018) 14 I/S: A Journal of Law and Policy for the Information Society 2, 227, 230.
176 Magali Eben, 'Market Definition and Free Online Services: The Prospect of Personal Data as Price' (2018) 14 I/S: A Journal of Law and Policy for the Information Society 2, 227, 231.

that "a product or service is provided free of charge does not prevent the offering of such a service from constituting an economic activity for the competition rules"[177] in the EU.

Additionally, John Newman expresses that the information used in data-driven markets where the price is zero and consumers pay for services with their attention or information is a property subject to commercial exchange.[178] Therefore, information becomes a currency for free services and products in data-driven markets.[179] In the *Google Search (Shopping)* case, the Commission expresses that even in the absence of monetary charges for the use of search services, users are charged in personal data by the service through every search query.[180] The Commission establishes that data-search service exchange is a contractual relationship between parties.[181] Therefore, more attention from consumers leads to more personal information exchange, and more data is collected. This way, data becomes an intangible asset in the new economy since it allows services to generate significant revenue through advertising channels.[182] By this means, zero prices for these services and products create network externalities intrinsically, and data becomes an indispensable part of online services.[183]

Free products and services have created novel problems for competition law. Traditional analysis methods for market power assessment are designed for goods with actual price tags.[184] When a product's price becomes zero, the price dimension of competition analysis becomes null, and reliance on these techniques diminishes[185] since two times zero or twenty times zero is zero. Therefore, David Evans stresses that free goods are "red flags" for the traditional competition models and that traditional methods do not apply to that type.[186] Evans adds that competition in a market is assessed on a basic finding in which competitive prices of a good tend to equal the marginal cost of production, and the marginal cost prices are indicators of dominance.[187] Therefore, an undertaking that enjoys monopolistic powers may raise prices and not lose demand. For this reason, dominance and market power are seen as an ability to raise prices out of the competitive zone.[188]

---

177 Case No COMP/AT.39740, *Google Search (Shopping)* C[2017] 4444 Final, para 152.
178 Newman, 'Antitrust in Zero-Price Markets: Applications' (2016) 54.
179 Gal and Rubinfeld (n 172) 522.
180 Case No COMP/AT.39740, *Google Search (Shopping)* C[2017] 4444 Final, para 158.
181 ibid.
182 David S Evans, 'Attention Rivalry Among Online Platforms' (2013) 9 Journal of Competition Law and Economics 2, 313; Howard A Shelanski, 'Information, Innovation, and Competition Policy for the Internet' (2013) 161 University of Pennsylvania Law Review 6, 1678; Gal and Rubinfeld (n 172) 522.
183 Gal and Rubinfeld (n 172) 522.
184 Ania Thiemann and Pedro Gonzaga, "Big Data: Bringing Competition Policy to the Digital Era" OECD 2016, DAF/COMP (2016) 15; Gal and Rubinfeld (n 172) 552.
185 Aleksandra Gebicka and Andreas Heinemann, 'Social Media & Competition Law' (2014) 37 World Competition 2, 149–72, 154.
186 David S Evans, 'The Antitrust Economics of Free' (2011) Competition Policy International 71, 81.
187 ibid 82.
188 Gal and Rubinfeld (n 172) 552.

In EU competition law, the demand and supply substitutability of a product and potential competition are measured to infer the market power of an undertaking. However, demand substitutability is the essence of market definition and the first step for market power assessment.[189] For instance, demand substitutability demonstrates that an undertaking in a competitive market cannot impose excessive terms and conditions or prices since consumers can easily switch to rival services or products.[190] Therefore, the main method to measure demand substitution or interchangeability of a product or service in the EU is an economic analysis called the hypothetical monopolist test (HMT).[191] In order to conduct the HMT test, an economic tool called the small but significant non-transitory increase in price (SSNIP) test is performed.

The HMT and SSNIP tests were initially designed for traditional markets in which monetary prices exist, which are the basic requirement for commercial transactions. As mentioned earlier, a hypothetical monopolist in a market can impose higher prices if their new pricing plan is still profitable for the business. In this sense, the SSNIP test aims to identify the relevant market and the undertaking's market power by assessing the slightest possible price change in the "possible" relevant markets through the lens of potentially substitute products or bundles.[192] The main idea behind the SSNIP test is to find that if there is an increase found to be unprofitable, then there must be other products in the given market, where consumers move towards these substitutes.[193] If so, both these products must be in the same market since they are interchangeable. This is also an implicit benchmark in identifying the smallest relevant market comprising these products.[194] Consequently, as John Newman states, "This analytical framework loses its coherence in zero-price markets, where the basic unit of value extracted from customers is not expressed as a price".[195] Along the same line, the Commission ruled in the *Google Search (Shopping)* case that "the SSNIP test would not have been appropriate in the present case because Google provides its services for free to users".[196]

Many academics argue that the problem regarding the application of the SSNIP test in multi-sided data-driven platforms is its nature.[197] The SSNIP test is designed

---

189 Richard Whish and David Bailey, *Competition Law* (8th edn, OUP 2015) 28; Stephen Weatherill, *Cases & Materials on EU Law* (6th edn, OUP 2003) 552.
190 Weatherill (n 189) 552.
191 Alison Jones and Brenda Sufrin, *EU Competition Law* (5th edn, OUP 2014) 67; Whish and Bailey (n 189) 27; Commission Notice on the Definition of Relevant Market for the purposes of Community competition law OJ [1997] C 372/5.
192 Jones and Sufrin (n 191) 67.
193 Lapo Filistrucchi and others, 'Market Definition in Two-Sided Markets: Theory and Practice' (2014) 10 Journal of Competition Law and Economics 2, 330.
194 ibid.
195 Newman (n 178) 65.
196 Case No COMP/AT.39740, Google Search (Shopping) [2017] 4444 Final, para 245.
197 Sebastian Wismer, Christian Bongard and Arno Rasek, 'Multi-Sided Market Economics in Competition Law Enforcement' (2017) 8 Journal of European Competition Law and Practice 4 Economist's Note 257, 260–61; David S Evans and Michael D Noel, 'Analyzing Market Definition and

for one-sided markets. Thus, the basic SSNIP test does not take into account the indirect network effects to reflect interdependencies between sides of a platform.[198] For this reason, Filistrucchi et al. underline the importance of addressing the price issue when performing the hypothetical monopolist test on different market sides where different prices are present.[199] In other words, the literature suggests that all sides of the platform should be analysed separately for a more accurate market power analysis since leaving out one group or side would lead to erroneous assumptions.[200] Dirk Auer and Nicolas Petit stress the importance of developing or adjusting the SSNIP test for multi-sided platforms to reflect all market sides for proper competition analysis.[201] However, all these studies are focused on multi-sided platforms like payment card systems, in which distinct prices are set for different groups on each side of the market. In the literature, multi-sided platforms like shopping malls, franchising and many others are studied to adjust the SSNIP test. Thus, solutions are addressed in terms of "distinct" prices on different sides of a platform. Therefore, another problem arises.

There are a vast number of unique multi-sided platforms containing different business strategies and different pricing structures today.[202] Some have indirect network effects as predominant characteristics, and some do not. As a result, performing a sole SSNIP test on all these various markets might not be useful.[203] In an economy in which new business models are constantly emerging, performing a one-size-fits-all test would be quite hard.[204] As mentioned earlier, the situation in data-driven multi-sided platforms is quite different from that in two-sided markets with different prices on each side of the market. Non-existence of monetary

---

Power in Multi-Sided Platform Markets' (2005) <https://ssrn.com/abstract=835504>; David S Evans and Michael D Noel, 'The Analysis of Mergers That Involve Multisided Platform Businesses' (2008) 4 Journal of Competition Law and Economics 3, 663–95; Renata B Hesse, 'Two-Sided Platform Markets and the Application of the Traditional Antitrust Analytical Framework' (2007) 3 Competition Policy International 191.

198 Wismer (n 197) 260–61; Renata B Hesse, 'Two-Sided Platform Markets and the Application of the Traditional Antitrust Analytical Framework' (2007) 3 Competition Policy International 191, 192–93; David S Evans, 'Two-Sided Market Definition' (2009) ABA Section of Antitrust Law, Market Definition in Antitrust: Theory and Case Studies 2 <https://papers.ssrn.com/sol3/papers.cfm?abstract_id=1396751>; Filistrucchi and others (n 193) 331–32; Gönenç Gürkaynak and others, 'Multisided Markets and the Challenge of Incorporating Multisided Considerations into Competition Law Analysis' (2017) 5 Journal of Antitrust Enforcement 100–29, 109.
199 Filistrucchi and others (n 193) 330.
200 Evans and Noel (n 197) 663–95; Lapo Filistrucchi, 'A SSNIP Test for Two-Sided Markets: The Case of Media' (2008) 34 NET Institute Working Papers; Renata B Hesse and Joshua H Soven, 'Defining Relevant Product Markets in Electronic Payment Network Antitrust Cases' (2006) 73 Antitrust Law Journal 709, 727–28; Filistrucchi and others (n 193); Gürkaynak and others (n 198) 109.
201 Dirk Auer and Nicolas Petit, 'Two-Sided Markets and the Challenge of Turning Economic Theory into Antitrust Policy' (2015) 60 Antitrust Bulletin 4, 30.
202 Gürkaynak and others (n 198) 110.
203 ibid.
204 ibid.

charges on at least one side of a market is the main reason the SSNIP is incompatible with data-driven markets. In addition to having no monetary charges on one side of a market, data-driven markets mainly exercise unlimited different prices on the advertising side.[205] Platform owners charge different prices in different situations, whether an advertisement for a keyword search, top page display advertisement or any other conditions in which prices are set by artificial intelligence for advertising purposes. In brief, there are billions of different prices for advertisers online, and the SSNIP or a similar test is not applicable on such a scale to identify the competitive structure.[206] In the opposite situation, when the SSNIP test is applied to the advertiser side of specific data-driven markets, it is inevitable that each pricing strategy for each individual search or display could be identified as a separate relevant market.[207] Also, indirect network effects make the SSNIP test incompatible with no monetary charges on one side of a market. The demand on one side is affected by the pricing strategy on the other; thus, a price increase that seems unrelated to the "determined" substitutability of a product affects the demand.[208] Consequently, if personal data object to a commercial transaction by being traded or sold, the SSNIP test can be the correct tool to assess competition.[209] Other than that, when data becomes the subject of a transaction, any price-centric tool becomes ill suited for market power analysis.[210] According to Petit, this was not seen as the inadequacy of price-centric competition tools but as an increased sophistication of price strategies in data-driven markets.[211]

Academics have discussed alternative methods for assessing demand-side substitutability.[212] The main idea is to move away from an analysis based on prices and focus on other aspects like consumer choice, privacy and quality, which are already in the framework of competition law analysis. Accordingly, the European Commission found quality to be a significant competition parameter in the absence of price.[213] In the Microsoft/Yahoo merger decision, the Commission expressed that competition predominantly occurs based on the quality of search results and the user interface of the service.[214] Therefore, priority must be given to parameters other than price. Along the same line, Aleksandra Gebicka and Andreas Heinemann

---

205 Sébastien Broos and Jorge Marcos Ramos, 'Google, Google Shopping and Amazon: The Importance of Competing Business Models and Two-Sided Intermediaries in Defining Relevant Markets' (2017) 62 The Antitrust Bulletin 2, 11.
206 ibid.
207 ibid 12.
208 Höppner (n 37) 349–66, 355–56.
209 Stucke and Grunes (n 121) 126.
210 ibid.
211 Nicolas Petit, 'Technology Giants, the Moligopoly Hypothesis and Holistic Competition: A Primer' (2016) 57 <http://dx.doi.org/10.2139/ssrn.2856502>
212 Gal and Rubinfeld (n 172) 553; Stucke and Grunes (n 121) 116; Gebicka and Heinemann (n 185) 149–72, 156; Thiemann and Gonzaga (n 184) 15.
213 Case No COMP/M.5727 *Microsoft/Yahoo! Search Business* C[2010] 1077 final, para 101; Case No COMP/M.6281 *Microsoft/Skype* C[2011] 7239 final, para 81.
214 Case No COMP/M.5727 *Microsoft/Yahoo! Search Business* C[2010] 1077 final, para 101.

advocate a cautious approach to the SSNIP test instead of withdrawing the test altogether since price is not an accurate benchmark in data-driven markets.[215] As a possible solution, they advise taking into account the quality of a product in order to execute the test.[216] This would be the SSNDQ (small but significant non-transitory decline in quality) test. Quality is a predominant parameter in markets such as the social network or search engine since most services' selling point is their reliability.[217] Consumers move away from the service when there is a slight decrease in reliability, like logging-in problems, crashes, excessive maintenance, hacking or spam. However, the decrease in quality must be small but significant and non-transitory and must not be wide scale.[218] Although the overall quality of a product or service can be quite easy to detect, the SSNDQ test is highly subjective. For instance, additional maintenance every month on a mobile app might not be perceived as a motive for consumers to leave the platform, or it might be for some.

Also, in a policy roundtable of OECD for competition, the Portuguese delegate proposed exercising the SSNDQ test in market definition and merger assessments.[219] However, the EU delegate found replacing the SSNIP test with the proposed SSNDQ test troublesome. A decrease in quality was found to be immeasurable since consumers reflect quality quite subjectively.[220] Additionally, it is argued that the traditional SSNIP test already incorporates an assessment of quality since consumers consider prices by evaluating the quality of the product or service before switching to substitute products.[221] In addition to these ideas, it can be deduced that tests like the SSNIP are fundamentally quantitative tests executed by measurable parameters. However, the SSNDQ test tries to achieve a qualitative analysis, which does not seem to be the initial objective of small but significant non-transitory change tests. Therefore, it can be concluded that it is quite hard to adopt any form of the HMT test or the SSNDQ test for competition law purposes in data-driven markets.

4.3.2 Digital Ecosystems and Market Shares Problem

The other issue about market power assessment for data-driven markets is the arguable prominence of market shares. In the traditional assessment method, the principles for assessing dominance include assessing the static market power of a given undertaking in a relevant market. Market shares are regarded as direct evidence of market power in competition law. For instance, a market share of 50%

---

215 Gebicka and Heinemann (n 185) 157.
216 ibid.
217 ibid 158.
218 ibid.
219 OECD, *Policy Roundtable: The Role and Measurement of Quality in Competition Analysis* (OECD Quality Report October 2013) 163 <http://www.oecd.org/competition/Quality-in-competition-analysis-2013.pdf>
220 ibid 164.
221 ibid.

is clear evidence of a dominant position, according to the CJEU.[222] Moreover, the European Commission stresses that an undertaking would likely be dominant if its market share is over 40%.[223] This approach is an economic one and is accepted as a shortcut to determining market power.[224] However, the sheer numbers do not accurately reflect the market power by itself. In order to analyse market shares, the real and potential competitors, characteristics and market structure should also be considered.[225] As a matter of fact, many commentators have lately criticised the economic analysis of market shares in the case of data-driven markets.[226]

Criticisms are based on the dynamic characteristic of data-driven markets. In an earlier study, Evans and Schmalensee argue that the static market power measured by shares might not be relevant for new economy industries for a couple of reasons. First, they argue the fragility of dominance in high-industry markets.[227] Market leadership in new economy markets is not an indicator of long-term dominance. Along the same line, Mandrescu underlines the dynamic character of data-driven markets and expresses that market shares change drastically over short periods.[228] Google's and Facebook's quick rise and established dominance in their respective markets, even though they were not first movers in the search engine or the social media market, prove the point. Therefore, a measurement of market shares might not deliver accurate conclusions for these online markets. Accordingly, the Commission stressed that market shares would provide a limited indication of market power in Microsoft/Skype.[229] This is due to the dynamic structure, fast changes in market shares and the free-of-charge price policy of the consumer communications market. Consequently, the market share assessment was found to be lacking as a proxy to evaluate market power and could only give a preliminary indication of the market's competitive structure.[230] The judgment was also enunciated before the

---

222 Case C-62/86 *AKZO Chemie BV/Commission* [1991] ECLI:EU:C:1991:286, para 60.
223 Communication from the European Commission, Guidance on the Commission's enforcement priorities in applying Article 82 of the EC Treaty to abusive exclusionary conduct by dominant undertakings (Text with EEA relevance) [2009] OJ C45/9, paras 13–14.
224 Schmidt (n 137) 63.
225 Richard Whish and David Bailey, *Competition Law* (8th edn, OUP 2015) 192.
226 Daniel Mandrescu, 'Applying EU Competition Law to Online Platforms: The Road Ahead – Part 2' (2017) 38 European Competition Law Review 9, 410–22, 413; Schmidt (n 137) 63–65; David S Evans and Richard Schmalensee, 'Some Economic Aspects of Antitrust Analysis in Dynamically Competitive Industries' in Adam B Jaffe, Josh Lerner and Scott Stern (eds), *Innovation Policy and the Economy*, vol 2 (1st edn, MIT Press 2002) 18; German Monopolies Commission (*Monopolkommission*), 'Competition Policy: The Challenge of Digital Markets' (2015) Special Report No 68, p 24 <https://www.monopolkommission.de/images/PDF/SG/s68_fulltext_eng.pdf>; David S Evans and Richard Schmalensee, 'The Antitrust Analysis of Multi-Sided Platform Businesses' in Roger Blair and Daniel Sokol (eds), *Oxford Handbook on International Antitrust Economics* (OUP 2013) 20–21; Jonathan Faull and Ali Nikpay, *The EU Law of Competition* (OUP 2014) 367–68.
227 Evans and Schmalensee (n 226) 19.
228 Mandrescu (n 226) 410–22, 413–14.
229 Case No COMP/M.6281 *Microsoft/Skype* C[2011] 7239 final, para 78.
230 ibid para 99.

General Court in the *Cisco v Commission* and *Microsoft* cases.[231] Like the Commission's decision, the CJEU also ruled that the consumer communications market is a fast-growing sector, and these markets are characterised by short innovation cycles.[232] Therefore, even large market shares cannot be relevant indicators for the market power assessment since it is not helpful to assess competition damages.

Second, Evans and Schmalensee relate the problem with market shares to the multi-sided structure of data-driven markets. As is apparent, cross-market connection and multi-sidedness make it challenging to measure the actual market shares of dominant undertakings.[233] Most undertakings are active in various linked markets, as mentioned in the "moligopoly" discussion.[234] Therefore, while the definition of relevant markets becomes obsolete due to diminishing boundaries between online markets, the determination of market shares cannot be indicative. Since undertakings are active on various platforms through different services, market shares often differ, creating complications while assessing competition individually and cumulatively.[235] In a later study, Evans and Schmalensee point out that market share measurements are often used to assess dominance for traditional single-sided undertakings.[236] The result is that it is not clear how to measure market shares of multi-sided platforms.[237]

Online advertisement–fuelled markets are the primary examples. Consider the search engine market. One of Google's main services is its general online search. Measuring shares of rivals by comparing total enquiries would reveal a conclusion in the absence of price in that market. Although the calculation cannot be done over a value-based market share, the total amount of enquiry would still give a relatively accurate conclusion. As a result, Google's market share is usually calculated as over 90% globally. However, the advertisement side of the market is an entirely different scenario, and even Google might have different market shares on different sides of the multi-sided platform. Therefore, measurements executed on specific market sides would not pinpoint a correct analysis of the market power of undertakings. Further, the Commission underlines that the dynamic link between online markets creates an inaccurate picture of the market reality in new economy industries since the significance of market shares differs in each market segment.[238] In a situation like this, the market power assessment should move the focus from market shares to the undertakings' overall strength as a whole in online ecosystems. This can be done by analysing specific characteristics of data-driven markets like the multi-sidedness, indirect network

---

231 Case T-79/12 *Cisco Systems, Inc. and Messagenet SpA v European Commission* [2013] ECLI:EU:T:2013:635, para 69.
232 ibid para 99.
233 Evans and Schmalensee (n 226) 20–21.
234 See Chapter 3.3.2.
235 Evans and Schmalensee (n 226) 20–21; Mandrescu (n 226) 413.
236 Evans and Schmalensee (n 226) 20.
237 ibid.
238 Case COMP/C-3/37.792 *Microsoft* 24 C[2004] 900 final, paras 437–47.

externalities, market barriers and Big Data capabilities. This suggests a huge paradigm shift in competition analysis when compared to traditional markets in terms of market power assessment.

In brief, market shares are deemed inaccurate indicators for market power analysis. Low or even high market shares cannot establish dominance in new economy markets. Especially in data-driven markets, where price is non-existent on at least one side of the platform, the competitive structure should not be assessed by market shares. In this sense, an overreliance on market shares could result in inaccurate conclusions. That being said, Mark Patterson argues that it would be a mistake if Google's market power were measured by its high market shares in the search engine market.[239] Similarly, Christian Kersting and Sebastian Dworschak state that Google's significant market share should not be an indicator for the market power analysis.[240] They also conclude that Google is not dominant in the search engine market in the EEA. This implication is erroneous.[241] Justification of this idea stems from the analysis of the Commission and the CJEU mentioned earlier. Although an undertaking's high market share measured by an online user base is not determinative in assessing dominance *per se*, a claim suggesting that Google is not dominant in the search engine market since a "search engine" market does not exist due to free-of-charge services seems to be incorrect also. That is to say, even following the decisions of competition authorities in the EU, which deem high market shares as impractical measures to assess dominance, this does not mean that undertakings which do have high market shares are not dominant. Methods like the "reverted" market share–based analysis, which claims undertakings cannot be dominant in free-of-charge markets even if they control the whole sector, should not be executed for data-driven markets. In conclusion, the irrelevance of the price-centric economic competition tools and market shares in complex data-driven markets reveals an urgent need to develop new tools to assess market power for data-driven markets. In this sense, could an assessment based on Big Data possession and the overall capability of undertakings across online platforms be used to measure market power?[242]

---

239 Mark R Patterson, 'Google and Search-Engine Market Power' (2013) Harvard Journal of Law and Technology 6–7.
240 Christian Kersting and Sebastian Dworschak, 'Does Google Hold a Dominant Market Position? Addressing the (Minor) Significance of High Online User Shares' (2014) 16 Ifo Schnelldienst 7.
241 ibid; James D Ratliff and Daniel L Rubinfeld, 'Is There a Market for Organic Search Engine Results and Can Their Manipulation Give Rise to Antitrust Liability?' (2014) 10 Journal of Competition Law and Economics 1–25, 2–3; Florence Thépot, 'Market Power in Online Search and Social Networking: A Matter of Two-sided Markets' (2013) 36 World Competition 2, 217–18; Florian Wagner-von Papp, 'Should Google's Secret Sauce Be Organic?' (2015) 16 Melbourne Journal of International Law 2, 609, 646–47; Marina Lao, 'Search, Essential Facilities, and the Antitrust Duty to Deal' (2013) 11 Northwestern Journal of Technology and Intellectual Property 275, 292; Andrea Renda, 'Searching for Harm or Harming Search? A Look at the European Commission's Antitrust Investigation Against Google' (2015) CEPS Special Report No. 118, 32.
242 See Chapter 6.

4.4 New Tests for Market Power Assessment in the Data-Driven Economy

The dynamics of the new economy require a change in the traditional concept of relevant markets for competition law analysis in both mergers and abuse of dominant position cases.[243] The traditional concept of defining a narrow product market seems less significant and irrelevant for the competition law analysis in data-driven markets.[244] Therefore, a broader understanding of market power analysis should be engaged. Competition Policy for the Digital Era, a European Commission report by Crémer et al., stresses that:

> In the digital world, market boundaries might not be as clear as in the "old economy". They may change very quickly. . . . In the case of multisided platforms, the interdependence of the "sides" becomes a crucial part of the analysis, whereas the traditional role of market definition has been to isolate problems. Therefore, we argue that, in digital markets, we should put less emphasis on analysis of market definition, and more emphasis on theories of harm and identification of anti-competitive strategies. . . . Where the firms' lock-in strategies are successful, and consumers find it difficult to leave a digital ecosystem, ecosystem-specific aftermarkets may need to be defined.[245]

Also, the current competition law tools to assess market power do not contain adequate mechanisms to identify Big Data–related market power. For instance, in the Commission Notice on the definition of relevant market,[246] multi-sided market structures or the ecosystem nature are not mentioned despite their prevalence and importance in the new economy.[247] Moreover, other aspects of data-driven markets, such as the importance of data accumulation, lock-in effects stemming from data utilisation and networks effects, the interrelationship between the two (or more) sides of a market and the implications of ecosystem business strategies, are not reflected in the assessment of market power and the definition of relevant markets in EU competition law. Accordingly, the dynamic nature of the new economy, innovative character, Big Data's role, the online ecosystem's structure and multi-sidedness should be at the centre of competition law analysis in this regard.

---

[243] Vanessa Turner and Agustin Reyna, 'Market Definition in EU Competition Law Enforcement: Need for An Update' BEUC's Response to the Public Consultation (2020) 3–4.
[244] ibid.
[245] Crémer, de Montjoye and Schweitzer (n 174) 4.
[246] European Commission Notice on the definition of relevant market for the purposes of Community competition law (Text with EEA relevance) [1997] OJ C 372/5.
[247] Turner and Reyna (n 243) 4.

4.4.1 Dynamic Nature of the New Economy

As mentioned in the previous chapter, data-driven markets have unique characteristics regarding the functioning of markets. Strong indirect network and feedback effects, Big Data accumulation and tipping markets are all identified as the main characteristics of data-driven markets. Consequently, the assessment of market power must differ to some extent from traditional markets. However, dynamic competition, fast-changing nature and indirect network externalities are not new to competition law, and discussion on the compatibility of defining a relevant product market for data-driven markets was started two decades ago.

For a study of the European Commission in the early 2000s, Alex Jacquemin underlined the emergence of new economy markets and their highly innovative character.[248] In the EU, the microeconomic theory tools and models of imperfect competition have been increasingly used for the assessment of market power. Jacquemin argues that the market power assessment method replaced the more static approaches of the past for the dynamic competition model.[249] However, in European competition law, market power assessment has not changed significantly, methodically speaking.[250] According to Van Gorp and Batura, the main problem of the relevant market analysis is the assumption that market definition is an obligatory step for the market power assessment procedure.[251] In data-driven markets, competition occurs on the grounds of progress, innovation and the creation of new market segments. Therefore, in markets where boundaries are continuously redefined and new segments are created, identification of a specific product market for market power assessment would not serve the purpose well.[252]

In data-driven markets, various issues can be encountered when analysis takes place to define a relevant product and geographical market in an abuse of a dominant position case.[253] First, due to its multi-sided nature, there might be more than one relevant product market in specific cases regarding data-driven markets. When there is more than one relevant market, market power might not be measured accurately. In many cases related to abuse of a dominant position or R&D acquisitions in data-driven markets, the Commission had to identify more than one relevant market for the market power assessment.[254] This inevitably caused misevaluations on the market power of intermediaries in multi-sided platforms: online ecosystems.

---

248 Alexis Jacquemin, 'Theories of Industrial Organisation and Competition Policy: What Are the Links?' (2000) European Commission Forward Studies Unit Working Paper 11.
249 ibid.
250 Nikolai Van Gorp and Olga Batura, 'Challenges for Competition Policy in a Digitalised Economy' A Study for the ECON Committee, Directorate General for Internal Policies, European Parliament, July 2015, IP/A/ECON/2014-12 PE 542.235, 50.
251 ibid.
252 ibid.
253 ibid 52.
254 See Chapter 5.

Second, due to the reliance on user data, many data-driven markets do not show characteristics of a traditional market, such as price competition. Many online services offered on multi-sided platforms are zero priced. As Ioannis Kokkoris underlines,

> In markets that are driven by innovation, neither price nor quantity plays any decisive role since the services are not monetized on the consumer side. . . . The only parameters that can be used as yardsticks to determine the effects on fair competition in such markets are quality, innovation and choice.[255]

Thus, price-based indicators are not relevant for data-driven markets. The price-based assessment of market power causes significant misevaluations. Also, it is highly unlikely to draw a boundary in terms of substitute products or geographical scope in data-driven markets. Boundaries of data-driven markets are mostly immeasurable due to the creation of ecosystems in the online world. All these problems are enunciated in the following subsections.

4.4.2 Innovative Character of the New Economy

In the early 2000s, Evans and Schmalensee highlighted the problems of defining relevant markets in the new economy. According to the study, a classic market definition analysis in which the price and output decisions, including the supply-and-demand analysis, create a misleading picture regarding the actual competition in new economy markets.[256] The main reason behind this is the dynamic competition occurring in the new economy.[257] Especially in data-driven markets, price and output competition do not seem to be prevalent; instead, undertakings compete by investing in R&D to create new products to address novel needs and demands of society. As mentioned in the previous chapter, new market segments are created as a result of an R&D race. In this sense, data-driven markets in which dynamic competition takes place differ significantly from static markets. Consequently, it cannot be assumed that a relevant market definition or a static market share examination is an essential part of market power assessment today.

Similarly, Ioannis Lianos underlines the importance of the new economy and complex processes, including new value-creation mechanisms. He expresses that questions on the role, function and scope of competition law in the digital age have not been expanded to cover new value-creation mechanisms and the complex economic links in the economy.[258] In the new economy, a dynamic system is created in which interacting players connect through feedback loops. In this system,

---

255 Ioannis Kokkoris, 'The Google Saga: Episode I' (2018) 14(2–3) European Competition Journal 464.
256 Evans and Schmalensee (n 226) 16.
257 ibid.
258 Ioannis Lianos, 'Competition Law for the Digital Era: A Complex Systems' Perspective' (2019) CLES Research Paper Series 6/2019, 8.

players interact in non-linear ways where small changes in parameters can create huge differences in behaviour. According to Lianos, references should be made to concepts such as tipping points, leverage points and increased returns.[259] He argues that the neoliberal price theories of 20th-century competition law are insufficient to capture market power and anti-competitive conduct. The complex structure of multi-sided data-driven markets and the players' complexity in the markets and their interactions should be engaged in the framework.[260] According to this idea, simple theories based on the supply-and-demand curves indicating market equilibrium, rational choice models or even business conduct are not adequate to identify the complex nature of the new economy.

In the new economy, the role of Big Data also should not be disregarded. Big Data takes the role of price analysis and market equilibrium of neoclassical economics. Big Data is the raw material for value creation in data-driven markets. Therefore, emphasis should be given to undertakings' Big Data utilisation capability. In addition, in data-driven markets, players in a market may change their roles due to the market's multi-sided nature.[261] That is to say, players can be both consumers and producers at the same time. This, in turn, would make classic supply-and-demand analysis quite troublesome. Also, a seller might be the marketplace owner and might govern rules for rival sellers in the same ecosystem. Thus, new methods need to be established for the market power assessment.

Evans and Schmalensee propose an assessment based on innovation and innovative threats since the race for market dominance occurs on innovation grounds.[262] According to their idea, assessment should include an examination of the potential innovative threats based on new technologies and the likelihood of how they radically change the product market.[263] However, there is no empirical evidence that the new technology's innovative possibilities and occurrence can be assessed under the market power assessment. More recently, Van Gorp and Batura reaffirmed the problems in the traditional approach of the current market power assessment. Defining a relevant market in data-driven markets as a starting point for power assessment should be abandoned in favour of a more dynamic concept.[264] An example of a more dynamic market analysis would be the examination of behaviours of undertakings. Like the proposal of Evans and Schmalensee, they also argue that competition authorities should focus more on business behaviours (in other words, business model substitutability) and potential competitors who may exist in the market.[265] Business behaviour analysis inevitably includes an examination of innovative threats in the form of various business models that may steal the proportion of the market and profits.[266]

---

259 ibid.
260 ibid.
261 ibid.
262 Evans and Schmalensee (n 226) 16.
263 ibid.
264 Van Gorp and Batura (n 250) 51.
265 ibid.
266 ibid.

Data-driven markets are innovative, and they have a dynamic character. However, the measurability of innovativeness is questionable for the market power assessment. There is no real-life evidence of how to assess possible innovative threats. In the previous chapter, the link between competition and innovation is analysed. Although a close relationship between innovation and competition has been found, this relationship cannot be deemed linear. As a result, the inconsistent findings on some market segments' innovative character would lead to erroneous assumptions on market power assessment. More important than that, it is highly unlikely for competition authorities and courts to examine future segmentation of potential new markets through the current innovation cycle. An examination would only reveal subjective prejudgments of decision makers about specific technologies or data-driven markets in general.

In addition to that, it is unclear how the behavioural examination of business strategies can reveal the competition possibilities in a market. Although business conduct would give preliminary ideas of a specific market's character, in general, to identify competition, such as Facebook's intentions regarding the privacy policy of WhatsApp and the assessment of market power, business behaviours might differ significantly. To exemplify, the analysis shows that many businesses in data-driven markets are in near-monopoly positions. In other words, they are super-dominant undertakings. However, these dominant undertakings are in blistering competition at the same time in regard to specific market segments related to online advertising. Therefore, tools to analyse which market segment in which undertaking has the market power to become dominant seem uncertain. In other words, determining market power through business behaviour in new economy markets seems as complex as determining market power through narrow, inaccurate product market definitions combined with the market share analysis.

Accordingly, Inge Graef also argues how the European Commission misunderstood the dynamics of data-driven markets.[267] As for the market power analysis in the merger decisions of Microsoft, Google and Facebook and the abuse of dominant position case of Google, relevant market analysis was the first step.[268] The Commission considered narrower relevant markets for data-driven markets in all of them. For instance, in Google/DoubleClick, the Commission discussed sub-segmentation of the online advertising market: display advertising market, search advertising market and ad intermediation market. Likewise, narrower relevant markets were also discussed for online communications and social network markets. According to Graef, this is an indication of how the Commission defines relevant markets based on functionality.[269] As mentioned earlier, even the rival services in the same market as WhatsApp and Facebook Messenger were not regarded as competitors due to assessment based on functionality. The interpretation of the Commission shows that the Authority reacts to the situation in data-driven markets

267 Graef (n 82) 110.
268 See Chapter 5.
269 Graef (n 82) 110.

to protect innovation by not extending the initial investigation in these high-technology markets.[270] However, narrower relevant market definitions based on functionality miss out on the disruptive character of new economy markets.

Christian Ahlborn criticises the approach of the Commission, which predominantly focuses on demand-side substitutability.[271] The short-term analysis of demand-side substitutability on specific products tends to miss the nature of innovation, resulting in superior, newer and unprecedented products.[272] As a result, the analysis also misses the future products that will create their own market segments and misses possible competitive pressures by potential competitors in broader markets. When a relevant market is defined as a narrow product market in data-driven markets, potential constraints, non-horizontal effects and new market segmentations cannot be examined in the market power assessment.[273] In other words, excessively narrow market definitions result in erroneous assumptions of market power and lead to incorrect findings, both false negatives and false positives, of dominance in data-driven markets.[274] In brief, innovation can be deemed the main parameter for data-driven markets even in arguably necessary relevant market analysis rather than neoclassical analysis of the short-term demand and supply-side substitutability regarding specific products. The business model substitutability also seems to be unclear since presumptions on innovation might give false results regarding the structure of markets and competition there.

4.4.3 Big Data as a Misleading Factor

Regarding the market power assessment, the role of Big Data is incontrovertible. However, there are many opposing views on Big Data regarding competition.[275] For the longest time, the Big Data issue was misunderstood: whether the technology is an input variable, a barrier to entry, confidential information that consumers cannot fully control or even a market itself. Unlike today, the perception of data was quite different in the previous decade regarding competition law and policy. In the general view, the Big Data issue was associated exclusively with consumer privacy itself. In other words, data collection, data processing and data analytics were

---

270 ibid.
271 Christian Ahlborn, David Evans and Atilano Jorge Padilla, 'Competition Policy in the New Economy: Is European Competition Law Up to the Challenge?' (2001) 22 European Competition Law Review 5, 161.
272 ibid.
273 Graef (n 82) 110.
274 Ahlborn, Evans and Jorge Padilla (n 271) 162.
275 Greg Sivinski, Alex Okuliar and Lars Kjolbye, 'Is Big Data a Big Deal? A Competition Law Approach to Big Data' (2017) 13 European Competition Journal 2–3; Robert P Mankhe, 'Big Data as a Barrier to Entry' (2015) 2 Competition Policy International Antitrust Chronicle; Nathan Newman, 'The Costs of Lost Privacy: Consumer Harm and Rising Economic Inequality in the Age of Google' (2014) 40 William Mitchell Law Review 849, 54; Maurice E Stucke and Allen P Grunes, 'No Mistake About It: The Important Role of Antitrust in the Era of Big Data' (2015) The Antitrust Source April, University of Tennessee Legal Studies Research Paper No. 269.

all privacy law and consumer protection matters.[276] Consumers of online services willingly or unwillingly provide information about themselves to platform owners; thus, any exploitation, including collecting data without the user's knowledge, must be addressed in privacy or consumer protection law rules. In other words, the trade or sale of consumer data without consumer consent is a matter of data privacy.[277] Therefore, competition authorities deliberately avoided all issues stemming from Big Data in their analyses. However, that idea has been overcome today.

The use of personal data for competition in a market or access to data that creates a market position itself moves away from the statement that the Big Data issue is peculiar to data privacy and consumer protection.[278] When access to and use of consumer data raise competition issues, it should become a competition law concern. Collection and utilisation of consumer data have recently become key components for companies to compete in data-driven markets in the age of the Internet of Things and Internet of Services.[279] In data-driven markets, personal data evolves into a tool, and companies harvest these datasets in order to provide customised and targeted services. It is important to note that services and products are often offered at zero price but require personal data to function. In other words, users must provide their data in order to use these services.

Moreover, consumers' free will and self-determination are likely to depend on the services they desire to use.[280] According to the data protection rules, users must be aware of what kind of information will be used by the service. However, the take-it-or-leave-it nature of these services – when someone does not want their data to be processed for advertising purposes and cannot access the website, for instance – left no other choice for consumers.[281] At this point, consumers exchange their personal data in order to use these services. Exposure of information about consumers to service/product owners should be regarded as a "hidden cost" for consumers. However, consumers do not tend to accurately assess the value of data and service exchange, and they do have quite a limited understanding of what companies could achieve with their data.[282] One can still argue that this is irrelevant to competition law. However, competition law today could well be applied in accordance with the data privacy norms as a part of the protection of consumers and consumer welfare.[283] Therefore, even matters pertaining to privacy can become competition issues. In terms of how undertakings establish dominance by accumulating Big

---

276 Maureen K Ohlhausen and Alexander P Okuliar, 'Competition, Consumer Protection and the Right (Approach) to Privacy' (2015) 80(1) Antitrust Law Journal 121, 156; David A Balto and Matthew Lane, 'Monopolizing Water in a Tsunami: Finding Sensible Antitrust Rules for Big Data' (2016) 9 <https://ssrn.com/abstract=2753249>
277 Schmidt (n 137) 35.
278 ibid 40.
279 Lianos (n 258) 9.
280 ibid.
281 ibid.
282 Schmidt (n 137) 37.
283 ibid 38.

Data in data-driven markets and its relation to privacy, Senator Al Franken, US Senator from Minnesota, underlines that:

> "The more dominant these companies become over the sectors in which they operate, the less incentive they have to respect your privacy. But the problem does not stop there. Because accumulating data about you is not just a strange hobby for these corporations. It is their whole business model. And you are not their client. You are their product".[284]

Frankly, increasing data collection improves a company's ability to compete in a data-driven market. Moreover, the future of the Internet of Things will contribute to the data advantage of companies that utilise data analytics and data collection through advanced algorithms and artificial intelligence systems.[285] Increasing data collection along with internet-based products or services that were not previously online will let companies collect massive amounts of data due to the Internet of Things.[286] A limited number of companies hold on to that data; thus, network effects and high switching costs are created due to the massive data collection and data analytics capabilities of these companies. Inevitably, the competitive advantage created by Big Data raises many competition concerns.

Today, it should be acknowledged that the aforementioned competition concerns can arise on issues related to confidential data, anonymous data or any accumulated data. In light of the information given here, it can be assumed that Big Data should play a crucial role in the market power assessment and become a matter of competition law.[287] As mentioned in the previous chapters, the joint report of German and French Competition Authorities stresses that Big Data should be regarded as an important source of market power in data-driven markets, which raises barriers to entry and results in several types of data-related anti-competitive conduct.[288] Although commentators argue that Big Data would not be a barrier to entry itself and instead would be quite beneficial for the data-driven economy,[289] when competitors rely on a similar input to their rivals to be in a market, Big Data then becomes a barrier to entry. Therefore, the evaluation of market shares would be misleading when Big Data is overlooked in the market power assessment.

Another matter regarding the Big Data-related market power assessment is the existence of a market for data itself. The existence of data markets has been a

---

284 Senator Alan Stuart Franken, 'How Privacy Has Become an Antitrust Issue' (29 March 2012) Speech at the American Bar Association Section of Antitrust Law Spring Meeting Dinner <https://www.huffpost.com/entry/how-privacy-has-become-an_b_1392580>
285 Lianos (n 258) 95.
286 ibid.
287 Schmidt (n 137) 35.
288 Autorité de la Concurrence (n 54) 11.
289 Renato Nazzini, 'Online Platforms and Antitrust: Where Do We Go from Here?' (2018) 5 Italian Antitrust Review 17.

widely discussed subject in recent years.[290] However, data is acknowledged as an input in data-driven markets and is not sold or traded in these markets. If data is input for other services or products, it cannot constitute a separate relevant market for competition law analysis.[291] Also, as input, data is not a product or service directly available to users on both sides of the platform, to advertisers or to consumers.[292] According to the current competition law, the only possible option to define a relevant market for data would be when online platforms sell personal data directly to advertisers or other users of the online service. Even so, there will be other issues pertaining to the characteristics of data. Behavioural user data, including traded data (like music charts), cannot be treated similarly, and a line must be drawn between them. For example, music data was not regarded as personal data[293] and could be licenced. However, behavioural user data cannot be licenced, traded or sold. Ioannis Lianos sheds light on the Apple/Shazam[294] merger decision and argues the difficulties in defining a relevant market for data available to be sold or traded to other parties, along with its structure as collected user data.[295]

However, trade commissioner Pamela Jones Harbour underlined a crucial point in her dissenting statement for the FTC's *Google/DoubleClick* decision, in which collected behavioural data was identified as a "special asset". The first recognition and proposed definition for data markets was given by Pamela Jones Harbour there. She expressed that Google's actual aim is to obtain DoubleClick's data before other rivals reach it.[296] In other words, Google's objective was to purchase the datasets, and not the other assets, of DoubleClick in the first place. If this was the case, then a proper analysis of the role of data must have taken place. In order to address the concern, Harbour expressed that "to define a putative relevant product market comprising data . . . may be useful to advertisers and publishers who wish to engage in behavioural targeting".[297] Following this idea, Harbour and Koslov published a study on data and the definition of data markets. They gave suggestions for defining relevant markets in data-driven markets. First, they separate data from data-driven markets like social networks, online advertising and search engines,

---

290 Graef (n 290) 489; Darren S Tucker and Hill B Wellford, 'Big Mistakes Regarding Big Data' (2014) 14 Antitrust Source 1, 4–5; Aleksandra Gebicka and Andreas Heinemann, 'Social Media & Competition Law' (2014) 37 World Competition 2, 149–72, 156; Pamela Jones Harbour and Tara Isa Koslov, 'Section 2 in a Web 2.0: An Expanded Vision of Relevant Product Markers' (2010) 76 Antirust Law Journal 769–97; D Daniel Sokol and Roisin Comerford, 'Antitrust and Regulating Big Data' (2016) 23 George Mason Law Review 5 1129, 1155–56.
291 Tucker and Wellford (n 290) 4; Lianos (n 258) 77.
292 Tucker and Wellford (n 290) 4.
293 Case No COMP/M 8788 *Apple/Shazam* C[2018] 5748 final.
294 ibid.
295 Lianos (n 258) 77.
296 Federal Trade Commission, Dissenting Statement of Commissioner Pamela Jones Harbour, In the matter of Google/DoubleClick F.T.C. File No. 071-0170 (2007) 9 <https://www.ftc.gov/sites/default/files/documents/public_statements/statement-matter-google/doubleclick/071220harbour_0.pdf>
297 ibid.

which are fuelled by the data itself.[298] Then, they argue that a relevant data market should be defined while recognising the increasing significance and value of data accumulation.[299] This would also enable us to distinguish the collected and processed data from each other.

Regarding the Google/DoubleClick merger, Harbour and Koslov argue that the market power assessment should have followed a more dynamic approach instead of defining narrow product markets, which was also observed in the European Commission's decision.[300] Therefore, in a market where Google holds significant power by collecting data through the Google search engine to fuel its online advertising services, the possibility of further data accumulation must be considered.[301] Therefore, a market for "data used for behavioural advertising" could be defined in this situation. In the relevant market for data used for behavioural advertising, Google's position could be concerning where Google continues to amass collected data to strengthen network effects and raise further barriers to entry.[302] Harbour and Koslov's proposal for defining a relevant data market for the Google/DoubleClick merger approaches data as a special asset for the market power assessment, equally important for merger control and abuse of dominant cases.

Even obtaining data in possession of DoubleClick might be the most important motivation for Google in the Google/DoubleClick merger. It would be hard to assume that online platforms compete *in* a data market or *for* a data market. Identifying a pure data market in the cornerstone abuse cases and mergers in data-driven markets is nearly impossible.[303] In none of the services, end-users' or advertisers' side of their businesses do Google, Microsoft or Facebook sell datasets or behavioural data to other parties. This makes it irrelevant to define a data market. However, stemming from the idea that Harbour and Koslov have identified market power for Google through their possession of Big Data, a slightly different approach could have been considered without defining a separate market for data. In this scenario, data can be used as an assessment tool to substitute the market share assessment, which is not a relevant indicator of market power in data-driven markets.[304]

4.4.4 Creation of Online Ecosystems

Due to their dynamic and innovative characteristics, data-driven markets are rapidly evolving. This resulted in a shift in which the way of competition was changed considerably. For most businesses, competition to out-innovate is a norm today.[305]

---

298 Harbour and Koslov (n 290) 773.
299 ibid.
300 ibid 784.
301 ibid.
302 ibid 785.
303 Lianos (n 258) 77.
304 See Chapter 6.3.2.
305 James F Moore, 'Predators and Prey: A New Ecology of Competition' (1993) 71 Harvard Business Review 3, 75.

Therefore, traditional assessment tools designed for a static market analysis fail for data-driven markets.[306] In other words, it does not seem logical to define a product market by considering the current substitutes of a specific product or its geographical scope, as did in the aforementioned investigations before the Commission. One of the main reasons behind it is the emergence of online ecosystems. The concept of ecosystem is relatively new to business life.[307] Business ecosystems follow a process similar to biological ecosystems, which is a constant evolutionary process in which only companies that follow well-adapted strategies and innovate can survive.[308]

In 1993, James Moore analysed the emergence of business ecosystems and explained it through four evolutionary stages. According to the study, companies create a revolutionary product backed by an innovation process, bring their product to consumers, and scale up supply to achieve substantial market coverage.[309] In a business ecosystem, companies work with third parties and innovators to bring new ideas, products or services to the ecosystem.[310] In other words, although there is usually one leading company initiating rapid improvements and drawing consumers to the ecosystem, ecosystems generally co-evolve.[311] Also, many other companies or institutions contribute to the creation and sustainment of new products and services.[312] David Teece expresses that "the co-evolution of the system is . . . reliant on the technological leadership . . . that provides a platform around which other system members, providing inputs and complementary goods, align their investments and strategies".[313]

Many online services and product providers aim to bring consumers into a comprehensive ecosystem. Online providers such as Google, Apple and Facebook offer a wide range of products and services to draw more consumers into their ecosystems. Therefore, they can maintain control over consumers' demands and meet consumers' needs with supplementary products and services without losing consumers.[314] For instance, Facebook arguably offers substitute products such

---

306 Gönenç Gürkaynak, Büşra Aktüre and Sıla Coşkunoğlu, 'Challenges of the Digital Age: The Relevant Product Market Definition in Online and Offline Sales' in Gönenç Gürkaynak (ed), *The Second Academic Gift Book of ELIG Gürkaynak Attorneys-at-Law on Selected Contemporary Competition Law Matters* (Legal Yayincilik 2019) 228; Crémer Report (n 245) 47; William F Baxter, 'The Definition and Measurement of Market Power in Industries Characterized by Rapidly Developing and Changing Technologies' (1984–1985) 53 Antitrust Law Journal 717.
307 David J Teece, 'Next-Generation Competition: New Concepts for Understanding How Innovation Shapes Competition and Policy in the Digital Economy' (2012) 9 Journal of Law, Economics and Policy 106; Lianos (n 258) 103; Moore (n 305) 75; Michael G Jacobides, Carmelo Cennamo and Annabelle Gawer, 'Towards a Theory of Ecosystems' (2018) 39 Strategic Management Journal 2255.
308 Teece (n 307) 106.
309 Moore (n 305) 77.
310 ibid.
311 ibid 79.
312 Teece (n 307) 104.
313 ibid.
314 Crémer Report (n 245) 47.

as Facebook and Instagram or WhatsApp and Facebook Messenger in order to compete with rivals such as Snapchat, Telegram, Viber and Signal. By offering Instagram, Facebook provides the best substitute for the Facebook application or WhatsApp for Facebook Messenger and does not lose consumers who lost interest in one of their applications.

Also, as long as consumers stay in an ecosystem, platform owners can effectively use personal data accumulated within the ecosystem.[315] For instance, Google and Apple have created ecosystems through their mobile operating systems (mobile OS). Also, they draw consumers into their ecosystems by providing cloud services, mail services and many more through smartphones and tablets. Therefore, smartphones are increasingly becoming access points to consumers for various services. Using services from one provider (ecosystem) allows better quality services since providers have access to all available consumer data to personalise services and offer content.[316] Consumers would find it difficult to leave these specific ecosystems in doing so. This also means that providers are quite successful in their lock-in strategies.

Ecosystems and lock-in strategies result in the creation of entry barriers to specific data-driven markets. Today, Apple iOS and Google Android are the most prevalent mobile operating systems through smartphones. Thus, most application developers create applications for Apple and Google's operating systems specifically, making it difficult for potential rivals to compete in the operating systems market. A company may even offer the highest-quality, superior mobile operating system with excellent privacy protection. That being said, many companies have offered mobile OSs for smartphones recently.[317] However, the existence of a rich variety of mobile applications through Android and iOS makes these ecosystems attractive to consumers. Recently, BlackBerry left its OS for Android in order to compete in the smartphone market, and Microsoft announced that it would not produce smartphones with the Windows Mobile OS due to the lack of applications and reluctance of application developers to develop apps for Windows Mobile.[318] In 2019, Microsoft announced that they killed off support for Windows Mobile in 2020 and suggested that Windows Mobile users switch to Android.[319]

Ioannis Lianos stresses that Big Data and its effects on markets require competition authorities to reconsider the dynamics of data-driven markets and reveal interactions beyond the traditional competition law regarding the relevant market analysis.[320] At this point, competition law and policy must deal not only with competitive struggle to gain an advantage on a specific product or geographical market

---

315 ibid.
316 ibid 48.
317 Tizen, Symbian, Bada, Windows 10 Mobile, KaiOS, Blackberry OS, Palm OS and others.
318 Furman (n 175) 40.
319 Todd Haselton, 'Microsoft Recommends Switching to iPhone or Android as It Prepares to KILL OFF Windows Phones' *CNBC* (18 January 2019) <https://www.cnbc.com/2019/01/18/microsoft-ending-windows-10-mobile-says-switch-to-iphone-or-android.html>
320 Lianos (n 258) 161.

Assessment of Data-Related Market Power in Data-Driven Markets 121

as traditional market power assessment does but also engage with the value creation mechanisms that are valued higher today, created in various new economy industries.[321] This means Big Data's innovative character and multi-sided nature must be considered to capture the ecosystem's dynamics and create an accurate analysis. In data-driven markets, competition analysis focused on the relevant product market analysis and price-centric tools should be abandoned due to the limited role of price competition[322] and other mentioned characteristics. Consequently, Lianos underlines the need for new tools to identify horizontal and vertical interactions in multi-sided data-driven markets.[323] Putting ecosystems into the centre of market power assessment and abandoning relevant product market definitions in favour of competition analysis on the platforms themselves should not seem unjustifiable.

4.4.5 Multi-Sided Market Confusion

In the data-driven economy, many markets are multi-sided. Therefore, assessing market power on both fronts plays an important role in finding dominance in data-driven markets.[324] Thus, defining a product market requires an analysis of every side of a multi-sided market. Hence, academics argue that defining more than one relevant market in data-driven markets is necessary.[325] However, Filistrucchi et al. underline the distinction between transaction and non-transaction markets as distinct types of multi-sided markets and propose that defining multiple relevant markets is relevant only for the non-transaction markets.[326] Thus, only one relevant market should be defined in two-sided transaction markets.[327]

According to the study, the difference between transaction and non-transaction two-sided markets is the absence or at least non-observance of a transaction between the two sides of the market.[328] In markets like social media or search engine, there are no transactions between the two sides since they are connected via an intermediary: an online platform. However, there is a direct link in markets such as payment

---

321 ibid.
322 See Section 5.4.
323 Lianos (n 258) 161.
324 Schmidt (n 137) 45; Lapo Filistrucchi and others (n 193) 293–339; Lapo Filistrucchi, Damien Geradin and Eric van Damme, 'Identifying Two-Sided Markets' (2012) TILEC Discussion Paper No. 2012-008; Robert Lind, Paul Muysert and Mike Walker, 'Innovation and Competition Policy, Part I, Conceptual Issues, Report Prepared for the Office of Fair Trading by Charles River Associates' (2002); Inge Graef 'Market Definition and Market Power in Data: The Case of Online Platforms' (2015) 38 World Competition 4, 473–506.
325 Nikolai Van Gorp and Olga Batura, 'Challenges for Competition Policy in a Digitalised Economy' A Study for the ECON Committee, Directorate General for Internal Policies, European Parliament, July 2015, IP/A/ECON/2014-12 PE 542.235, 53; Filistrucchi and others (n 193) 293–339; Lapo Filistrucchi, Damien Geradin and Eric van Damme, 'Identifying Two-Sided Markets' (2012) TILEC Discussion Paper. No. 2012-008; Ratliff and Rubinfeld (n 241) 1–25, 21.
326 Filistrucchi and others (n 193) 302.
327 ibid.
328 ibid 298.

cards, a transaction between groups using the same platform. Also, another difference between the two types of multi-sided markets is the "usage externalities".[329] Although indirect network effects characterise both markets, transaction markets have usage externalities, unlike non-transaction markets. The usage externalities or usage effects occur from using the platform itself. For instance, a user who sells or buys something through their credit card directly benefits the payment system companies in the payment card market. However, a social media user does not benefit the advertiser, despite creating value by contributing to the intermediary. In brief, in non-transaction markets, the usage externalities and transactions between parties on different market sides are non-existent.

Many identified data-driven markets where the price is zero on one side can be categorised as non-transaction markets, according to the Filistrucchi analysis. Therefore, data-driven markets such as search engine and social media markets can be separated into the users' and advertisers' sides. Regarding market power assessment, the users' and advertisers' sides of the market should be assessed, and authorities should consider both sides.[330] In light of this idea, Filistrucchi et al. argue the Commission's interpretation in Google/DoubleClick is insufficient to capture the potential aim of Google to acquire the datasets of DoubleClick.[331] First, the Commission correctly identified that Google is an online intermediary active in the online advertising market. In the analysis, the online advertising market was not separated into the users' and advertisers' sides and was regarded as one single market. However, as Filistrucchi et al. suggest, the online advertising market could be separated into several non-transaction markets from the advertisers' side, and this could make it possible to reveal how and why Google tries to acquire the datasets of DoubleClick to improve its advertising services across all platforms, devices, and applications.[332]

On the other hand, although academics argue that analysis on both sides of the market is crucial for the relevant market definition,[333] recent case law has identified no need for the sub-segmentation in multi-sided markets from users' and advertisers' sides of the markets.[334] At this point, it is important to note that analysis that

---

329 ibid.
330 ibid 322.
331 ibid 307–8.
332 ibid 308.
333 Höppner (n 37) 3, 349–66, 354; David S Evans, 'The Antitrust Economics of Multi-Sided Platform Markets' (2003) 20 Yale Journal on Regulation 2, 357–60; Francesco Russo and Maria Luisa Stasi, 'Defining the Relevant Market in the Sharing Economy' (2016) 5 Internet Policy Review 2, 8; Miguel S Ferro, 'Ceci n'est pas un marché: Gratuity and Competition Law' (2015) Concurrences 10, 10–13; Christian Kersting and Sebastian Dworschak, 'Does Google Hold a Dominant Market Position? Addressing the (Minor) Significance of High Online User Shares' (2014) 16 Ifo Schnelldienst 7; Schmidt (n 137) 47, citing: Pinar Akman 'Market Definition in Online Markets: Mission Impossible' Presentation 9 September 2016 at University of Leeds Conference on 'Competition and Regulation in Digital Markets'.
334 Case No COMP/M.4731 Google/DoubleClick C[2008] 927 final; Case No COMP/M.5727 Microsoft/Yahoo! Search Business C[2010] 1077 final.

identifies both sides of the market should always be done on a case-by-case basis in data-driven markets. Nevertheless, the interaction between both sides of the market seems to be an important point. Thomas Höppner expresses that in order to define a relevant sub-market, a separate interaction must be identified.[335] Moreover, he adds that data-driven markets could have more than two sides. In the case of online search engines, Höppner identifies three distinct sides.[336] As an intermediary itself, a search engine is not regarded as a side of the business. Instead, three sides are identified: search, advertising and content.[337] According to the classification, search engines used by internet users who desire to find information on the web constitute the market's user/search side. Advertisers who buy advertising space are on the advertisers' side of the market. Furthermore, providers of online content on the web are on the content side of the market. Unlike the social media market, where providers and users are the same, they are on different sides in the search engine market. As a result, the interaction between all these groups must be identified together in the market power analysis.

To sum up, the price analysis or substitutability analysis, which is performed on every side of the market, seems to be an adequate response for emerging data-driven markets in the eyes of many academics. However, as mentioned previously, the relevant market analysis defines the "boundaries" of a market in terms of product and geographical scope. The traditional approach does not seem to work in markets where companies continuously redefine boundaries or create new market segments.[338] For instance, regarding the *Google Search (Shopping)* case, Ratliff and Rubinfeld concluded that the relevant market for Google should be defined as at least as broad as the online advertising market, including organic search engines.[339] The reason behind this is the indirect network effects between search-related advertising and organic searches inside the search engine.[340] Network effects stemming from organic searches are vital for the functioning of online advertising.

Moreover, online search services would be quite unprofitable without advertising services as a freestanding service.[341] As a reminder, the Commission concluded that the online comparison-shopping and search engine markets are two separate relevant markets in the EU for that abusive behaviour case. That is to say, the platform itself or the online advertising market could be defined as the sole, broad relevant market for the abuse of dominant position analysis. In this manner, interactions, dependency, network effects and the value chain could have been identified correctly for the analysis. In the same vein, regarding the *Google Search (Shopping)* case, Broos and Ramos advocate that Google operates in only

---

335 Höppner (n 37) 349–66, 354.
336 ibid 356.
337 ibid.
338 Antonio Capobianco and Anita Nyeso, 'Challenges for Competition Law Enforcement and Policy in the Digital Economy' (2018) 9 Journal of European Competition Law and Practice 1, 19–27, 23.
339 Ratliff and Rubinfeld (n 241) 1–25, 1.
340 ibid 22.
341 ibid 22.

one market where Google links two sides to each other; users and advertisers (or three sides, if Höppner's analysis is implemented).[342] In other words, the relevant market consists of search services, shopping services and advertising services, which operate together.[343]

In conclusion, the static product market definition should be avoided in data-driven markets primarily due to these markets' fast-changing and innovative character. Also, the multi-sided nature of online platforms makes narrower product market definitions null. Hence, data-driven markets must be analysed as ecosystems to infer the correct results for the market power analysis. The most important reason competition authorities should avoid traditional market power analysis is the role of Big Data as a value-creation mechanism there. Big Data and the power stemming from data utilisation are the lost links between services operating in data-driven markets for users, advertisers and other identified platform sides.

4.5 Concluding Remarks

In data-driven markets, the traditional approach to market power assessment is not as useful as lawmakers intended. There were many important data-driven acquisitions and abuse of dominant cases in which authorities and courts had difficulty applying traditional tools of competition to cases and investigations. In these investigations, authorities defined relevant markets by segmenting and narrowing proposed markets for specific products. Therefore, in most cases, more than one relevant market was identified. Apart from the market definition, authorities were sceptical about market share measurements. Nevertheless, many critical issues were overlooked.

The main reason behind the problems is that data-driven markets have some novel characteristics which pose difficulties while assessing market power. In the new economy, markets are characterised by fast innovation cycles and competition *for* the market. This is not a new phenomenon. However, these markets have multi-sided nature, and in many of these markets, price/monetary charges are non-existent on at least one side of the market. Another important feature is the creation of ecosystems. The valuable data led to the creation of online ecosystems where companies attract consumers to extract information from them to serve them better products and services, thus monetising these services through online advertising. As a result, product markets connected and relevant markets widened considerably. Overall, due to the innovative character, dynamic competition, creation of ecosystems and Big Data value chain, competition tools to assess market power are insufficient for data-driven markets. Undervaluation of the power of data in the online world resulted from using traditional competition assessment tools for data-driven markets.

---

342 Sébastien Broos and Jorge Marcos Ramos, 'Google, Google Shopping and Amazon: The Importance of Competing Business Models and Two-Sided Intermediaries in Defining Relevant Markets' (2017) 62 The Antitrust Bulletin 2, 11–13.
343 ibid.

Traditional competition tools for the assessment are mainly price-centric. The hypothetical monopolist and SSNIP tests to identify monopolistic powers under the HMT umbrella are based on price as the main parameter of competition law. Thus, these methods are primarily designed for products and services with price tags. Therefore, products and services in data-driven markets are "red flags" for traditional competition models since these methods cannot be sufficiently applied to free online products or services. Another problem is the irrelevance of competition law's static market share analysis. As mentioned earlier, data-driven markets are quite complex; thus, static market shares in narrowly defined relevant markets do not contribute to the market power analysis. Instead of relying on market shares and other price-centric tools, new methods should be developed.

In most digitalised and newly emerged markets, Big Data has become a significant input and a source of market power. The significance of data as an input and a source of market power also reveals an urgent need to develop new methods to measure the market power of undertakings and the general competitive structure of data-driven markets. As a proposal, an assessment through Big Data could take the place of the neoclassical economic tools gathered around price analysis. Big Data capabilities and data possession of technology giants and other companies in the new economy could well contribute to competition analysis. It could lead to a well-defined competitive structure based on the current competition methods of competitors. Data collection → data analytics → better services/products → better-targeted advertisements → more consumers and advertisers → network effects → the creation of ecosystems → tipping effects and finally monopolisation chain is the main mechanism in data-driven markets. In brief, Big Data fuels the mechanism for creating market power across the online world.

Consequently, the assessment of Big Data possession and data analytics capabilities of undertakings must be primarily identified in the market power analysis. Conclusions based on "data power" as a new form of "market power" would give accurate results regarding the competitive structure of data-driven markets. Such an analysis will also serve a wider goal than the competition for the community, the total welfare of consumers. Well-identified data collection methods, data possession, analytics and targeted advertisements will also provide great transparency throughout data-driven markets. Consequently, any privacy-related concern regarding data collection by technology giants can be addressed relatively more accurately.

5 Abusive Behaviour in Data-Driven Markets

5.1 Abuse Through Leveraging Market Power

In competition law, leveraging market power is a unique abuse type since abuse and dominance are expected to happen in different markets, such as neighbouring or downstream markets, as a prerequisite for this kind of abuse.[1] Other abuses mostly harm competitors or competition in general in the same market where dominant undertakings' conduct happens. In data-driven markets, leveraging market power abuse occurs in a segment of the ecosystem of dominant undertakings. As discussed in Chapter 4, segments of the online advertising sector merged with search engines and social media are the primary examples of the data-driven market structure. Thus, the main problem is that data-rich undertakings do not use their market power, relying on scale economies or lower prices to leverage power.[2] The main method is to leverage their "data advantage" into new market segments and utilise personal information to swallow new platforms and businesses.

Apart from linking new business platforms or market segments into a bigger ecosystem, leveraging market power could well occur where dominant undertakings try to gain ground in a market unrelated to the original ecosystem. For instance, these data-rich undertakings such as Google, Apple or Amazon jump to other sectors out of the online world, like automotive, white appliances or even energy, to extend their businesses to take advantage of the Internet of Things (IoT).[3] Data-rich undertakings are experts in data processing, algorithms and new business models; thus, they leverage their qualities into other industries.[4] The application of digital technology introduces new data-driven platforms and businesses connected with

---

1 Aleksandra Gebicka and Andreas Heinemann, 'Social Media & Competition Law' (2014) 37 World Competition 2, 149–72, 170.
2 ibid.
3 For more information of leveraging market power: Giorgio Monti, *EC Competition Law* (1st edn, CUP 2007) 186–95.
4 Nikolai Van Gorp and Olga Batura, 'Challenges for Competition Policy in a Digitalised Economy' A Study for the ECON Committee, Directorate General for Internal Policies, European Parliament, July 2015, IP/A/ECON/2014-12 PE 542.235, 61; Antonio Capobianco and Anita Nyeso, 'Challenges for Competition Law Enforcement and Policy in the Digital Economy' (2018) 9 Journal of European Competition Law & Practice No. 1, 26.

DOI: 10.4324/9781003458791-5

the core online ecosystems of these undertakings. These undertakings compete for market presence based on their merits.[5] They force other undertakings in those industries to innovate into data-driven business models and technologies. Therefore, innovation and data-driven business strategies expand in these industries as well.[6] However, harm to innovation and exclusionary effects are inevitable when the conduct becomes abusive. In its *Microsoft* decision, the European Commission has decided that leveraging market power reduces consumers' choices and causes great harm to innovation.[7]

Leveraging market power in data-driven markets can occur in diverse ways: leveraging or self-preferencing. Leveraging can be offensive or defensive.[8] Offensive leveraging is a business strategy that aims to generate more profits and expansion.[9] On the other hand, defensive leveraging is a strategy of undertakings trying to prevent entry into a market where dominance is already established.[10] Data-rich undertakings controlling bottlenecks may abuse their positions through defensive leveraging. Instead of reaping more profits from neighbouring markets, it is purely an attempt to protect their dominant positions.[11] Thus, characteristics of data-driven markets, such as strong indirect network effects and access to data, also contribute to defensive leverage strategies.[12] However, there are no legal or analytical differences between offensive and defensive leveraging in competition law.[13] When a data-rich undertaking leverages its market power, competition law should effectively identify these abuses.

The other type of leveraging is called self-preferencing. Self-preferencing is not as straightforward as defensive leveraging. It is mainly about undertakings that give favoured treatment to their own products while competing with rivals within the same platform of an ecosystem. According to EU competition law, self-preferencing is not an abuse of a dominant position situation *per se*. Article 102 TFEU does not prohibit dominant undertakings from self-preferencing their products. There seem to be a couple of exceptions to the main rule. First is the special responsibility that the essential facility owner dominant undertakings have. According to the CJEU, owning an essential facility requires not engaging in self-preferencing practices.[14] The second exception should be the platform owners themselves in the online ecosystems. According to Crémer et al., in data-driven

---

5 Van Gorp and Batura (n 4) 61; Capobianco and Nyeso (n 4) 26.
6 ibid.
7 Case T – 201/4 *Microsoft Corp. v Commission of the European Communities* [2007] ECLI:EU:T:2007:289, para 1095.
8 Jacques Crémer, Yves-Alexandre de Montjoye and Heike Schweitzer, *Competition Policy for the Digital Era: Final Report* (Publications Office of the European Union 2019) 7.
9 ibid.
10 ibid.
11 Van Gorp and Batura (n 4) 61.
12 Crémer, de Montjoye and Schweitzer (n 8) 66.
13 ibid 8.
14 Case T – 201/4 *Microsoft Corp. v Commission of the European Communities* [2007] ECLI:EU:T:2007:289, para 1088.

markets where platforms serve as intermediary services and platform owners act as intermediaries who compete in the platforms, these undertakings become *de facto* regulators of the ecosystem.[15] In these integrated online platforms, dominant undertakings must prove that self-preferencing does not contain any exclusionary effects or demonstrate any pro-competitive rationale behind self-preferencing.[16] In other words, the burden of proof should be shifted to dominant undertakings in that case.

Abuse through self-preferencing was relevant and discussed in detail in the *Google Search (Shopping)* case.[17] As discussed in Chapter 4, the Commission found that Google promotes its own services by decreasing traffic to rival shopping services from the Google search results page. Instead, a systematic replacement to Google's own shopping service in search results occurred for a long time. The Commission added that traffic to comparison shopping services is mostly through the general search services of Google, and the conduct of Google creates a situation in which rival comparison shopping services are excluded from the market. Therefore, the abusive conduct was labelled as "self-preferencing" since Google promotes and gives favoured treatment to its own shopping service on its own platform where it competes with rivals. Self-preferencing as abuse is also discussed by the Commission and the *Bundeskartellamt* in Amazon's case.

5.1.1 Self-Preferencing

In data-driven markets, self-preferencing is an important competition concern. Self-preferencing as an abuse is widely discussed during and after the Commission's key investigation against Google's comparison shopping services.[18] As mentioned in Chapter 4, the investigation started back in 2010 in order to find out whether Google abuses its dominant position by showing the Google Shopping links more prominently on the Google search screen by giving systematic favourable treatment to the Google Shopping service and demoting rival comparison shopping services in the search results page at the same time.[19] After a lengthy investigation almost ended with commitments in 2014, Google was fined €2.42 billion by the European Commission in 2017, and the General Court of the CJEU dismissed Google's action and upheld the fine that the Commission issued.[20]

---

15 Crémer, de Montjoye and Schweitzer (n 8) 66.
16 ibid.
17 Case No COMP/AT.39740, *Google Search (Shopping)* [2017] 4444 Final.
18 ibid.
19 European Commission, Press Release, 'Antitrust: Commission Fines Google €2.42 Billion for Abusing Dominance as Search Engine by Giving Illegal Advantage to Own Comparison Shopping Services' (Brussels, 27 June 2017) <https://ec.europa.eu/commission/presscorner/detail/en/IP_17_1784>
20 Case T-612/17 *Google and Alphabet v Commission (Google Shopping)* [2021] ECLI:EU:T:2021:763; European Commission, Press Release, 'Antitrust: Commission Obtains from Google Comparable Display of Specialised Search Rivals' (Brussels, 5 February 2014) <https://ec.europa.eu/commission/presscorner/detail/en/IP_14_116>

In its decision, the Commission reported that Google had abused its dominant position in the search engine market by diverting traffic from rival shopping services to its own service.[21] The abuse was done by decreasing traffic to the rival comparison shopping services from the Google search engine.[22] According to the Commission, the conduct did not fall within the scope of competition on merits since the conduct excluded rivals by diverting the traffic and had anti-competitive effects on both the search engine and comparison shopping service markets. Google was not the inventor of comparison shopping services, and its shopping service was not gaining significant traffic before the favoured appearance on the search results page.[23] Google is the super-dominant undertaking in the search engine market, and being on the general search results page affects online comparison shopping services greatly.

Regarding the dominance of Google in the search engine market and holding the largest proportion of traffic for comparison shopping services, the Commission underlined that although multi-homing could be frequent in theory, most consumers who use the Google search engine in the EEA do not multi-home in reality.[24] In other words, a significant number of consumers would likely continue to use Google's search engine even if the quality of the service Google provides lowered.[25] In addition, as a result of the anti-competitive conduct, the Commission found evidence of huge drops in traffic to certain comparison shopping services which are rivals of Google in the EEA, such as 92% in Germany, 85% in the United Kingdom and 80% in France.[26] According to the Commission,

> The evidence shows that consumers click far more often on . . . the results appearing higher up in Google's search results . . . the ten highest-ranking generic search results on page 1 together generally receive approximately 95% of all clicks on generic search results.[27]

---

21 Summary of Commission decision of 27 June 2017, Relating to a Proceeding Under Article 102 of the Treaty on the Functioning of the European Union and Article 54 of the EEA Agreement (Case AT.39740 *Google Search (Shopping)*) para 10; Case No COMP/AT.39740, *Google Search (Shopping)* [2017] 4444 Final, para 341.
22 Case No COMP/AT.39740, *Google Search (Shopping)* [2017] 4444 Final, para 341.
23 ibid para 343.
24 ibid paras 306–12.
25 ibid para 312; Konstantina Bania, 'The European Commission's Decision in Google Search: Exploring Old and New Frontiers of Competition Enforcement in the Digital Economy' in Björn Lundqvist and Michal S Gal (eds), *Competition Law for the Digital Economy* (1st edn, Edward Elgar Publishing 2019) 280.
26 European Commission Press Release, 'Antitrust: Commission Fines Google €2.42 Billion for Abusing Dominance as Search Engine by Giving Illegal Advantage to Own Comparison Shopping Services' (Brussels, 27 June 2017) <https://ec.europa.eu/commission/presscorner/detail/en/IP_17_1784>
27 ibid.

Therefore, favourable treatment of the Google shopping service on the search results page had exclusionary effects and ultimately led to market foreclosure. The main reason the conduct forecloses the market is that the traffic for comparison shopping services largely flows through the Google search results page. This cannot be replaced by other sources currently available for comparison shopping services.

The investigation also highlights the power of Google in determining access to specific online services and ultimately deciding the fate of its rivals who rely on Google's services, such as its search engine.[28] As mentioned earlier, in an online ecosystem where platform owners are both competitors and intermediaries (service providers), there are huge risks since platform owners become regulators of an ecosystem. In the online world, technology giants can decide the fates of smaller competitors, businesses and start-ups. For this very reason, the Commission should impose special responsibilities on dominant undertakings.

In the *Google* case, the Commission asked the company to give "equal treatment" to rival comparison shopping services and use the same processes and methods in deciding the display results of shopping links on the search results page.[29] As the remedy stands next to the search neutrality principle, the actual remedy is a form of duty to deal. This remedy is important to reveal how intermediaries can regulate the ecosystem in the online world. Thus, they must have special responsibilities not to distort competition.[30] In 2018, Margrethe Vestager stressed that behavioural remedies of the Commission on Google search and comparison shopping services have had an effect and are beginning to bear fruit.[31] This can be seen from the increasing number of rival comparison shopping services appearing on the first pages of search results and from the rival companies' traffic.[32]

Similar concerns were raised in a more recent investigation against the Amazon marketplace before the European Commission and the Federal Cartel Office of Germany (the *Bundeskartellamt*). The European Commission started investigating Amazon's use of sensitive data collected from independent retailers on Amazon's marketplace.[33] Amazon has a dual role as an intermediary between online retailers and consumers and an online retailer in a marketplace platform called a "hybrid

---

28 Ariel Ezrachi and Maurice Stucke, 'Emerging Antitrust Threats and Enforcement Actions in The Online World' (2017) 13 Competition Law International 2, 8.
29 Case No COMP/AT.39740, *Google Search (Shopping)* [2017] 4444 Final, para 671.
30 Dominant players that have *de facto* regulatory roles in ecosystems are discussed in detail in Chapter 6.
31 Pallavi Guniganti, 'Google Shopping Remedies Have Had Effect, Vestager Says' *Global Competition Review* (18 June 2018) <https://globalcompetitionreview.com/google-shopping-remedies-have-had-effect-vestager-says>
32 ibid.
33 European Commission, Press Release, 'Antitrust: Commission Opens Investigation into Possible Anti-Competitive Conduct of Amazon' (Brussels, 17 July 2019) <https://ec.europa.eu/commission/presscorner/detail/en/IP_19_4291>

platform".[34] Possible anti-competitive conduct is related to Amazon's collection and the utilisation of retail data to maximise profits. Amazon can collect and analyse all available data on the marketplace regarding every single transaction and thus can learn which products sell most at what price.[35] Therefore, Amazon can gain a crucial competitive advantage over its rivals dependent on Amazon's marketplace to continue their business. In other words, operating on both sides of the platform (upstream merchant intermediation side and downstream retail market side) creates an advantageous position for Amazon.

Margrethe Vestager stated:

> The question here is about the data. If you as Amazon get the data from smaller merchants that you host . . . do you then also use this data to do your own calculations, as to what is the new big thing, what is it that people want, what kind of offers do they like to receive, what makes them buy things?[36]

The Commission stresses that by providing a marketplace for third-party retailers, Amazon has all available data for their use regarding the marketplace, which its rivals cannot have.[37] The Commission identified that Amazon competitively uses sensitive information regarding retailers, sales, products and transaction information and possibly leverages market power in the preliminary findings.[38]

Accordingly, the *Bundeskartellamt* raised concerns about abuse through self-referencing in 2018 towards the Amazon marketplace. The president of the German Competition Authority, Andreas Mundt, expressed that

> Amazon is the largest online retailer and operates by far the largest online marketplace in Germany. Many retailers and manufacturers depend on the reach of Amazon's marketplace for their online sales. Amazon functions as a kind of "gatekeeper" for customers.[39]

There are many concerns that Amazon could behave in an abusive way in its own marketplace. As mentioned earlier, Amazon has a dual role as a dominant undertaking in its own platform, where it has access to all available data but, at the same

---

34 Thomas Höppner and Philipp Westerhoff, 'The EU's Competition Investigation into Amazon Marketplace' *Kluwer Competition Law Blog* (30 November 2018) <http://competitionlawblog.kluwercompetitionlaw.com/2018/11/30/the-eus-competition-investigation-into-amazon-marketplace/?doing_wp_cron=1591716526.0472819805145263671875>
35 ibid.
36 Natasha Bernal and James Titcomb, 'EU Opens Formal Competition Investigation into Amazon Over Use of Merchant Data' *The Telegraph* (San Francisco, 16 July 2019) <https://www.telegraph.co.uk/technology/2019/07/16/eu-open-formal-competition-investigation-amazon-within-days/>
37 European Commission Press Release (n 33).
38 ibid.
39 *Bundeskartellamt*, News, '*Bundeskartellamt* Initiates Abuse Proceeding Against Amazon' (29 November 2018) <https://www.bundeskartellamt.de/SharedDocs/Meldung/EN/Pressemitteilungen/2018/29_11_2018_Verfahrenseinleitung_Amazon.html>

132 *Abusive Behaviour in Data-Driven Markets*

time, as a rival to other online sellers.[40] Amazon not only has the dual role as a business but also the risk when it cooperates with manufacturers to offer the same products cheaper and faster than smaller businesses; these independent businesses may find themselves in a disadvantaged, unfavoured position in the market or even squeezed out.[41] The *Bundeskartellamt* evaluated most of the concerns regarding the dual role and power of Amazon, and a year later, the *Bundeskartellamt* ended its investigation of Amazon after Amazon agreed to improve business terms for independent sellers in the marketplace.[42] In response to the concerns raised by the authority, Amazon agreed to amend the liability, termination and blocking of accounts, returns and reimbursements, product information and rights of use, confidentiality, transparency, product reviews and seller rating provisions of its terms for business sellers.[43]

Thomas Höppner explains the possible anti-competitive conduct related to Amazon and its use of sensitive data. The overarching theory of harm is related to leveraging market power and, consequently, self-preferencing.[44] As regards dominance, Amazon, as a platform owner, definitely has a dominant position in the e-commerce market. Therefore, collecting and utilising all merchant data creates an edge for Amazon as a retailer. Moreover, this advantage seems to be quite an important concern since Amazon extracts data directly from its competitors.[45] None of the independent retailers is in a similar position, and Amazon can easily outperform and outcompete its rivals. Amazon's data policy and terms of service are somewhat similar to those in the investigation against Facebook,[46] in which extracted data provides an inherent advantageous position when used as a competitive tool. The use of commercially sensitive data exceeding competition on

---

40 Damien Geradin and Dimitrios Katsifis, 'An EU Competition Law Analysis of Online Display Advertising in the Programmatic Age' (2018) 15 European Competition Journal 55–96, 90.
41 *Bundeskartellamt*, 'Competition Restraints in Online Sales After Coty and Asics – What's Next?' (2018) Series of Papers on "Competition and Consumer Protection in the Digital Economy 4 <https://www.bundeskartellamt.de/SharedDocs/Publikation/EN/Schriftenreihe_Digitales_IV.pdf?__blob=publicationFile&v=2>
42 *Bundeskartellamt*, News, '*Bundeskartellamt* Obtains Far-Reaching Improvements in the Terms of Business for Sellers on Amazon's Online Marketplaces' (17 July 2019) <https://www.bundeskartellamt.de/SharedDocs/Meldung/EN/Pressemitteilungen/2019/17_07_2019_Amazon.html;jsessionid=98F173CFCF40CBB4E3AA149FF088832E.1_cid362>; Silke Heinz, '*Bundeskartellamt* Ends Abuse Probe After Amazon Agrees to Changing Business Terms for Dealers' *Kluwer Competition Law Blog* (30 July 2019) <http://competitionlawblog.kluwercompetitionlaw.com/2019/07/30/bundeskartellamt-ends-abuse-probe-after-amazon-agrees-to-changing-business-terms-for-dealers/?doing_wp_cron=1590500147.1006309986114501953125>
43 *Bundeskartellamt*, B2-88/18, 'Case Summary from 17 July 2019: Amazon Amends Its Terms of Business Worldwide for Sellers on Its Marketplaces – *Bundeskartellamt* Closes Abuse Proceedings' (17 July 2019) <https://www.bundeskartellamt.de/SharedDocs/Entscheidung/EN/Fallberichte/Missbrauchsaufsicht/2019/B2-88-18.html;jsessionid=6F46AFC4DECD4268BD11E5D792299FD1.1_cid362?nn=3600108>
44 Höppner and Westerhoff (n 34).
45 ibid.
46 See Chapter 5.2.2.

merits would create a situation in which Amazon uses the data for exclusionary and exploitative purposes.

Like the *Google Search* case, Amazon favoured its own services in the marketplace as the abuse. Many merchants, including Amazon itself, commonly sell the same products on the marketplace. Consequently, a conflict of interest stems from Amazon's dual role in e-commerce and its downstream market, online retail services.[47] Google was also in a similar position as an intermediary as the search engine and a competitor in online shopping services. The investigation has revealed one of the most important abuses related to data and the online world. The investigation against Amazon could also reveal abuse regarding Amazon favouring its online retailer in the marketplace and exclusionary effects on third-party sellers on the platform. This case would contribute to establishing case law against data-driven abuses in online ecosystems.

5.1.2 Google's Abuse and Theory of Harms

Specifically, the *Google Shopping* case has led to a wide debate in academia regarding the theory of harm and self-preferencing. As mentioned earlier, the European Commission based its decision on the theory of leveraging market power. Not only abuse of dominant position in the same relevant market but also the conduct of a dominant undertaking that aims to extend its dominance into neighbouring markets are found to be anti-competitive in competition law theory.[48] In the *Google* case, the Commission added that the conduct of a dominant undertaking to extend its position in a market to another is not novel and is a well-established form of abuse in EU competition law.[49] According to the Commission, Google abused its dominant position by favouring its services in one market by abusing its power in another: in other words, diverting traffic from rivals' services and decreasing their traffic in order to increase the traffic of its own comparison-shopping service. Google's conduct has anti-competitive effects on comparison shopping services through self-preferencing. Self-preferencing could be regarded as abusive if the conduct falls outside competition on merits, lacks justification or has exclusionary effects on the market and detrimental effects on consumers ultimately.[50]

However, during and after the investigation, commentators examined the conduct of Google and the Commission's ruling in terms of existing case law and types

---

47 Höppner and Westerhoff (n 34).
48 Case No COMP/AT.39740, Google Search (Shopping) [2017] 4444 Final, para 334.
49 ibid para 649.
50 European Commission, Guidance on the Commission's enforcement priorities in applying Article 82 of the EC Treaty to abusive exclusionary conduct by dominant undertakings, C (2009) 864 Final, paras 19–22.

of abusive behaviour.[51] Article 102 TFEU provides a list of abusive conduct.[52] Similarly, the guidance on the Commission's enforcement priorities in applying Article 102 TFEU mentions specific abusive behaviour: namely, exclusive dealing, tying and bundling, predation and refusal to supply and margin squeeze.[53] However, these lists are not exhaustive, and if their criteria are met, novel abuses are also considered anti-competitive in EU competition law. However, Pinar Akman conducted a positive and normative law assessment of the alleged abuse in the *Google Search* case. She found no specific abuse for the application of EU competition law.[54] The positive assessment is based on the three types of abusive behaviour: refusal to supply, tying and discrimination.[55] According to the study, the alleged abusive behaviour does not fit any of these types of abuse based on case law. Likewise, the normative assessment found that abuse does not fit into the framework of Article 102 at all.[56] Akman argues that exploitative and exclusionary effects are non-existent in the *Google Search* case, along with possible decreases in efficiency.

The discussion clearly demonstrates that assessing novel abuses through existing abuse types and assessment criteria for abuse of a dominant position is inefficient. Existing abuse types and criteria for anti-competitive conduct are not well suited for data-driven markets. As discussed in Chapter 4, even criteria to assess dominance and market definition are problematic in data-driven markets. These markets are multi-sided and form online ecosystems where dominant undertakings are the actual decision-makers for everything in their ecosystems. For instance, Google is the dominant undertaking in the search engine market, where many segments, such as vertical search engines, video sharing, online shopping, navigation and email services fight over consumers' attention. In such a circumstance, undertakings such as Google or Amazon (for the e-commerce platforms) have the power to act as regulators and enforce their own rules on that platform. The Commission has underlined on several occasions that Google leveraged its dominance on the platform (Google Search) into another segment of it (comparison shopping

---

51 Pinar Akman, 'A Preliminary Assessment of the European Commission's Google Search Decision' (2017) 3 CPI Antitrust Chronicle 7; Pinar Akman, 'The Theory of Abuse in Google Search: A Positive and Normative Assessment Under EU Competition Law' (2017) 2 Journal of Law, Technology and Policy 301; Ioannis Kokkoris, 'The Google Saga: Episode I' (2018) 14(2–3) European Competition Journal 462–90; Nathan Newman, 'Search, Antitrust, and the Economics of the Control of User Data' (2014) 31 Yale Journal on Regulation 2; Bo Vesterdorf, 'Theories of Self-preferencing and Duty to Deal – Two Sides of the Same Coin' (2015) 1 Competition Law and Policy Debate 5; Renato Nazzini, 'Google and the (Ever-Stretching) Boundaries of Article 102' (2015) 6 Journal of European Competition Law and Practice 5, 301; Ioannis Lianos and Evgenia Motchenkova, 'Market Dominance and Search Quality in the Search Engine Market' (2013) 9 Journal of Competition Law and Economics 419; Nicolas Petit, 'Theories of Self-Preferencing Under Article 102TFEU: A Reply to Bo Vesterdorf' (2015) SSRN Electronic Journal <https://plu.mx/ssrn/a/?ssrn_id=2592253>
52 Article 102 of the TFEU.
53 European Commission (n 50).
54 Pinar Akman, 'A Preliminary Assessment of the European Commission's Google Search Decision' (2017) 3 CPI Antitrust Chronicle 7; Akman (n 51) 301.
55 Akman (n 51) 307–55.
56 ibid 355–70.

services), which resulted in market foreclosure and a decrease in the relevancy of search results.[57] In such a situation, examining the conduct of Google through specific abuse types and traditional methods is irrational. The characteristics and structures of online ecosystems make it difficult to assess dominance to define a relevant market, assess and determine the type of anti-competitive conduct, and establish a theory of harm for competition authorities.[58]

Ioannis Kokkoris stresses that alleged abuse is a novel type not found in the existing case law regarding Google's abuse.[59] In other words, the Commission added a new type of abuse to EU case law. Kokkoris underlines the importance of a clear analysis and legal certainty regarding alleged abuse while investigating whether a new abuse should be added to the menu.[60] In the study, the criticism gathers around possible consumer harms, which are found non-existent in the *Google Search* case, according to Kokkoris. Although the Commission argues that Google has diverted traffic from rivals into its own service, and Google might have foreclosed a market from rivals where users do not see the most relevant results in search queries, the conduct might not constitute abuse under Article 102.[61] The study claims that Google's search service relying on innovation and development creates consumer benefits for which consumers are able to conduct much higher-quality searches than in the past.[62] In such a situation, Kokkoris expresses that claiming competition is distorted becomes a question mark.[63] Therefore, claims directed at consumer harm must be examined to demonstrate the difference in consumer experience when the alleged abuse is non-existent. The study claims that the same analogy must be applied to competitors where merchant harm must be demonstrated through causality for the alleged abuse. Thus, the exclusion of rivals is not necessarily linked to abuse, and exclusion could result from an outdated business strategy in these innovative markets.[64] In other words, to conduct a clear analysis, the Commission must ensure that market foreclosure results from the actual effects of Google's abusive behaviour and not from Google's successful innovation investments which rivals cannot compete with or respond to.[65]

As mentioned before, dominant undertakings that control ecosystems in the online world have executive powers, including *de facto* regulatory powers. Therefore, competition in any segment of an ecosystem is in danger of abusive behaviour from the dominant undertaking if that undertaking also competes in one or more platform segments. This seems to be a broad anti-competitive

---

57 Lesser relevant search results mean decreased product/service quality for consumers.
58 Ebru Gökçe, 'Competition Issues in the Digital Economy' (2019) UNCTAD Background Note 9 <https://unctad.org/system/files/official-document/ciclpd54_en.pdf>
59 Kokkoris (n 51) 462–90, 469.
60 ibid 470.
61 ibid 472.
62 ibid 475.
63 ibid.
64 ibid 483.
65 ibid 489.

concern in competition law. For instance, Foundem and other parties accused Google of making them disappear from the organic search results page for a long time when the investigation started against Google.[66] The business strategy of undertakings in data-driven markets such as Google's or Amazon's is somewhat unique. Unlike other industries, they can collect and analyse all available data in the platform to compete with their rivals. Moreover, they create a "single-user data profile" system across the ecosystem, using the same collected data for numerous services and products.[67] This provides an unprecedented competitive edge to dominant undertakings. Excessive data collection also contributes to abusive self-preferencing behaviour in which dominant undertakings benefit from data processing. Their ability to offer higher quality products increases, and they exclude rivals in the platform.

Bork and Sidak argue that using datasets to gain revenue from favoured services such as vertical search engine advertising significantly decreases the undertaking's income in general search engine advertising services.[68] The reasoning behind this is the "single-monopoly-profit theorem". According to this Chicago School theorem,[69] in a vertically integrated market, monopolists cannot profit from both markets; they only profit from one market, upstream or downstream.[70] Bork and Sidak explain the reasoning: "When the upstream supplier begins producing the downstream product, it will increase its joint profits by lowering the price of the downstream product. . . . Total profits cannot exceed the monopoly profits from any one stage".[71] Therefore, it can be deduced that when Google tries to maximise its profits in comparison shopping services, its revenue from the general search engine should decrease significantly. However, the Chicago School theory is insufficient when applied to markets in which Big Data is a core competition component. Nathan Newman points out that the Chicago School model ignores the platform owners' ability to collect sensitive data directly from competitors' transactions.[72] Unlike the theory suggests, dominant undertakings' revenue would not drop since the collected data from general search services and comparison shopping services significantly reinforce each other and increase the revenue of both services at the

---

66 Nathan Newman, 'Search, Antitrust, and the Economics of the Control of User Data' (2014) 31 Yale Journal on Regulation 2, 432.
67 ibid.
68 Robert H Bork and J Gregory Sidak, 'What Does the Chicago School Teach About Internet Search and the Antitrust Treatment of Google?' (2012) 8(4) Journal of Competition Law and Economics 663–700, 675.
69 Robert H Bork, *The Antitrust Paradox: A Policy At War With Itself* (2nd edn, Basic Books 1993) 229; Phillip E Areeda and Herbert Hovenkamp, *Antitrust Law: An Analysis of Antitrust Principles and Their Application* (2nd edn, Wolter Kluwer International 2002) 30; Aaron Director and Edward H Levi, 'Law and the Future: Trade Regulation' (1956) 51 Northwestern University Law Review 281, 290; Richard A Posner, 'The Chicago School of Antitrust Analysis' (1979) 127 University of Pennsylvania Law Review 925, 926–27.
70 Bork and Sidak (n 68) 675.
71 ibid 676.
72 Newman (n 66) 434.

cost of distorting competition on the segments of the online platform. The added value of using datasets for both services exponentially increases when the dominant undertaking favours its own services. Google's or Amazon's ability to process information available on their ecosystems creates a barrier, and their rivals cannot overcome and respond with their competitive services. Ultimately, the fate of rivals and competition remain solely in the dominant undertakings' hands in such circumstances.

In light of this situation, consumer harm becomes detectable: a decrease in quality and a decrease in the relevance of search results. As the Commission highlighted, foreclosing rival shopping services and favouring their own services will lead to higher fees for merchants.[73] Google can raise participation costs for its rivals, or rivals need to invest more to get consumers' attention, resulting in higher product prices for consumers, especially the products of rival companies. In the second phase, incentives for innovation are expected to decrease in comparison shopping services or similar services. Rival companies will not invest in their services if they cannot attract a reasonable number of consumers and make transactions.[74] In a situation in which Google diverts traffic from rival services, a decrease in innovation investment will likely occur. At the same time, Google's incentives to improve its own services will also decrease since Google does not face any serious competition in the market.[75] Consequently, the quality of Google's service will also be reduced. In addition to decreased quality when innovation investments fall, lesser relevant search results become another consumer harm. Google's conduct is likely to reduce choices for the consumer by limiting search results in favour of its own services, which must be deemed anti-competitive.[76]

The Commission's decision and theories on leveraging market power and self-preferencing play a key role in the following investigations of Google Android and AdSense.[77] The Commission opened an investigation concerning Google's alleged abuse inside the Android ecosystem in 2015. Related to a previous investigation of Google Search, Commissioner Vestager reported:

> I have also launched a formal antitrust investigation of Google's conduct concerning mobile operating systems. . . . Smartphones, tablets and similar devices play an increasing role in many people's daily lives, and I want to make sure the markets in this area can flourish without anticompetitive constraints imposed by any company.[78]

---

73 Case No COMP/AT.39740, Google Search (Shopping) [2017] 4444 Final, para 594.
74 ibid para 595.
75 ibid para 596.
76 ibid para 597.
77 Ariel Ezrachi and Maurice Stucke, 'Emerging Antitrust Threats and Enforcement Actions in The Online World' (2017) 13 Competition Law International 2, 8.
78 European Commission, Press Release, 'Antitrust: Commission sends Statement of Objections to Google on Comparison Shopping Service; Opens Separate Formal Investigation on Android' (Brussels, 15 April 2015) <https://ec.europa.eu/commission/presscorner/detail/en/IP_15_4780>

138 *Abusive Behaviour in Data-Driven Markets*

Like the search engine market, Google holds worldwide dominance in the mobile operating systems market via Android. Google acquired the original Android Inc. back in 2005, and the first commercial Android phones were released in 2008.[79]

The Android system is based on Linux, and the source code of Android is freely available through the Android open-source project (AOSP). As a result, developers and companies can freely use the system theoretically. The majority of mobile device manufacturers in the world use Google's mobile operating system on their tablets and smartphones, which indicates the dominance of Google in the market.[80] In the market of mobile operating systems, Google and Apple have their own ecosystems, consisting of a wide array of applications and libraries.[81] Although using the Android OS is free of charge, the Commission found that Google controls its operating system through various licensing agreements with device manufacturers. Through the AOSP licences, Google gives device manufacturers the Google Play Store and Google Play Service licences.[82] According to these contractual conditions, Google incentivises and requires device manufacturers to exclusively pre-install the Google search application and Chrome browser as a result of licensing the Google Play Store to manufacturers. Moreover, Google shares revenue with certain manufacturers that do not pre-install rival applications.

The requirements imposed by Google on manufacturers were ultimately found to be anti-competitive since the conduct significantly distorted competition by disincentivising manufacturers to pre-install other search and web browser applications. The conduct also reduces consumers' incentives to download third-party applications.[83] According to Vestager, people who buy Android smartphones do not change the default applications of search and browsers in their phones.[84] Therefore, a "choice evasion" problem arises since the abusive practice reduces consumers' choices.[85] Since most consumers do not change default applications on their phones, Google sees the opportunity to require device manufacturers to pre-install Google apps and not install rival applications; thus, Google leverages its market power by tying practices.[86]

In addition to tying its services to the Google Play Store licences, the *Google Android* case also draws attention to conditions in which device manufacturers who want to install their own services or Google's rival services will not get a licence for

---

79 Case No. COMP/AT.40099, *Google Android* [2018] 4761 Final, para 123.
80 European Commission Press Release (n 78).
81 Web browser, email, alarm, media player, SMS/MMS service, photo service, games, OpenGL/ES, SSL, WEBKIT and many others.
82 Case No. COMP/AT.39740, *Google Search (Shopping)* [2017] 4444 Final, paras 155–56.
83 Ariel Ezrachi and Maurice Stucke, 'Emerging Antitrust Threats and Enforcement Actions in The Online World' (2017) 13 Competition Law International 2, 8.
84 Only 1% of consumers change their search apps, and only 10% of them change their mobile web browser. Matthew Cole, 'Does the EU Commission Really Hate the US? Understanding the Google Decision Through Competition Theory' (2019) 44 European Law Review 4, 487.
85 Cole (n 81).
86 ibid 488.

the Google Play Store, where Google's dominance characterises the market.[87] Even Microsoft's and BlackBerry's own stores could not compete with Android and Apple, which led them to use Android OS by acquiring various licences from Google. In such a situation, Google dominates the mobile operating system market and can leverage its market power into integrated markets in the ecosystem and exclude rivals' services both in the upstream operating system and the downstream integrated markets. In other words, concerns are not only about Google tying its mobile applications to the Android OS but also include a competition problem that device manufacturers face if they want to pre-install third-party applications and want access to the Google Play Store.[88] As a result, Google was fined €4.3 billion by the Commission a year after the *Google Search* decision. This case is important specifically because both decisions demonstrate a special responsibility and legal obligation under which dominant undertakings in the online world, such as Google, Amazon, Apple and Microsoft, should not exclude rival services from their ecosystems by leveraging their market power as platform owners through tying or self-preferencing practices.

Regarding the Google Search investigation, Frank Pasquale focuses on claims made by Foundem (Infederation Ltd.), a UK-based vertical search advertising company that filed a complaint against Google in 2010. According to claims, Foundem does not have the mass user base and critical data to be able to compete with Google; thus, they are excluded from the market by Google. Only six months after Foundem launched, it was claimed that Google blocked Foundem from appearing on the first page of organic search results (Google Search) regarding price comparison services.[89] Google defended itself by claiming Foundem has a lower-quality, inferior service; Google's algorithms distinguish better services before they create organic results and show them to consumers.[90] In addition, the main role of a search engine should be to serve the best possible search results to consumers at the top of the results page. However, this means that smaller rivals are excluded from the top of the results page, which is necessary for them to be present in the market. In addition, Google seems to divert traffic from smaller companies to discourage them from succeeding as online advertisement providers. In other words, Google controls the market and limits its rivals' access to the end consumers, where Google's own service is always prevalent and is seen at the top of the page in every search query. Therefore, feedback loops feed Google with more data, which, in turn, is used for better-quality services. At the same time, rivals such as Foundem are downranked, reducing their visibility on the organic search results page.[91] Regarding the paid results section of the search page, Google seems to cut off rival companies' ability to reach end consumers.[92]

---

87 Inge Graef, 'Rethinking the Essential Facilities Doctrine for the EU Digital Economy' (2019) 53(1) Revue juridique Thémis de l'Université de Montréal 33–72, 49.
88 ibid.
89 Frank Pasquale, *The Black Box Society: The Secret Algorithms That Control Money and Information* (1st edn, Harvard UP 2015) 67.
90 ibid.
91 ibid.
92 ibid.

On the other hand, Bork and Sidak argue that allegations about Google depriving its competitors of achieving scale are actually not true. One of the base arguments in the study is the necessity of scale. Google was not the first-mover undertaking in the search engine market. It started its business after AltaVista, Yahoo! and many others.[93] However, Google has still managed to surpass its rivals. In the same way, newcomers could well surpass Google also. The study emphasized that the difference between "necessary to compete" and "necessary to succeed" would not change competition law assessment since competition does not impose a duty on dominant undertakings to ensure the profitability of their smaller rivals.[94] In other words, the study stresses that achieving an "efficient scale" cannot be a benchmark for the analysis.

The first reason is that the user data required to be competitive or serve quality products is not that much. They give the example of Google from 2003, when Google only had 42.9 million users but had market dominance.[95] On the other hand, Google's biggest rival, Bing, had 122 million users in 2012.[96] However, the numbers do not support the argument. Conversely, numbers demonstrate how the accumulation of user data was important during the early 2000s, creating a huge barrier for Google's rivals in time. In other words, the data of 40 million and more users accumulated each year and contributed to the creation of an enormous competitive advantage for Google, also thanks to improvements in data-collection and processing methods. Later, in the Microsoft/Yahoo! merger, the Commission correctly identified that Yahoo! and Microsoft lacked the scale to compete with Google.[97]

Bork and Sidak stress the necessity of advertising revenues for innovation in the online search advertising market. They argue that scale is unnecessary to gain advertising revenues; thus, these revenues cannot be decisive in funding product improvements and innovation.[98] In addition, indirect network effects in the market do not create barriers for newcomers.[99] In a sense, funding for improvements and innovation can be substituted when advertising revenues are significantly lacking. However, it has already been proven wrong in Chapter 4 that indirect network effects are barriers to entry in data-driven markets. Moreover, the indirect network effect structure is the predominant structure and one of the unique characteristics of data-driven markets. Therefore, the claim that search engines do not benefit from indirect network externalities is wrong.[100] All this information suggests that the structures of the search engine and online advertising markets are shaped by indirect network effects. Multi-sidedness requires market players to achieve an

93 Bork and Sidak (n 68) 666.
94 ibid 687.
95 ibid 690.
96 ibid.
97 Case No COMP/M.5727, Microsoft/Yahoo! Search Business C [2010] 1077 Final, paras 136–49.
98 Bork and Sidak (n 68) 692.
99 ibid.
100 ibid.

"efficient scale" to compete online. Therefore, without achieving the necessary scale, smaller rivals cannot attract consumers to their services, cannot gain revenues through online advertising, and cannot fund their services for improvements. Although advertisement revenues are not the only source, they are needed for almost all newcomers with no significant capital or funds.

5.1.3 "Frenemy" Situation in Multi-Sided Markets

Companies such as Google and Apple own and control vast online ecosystems where hundreds and thousands of independent companies compete against each other in the mobile device application markets.[101] Moreover, both companies rely on advertisement revenues. Almost all Google's revenue flows through 'targeted advertisements', in which the company relies on data collection and processing methods to maintain its competitive advantage.[102] With an inherent competitive advantage due to the data collection and processing techniques, platform owners have many opportunities to introduce and serve their own products in their ecosystems that foreclose rival third-party suppliers.[103] A platform owner can exclude or destroy the rival applications inside its platform.[104] In other words, third-party providers' fates are in the hands of platform owners. In addition, the introduction of additional applications and services provides more sources of fresh data for collection purposes to platform owners, which ultimately strengthens the positions of the companies.

The situation indicates a "frenemy" situation.[105] Ariel Ezrachi and Maurice Stucke proposed the word in order to capture the "dual role" of platform owners since horizontal, vertical or conglomerate phrases are not flexible enough to capture the dynamics of the new economy.[106] The rise of ecosystems and platform-based competition indicates an increasing "friend" and "enemy" situation in data-driven markets. On one side, the platform owners and independent content providers/sellers have a friendly relationship in which third parties benefit from being on the platform. As a result, the traffic increases. As discussed in Chapter 4, indirect network externalities are present in these ecosystems. On the other side, the "enemy" relationship refers to rivalry against platform owners and independent sellers/providers. Platform owners are direct rivals for third parties on platforms

---

101 OECD, *Exploring the Economics of Personal Data: A Survey of Methodologies for Measuring Monetary Value*, OECD Digital Economy Papers, No. 220 (OECD Publishing 2013) 15 <https://www.oecd-ilibrary.org/science-and-technology/exploring-the-economics-of-personal-data_5k486qtxldmq-en>
102 Maurice E Stucke and Allen Grunes, *Big Data and Competition Policy* (1st edn, OUP 2016) 293.
103 ibid.
104 Keith Hylton, 'Digital Platforms and Antitrust Law' (2019) Boston University School of Law, Law and Economics Research Paper No. 19-8, 7.
105 Ariel Ezrachi and Maurice Stucke, *Virtual Competition: The Promise and Perils of the Algorithm-Driven Economy* (1st edn, Harvard UP 2016) Part IV.
106 ibid 147.

where competition occurs multi-dimensionally.[107] For instance, within these ecosystems, web browser application creators compete on the platform (in an app market such as Apple Store). These applications compete not only on that platform but also with other applications on other ecosystems (the other app market, Google Play). On top of that, both these ecosystems also compete against each other.[108] Commentators argue that the future of online ecosystems lies in digital personal assistants and advanced artificial intelligence products.[109] Personal assistants such as Siri (Apple), Cortana (Microsoft), Alexa (Amazon), M (Facebook) and Google Assistant will become gatekeepers for humans to reach the online world for communication, news, restaurant searches, hotels, shopping and basically everything.[110] Transformation is happening, and each is ultimately the "mouth" of the ecosystem where almost all digital competition occurs.

One of the first examples of frenemy abuse in data-driven markets is Microsoft's browser strategy on desktop computers in the 1990s. Microsoft had the monopoly position in the Intel- based computer operating systems market through its platform, Windows OS. In its platform, many third-party software creators designed applications for Windows. That said, Netscape was a successful web browser designed for Windows in the 90s. However, Microsoft saw the opportunity and introduced a free browser, Internet Explorer, which also operates as a part of the Windows OS. According to Microsoft, the move was a successful innovation that improved the quality of services by integrating the two services, and consumers eventually benefited from it.[111] However, as an inevitable end, Microsoft's rivals, such as Netscape and Opera, were excluded from the market, and Microsoft restricted access to the market due to Internet Explorer. Consequently, the conduct of integrating the web browser into the operating system was found to be abusive by the US Supreme Court.[112]

In the 2000s, companies like Google and Apple followed the same route. These companies integrated many services into their platform by introducing new applications or data-driven acquisitions. For instance, an independent developer (a former PayPal employee) innovated a vertical search engine called Yelp, with which consumers can search for nearby restaurants with integrated reviews.[113] Soon after, Google, as the ultimate platform owner of search engines, integrated service to the horizontal search engine, where consumers can search for nearby restaurants introduced with Google reviews. Due to Google's competitive advantage (scale, data and the gateway to the internet and the main horizontal search engine), the traffic was diverted from independent applications to Google. In other words, Google also took advantage of successful innovation and expanded its business to that

---

107 ibid.
108 ibid 149.
109 ibid 191.
110 ibid.
111 Hylton (n 104) 7.
112 Case *United States v Microsoft Corporation*, 253 F.3d 34 (D.C. Cir. 2001).
113 Hylton (n 104) 7.

market segment. This clearly indicates that any innovation and sub-platform is under Google's kill zone.[114]

Ecosystem owners have the luxury of sitting and waiting for a productive innovation that may occur in their ecosystems.[115] When the innovation starts to monetise, the platform owner moves in and integrates the service into its platform via its applications. Due to the network effects, efficient scale, and Big Data abilities, none of the independent developers would have a competitive advantage over platform owners. Alternatively, as in the case of YouTube and Google, the platform owner acquires the most successful service and integrates it into their ecosystem. In a word, platform owners such as Google have the market power to discriminate and exclude rival service providers from their platforms. In the US, in a dissenting opinion, Commissioner Thomas Rosch of the Federal Trade Commission expressed that "Vertical search engines – including the alleged 'victims' of Google's scraping – have continued to thrive and expand".[116] There is always a chance for healthy competition in these ecosystems, even if there is no explicit mitigation for the unhealthy structure and the possible discriminatory and exclusionary conduct.

In the absence of special responsibilities for the intermediaries – platform owners – with a dual role, possible discriminatory practices occur against independent product or service suppliers that rely on the platform of technology giants. As mentioned earlier, dominant undertakings acting as sellers and intermediaries for other sellers have an inherent competitive advantage over rivals by collecting and using data only available to them on the platform. European competition authorities try to unveil the systematic abuse of dominant undertakings involving data collection-processing methods and favouring practices (self-preferencing). As a result, a need for possible regulatory action for data-driven markets is revealed. Possible novel abuses and theories of harm were widely discussed in the Commission's Google investigation. Also, both the European Commission and the *Bundeskartellamt* investigated Amazon's conduct in the e-commerce market. Having a dual role just like Google, Amazon's role in e-commerce and its rivals' dependence on Amazon are alarming for healthy competition in the online world. Both companies' self-favouring practices in ecosystems where their rivals depend on them were found discriminatory.

In this sense, Pinar Akman examines Google's conduct in light of the current legal framework in order to reveal the relevance of self-preferencing conduct with discrimination. In a non-exhaustive list, Article 102 indicates that "applying dissimilar conditions to equivalent transactions with other trading parties, thereby

---

114 ibid.
115 ibid 8.
116 Federal Trade Commission, Concurring and Dissenting Statement of Commissioner J Thomas Rosch Regarding Google's Search Practices, FTC File No. 111-0163 (2012) <https://www.ftc.gov/sites/default/files/documents/public_statements/concurring-and-dissenting-statement-commissioner-j.thomas-rosch-regarding-googles-search-practices/130103googlesearchstmt.pdf>

placing them at a competitive disadvantage" may be abusive.[117] As the Commission found Google's favouring abusive and remedied the abuse by equal treatment of comparison shopping services by Google, Akman suggests discussing several factors concerning the applicability of this rule to the relevant case.[118] According to the study, conditions of "transaction with other parties", "competitive disadvantage", "applying dissimilar conditions" and "relevance of vertical integration" do not apply to the case, and discrimination is non-existent in Google's conduct.

First, the study suggests that transactions with other parties are non-existent since there are no identifiable transactions between Google and other comparison shopping services.[119] However, there is a clear commercial link and transaction where Google provides space on its search results page to the suppliers of advertisements (from third-party advertisers), recognised as comparison shopping services just like Google. On top of that, there are no plausible alternatives for the "provided space" since 90% of the EU uses the service for online search and shopping. The absence of a contract or a fee between the parties does not reverse the situation since nearly all online shopping traffic flows from Google's search engine, and Google is also a trading party with other comparison shopping services. As a result, a clear competitive advantage occurs when Google favours its own services in the ecosystem, unlike the study suggests. However, due to the competition regulation being inherently lacking in identifying the dual roles of ecosystem owners and also free-of-charge transactions in the online world, it can be deduced that the main problem stems from the current legal framework.

Additionally, applying dissimilar conditions to equivalent transactions in a vertically integrated market clause is the reason Google's conduct does not fit into the case law under Article 102, according to the study.[120] Akman suggests that discrimination theory can only be relevant if Google is vertically integrated on more than one level of services.[121] In other words, Google comparison shopping services and the Google search engine must be separate markets first, and then they must also be vertically integrated.[122] Akman also questions the vertical relationship between Google's services. The problem here is also related to regulatory shortcomings. First, the relevant market definition is problematic for these types of online ecosystems. Second, searching for a horizontal or vertical relationship in a platform where the whole platform could be just one relevant market or segments that function as a single market is also problematic. For this reason, the Commission underlines that: "Google's conduct would also have potential anti-competitive effects even if comparison shopping services did not constitute a distinct relevant product market, *but rather a segment of a possible broader relevant product market* comprising

---

117 Article 102 of the TFEU.
118 Akman (n 51) 301, 327.
119 ibid 329–30.
120 ibid 339.
121 ibid.
122 ibid.

both comparison shopping services and merchant platforms".[123] Contrary to the argument which suggests self-preferencing cannot be deemed abusive if there is no upstream or downstream relation between Google's services, the problem clearly shows that "the theory of discrimination" in the current legal framework is not effective enough.

The most recent investigation involving the dual role of an intermediary can be found in the complaint Spotify filed with the European Commission against Apple music streaming, followed by another complaint regarding Apple audiobooks and e-books in June 2020.[124] Both investigations are about the possible abuse by Apple in its ecosystem. In Margrethe Vestager's words:

> Mobile applications have fundamentally changed the way we access content. Apple sets the rules for the distribution of apps to users of iPhones and iPads. It appears that Apple obtained a "gatekeeper" role when it comes to the distribution of apps and content to users of Apple's popular devices. We need to ensure that Apple's rules do not distort competition in markets where Apple is competing with other app developers, for example with its music streaming service Apple Music or with Apple Books.[125]

The CEO of Spotify expresses that since Apple is both a competitor and an intermediary, it continuously gives itself an unfair advantage, such as excessively taxing its rivals, which puts them in a disadvantageous position.[126] In the long run, this exclusionary and discriminatory conduct limits choices for consumers while also stifling innovation.[127]

In this sense, the *Google AdSense* case is another important competition investigation Google faced in the EU in addition to the *Search* and *Android* cases. In the AdSense investigation, Google was found to be conducting abusive behaviour by preventing rivals from competing in the search advertising intermediation market and imposing contractual restrictions on third-party websites.[128] "AdSense for Search" is an intermediary platform of Google that operates in online search advertising. In the EEA, both Google and AdSense held market shares of over 75% at

---

123 Summary of Commission decision of 27 June 2017, relating to a proceeding under Article 102 of the Treaty on the Functioning of the European Union and Article 54 of the EEA Agreement (Case AT.39740 *Google Search (Shopping)*) para 25 (emphasis added).
124 European Commission, Press Release, 'Antitrust: Commission Opens Investigations into Apple's App Store Rules' (Brussels, 16 June 2020) <https://ec.europa.eu/commission/presscorner/detail/en/ip_20_1073>
125 ibid.
126 Daniel Ek, 'A Level Playing Field, Consumers and Innovators Win on a Level Playing Field' *Newsroom Spotify* (13 March 2019) <https://newsroom.spotify.com/2019-03-13/consumers-and-innovators-win-on-a-level-playing-field>
127 ibid.
128 European Commission, Press Release, 'Antitrust: Commission Fines Google €1.49 Billion for Abusive Practices in Online Advertising' (Brussels, 20 March 2019) <https://ec.europa.eu/commission/presscorner/detail/en/IP_19_1770>

the time of the investigation. The situation indicates how much power Google has over the European ad intermediation market. Google negotiates and agrees with third-party publishers in online search advertising intermediation services. The Commission has found hundreds of agreements that include exclusivity clauses on third-party publishers in its investigation.[129]

The ruling has revealed that Google started to prohibit publishers from placing any advertisements from Google's competitors in the Google ecosystem starting in 2006.[130] Three years later, Google introduced the "Premium Placement" clause in its contracts with publishers, requiring publishers to promote Google-related advertisements and put them in the best possible places on the Google search results page. Therefore, almost all first-seen advertisements belonging to Google and rivals were prevented from being in a visible spot on the search results page. New contracts for third-party advertisement providers also include clauses requiring these publishers to obtain Google's authorisation before making any changes to promoting its rivals' advertisements. Overall, Google has taken control of the online search advertising intermediation market due to its super dominance in the search engine and online advertising markets. It has also shielded its dominance from the competition through exclusivity contracts imposing contractual restrictions on third-party advertisements provided online.[131] The abusive conduct lasted at least a decade and negatively affected healthy competition and innovation. As a result, Google was fined €1.49 billion by the Commission for abusing its dominance by vertically integrating its search services and online advertising intermediation services and creating exclusivity contracts with advertisement publishers in its ecosystem.

These cases show that competition law assessment must be engaged with extreme caution regarding online ecosystems by considering the multi-sided nature of the markets and the ecosystem structures, as stressed in Chapter 4. To draw an analogy, a soccer team cannot compete with its rival if the other team also regulates the rules of the match; holds all data which is not available for them regarding wind, stadium, players and other instruments; and even becomes the referee as well as being a soccer team. The investigations against Google, Apple and Amazon and the given decisions hopefully set a precedent for the dual-role abuses and leveraging market power theories in data-driven markets, ultimately opening the way for possible regulatory action in the future.

5.2 Abuse Through Access to Data

The previous discussion demonstrates how data-rich undertakings take advantage of their datasets and leverage their market power in various ways. Data-driven markets are multi-sided, and data-rich undertakings form online ecosystems where dominant undertakings become the actual decision-makers for the ecosystem.

---

129 ibid.
130 ibid
131 ibid.

Thus, assessing these abuses through the current tools, such as existing abuse types and assessment criteria for abuse of dominant position, is found to be inefficient. That means the existing abuse types and criteria for anti-competitive conduct are not well suited to data-driven markets. In addition to the findings in Chapter 4, which are the economic tools' ineffectiveness in assessing dominance and defining relevant product markets in data-driven markets, the identification of data-related abuse is also highly challenging. In other words, data is not just used for leveraging market power strategies, as discussed earlier. Refusal to supply critical data might also become an abusive behaviour of data-rich undertakings.

5.2.1 Refusal to Access and Discriminatory Access

As Chapter 3 identifies Big Data as the most important component for creating new value chains in the online world, data exploitation may become a huge risk for the market economy and competition. The starting point should be to understand data-driven businesses' core structure and strategies.[132] Commentators argue that undertakings such as Google aim to prevent their rivals from utilising data that fuels AI-driven algorithms.[133] The emphasis should be on how much competitive advantage the data provided to these companies.[134]

As examined in the previous sections of this chapter, data was mostly a tool for the abuse scenarios. Moreover, data can be the subject of the abuse itself. Possessing huge datasets unavailable for rivals or entrants leads to market dominance.[135] However, the dominance based on data possession is related to data's substitutability,

---

132 Vikas Kathuria and Jure Globocnik, 'Exclusionary Conduct in Data-Driven Markets: Limitations of Data Sharing Remedy' (2019) Max Planck Institute for Innovation and Competition Research Paper No. 19-04, 3.
133 ibid.
134 David S Evans, 'Antitrust Issues Raised by the Emerging Global Internet Economy' (2008) 102 Northwestern University Law Review; Inge Graef, 'Market Definition and Market Power in Data: The Case of Online Platforms' (2105) 38 World Competition *2015 4, 479–80, 483–89; Nathan Newman, 'Search, Antitrust, and the Economics of the Control of User Data' (2014) 31 Yale Journal on Regulation 2; Andres V Lerner, 'The Role of "Big Data" in Online Platform Competition' (2014) SSRN Working Paper* August 2014 <http://papers.ssrn.com/sol3/papers.cfm?abstract_id=2482780>; Darren S Tucker and Hill B Wellford, 'Big Mistakes Regarding Big Data' [2014] 14 Antitrust Source 1; Maurice E Stucke and Allen P Grunes, 'No Mistake About It: The Important Role of Antitrust in the Era of Big Data' (2015) The Antitrust Source April, University of Tennessee Legal Studies Research Paper No. 269; Daniel D Sokol and Roisin E Comerford, 'Does Antitrust Have a Role to Play in Regulating Big Data?' in Roger D Blair and Daniel D Sokol (eds), *Cambridge Handbook of Antitrust, Intellectual Property and High Technology* (CUP 2017); David A Balto and Matthew Lane, 'Monopolizing Water in a Tsunami: Finding Sensible Antitrust Rules for Big Data' (2016) SSRN Working Paper March 2016 <https://ssrn.com/abstract=2753249>
135 Jacques Crémer, Yves-Alexandre de Montjoye and Heike Schweitzer, *Competition Policy for the Digital Era: Final Report* (Publications Office of the European Union 2019) 49 <http://ec.europa.eu/competition/information/digitisation_2018/report_en.html>; Pinar Akman, 'Competition Policy In A Globalized, Digitalized Economy' White Paper Series (World Economic Forum 2019) 10 <https://www.weforum.org/whitepapers/competition-policy-in-a-globalized-digitalized-economy>

utilisability and effects on scale economies.[136] As it is generally considered that data collection has diminishing returns to scale where the benefits of having extra data do not give additional value depending on the volume of personal information,[137] it is argued that if the additional value only starts to diminish at astronomical levels, then a competitive advantage can easily be observed for the dominant players.[138] In addition to the volume of data, the variety and velocity of data also contribute to the market power in this sense.[139] Regarding the variety of data, the European Commission expresses that "Competition based on the quality of collected data ... is not only decided by virtue of the sheer size of the respective databases, but also determined by the different types of data the competitors have access to".[140]

The Furman Report focuses on possible competitive advantages provided by the possession of exclusive data.[141] For instance, the study mentions the competitive scene in the search engine market. A potential rival to Google which has fewer search queries to process has fewer data for its algorithms and organic results. This, in turn, results in less accurate search results for consumers.[142] As a matter of course, consumers who choose to use Google fuel the problem in the market in terms of excessive data collection and processing.[143] However, the Furman Report also expresses that the available evidence for having exclusive data or huge levels of data advantage for competition and barriers to entry is actually mixed.[144] For instance, in the cases of Netflix,[145] Uber, Airbnb,[146] Facebook, Snapchat and Tinder,[147] the returns to scale of data in their markets seemed to diminish rapidly

---

136 Jason Furman, 'Unlocking Digital Competition: Report of the Digital Competition Expert Panel' (2019) 33 <https://www.gov.uk/government/publications/unlocking-digital-competition-report-of-the-digital-competition-expert-panel>
137 Elena Argentesi and others, 'Ex-Post Assessment of Merger Control Decisions in Digital Markets' LEAR Final Report (2019) 139 <https://www.learlab.com/publication/ex-post-assessment-of-merger-control-decisions-in-digital-markets/>; Andres V Lerner, 'The Role of Big Data in Online Platform Competition' (2014) SSRN Working Paper August 2014, 41–44 <http://papers.ssrn.com/sol3/papers.cfm?abstract_id=2482780>; Howard A Shelanski, 'Information, Innovation, and Competition Policy for the Internet' (2013) 161 University of Pennsylvania Law Review 6, 1681.
138 Inge Graef, 'Data as Essential Facility: Competition and Innovation on Online Platforms' (PhD Thesis, KU Leuven Faculty of Law 2016) 247.
139 Furman Report (n 136) 34; Graef (n 138) 247.
140 Case No COMP/M.4731 *Google/DoubleClick* C[2008] 927 final, para 273.
141 Furman Report (n 136).
142 ibid; also Marc Bourreau, Alexandre de Steel and Inge Graef, 'Big Data and Competition Policy: Market Power, Personalised Pricing and Advertising' (2017) Centre on Regulation in Europe Project Report.
143 ibid.
144 ibid.
145 Xavier Amatriain, '10 Lessons Learned from Building Machine Learning Systems' (2014) MLconf 2014 San Francisco <https://mlconf.com/sessions/10-lessons-learned-from-building-real-life-large-s/>
146 Pinar Akman, 'Competition Policy IN A Globalized, Digitalized Economy' White Paper Series (World Economic Forum 2019) 10 <https://www.weforum.org/whitepapers/competition-policy-in-a-globalized-digitalized-economy>
147 Maren Tamke, 'Big Data and Competition Law' (2017) Zeitschrift für Wettbewerbsrecht 4, 366.

as time has revealed. Ultimately, these companies have managed to disrupt incumbents and even acquired market dominance for themselves due to the fact that their fewer datasets did not hinder their growth in the online world.[148] The inclusion of indirect network effects and ecosystem structures in the equation supports the idea that large datasets provide incumbents with a competitive advantage. Therefore, Akman et al. argue that further empirical research is necessary in engaging market power and abuse of dominant position in the online world to understand the characteristics of Big Data that could easily lead to barriers to entry and dominance.[149]

In a case in which a dominant company holds exclusive data or huge datasets that are incomparable to those of its rivals, which includes information on consumers, shopping habits or the market itself, there might be certain liabilities for the dominant player. In the previous chapters, the prominent role of Big Data in the operation of online businesses has been discussed. In light of this, refusal to supply crucial and necessary data to competitors may become a huge concern since dominant undertakings can take control of how much personal information their rivals can access inside an ecosystem. In EU competition law, exclusive supply liability is not a new phenomenon.[150] Monopolies or dominant players deprive their rivals through exclusive dealing and refusal to supply critical outputs. In its guidelines for Article 102 cases, the Commission expresses that the dominant players may try to foreclose the market by hindering the ability of their rivals to enter into commercial transactions.[151] Exclusive supply obligations are a part of exclusive dealings, and the Commission considers that these anti-competitive actions both have the same foreclosure effects.[152] In these scenarios where refusal to supply is engaged by dominant players, rivals might not find alternative sources for crucial input supply. Therefore, production or sales become impossible for competitors. At this point, the conduct of the dominant undertaking becomes anti-competitive due to the foreclosure effects.

As discussed in Chapter 3, the accumulation of Big Data is a real concern for data-driven markets. Thus, the results of having vast numbers of datasets are not limited to leveraging market power theories. Competitive concerns may arise for refusal to access or discriminatory access to data situations. Commissioner Pamela Jones Harbour expresses that "Google aims to merge not only the two leading technology companies but also aims to combine their data for advertising purposes

---

148 Sokol and Comerford (n 134) 5.
149 Akman (n 146) 10.
150 Damien Geradin, 'Limiting the Scope of Article 82 of the EC Treaty: What Can the EU Learn from the U.S. Supreme Court's Judgment in Trinko in the Wake of Microsoft, IMS, and Deutsche Telekom' (2004) 41 Common Market Law Review 1519.
151 Communication from the European Commission, Guidance on the Commission's enforcement priorities in applying Article 82 of the EC Treaty to abusive exclusionary conduct by dominant undertakings (Text with EEA relevance) [2009] OJ C45/9, para 32.
152 ibid para 32 footnote 4.

150 Abusive Behaviour in Data-Driven Markets

in its ecosystem".[153] Then how could Google make use of this data? Could they limit access to this data and foreclose the market? The Guidelines of the European Commission in applying Article 102 TFEU to abusive conduct state that several circumstances need to be present for a refusal to supply, which could be considered an enforcement priority. According to paragraph 81, the refusal of a product or service must be objectively necessary for the transactions on a downstream market; thus, the refusal must lead to the elimination of competition there, and there must be consumer harm.[154] Therefore, if a dominant player does not allow its current and potential competitors to access critical data in a downstream market inside an ecosystem, there might be special obligations for dominant players.

Regarding refusal to deal cases, even though many academics from the Chicago School advocate a non-interventionist approach since competition law is flawed in nature and markets tend to correct themselves,[155] Professor Dennis Carlton from the Chicago School expresses that competition law has a legitimate role in the refusal to deal type of anti-competitive conduct, especially in the new technology markets.[156] According to Carlton, the competition law intervention is plausible for dynamic industries since scale economies and network effects are key points there.[157] In these markets, small strategies designed to discriminate or to prevent rivals from growing can create huge competitive advantages for dominant players, like a snowball effect.[158]

In data-driven markets, the question of whether personal information is a critical input occurs for supply obligations. The main point is the necessity of data. If data is objectively indispensable for competition and the continuation of commercial transactions, then refusal to access data cases can be considered competition law infringements. Suppose data is an indispensable part of online businesses. In that case, denial of necessary data, refusal to give access to critical data or giving discriminatory access to critical data constitutes an abuse of a dominant position in terms of Article 102. At this point, the applicability of the "essential facilities doctrine" becomes an inseparable discussion for access to the data issue.[159] In the

---

153 Dissenting Statement of Commissioner Pamela Jones Harbour, In the Matter of Google/DoubleClick F.T.C. File No. 071-0170 (2007) <https://www.ftc.gov/sites/default/files/documents/public_statements/statement-matter-google/doubleclick/071220harbour_0.pdf>
154 Communication from the European Commission, Guidance on the Commission's Enforcement Priorities in Applying Article 82 of the EC Treaty to Abusive Exclusionary Conduct by Dominant Undertakings [2009] OJ C45/9, para 81.
155 Richard A Posner, *Antitrust Law* (2nd edn, Chicago UP 2001); Richard A Posner, *Economic Analysis of Law* (7th edn, Wolters Kluwer 2007); Robert H Bork, *The Antitrust Paradox: A Policy at War with Itself* (2nd edn, Basic Books 1993); Frank H Easterbrook, 'Limits of Antitrust' (1984) 63 Texas Law Review 1.
156 Dennis W Carlton, 'A General Analysis of Exclusionary Conduct and Refusal to Deal: Why Aspen and Kodak Are Misguided' (2001) 68 Antitrust Law Journal 3, 659–83.
157 ibid 668.
158 ibid.
159 Inge Graef, Sih Yuliana Wahyuningtyas and Peggy Vackle, 'Assessing Data Access Issues in Online Platforms' (2015) 39 Telecommunications Policy 5, 383; Damian Geradin and Monika Kuschewsky, 'Competition Law and Personal Data: Preliminary Thoughts on a Complex Issue' (2013) 2 Concurrences; Inge Graef, *EU Competition Law, Data Protection and Online Platforms: Data as Essential Facility* (1st edn, Kluwer Law International 2016).

following subsections, the ideas on remedies such as enforcing the essential facilities doctrine, mandatory data sharing and data portability as remedies are discussed in detail.

In addition to the refusal to supply cases, discriminatory access to critical data may lead to anti-competitive conduct as well. In their joint report, the *Bundeskartellamt* and the *Autorité de la Concurrence* state that discriminatory access to data is a type of abusive conduct which involves the exploitation of Big Data, just like refusal to supply and leveraging data advantage cases.[160] The report mentions the French case of Cegedim as an example.[161] Cegedim was challenged by the *Autorité de la Concurrence* back in 2014 for refusing to provide (sell) information from its medical database, which is called One Key, to its competitors. Cegedim was the leading provider of medical information datasets in France. However, customers for the medical databases of Cegedim were using customer relationship management software by a company called Euris, which is a rival of Cegedim.[162] To be clear, there are two levels of competition: one is for the software for customer relationship management in the health sector (between Cegedim and Euris), and the other is for providing healthcare solutions based on medical information, also a different market in the health sector. As the dominant player, Cegedim refused to sell medical information to undertakings that used the rival service Euris. By this means, Cegedim aimed to foreclose the software market. As a consequence, the discriminatory access to medical data hampered the development of Euris and distorted competition in the market between 2008 and 2012.[163]

A vertical relationship does not necessarily have to be present in the market for discriminatory access to data abuses.[164] The intention of providing an unduly competitive advantage to an undertaking over its rivals, such as a platform owner or an intermediary which is a direct competitor of other retailers in the market, may obtain data advantage, discriminate access to that data and foreclose the market.[165] The previous section already mentioned that a dominant player and an intermediary such as Amazon or Google have access to sensitive information that other competitors do not have since they have no control over the ecosystem. These dominant players can use the information about the transactions and consumer behaviour in favour of themselves to identify the market tendencies and trends better and efficiently adjust their products based on that data, whereas independent retailers cannot use these data. In theory, a similar outcome can also be achieved through discriminatory access to the same datasets.

---

160 *Bundeskartellamt* and *Autorité de la Concurrence* (n 160) 18–19.
161 French Competition Authority, Decision No: 14-D-06 Cegedim, 8 July 2014.
162 ibid.
163 *Bundeskartellamt* and *Autorité de la Concurrence* (n 160) 19.
164 OECD, Ania Thiemann and Pedro Gonzaga, 'Big Data: Bringing Competition Policy to the Digital Era' (2016) DAF/COMP (2016)14, 21, para 67.
165 ibid.

5.2.2 Applicability of Essential Facilities Doctrine

In their joint report, the *Bundeskartellamt* and the *Autorité de la Concurrence* express that if dominant players restrict access to such necessary data for the functioning of an online platform where their rivals are also operating, then possible limitations to required data might have distorting effects on competition.[166] In other words, abusive behaviour can deprive competitors of access to data and lead to their exclusion. In this situation, the joint report of German and French Competition Authorities expresses that refusal to access data becomes anti-competitive if data is an "essential facility" to the business activity.[167] Hence, the questions are: Is data an essential input for businesses? If yes, is applying the essential facilities doctrine suitable for data-driven markets?

In the recent past, some commentators argued that the collected personal information – or, to be exact, Big Data – does not have the qualifications to become an essential facility in terms of competition law. For instance, Andres Lerner stresses the non-exclusivity of user data and claims that all businesses can collect the same data that the incumbent already holds in the online world.[168] According to Lerner, the evidence can be found in "multi-homing" practices in which users share the same data with various platforms in the online world.[169] Thus, data becomes a non-rivalrous good for businesses. Balto and Lane also advocate that personal data is not, or at least should not be, essential for businesses, and the exclusivity of data is not possible for undertakings for acquisition purposes.[170] However, the Facebook/WhatsApp merger is a clear example of a data acquisition, in which WhatsApp had exclusive information which Facebook intended to monetise through online advertising. Today, the datasets of specific undertakings, such as super-dominant platform owners, should be regarded as exclusive to some extent. As mentioned several times before, entrants or even smaller rivals (independent sellers on a platform, for example) cannot collect the same data as ecosystem owners.

Secondly, Lerner argues that no one business could hold on to a massive amount of data, potentially creating a bottleneck. For example, Bing has vast datasets which could enable them to compete with Google.[171] To note, it was discussed in the previous chapter that the European Commission acknowledges Bing lacked the scale and also network externalities to compete with Google. This was one of the main reasons the Commission gave the green light to the Microsoft/Yahoo merger. Supporting Lerner's idea, Tucker, Wellford, Sokol and Comerford advocate the non-rivalrous nature of data, express that data is a critical input and state that even

---

166 *Bundeskartellamt* and *Autorité de la Concurrence* (n 160) 19.
167 ibid 17.
168 Lerner (n 137) 20–21.
169 ibid 21.
170 David A Balto and Matthew Lane, 'Monopolizing Water in a Tsunami: Finding Sensible Antitrust Rules for Big Data' (2016) 3, SSRN Working Paper March 2016, SSRN <https://ssrn.com/abstract=2753249>
171 Lerner (n 137) 23–24.

companies without a sizeable amount of data could have expanded in the online world and become dominant players.[172] Sokol and Comerford mention companies such as Facebook, Snapchat, Tinder and Slack, which all accomplished rapid success while lacking a clear data advantage and without any established network effects.[173] Additionally, Lambrecht and Tucker argue that Big Data is a substitutable input for undertakings. They relate the success of online service providers such as Facebook and Tinder to successfully understanding and meeting consumers' needs.[174] According to them, there is just a little evidence that indicates the success of digital businesses in providing better products or services that stem from the possession of Big Data.

Although the new entrants mentioned here have succeeded in the online world, arguments based around data that downplay Big Data's role are an outcome of the newness of the phenomenon itself. OECD underlines that business strategies based on Big Data and other technological developments such as machine learning and algorithms are fairly new, and the market structures are quite different now from when companies like Facebook, Google, Snapchat and Tinder first entered the market.[175] Therefore, it is quite possible that data-driven markets have already reached a point where new entrants cannot exert competitive pressure over incumbents. Due to ecosystem characteristics, it becomes even harder for new companies to dethrone established ones.[176] Nevertheless, it is necessary to discuss the essential facilities doctrine as a remedy if Big Data is an indispensable input, as commentators claim.[177] On top of that, indispensability is not enough for the essential facilities doctrine to be applied in data-driven markets. Established case law must be studied in the first place.

Although the essential facilities doctrine has never been formally recognised by the CJEU in their judgments,[178] it is applied narrowly only in situations where there is no alternate way for competitors to operate in the market due to the lack of input.[179] In the EU, the first case related to the essential facilities doctrine was the *Commercial Solvents* case.[180] The case was about the abuse of a dominant position

---

172 Darren S Tucker and Hill B Wellford, 'Big Mistakes Regarding Big Data' (2014) 14 Antitrust Source 1, 7–8; D Daniel Sokol and Roisin Comerford, 'Antitrust and Regulating Big Data' (2016) 23 George Mason Law Review 5 1129, 1136.
173 Sokol and Comerford (n 172) 1136.
174 Anja Lambrecht and Catherine E Tucker, 'Can Big Data Protect a Firm from Competition?' (2015) SSRN Paper 15 <https://ssrn.com/abstract=2705530>
175 Thiemann and Gonzaga (n 164) 22.
176 ibid.
177 Graef, Yuliana Wahyuningtyas and Vackle (n 159) 375–87.
178 Inge Graef, 'Rethinking the Essential Facilities Doctrine for the EU Digital Economy' (2019) 53(1) Revue juridique Thémis de l'Université de Montréal 33–72, 34.
179 Vikas Kathuria and Jure Globocnik, 'Exclusionary Conduct in Data-Driven Markets: Limitations of Data Sharing Remedy' (2019) Max Planck Institute for Innovation and Competition Research Paper No. 19-04, 6; for more information: Geradin (n 159) 1519–53.
180 Cases 6 and 7/73 *Istituto Chemioterapico Italiano and Commercial Solvents v Commission* [1974] ECLI:EU:C:1974:18.

and liabilities due to having a dominant position in the market. Commercial Solvents produces a chemical material used to produce ethambutol, a medication for tuberculosis. At that time, the rival of Commercial Solvents, Zoja, was dependent on the raw chemical from Commercial Solvents to produce ethambutol. However, Commercial Solvents refused to supply the material to Zoja. The Court of Justice ruled that Commercial Solvents, as the dominant player, abused its position by declining to supply the chemical substance to Zoja and tried to eliminate them from the ethambutol market. The Court expressed that:

> an undertaking being in a dominant position as regards the production of raw material and therefore able to control the supply to manufacturers of derivatives, cannot... act in such a way as to eliminate their competition which... amount to eliminating one of the principal manufacturers of ethambutol in the Common Market.[181]

This was the first case related to abuse through an essential input used by rivals in the market. Although many cases followed reasoning similar to the *Commercial Solvents* case,[182] the fundamental conditions in applying essential facilities doctrine were established by the CJEU in the *Bronner*,[183] *Microsoft*,[184] and *IMS Health*[185] cases.

In the *Bronner* case, the CJEU set conditions more clearly for the claims in which dominant undertakings refuse to share or refuse access to an essential input for products or services.[186] Most importantly, the indispensability requirement was brought to the application of the doctrine in the *Bronner* Case.[187] The case was about a publisher of a couple of newspapers, Mediaprint, and its rival in the newspaper market, a local newspaper company, Bronner, which was denied access to Mediaprint's national delivery scheme.[188] In its ruling, the CJEU repeated the already-established requirements: (1) the elimination of competition in the downstream or the secondary market and (2) the lack of objective justification.[189]

---

181 ibid para 25.
182 Case C-311/84 *CBEM v CLT & IPB (Télémarketing)* [1985] ECLI:EU:C:1985:394; Case C-53/87 *Renault v Maxicar* [1988] ECLI:EU:C:1988:472; Case C-238/87 *Volvo v Eric Veng* [1988] ECLI:EU:C:1988:477; Joined cases C-241/91 and C-242/91 *Telefis Eireann and Independent Television Publications Ltd v Commission of the European Communities (Magill)* [1995] ECLI:EU:C:1995:98.
183 Case C-7/97 *Oscar Bronner GmbH & Co. KG v Mediaprint Zeitungs- und Zeitschriftenverlag GmbH & Co. KG and others* [1998] ECLI:EU:C:1998:569.
184 Case T-201/4 *Microsoft Corp. v Commission of the European Communities* [2007] ECLI:EU:T:2007:289.
185 Case C-418/01 *IMS Health GmbH & Co. OHG v NDC Health GmbH & Co. KG.* [2004] ECLI:EU:C: 2004:257.
186 Paul Lugard and Lee Roach, 'The Era of "Big Data" and EU/U.S. Divergence for Refusals to Deal' (2017) 31(2) Antitrust 60.
187 Graef (n 178); Inge Graef, 'Data as Essential Facility: Competition and Innovation on Online Platforms' (PhD Thesis, KU Leuven Faculty of Law 2016) 170.
188 Case C-7/97 *Oscar Bronner GmbH & Co. KG v Mediaprint Zeitungs- und Zeitschriftenverlag GmbH & Co. KG and others* [1998] ECLI:EU:C:1998:569, para 8.
189 ibid para 41.

On top of that, as the third requirement, the CJEU ruled that access to necessary input must be indispensable where there are no economically viable actual or potential substitutes that could be chosen alternatively.[190]

In this sense, the indispensability requirement has an objective character where refusal to access an essential input must put rivals into a situation in which replicating the facility or producing the product is not economically viable. Consequently, replication or substitution cannot be expected from them.[191] Later, in the *IMS Health* case, these three conditions were repeated. According to the CJEU:

> It is clear from that case law that, in order for the refusal by an undertaking which owns a copyright to give access to a product or service indispensable for carrying on a particular business to be treated as abusive, it is sufficient that three cumulative conditions be satisfied, namely, that that refusal is preventing the emergence of a new product for which there is a potential consumer demand, that it is unjustified and such as to exclude any competition on a secondary market.[192]

More recently, the *Microsoft* case before the General Court demonstrates that the view of the court is to apply essential facilities doctrine only under exceptional circumstances.[193] According to the ruling in *Microsoft*, the General Court held that the following circumstances must be considered exceptional, and potential infringements could only be present when there are no objective justifications.[194] These are:

> (1) the refusal relates to a product or service indispensable to the exercise of a particular activity on a neighbouring market; (2) the refusal is of such a kind as to exclude any effective competition on that neighbouring market; (3) the refusal prevents the appearance of a new product for which there is potential consumer demand.[195]

In light of this information regarding the refusal-to-deal in case law and its application in the EU law, it can be deduced that the duty-to-deal obligations for the refusal to access cases in the online world or so-called essential facilities doctrine should be applied cautiously, especially for the Big Data—related competition law infringements. The main problem here is whether Big Data is subject to a

---

190 ibid para 46.
191 Lugard and Roach (n 186) 60.
192 Case C-418/01 *IMS Health GmbH & Co. OHG v NDC Health GmbH & Co. KG.* [2004] ECLI:EU:C: 2004:257, para 38.
193 Kathuria and Globocnik (n 179) 7.
194 Case T-201/4 *Microsoft Corp. v Commission of the European Communities* [2007] ECLI:EU: T:2007:289, paras 332–33.
195 ibid.

duty-to-deal obligation. In other words, could Big Data be regarded as an essential facility in the new economy?

Paul Lugard and Lee Roach emphasise the unique characteristics of Big Data. Through the direct and indirect network effects and the impact of Big Data, consumer and business relationships changed significantly in the online world. According to them, the emergence of Big Data has brought a diverse treatment of the essential facilities doctrine in the EU law.[196] It is clear that the collected data constitutes a source of competitive advantage since some companies amass such data and leverage their data power over rivals and consumers.[197] A necessary analysis should be conducted on a case-by-case basis, and appropriate remedies must be revealed. Otherwise, several problems might occur, such as forced data sharing in situations where data is ubiquitous. In such cases, data sharing as a remedy could become a tool for collusion or could grant unfair advantage to rivals.

Accordingly, Vikas Kathuria and Jure Globocnik advocate the ubiquitous and non-rivalrous nature of Big Data. The idea is as follows: since Big Data is not unique and several market players can also collect the same kind of data, Big Data cannot be regarded as indispensable, which is one of the three main requirements[198] for the application of the essential facilities doctrine in the EU law.[199] According to the claim, users provide the same kind of data to various service providers, such as personal information or geographical location. For instance, regarding Google's abuse of dominant position case, rivals should be able to collect similar data in a climate where Google does not deny any access to data. As a result, data becomes a non-rivalrous input and cannot be the subject matter for the application of the essential facilities doctrine in the *Google Search* case.[200]

Ioannis Kokkoris also underlines that none of Google's rivals has been denied access to any data. However, he expresses that the refusal to deal and essential facilities doctrine does not apply to the *Google Search* case.[201] He focuses on the "necessity" of the Google search engine itself while moving away from Big Data and the characteristics of data-driven markets. He argues that rivals of Google are free to invest in the search engine market to create vertical or horizontal search engines. According to Kokkoris, numerous active search engines in the market are the primary proof.[202] Referring to the requirement of indispensability

---

196 Lugard and Roach (n 186) 62.
197 ibid.
198 Case C-7/97 *Oscar Bronner GmbH & Co. KG v Mediaprint Zeitungs- und Zeitschriftenverlag GmbH & Co. KG and others* [1998] ECLI:EU:C:1998:569; Case C-418/01 *IMS Health GmbH & Co. OHG v NDC Health GmbH & Co. KG.* [2004] ECLI:EU:C: 2004:257; Case T-201/4 *Microsoft Corp. v Commission of the European Communities* [2007] ECLI:EU:T:2007:289.
199 Kathuria and Globocnik (n 179) 7.
200 ibid.
201 Ioannis Kokkoris, 'The Google Saga: Episode I' (2018) 14(2–3) European Competition Journal 462–90, 466.
202 ibid 467.

of an input, claims were made: "Search engines are not essential portals from the perspective of any side in the multi-sided search engine platform. Thus, a search engine is a replicable asset and the criteria for the essential facilities doctrine are not met".[203]

The same method can be seen in Pinar Akman's reasoning. Akman also underlines that data and refusal to deal are not subject matters in the relevant case.[204] Instead, the case deals with a situation in which Google denies its rival access to its search page. In a sense, the key discussion should be the indispensability of the Google search engine since the rival comparison shopping services need a proportion of display on the search engine's results page.[205] As mentioned before, the duty-to-deal and application of the essential facilities doctrine can only be justified when the dominant player has an essential input that cannot be replicated or substituted by rivals.[206] In light of this, some commentators advocate for the Google search engine to be regarded as an indispensable input for comparison shopping services; thus, it can become an essential facility to which rivals also should have access.[207] However, the *Monopolkommission* (German Monopolies Commission) claims that search engines should not meet indispensability requirements and become essential facilities.[208] Although Google Search's market presence is huge, a search engine should not be regarded as an essential facility regardless of its market share.[209] There are still many alternative search engines for comparison shopping services. It is arguable to call a single search engine indispensable to apply the essential facilities doctrine.

Additionally, Bork and Sidak focus on the problems regarding the application of the essential facilities doctrine in the EU. They introduce the essential facilities doctrine as the unicorn of competition law.[210] In this sense, everyone knows about the doctrine, but even the CJEU does not corroborate the doctrine itself.[211] As a result, the application of the doctrine in the correct way becomes a huge problem. Regarding Google's abuse of dominant position, Bork and Sidak express that none of the requirements of the essential facilities doctrine are met for a

---

203 ibid.
204 Pinar Akman, 'The Theory of Abuse in Google Search: A Positive and Normative Assessment Under EU Competition Law' (2017) 2 Journal of Law, Technology and Policy 301, 311–27.
205 ibid 316.
206 Renato Nazzini, 'Google and the (Ever-Stretching) Boundaries of Article 102' (2015) 6 Journal of European Competition Law and Practice 5, 309.
207 Ioannis Lianos and Evgenia Motchenkova, 'Market Dominance and Search Quality in the Search Engine Market' (2013) 9 Journal of Competition Law and Economics 434; Lisa Mays, 'The Consequences of Search Bias: How Application of the Essential Facilities Doctrine Remedies Google's Unrestricted Monopoly on Search in the United States and Europe' (2015) 83 The George Washington Law Review 2, 721–60, 751.
208 German Monopolies Commission (*Monopolkommission*), 'Competition Policy: The Challenge of Digital Markets' (2015) Special Report No. 68, 58.
209 ibid.
210 Bork and Sidak (n 68) 679.
211 ibid.

competition intervention and duty to deal.[212] First, shopping advertisement placements on the Google search page should be discussed as an "essential facility" in the relevant case. Therefore, in terms of indispensability, the question is whether rivals of Google could duplicate or substitute the facility. Google is not the only search engine; thus, it cannot be regarded as an indispensable facility.[213] In the presumption of the Google search results page as the essential facility, it is not clear how the essential facilities doctrine could be applied to the relevant case since the facility is not a product that could be provided simultaneously to all providers, like data or something else. Only one link can be shown in the best spot for consumers, and then only another link can be placed in the second-best place on the results page. According to Bork and Sidak, providing the top of a result page to every company to apply the essential facilities doctrine is technologically impossible because not every comparison shopping link can earn the highest spot on the results page.[214]

As seen earlier, applying the essential facilities doctrine is centred around the so-called ubiquitous, non-rivalrous nature of Big Data or the Google search engine itself, which cannot be regarded as an indispensable facility. However, Giuseppe Colangelo and Mariateresa Maggiolino bring another crucial point to the discussion. They analyse the impact of Big Data rather than the data itself on the characterisation of data as an essential facility in the EU law. Thus, Big Data as an essential facility does not seem relevant for the application of the doctrine since the importance of data derives not from its pure volume or variety but from its value.[215] The idea is that online intermediaries succeed because they develop better, higher-quality products or services when they derive value from Big Data using particular analytical tools to extract information from consumer data.[216] In other words, it is not Big Data itself but the value extracted from that data that is useful for companies. Therefore, instead of Big Data, the "valued" data should be the focus of the application of the essential facilities doctrine.[217] The differentiation of Big Data and the 4Vs[218] becomes important at this point. Big Data must be examined through its distinctive features. Thus, whether Big Data or the information extracted from this data is essential should be revealed case by case. Colangelo and Maggiolino emphasise that if the competitive advantage derives from the value of data, then controlling a mass amount of data might not hold as much importance as anticipated.[219]

---

212 ibid 678.
213 ibid 682.
214 ibid 683.
215 Giuseppe Colangelo and Mariateresa Maggiolino, 'Big Data as Misleading Facilities' (2017) 13 European Competition Journal 2–3, 249–81.
216 ibid 272–73.
217 ibid.
218 See Chapter 2.1.1.
219 Colangelo and Maggiolino (n 215) 272–73.

For instance, it is impossible to assess whether Big Data is an essential facility by just looking at its sheer volume; ignoring what pieces of information are waiting to be extracted could be the main reason for the imbalanced competitive advantage in the online world. If this is the reason, then the discussion comes to the point where specific "characteristics" of Big Data could have the final word on the essential facility problem. In that case, some steps of the Big Data value chain might be less important than others, such as data collection having a minor effect compared to data processing.[220] Additionally, the differentiation of data processing techniques by different companies may create a situation in which similar datasets might be equally useful for all rivals. In this regard, Tim Cowen comments on the Commission's inadequate examination of the Facebook/WhatsApp merger regarding the importance of Big Data and data collection:

> In perhaps the weakest part of its decision, it referred to the generic collection of data and took no account of the unique nature of user data held by WhatsApp on its users. The Commission pointed to user data as a type of undifferentiated raw material ("internet data"). . . . The Commission provided an overview of the estimated share of data collection across the web by those different companies. This shows that the Commission probably failed to appreciate that data about one consumer preference collected by one company in one situation is not much use as a substitute for data about something else collected by another. In addition, data from different sources may . . . give rise to different knowledge, and if so, the fact that an alternative raw material is available will be of no significance in the market for the intermediate knowledge products.[221]

The velocity of Big Data must also be discussed at this point. In other words, up-to-date information is the most important component for data-driven companies, which use valuable data as fast as possible. In other words, the newness or freshness[222] of data is the most crucial attribute for companies in the data-driven online world.[223] Not only the volume or variety but also real information and the valuable data extraction at fast speeds enables better quality products and services.[224] Furthermore, relatively old datasets might lose their fundamental importance quickly and become obsolete since the old information regarding the past might not be sufficient. For instance, if a search engine company had bought Google's complete 2019 data, in theory, they would not have gained the ability to serve the same

---

220 ibid.
221 Tim Cowen, 'Big Data as a Competition Issue: Should the EU Commission's Approach Be More Careful' (2016) 4 European Networks Law and Regulation Quarterly 14, 22.
222 Daniel L Rubinfeld and Michal S Gal, 'Access Barriers to Big Data' (2017) 59 Arizona Law Review 339, 346.
223 See Chapter 2.
224 Maurice Stucke and Allen Grunes, *Big Data and Competition Policy* (1st edn, OUP 2016) 19; OECD, *Data-Driven Innovation, Big Data for Growth and Well-Being* (OECD Publishing 2015), 4 <https://www.oecd-ilibrary.org/science-and-technology/data-driven-innovation_9789264229358-en>

quality of service as Google. Therefore, it becomes a crucial task to analyse the initial structure of Big Data and its way of utilisation before mandating duty to deal based on the essential facilities doctrine. As the OECD study suggests: "It may not be the collection of the data, as much as the ability to timely and swiftly extract useful information from a large volume and variety of data that leads to a competitive advantage being gained".[225]

In summary, applying the essential facilities doctrine to Big Data—related infringements follows several mandatory steps. First, the refusal must relate to an indispensable product or service. In this case, Big Data must be regarded as an indispensable facility. In order to claim that necessity or essentiality is not sufficient, it is also necessary to prove that it cannot be reasonably duplicated or replicated.[226] Even if the creation of new data (duplication or replication) is possible, only if it is not economically viable could indispensability be possible.[227] In terms of data-driven markets, it must be demonstrated that Big Data is truly unique, and competitors do not have any other opportunities to access this data to operate their online services.[228] When all requirements are met, including the elimination of competition, and the lack of objective justification, then remedies such as mandatory data sharing could be applied to competition infringements. However, access to data might create several problems, including privacy if the consumers' information is shared with third parties without the consumers' consent and disincentivising rivals to collect data, which hinders innovation from developing better methods and products for data collection, data processing, algorithms and even machine learning.

5.2.3 Mandatory Data Sharing as a Remedy

If the essential facilities doctrine is found to be relevant for Article 102 infringements in data-driven markets, mandatory data sharing comes to mind as a potential remedy. Nevertheless, it is difficult to approve mandatory sharing as a competition law "sanction" since it aims to end the infringement itself, and it is not like imposing a fine on the dominant company.[229] For example, Google has already been fined almost €9 billion by the European Commission in its *Search(Shopping)*,[230]

---

225 Thiemann and Gonzaga (n 164) 22.
226 J Gregory Sidak and Abbott B Lipsky, 'Essential Facilities' (1999) 51 Stanford Law Review 5, 1187–249, 1203.
227 Case C-7/97 *Oscar Bronner GmbH & Co. KG v Mediaprint Zeitungs- und Zeitschriftenverlag GmbH & Co. KG and others* [1998] ECLI:EU:C:1998:569, para 46.
228 Gönenç Gürkaynak, Ali Kağan Uçar and Zeynep Buharali, 'Data-Related Abuses in Competition Law' in Nicolas Charbit and Sonia Ahmad (eds), *Frédéric Jenny Liber Amicorum, Standing Up for Convergence and Relevance in Antitrust* (Concurrences 2019) 301; Bundeskartellamt and Autorité de la Concurrence (n 160) 18.
229 Article 7 of the Regulation 1/2003; Kathuria and Globocnik (n 179) 5.
230 €2.5 billion.

Android[231] and *AdSense*[232] cases, and it seems that even astronomical fines are not effective sanctions as a remedy for competition matters, especially regarding the data-rich technology giants. In this sense, companies like Google could pay the fine and continue their behaviour. There could be circumstances in which dominant companies keep reaping the benefits of their abusive behaviour and continue engaging in similar abusive behaviour after paying the fines.[233] To stop the violation, authorities should engage in the necessary steps to stop infringements entirely. In this regard, the European Council imposes the following:

> This Regulation should make explicit provision for the Commission's power to impose any remedy, whether behavioural or structural, which is necessary to bring the infringement effectively to an end, having regard to the principle of proportionality. Structural remedies should only be imposed either where there is no equally effective behavioural remedy or where any equally effective behavioural remedy would be more burdensome for the undertaking concerned than the structural remedy. Changes to the structure of an undertaking as it existed before the infringement was committed would only be proportionate where there is a substantial risk of a lasting or repeated infringement that derives from the very structure of the undertaking.[234]

That being said, mandating a data-sharing remedy could lead to different conclusions, including restoring competition in data-driven markets or disincentivising companies to innovate. Recently, European national competition authorities mandated data-sharing remedies to Big Data–related competition infringements. Although not mentioning the essential facilities doctrine, both the French Competition Authority and the Belgian Competition Authority required dominant companies to share their data with rivals in the *GDF-Suez* and *Belgian National Lottery* cases.[235]

GDF Suez was a former legal monopoly in the energy market as well as the Belgian National Lottery in the market of organising nationwide public lotteries. Due to their monopoly positions, both undertakings had control over a massive amount of personal data regarding their services. After the liberalisation of the energy supply market in France, GDF Suez was found to be abusing its dominant

---

231 €4.3 billion.
232 €1.5 billion.
233 Kathuria and Globocnik (n 179) 8.
234 Article 12 of the Regulation 1/2003.
235 French Competition Authority, Decision No. 14-MC-02 (GDF-Suez Decision) 9 September 2014. Belgian Competition Authority, Beslissing nr. BMA-2015-P/K-27-AUD (van 22 September 2015, Zaken nr. MEDE-P/K-13/0012 en CONC-P/K-13/0013, Stanleybet Belgium NV/Stanley International Betting Ltd en Sagevas S.A./World Football Association S.P.R.L./Samenwerkende Nevenmaatschappij Belgische PMU S.C.R.L.t. Nationale Loterij NV).

position by utilising an established database.[236] As a remedy, the French Competition Authority mandated GDF Suez to share its database with rivals under objective and transparent terms.[237] In a similar vein, the Belgian Competition Authority ruled the Belgian National Lottery had to share its database and imposed a fine for an Article 102 infringement in which the Belgian Lottery used the contact information of its consumers to promote its new betting product, Scooore![238] However, the Belgian Competition Authority revoked the data-sharing remedy because the National Lottery just used the data once for promotion purposes, and the infringement was found to be a one-off.[239] It is also important to note that both the *GDF Suez* and *Belgian National Lottery* cases were related to legal monopolies. The "necessary" facility does not fit the essential facility doctrine in these cases.

Although there are possible positive outcomes in terms of maintaining healthy competition after liberalising a former monopoly market, mandating a data-sharing remedy by the courts or the Commission as a kind of intervention relevant to the infringement through the application of the essential facilities doctrine might bring various problems including stifling innovation, the irrelevance of the data sharing remedy to the situation and privacy concerns in some data-driven markets. The first concern, innovation, is definitely a result of data-sharing remedies in data-driven markets. As a result of mandatory sharing, rivals of dominant undertakings would easily use huge datasets without actually collecting and improving their algorithms. This would disincentivise new entrants in investing in methods that might lead to technological developments since they could enjoy this advantage through competition law intervention. Not only smaller rivals but also dominant undertakings may also abandon their practices on Big Data if they cannot enjoy their innovation and success in terms of being innovative and competitive.

Especially in data-driven markets where rapid innovation occurs and data is the most important input, mandating the sharing of collected data through commercial activities will bring less investment in data-related technologies. Since the data collection and analysis require a serious investment before even being profitable, huge investment costs would not be desirable for companies to undertake. In addition to this, data-rich undertakings such as Google may stifle innovation in order not to bestow a competitive advantage on its rivals in the search engine market.[240] Ultimately, less innovation leads to lesser quality products and services; thus, it leads to consumer harm.[241]

---

236 French Competition Authority, Decision No. 14-MC-02 (GDF-Suez Decision) 9 September 2014, paras 147–72.
237 ibid para 292.
238 Belgian Competition Authority, Beslissing nr. BMA-2015-P/K-27-AUD.
239 Kathuria and Globocnik (n 179) 15; Inge Graef, *EU Competition Law, Data Protection and Online Platforms: Data as Essential Facility* (1st edn, Kluwer Law International 2016) 273.
240 Kathuria and Globocnik (n 179) 15.
241 John E Lopatka and William H Page, 'Devising a Microsoft Remedy That Serves Consumers' (2001) 9 George Mason Law Review 3, 691–726, 700.

Abusive Behaviour in Data-Driven Markets 163

The second concern is the irrelevance of data-sharing remedies in data-driven markets. Even in the scenario in which dominant undertakings still compete under the mandatory data-sharing remedies of the competition authorities and courts, rivals could make use of shared data to leverage data power into adjacent markets. In other words, shared data could be used by third-party undertakings in other online ecosystems. For example, in the case of *Google Shopping*, if the defendant is forced to share its data with other comparison shopping services, these companies could make use of Google's huge search databases to create market power in adjacent markets. According to Kathuria and Globocnik's example regarding leveraging data power, rivals of Google in the search engine market, such as Bing, could acquire Google's data and use it through different algorithms in other data-driven markets, like the social network market.[242] Google's social media product, Google+, was unsuccessful against Facebook. However, this does not mean that Bing (Microsoft) will also suffer the same problems if they use different algorithmic methods to create a market presence and competitiveness in the social network market. Therefore, the data-sharing remedy will not be useful in ceasing the infringement and could also distort competition in other data-driven markets and online ecosystems.[243]

Regarding the irrelevance of the mandatory data-sharing remedy, Big Data's velocity must be mentioned again as a contradictory situation in which shared data becomes quite useful for rivals. As explained earlier, old datasets might not be as useful as predicted. As the OECD stresses, it is not the volume of the data but the ability to timely extract relevant information from huge datasets that allows undertakings to gain great competitive advantage.[244] To put it another way, it is not Big Data itself but the utilisation methods and the freshness of data that are important for gaining market power and abusing a dominant position. Consequently, rivals acquiring huge but obsolete datasets through data-sharing remedies may not utilise this data successfully. For instance, Google's rivals which acquire past data from Google might not gain the ability to serve better products due to the lack of superior data analysis methods with fresh data and the velocity of data. In this circumstance, the data-sharing remedy becomes an inferior method and a tool to stop the actual abuse other than providing consumer information to third parties without consumers' consent. This brings another concern: privacy.[245]

The 2016 report of the *Bundeskartellamt* and the *Autorité de la Concurrence* states that:

> Access to a company's data may raise privacy concerns as forced sharing of user data could violate privacy laws if companies exchange data without

---

242 Kathuria and Globocnik (n 179) 18.
243 ibid.
244 Thiemann and Gonzaga (n 164) 22.
245 Bundeskartellamt and Autorité de la Concurrence (n 160) 18.

asking for consumer's consent before sharing their personal information with third companies with whom the consumer has no relationship.[246]

Although the subject of the abuse is data, data sharing must comply with the GDPR provisions in the EU. However, it is also crucial to implement any necessary data-sharing remedies under competition law instead of privacy or consumer protection law provisions, even though data-sharing remedies involve transferring and processing personal information. The reason for this is the irrelevance of privacy agencies in mergers and abuse of dominant position cases. Privacy agencies normally do not enjoin and are not even be notified before a merger.[247] Also, remedies provided by privacy and consumer protection laws are often behavioural, which have lesser effects on the market than competition remedies.[248] Intrinsically, moves from privacy authorities do lack structural remedies.[249] Most commonly, a fine will likely be the sanction and remedy for a privacy violation. As mentioned earlier, even as a competition remedy, huge fines are not enough to stop a competition law infringement when strong direct and indirect effects are present. Therefore, competition authorities must step in and provide accurate remedies for data-related infringements. Would mandatory data sharing as a competition remedy harm consumers from a privacy point of view?

Article 6(1)(c) of the GDPR expresses that data processing (data collection, analytics, use, sharing and storage, according to Article 4[250]) must comply with a legal oblation to which the controller is subject.[251] In this case, a remedy imposed by competition authorities or courts in the EU regarding data sharing should be regarded as a legal obligation. Thus, Article 6(1)(f) states that data processing or data sharing as a competition remedy must include a legitimate interest of the controller or third parties.[252] In terms of a mandatory data-sharing remedy, it is inarguable that rivals have legitimate interests if there is a competition violation. However, the same article mentions exceptions in which the interests or fundamental rights of sensitive consumer groups such as children might have been violated. In this case, data sharing with third parties will endanger the fundamental rights of specific consumer groups. This brings another compliance issue: the consent of consumers. Articles 7 and 8 of GDPR explicitly state that data subject consent[253] is obligatory

---

246 ibid; also mentioned in Darren S Tucker and Hill B Wellford, 'Big Mistakes Regarding Big Data' (2014) 14 Antitrust Source 1, 11.
247 Maurice E Stucke and Allen Grunes, *Big Data and Competition Policy* (1st edn, OUP 2016) 254.
248 ibid.
249 ibid 255.
250 Article 4 of the GDPR.
251 Article 6(1)(c) of the GDPR.
252 Article 6(1)(f) of the GDPR.
253 Data subjects are defined by the GDPR as: "an identified or identifiable natural person" and "an identifiable person is one who can be identified . . . in particular by reference to an identifier such as a name, an identification number, location data, online identifier or to one or more factors specific to the physical, physiological, genetic, mental, economic, cultural or social identity of that natural person". Article 4(1) of the GDPR.

for data processing, including data sharing.[254] The legal obligation mandated by competition authorities to share data with rivals must also comply with these provisions. Moreover, any consent given to the controller during the initial data collection would not be enough to share data with third parties. Thus, another consent should be situated in order to comply with the GDPR rules at the time of the ruling.

These difficulties show that mandatory data sharing as a remedy through the essential facilities seems quite inaccurate. To sum up, even in the hypothetical situation in which the essential facilities doctrine can be applied to Big Data in competition cases, there are no explicit norms or regulations on how mandatory data sharing remedy can be applied through the GDPR. This seems to be a legal gap during the creation of new data protection regulations in the EU. Therefore, extensive research must be conducted by both privacy and competition authorities on how personal and sensitive data (especially de-anonymised data) can be subject to the essential facilities doctrine remedies in Europe if the doctrine is found to be fit for data-driven abuses. As a side note, in 2018, the leader of the Social Democrat Party of Germany (SDP) called for legislation mandating dominant technology companies to share a certain part of their Big Data with the public.[255] According to her, this type of obligation would ensure healthy competition while reducing inequalities between companies.[256]

5.2.4 Data Portability as an Alternate Remedy

Data portability, also regulated in the GDPR, could be less harmful than a data-sharing obligation through the essential facilities doctrine as a remedy.[257] Data portability mainly refers to the right of consumers to obtain a copy of their data from the data controller and transfer it to another provider.[258] Article 20 of the GDPR gives the right to the data subjects[259] to transfer their data from one online platform

---

254 Article 7 and 8 of the GDPR.
255 Claudia Biancotti and Paolo Ciocca, 'Opening Internet Monopolies to Competition with Data Sharing Mandates' (2019) Policy Brief 19-3, Peterson Institute for International Economics 6, citing: <https://www.handelsblatt.com/meinung/gastbeitraege/gastkommentar-die-tech-riesen-des-silicon-valleys-gefaehrden-den-fairen-wettbewerb/22900656.html>
256 ibid 6.
257 Barbara Engels, 'Data Portability Among Online Platforms' (2016) 5 Internet Policy Review 2; Peter Swire and Yianni Lagos, 'Why the Right to Data Portability Likely Reduces Consumer Welfare: Antitrust and Privacy Critique' (2013) 72 Maryland Law Review 2, 335–80; Inge Graef, Jeroen Verschakele and Peggy Valcke, 'Putting the Right to Data Portability into a Competition Law Perspective' [2013] The Journal of the Higher School of Economics, Annual Review 53–63; Ayşem Diker Vanberg and Mehmet Bilal Ünver, 'The Right to Data Portability in the GDPR and EU Competition Law: Odd Couple or Dynamic Duo?' (2017) 8 European Journal of Law and Technology 1.
258 Vanberg and Ünver (n 257) 2.
259 Data subjects are defined by the GDPR as "an identified or identifiable natural person" and "an identifiable person is one who can be identified . . . in particular by reference to an identifier such as a name, an identification number, location data, online identifier or to one or more factors specific to the physical, physiological, genetic, mental, economic, cultural or social identity of that natural person". Article 4(1) of the GDPR.

to another.[260] It also mentions that the data subject to portability is either based on the data processed by means of Article 6(1) of the GDPR or the data processed by automated means.[261] The right to data portability can be an obligation to online service providers in data-driven markets where anti-competitive conduct is present or potential risks of competition harm are suspected.

In a 2012 speech, Competition Commissioner Joaquín Almunia stressed the importance of the right to data portability. He believes that the right to portability in the GDPR goes to the heart of competition policy, and healthy competition can be established if consumers have the ability to transfer their own data easily and cheaply between service providers:[262] "In those markets that build on users uploading their personal data or their personal content, retention of these data should not serve as barriers to switching", and "customers should not be locked in to a particular company just because they once trusted them with their content".[263]

Similarly, in their 2014 report on the interplay between data protection, competition law and consumer protection in the digital economy, the European Data Protection Supervisor (EDPS) suggested an implementation of the right to data portability, promoting competition in data-driven markets and also empowering individuals in terms of relieving the possible switching costs that the dominant player might create.[264] The EDPS suggests that the right to portability can bring synergies to competition and data protection laws due to the interplay between these laws.[265] According to the EDPS's study, data portability can bring an end to and prevent abusive behaviour (both exclusionary and exploitative) in data-driven markets.[266] Consumers would not be locked into specific online providers, and rivals would be less prone to dominant undertakings' exclusionary and exploitative conduct. At the same time, consumers gain power over their own data in the online world in terms of data privacy and can take advantage of third-party services while facilitating access to rival services in a market.[267]

In a similar vein, Barbara Engels advocates the accuracy of data portability as mitigation in data-driven markets. In her study, Engels analysed various platform-data model simulations regarding data portability in the online world. Simulations demonstrate that in markets where anti-competitive conduct is present, data portability mitigates problems or is at least not harmful to the competition and the

---

260 Article 20 of the GDPR.
261 ibid.
262 Joaquín Almunia, 'Competition and Personal Data Protection' SPEECH 12/860 of 26 November 2012 <https://ec.europa.eu/commission/presscorner/detail/en/SPEECH_12_860>
263 ibid.
264 Preliminary Opinion of the European Data Protection Supervisor, 'Privacy and Competitiveness in the Age of Big Data: The Interplay Between Data Protection, Competition Law and Consumer Protection in the Digital Economy' (March 2014), paras 72, 82 <https://edps.europa.eu/sites/edp/files/publication/14-03-26_competitition_law_big_data_en.pdf>
265 ibid para 83.
266 ibid.
267 ibid.

rival companies.[268] Therefore, an obligation of data portability in platform markets such as search engines, online marketplaces and social networks is easily recommendable as an alternative remedy to ensure healthy competition.[269] However, Engels advocates for stricter remedies in the search engine market than in other data-driven markets such as social networks and online marketplaces[270] because of the concentration level of the search engine market. In markets with much higher concentrations, such as the search engine market, the harms of anti-competitive conduct will be much higher. Therefore, as a remedy, the study suggests a data portability regulation for the search engine market and a lighter obligation to provide data portability for social networks, online marketplaces and others.[271]

Although this study claims that there is no direct correlation between innovation and data portability remedy in terms of promoting or hampering innovation,[272] Peter Swire and Yianni Lagos express concerns over data portability or sharing obligations that could hamper innovation in data-driven markets.[273] First movers or the main data collectors that became dominant over time would have lower expected profits if they started sharing even a small portion of their collected data with competitors.[274] Besides, a data portability remedy means lower consumer loyalty to any online platform. Thus, due to the loss of network effects, companies will not be able to gain expected profits from their investments. Therefore, companies might be disincentivised from investing and collecting data.

Contrary to these supportive ideas, Ayşem Diker Vanberg does not find the data portability of Article 20 of the GDPR an appropriate remedy for Article 102 TFEU–related situations.[275] The study suggests that the right to data portability regulated in the GDPR has inherent limitations for competition law applications, such as the rights and freedoms of the data subjects.[276] For instance, the right to data portability mentioned in the GDPR concerns only consumers: in other words, natural persons and not legal persons.[277] There are no governing rules for legal persons in the GDPR; therefore, Article 20 is inapplicable, and legal persons do not have the right to data portability. However, online service providers such as Google and other companies also collect data from both natural and legal entities in massive amounts.[278] In this sense, there would be two "types" of data: the portable data

---

268 Engels (n 257) 9.
269 ibid.
270 ibid 13.
271 ibid.
272 ibid.
273 Peter Swire and Yianni Lagos, 'Why the Right to Data Portability Likely Reduces Consumer Welfare: Antitrust and Privacy Critique' (2013) 72 Maryland Law Review 2, 335–80, 357–58.
274 ibid.
275 Vanberg and Ünver (n 257) 10.
276 ibid.
277 Stefano Lucchini and others, 'Online Digital Services and Competition Law: Why Competition Authorities Should be More Concerned About Portability Rather than About Privacy' (2018) 9 Journal of European Competition Law and Practice 9, 565.
278 ibid.

of natural persons and the unportable data of legal persons. Accordingly, the data source is irrelevant for competition law purposes when there is abuse, and the lack of a wider application of Article 20 of the GDPR seems to be an intrinsic limitation for competition law–related applications.[279]

Second, the consent of data subjects makes the applicability of data portability even less since consumers must be aware of data portability options and give consent to it in the first place for a competition authority to enforce the obligation of dominant undertakings. In other words, the right to data portability can be the solution at the request of the data subject and not data controllers or third parties such as rivals.[280] The third shortcoming can be found in Recital 68 of the GDPR, which expresses that this right does not require data controllers to adopt "technically compatible" processing systems into their systems.[281] This means collected data might not be transferable; thus, data portability cannot be possible in every scenario.

It is also important to underline the difference between the competition rules and the general application of the GDPR. Although the GDPR rules are applicable at all times for all service providers, including the smallest ones, without looking at their size or market presence, data portability as a competition remedy can only be applied through Article 102 TFEU when there is an explicit market power of dominant undertakings and a risk of harm to competition and consumers.[282] Therefore, the applicability of data portability as a competition remedy is quite low, especially as a substitute for the essential facilities doctrine. Although there are almost no risks of leveraging market power in the application of data portability, authorities will face the same problems of mandatory data sharing through the essential facilities doctrine, such as relevancy, the velocity of data and the consent of data subjects. A better option would be imposing an obligation on all online providers, even without an Article 102 violation. However, this cannot be considered a remedy for Article 102 violations by competition authorities. It needs a cooperative and comprehensive study that must be conducted by both privacy and competition authorities together.

Additionally, data portability should not be confused with data interoperability, which is stricter than data portability.[283] Although there are no risks regarding leveraging data power in the right of data portability, data interoperability inherently consists of this risk if it becomes a competition law remedy. When data interoperability is used in the social network market, for example, users can access their profiles and message histories from Facebook, Google+ or any other network, irrespective of the original contents service provider.[284] This means that users of various social networks can be connected without creating a new account on rival platforms. For example, Facebook users could share posts or write messages to

---

279 ibid.
280 ibid.
281 Recital 68 of the GDPR.
282 Vanberg and Ünver (n 257) 10; Swire and Lagos (n 273) 351.
283 Engels (n 257) 4.
284 ibid.

Google+ users. The situation in which all companies have access to the same user data will lead to problems in which third-party social network providers enter the market to take advantage of users' data in adjacent markets. Therefore, data interoperability contains higher risks, such as mandatory data sharing in terms of competitive effects, than data portability.

5.3 Abuse Through Data Privacy

Big Data–related anti-competitive conduct is not limited to the abuses mentioned here, such as leveraging market power, vertical integration, and abuse through access to data in data-driven markets. The common characteristic of the mentioned abuses is predictability. They can all be anticipated by competition authorities, courts or market players since most are regulated and well-known abuse types in case law. The most challenging part is assessing the role of Big Data as a source of market power and a tool to distort competition in the online world. However, there might be more abuse types in data-driven markets in the age of Big Data and algorithms. As a novel abuse in data-driven markets, abuse through data privacy must be discussed.

5.3.1 A Novel Abuse

Data privacy is already a grey zone between privacy, consumer protection and competition laws. Data privacy as a competition concern was first raised during the Google/DoubleClick merger in 2007. Commissioner Pamela Jones Harbour of the Federal Trade Commission (FTC) expressed her belief that undertakings in data-driven markets also compete on privacy protection and other non-price dimensions.[285] Citing Peter Swire's testimony, Harbour underlined in her dissenting opinion in the *Google/DoubleClick* case that privacy can be a non-price dimension of competition in the search engine market.[286] Since nobody knows the limits of what Google can achieve with its trove of information regarding consumer preferences after the *DoubleClick* merger, consumer preferences and consumers privacy could well be at stake. Harbour states that privacy disclosure is not limited to identifiable information such as name or age. However, all types of data that Google collected are also included in consumer preferences, such as behavioural information (web browsing through Google search), contacts (Gmail), location (Google Maps), shopping behaviours and others.[287]

Although it is still highly debated whether data privacy should be evaluated as a non-price competition parameter, abuse related to data privacy might actually

---

[285] Dissenting Statement of Commissioner Pamela Jones Harbour, In the Matter of Google/DoubleClick F.T.C. File No. 071-0170 (2007) 9–10 <https://www.ftc.gov/sites/default/files/documents/public_statements/statement-matter-google/doubleclick/071220harbour_0.pdf>
[286] ibid citing: Testimony of Peter J Swire, 'Submission to the Federal Trade Commission, Town Hall on "Behavioural Advertising: Tracking, Targeting, and Technology"' (18 October 2007).
[287] Harbour (n 285) 10, footnote 24.

be present in data-driven markets. Suppose privacy violations are used to gain or abuse market power through exclusionary and exploitative conduct in markets where indirect network effects are prominent. In that case, competition authorities need to step in.[288] For example, the OECD report on Big Data and competition policy mentions a situation in which consumers' private data could be extracted and utilised to foreclose rivals and raise entry barriers into a market.[289] In this scenario, exclusionary abuse could amount to a privacy violation at the same time.

The most important example of privacy violation as an abuse type is the investigation of Facebook by the *Bundeskartellamt* (the German Federal Cartel Office). The *Bundeskartellamt* has opened an abuse of a dominant position investigation into Facebook. According to the preliminary assessment of the *Bundeskartellamt*, Facebook abused its dominant position in the social network market by transferring and utilising data from its other services, such as Instagram, WhatsApp, websites, embedded games and application programming interfaces (APIs) to its main service Facebook for behavioural advertising purposes.[290] Therefore, it is argued that Facebook breached competition law by violating its consumers' privacy.[291]

Andreas Mundt, the president of the German Competition Authority, stressed the need to examine Facebook's behaviour in the social network market. He expressed that there might be a violation of Article 102 TFEU by violating consumers' privacy.[292] Similarly, Margrethe Vestager mentioned the German investigation into Facebook on Bloomberg TV. She described Facebook's market presence as "a very dominant" undertaking in the social network market and mentioned the investigation's stance as a "gray zone between competition and privacy".[293] Vestager added: "Data as such is one of the more important things because that is the new line of business.... [B]oth knowledge and data are another kind of currency, another asset than just the turnover of the company".[294] Also, Maximilian Volmar and Katharina Helmdach underlined the importance of the investigation in terms of tightening the relationship between competition law and data protection law, and even this novel abuse type might lead to a rethinking of abuse of dominant position cases and Article 102 of the TFEU in the age of Big Data.[295] It is necessary to discuss the Facebook probe of the German Competition Authority in detail.

288 Thiemann and Gonzaga (n 164) 21.
289 ibid.
290 *Bundeskartellamt* (FCO) Press Release, 'Preliminary Assessment in Facebook Proceeding: Facebook's Collection and Use of Data from Third-Party Sources Is Abusive' (19 December 2017) <https://www.bundeskartellamt.de/SharedDocs/Meldung/EN/Pressemitteilungen/2017/19_12_2017_Facebook.html>
291 ibid.
292 Thiemann and Gonzaga (n 164) 21, para 69.
293 Aoife White and Francine Lacqua, 'Facebook Probe Is in Antitrust, Privacy Gray Zone, EU Says' *Bloomberg Tech* (14 September 2016) <https://www.bloomberg.com/news/articles/2016-09-14/facebook-probe-in-antitrust-and-privacy-gray-zone-vestager-says>
294 ibid.
295 Maximilian N Volmar and Katharina O Helmdach, 'Protecting Consumers and Their Data Through Competition Law? Rethinking Abuse of Dominance in Light of the Federal Cartel Office's Facebook Investigation' (2018) 14 European Competition Journal 2, 200–1.

5.3.2 The Bundeskartellamt's Facebook Investigation

The German Competition Authority opened an investigation into Facebook in March 2016 based on the suspicion that Facebook was abusing its power in the social network market. The Authority also launched a sector inquiry into the online advertising sector and its market conditions.[296] Facebook was alleged to use the personal information collected from its other online services such as WhatsApp, Instagram, Masquerade, Oculus, Onavo, Crowd Tangle and Moves in order to utilise the information for advertising services under the Facebook.com umbrella.[297] Facebook had 1.5 billion daily and 2.3 billion monthly active users globally in December 2018 and 23 million daily active users and 32 million monthly active users in Germany in November 2018.[298] Daily active users indicate Facebook's power and dominant position in the social network market in both Germany and the world.[299] According to the investigation, Facebook's user-based market share in Germany is over 95%.

Also, the investigation revealed that 98% of the total turnover of Facebook in 2018 was generated through advertising.[300] Thus, online advertising is the main source of funding for Facebook and other Facebook-owned applications. These online advertisements are published on Facebook.com, Facebook Messenger and Instagram and on third-party websites that are part of Facebook's advertising network.[301] The direct and indirect network effects Facebook has already established fuel online advertising with data and create a huge advantage over rivals.[302] The investigation claims:

> [V]ia indirect network effects, the increasing installed base, and the ensuing amount of data have an impact on the advertisers' side of the market. If . . . users spend much time on the Facebook website, this improves targeting options which in turn attracts a large number of advertisers who contribute their own data sources, generate further data by means of the Facebook measurement tool and make these available to Facebook.[303]

Therefore, Facebook was allegedly abusing its dominant position pursuant to Section 19(1) GWB,[304] which is the equivalent of Article 102 TFEU, by gathering the user's personal, behavioural and device-related data from its online services

---

296 *Bundeskartellamt*, Press Release, '*Bundeskartellamt* Launches Sector Inquiry into Market Conditions in Online Advertising Sector' (1 February 2018) <https://www.bundeskartellamt.de/SharedDocs/Meldung/EN/Pressemitteilungen/2018/01_02_2018_SU_Online_Werbung.html>
297 B6-22/16, *Facebook Inc., Facebook Ireland Ltd., Facebook Deutschland GmbH, Verbraucherzentrale Bundesverband e.V.* Bundeskartellamt 6th Decision Division (6 February 2019) paras 1–12.
298 ibid para 17.
299 ibid paras 374–89.
300 ibid para 13.
301 ibid para 37.
302 ibid para 492.
303 ibid para 497.
304 Section 19(1) GWB.

such as WhatsApp, Facebook, Instagram and others and combining these datasets without the users' consent for advertising purposes.[305] In other words, implementing its data policy allows Facebook to gather personal and behavioural data from sources other than Facebook and merge it with Facebook's dataset (data collected on Facebook).[306] Facebook's data policy was found to be exploitative and to constitute an abuse of a dominant position under Section 19(1) GWB on the social network market. Facebook abused its dominant position by using and implementing its online terms of service (TOS).

In addition, the investigation reveals that these TOS also violate the data protection rules pursuant to the GDPR by imposing terms detrimental to consumers and their privacy.[307] Ultimately, violation of the data protection rules becomes an abusive practice at the same time. The *Bundeskartellamt* examined the relationship between the harmonised consumer protection laws of the EU (the GDPR) and the competition law provisions regarding abuse of a dominant position and concluded that when there is a data privacy violation through data collection and processing methods which resembles the market power of dominant undertakings and is also detrimental to the competition in the market, then the conduct becomes relevant for the competition intervention.[308] Therefore, the *Bundeskartellamt* holds the view that the data protection and competition rules should be assessed together in a case of data-related abuse. It adds that the abuse of the dominant position rules of the GWB is fully applicable to data protection violations if the conduct has an abusive nature and causes consumer harm.[309] Regarding the application of competition law to data privacy violations, Hamburg's Commissioner for Data Protection and Freedom of Information stresses:

> Abusive market behaviour which violates data protection rules and leads to a situation where fair competition is no longer possible in digital markets must be stopped. In this respect, data protection and competition law are two sides of the same coin. The activities of the Bundeskartellamt strive to ensure that it will no longer pay off to violate data protection rules in order to gain market power.[310]

In light of these findings, the data processing policies and abusive TOS of Facebook are prohibited by the *Bundeskartellamt*, and the Authority ordered the termination of the abusive conduct in February 2019.[311] According to the Authority,

---

305 B6-22/16, *Facebook Inc.*, para 522.
306 Case Summary B6-22/16, Facebook, Exploitative Business Terms Pursuant to Section 19(1) GWB for Inadequate Data Processing (15 February 2019) 7 <https://www.bundeskartellamt.de/SharedDocs/Entscheidung/EN/Fallberichte/Missbrauchsaufsicht/2019/B6-22-16.html>
307 ibid.
308 B6-22/16, *Facebook Inc.*, paras 525–58.
309 ibid.
310 ibid para 548.
311 ibid para 741–54, 916–49.

the consumer data collected through different online services constitutes a huge competitive risk on the market and creates market barriers as well as high switching costs.[312] The prohibition ruled by the Authority refers to TOS, including data and the cookie policy of Facebook, as the infringement itself since the abusive conduct consists of the implementation of this terms of service and data policy.[313] The *Bundeskartellamt* also prohibited the application of these terms of service and data policy in actual data processing procedures performed by Facebook based on its data and cookie policies.[314] Facebook has processed (collected, utilised and used) consumers' data from sources outside Facebook, violating consumers' privacy and hindering competition by exploiting consumer data. The *Bundeskartellamt* covered two types of data; one from Facebook-owned services like WhatsApp and Instagram, which can only be processed after the users' voluntary consent. However, data processing must remain with the respective service and cannot be utilised or moved in any combination with Facebook's collected data.[315] The second type of data covered in the investigation is collected from other services but assigned to a Facebook user account.[316] For instance, consumer data from WhatsApp and Instagram are directly linked to the Facebook database by an application called Family Device ID that WhatsApp and Instagram install on the users' devices.[317] According to the Authority, when there is no consent, Facebook will not be able to process and combine these data. Eventually, Facebook appealed the decision.

In its appeal decision, the Düsseldorf Higher Regional Court ruled that there was no actual abusive behaviour stemming from the data and cookie policies of Facebook or other Facebook-owned online services.[318] The Court also brought case before the CJEU for preliminary ruling. In his opinion Advocate General Athanasios Rantos stated that a competition authority does not have jurisdiction to rule on an infringement of the GDPR. However, he added that, in the exercise of their own powers, competition authorities can take account of the compatibility of a commercial practice with the GDPR. In that respect, the advocate general emphasised that the non-compliance of a behaviour related to the GDPR could be an important indication of whether that conduct amounts to a breach of competition rules.[319]

---

312 ibid para 749.
313 ibid para 918.
314 ibid para 940; Case Summary B6-22/16, Facebook, Exploitative Business Terms Pursuant to Section 19(1) GWB for Inadequate Data Processing (15 February 2019) 12 <https://www.bundeskartellamt.de/SharedDocs/Entscheidung/EN/Fallberichte/Missbrauchsaufsicht/2019/B6-22-16.html>
315 *Bundeskartellamt*, News, '*Bundeskartellamt* Prohibits Facebook from Combining User Data from Different Sources (7 February 2019) <https://www.bundeskartellamt.de/SharedDocs/Meldung/EN/Pressemitteilungen/2019/07_02_2019_Facebook.html>
316 ibid.
317 B6-22/16, *Facebook Inc.*, paras 942–44.
318 Case VI-Kart 1/19 (V) *Facebook/Bundeskartellamt*, The Decision of the Higher Regional Court of Düsseldorf (26 August 2019) <https://www.d-kart.de/wp-content/uploads/2019/08/OLG-D%C3%BCsseldorf-Facebook-2019-English.pdf>
319 Case C-252/21 Meta Platforms vs. Bundeskartellamt [2022] ECLI:EU:C:2022:704; PRESS RELEASE No 158/22 Luxembourg, 20 September 2022 Advocate General's Opinion C-252/21 | Meta Platforms and Others (General terms of use of a social network).

The Regional High Court's decision is arguable. The court found no causal link between the violation of data privacy and market power where a breach of data protection rights may constitute an abuse of a dominant position.[320] According to European and German competition laws, behavioural causality must be established, and a link between the market power of the dominant undertaking and its abusive conduct must be visible, or at least the anti-competitive effects of Facebook's conduct can be traced back to dominance.[321] In this case, the high court ruled that it is not the market power that enabled Facebook to impose terms of service on its consumers; thus, exploitative abuse cannot be linked to the terms of service of Facebook or any Facebook-owned online services.

Moreover, all consumers of Facebook were well aware of its data-processing conduct, and they consented while registering on Facebook to any processing and combining of data. The court added:

> There is no point in Facebook obtaining the user's consent through coercion, pressure, exploitation of a weakness of will or other unfair means or the company using the additional data contrary to the agreement beyond the agreed scope. The fact that the use of the Facebook network is linked to the consent to the use of additional data does not imply any compulsion and does not constitute a predicament for the user.[322]

Therefore, judges argued that users are not dependent on Facebook by any means at the time of registration, and they can accept or leave Facebook.[323] The appeal decision is quite important since it cripples the efforts of the *Bundeskartellamt* to break new ground regarding competition and data privacy laws.[324] However, this investigation and reasoning should be welcomed as a true step in identifying Big Data–related abuses.

Nevertheless, the investigation into Facebook clearly demonstrates a need to interpret competition rules from a different point of view in the age of Big Data since there might be critical abusive conduct that is novel for the competition law assessment. As discussed before, the interaction between competition and data protection laws in data-driven markets is an ongoing debate many scholars have studied.[325] In order to achieve competition-data protection cooperation, which could

---

320 Case VI-Kart 1/19 (V) *Facebook/Bundeskartellamt* 15–16.
321 ibid 16.
322 ibid 22.
323 Denis Schlimpert, 'Victory for Facebook as Düsseldorf Court Suspends the *Bundeskartellamt*'s Decision' *CMS Law Now* (30 August 2019) <https://www.cms-lawnow.com/ealerts/2019/08/victory-for-facebook-as-duesseldorf-court-suspends-the-bundeskartellamts-decision?cc_lang=en>
324 ibid.
325 Giulia Schneider, 'Testing Art. 102 TFEU in the Digital Marketplace: Insights from the Bundeskartellamt's Investigation Against Facebook' (2018) 9 Journal of European Competition Law and Practice 4, 213; Maureen K Ohlhausen and Alexander P Okuliar, 'Competition, Consumer Protection and the Right (Approach) to Privacy' (2015) 80 Antitrust Law Journal 1; Marco Botta and Klaus Wiedemann, 'The Interaction of EU Competition, Consumer, and Data Protection Law in

be much more effective for data-related abuses in the new economy, the German Competition Authority utilised European data protection provisions to examine exploitative abuses in data-driven markets, and they also closely cooperated with data protection authorities thereof.[326] To be more precise, the *Bundeskartellamt* linked abusive conduct to data privacy violations and concluded that violation of data protection laws could be an abusive practice.

In the same vein, the UNCTAD Secretariat's study of competition issues in the digital economy also stresses the need for a more flexible approach to the abuse of dominance assessments in data-driven markets.[327] The study underlines the two important points that the Facebook investigation by the *Bundeskartellamt* revealed: first, a need for integration between competition, consumer protection and data protection laws since they have all become intertwined due to Big Data, the Big Data–driven market power and data privacy–related abuse of dominant position cases.[328] Second is the need to ensure that the particularities of online ecosystems and data-driven businesses are reflected in competition law assessment and enforcement without any errors.[329]

However, according to many scholars, the *Bundeskartellamt*'s method of assessing Facebook's terms of service through competition law instead of consumer or data protection laws was peculiar.[330] According to this contrary idea, as a policy

---

the Digital Economy: The Regulatory Dilemma in the Facebook Odyssey' (2019) 64 The Antitrust Bulletin 3, 428–46; Lisa Kimmel and Janis Kestenbaum, 'What's Up with WhatsApp? A Transatlantic View on Privacy and Merger Enforcement in Digital Markets' (2014) 29 Antitrust 48; Geoffrey A Manne and Joshua D Wright, 'Google and the Limits of Antitrust: The Case Against the Antitrust Case against Google' (2011) 34 Harvard Journal of Law and Public Policy 171, 212; Daniel Sokol and Roisin Comerford, 'Does Antitrust Have a Role to Play in Regulating Big Data?' in Roger D Blair and Daniel Sokol (eds) *The Cambridge Handbook of Antitrust, Intellectual Property and High Tech* (CUP 2017) 271, 277; Damien Geradin and Monika Kuschewsky, 'Data Protection in the Context of Competition Law Investigations: An Overview of the Challenges' (2014) 37 World Competition 69; Francisco Costa-Cabral and Orla Lynske, 'Family Ties: The Intersection Between Data Protection and Competition EU Law' (2017) 54 Common Market Law Review 11, 17; Joaquin Almunia, 'Competition and Privacy in Markets of Data' Speech at Privacy Platform Event: Competition and Privacy in Markets of Data, Brussels, 26 November 2012 <http://europa.eu/rapid/press-releaseSPEECH-12-860_en.htm>; David S Evans and Richard Schmalensee, 'The Antitrust Analysis of Multi-Sided Platform Businesses' in R Blair and D Sokol (eds), *Oxford Handbook on International Antitrust Economics*, vol 1 (OUP 2015) 404.
326 *Bundeskartellamt*, News, '*Bundeskartellamt* Prohibits Facebook from Combining User Data from Different Sources (7 February 2019) <https://www.bundeskartellamt.de/SharedDocs/Meldung/EN/Pressemitteilungen/2019/07_02_2019_Facebook.html>
327 Ebru Gökçe, 'Competition Issues in the Digital Economy' (2019) UNCTAD Background Note, para 23 <https://unctad.org/system/files/official-document/ciclpd54_en.pdf>
328 ibid.
329 ibid.
330 Marco Botta and Klaus Wiedemann, 'The Interaction of EU Competition, Consumer, and Data Protection Law in the Digital Economy: The Regulatory Dilemma in the Facebook Odyssey' (2019) 64 The Antitrust Bulletin 3, 428–46, 440; Giuseppe Colangelo and Mariateresa Maggiolino, 'Data Protection in Attention Markets: Protecting Privacy Through Competition?' (2017) 8 Journal of European Competition Law and Practice 363.

choice, data protection law would fit the investigation of Facebook better before the civil courts.[331] Some scholars also reject the idea that data protection concerns are addressable under competition law.[332] In this sense, Facebook is already under scrutiny by the data protection authorities in Europe.[333] Many data protection authorities throughout Europe, including those in Belgium, Germany, Italy, the Netherlands and Spain, have opened investigations into the data processing methods of Facebook and Facebook-owned online services.[334] However, if the conduct of dominant Facebook is abusive and Facebook abuses this position through its data power, competition law needs to step in.

The key point is the relevancy of competition law to the data violations of dominant undertakings in data-driven markets. As examined earlier, the European Commission cleared the Facebook/WhatsApp merger in 2014. In the investigation, almost all dangers and risks of data merging and processing were on the table. Still, erroneously, the Commission cleared the merger and ruled that data protection concerns are not related to competition law, and privacy concerns must be addressed outside competition law.[335] As a result, Facebook changed its privacy policies just after the merger, and exploitative abuse followed, triggering the attention of competition authorities.

More importantly, the *Bundeskartellamt* took a novel approach in its investigation. Rather than analysing the alleged abuse by focusing on the existing case law and regulation-established exclusionary conduct, the authority took on the challenging task of analysing competition infringement by also taking data protection concerns into consideration. The *Bundeskartellamt*'s way of approaching the issue demonstrates how competition is evolving in the age of Big Data and how the authorities should shift their assessments of abuses in data-driven markets.

To sum up, the possibility of abuse through the violation of data protection rules in data-driven markets reveals the need for a more flexible approach in the assessment of abuse cases and merger control. Today, more companies successfully utilise Big Data for their services throughout the online world, and data provides market power for these undertakings. Where the processing of data (collecting, analysing, utilising) becomes a part of gaining market power, for anti-competitive conduct (which is abuse through exclusionary and discriminatory practices, abuse through access to data and other novel abuses such as abuse through data privacy) or subject to a merger, then competition law must be applied to these situations. Moreover, competition authorities must closely monitor dominant technology giants' data collection, analytics and utilisation activities since many competition

---

331 Botta and Wiedemann (n 330) 440.
332 Geoffrey A Manne and Joshua D Wright, 'Google and the Limits of Antitrust: The Case Against the Antitrust Case Against Google' (2011) 34 Harvard Journal of Law and Public Policy 250, 258; Wolfgang Kerber, 'Digital Markets, Data, and Privacy: Competition Law, Consumer Law, and Data Protection' (2016) 11 Journal of Intellectual Property Law and Practice 856.
333 Jordan Ellison and others, 'A New Frontier for Privacy and Competition' Slaughter and May Report (March 2018) 3.
334 ibid.
335 Case No COMP/M.7217 *Facebook/WhatsApp* C [2014] 7239 final, para 164.

risks arise from the data power of technology giants. Data privacy or consumer protection authorities cannot conduct this task since they do not have capacity in cases of competition law. However, competition authorities should cooperate with consumer protection and data protection officials if there is a need to assess the Big Data issue from a privacy point of view. Moreover, privacy policies can also be an internal part of competition law if privacy becomes a parameter of competition law as a non-price dimension of the market power assessment.

5.3.3 Discussion of Privacy Policies Under Article 102 of the TFEU

The possible application of privacy as a non-price dimension of market power assessment is discussed in detail in Chapter 4. The reason behind it is clear: privacy protection is becoming more of a concern in data-driven markets due to anti-competitive practices such as Facebook's abuse. Privacy protection also becomes more of a concern in data-driven markets in general. According to the study of ECORYS, less incentive to protect consumers and violation of consumer privacy form the theory of harm of competition law in the highly concentrated data-driven markets.[336] In other words, undertakings do not protect the privacy of their consumers while processing (collecting and utilising) data. Marco Botta and Klaus Wiedemann specified a problem on the users' side of markets: the privacy paradox.[337] The privacy paradox creates several problems. First, although users care about their privacy, they do not protect their data and often give out their personal and behavioural information by clicking their consent right away in order to use online services without even reading the terms of service.[338] A European Commission survey indicates that 31% of consumers do not read online privacy policies, while 49% only read these policies partially.[339] Online service providers often provide long terms of service in the smallest font possible, which are basically unreadable by users. Even if consumers read them, they probably do not understand them. The second problem that the privacy paradox creates is the lack of transparency. In the scenario in which users give consent comprehendingly, they probably do not know what undertakings will or could achieve with their data.[340] In other words, like Facebook's conduct, consumers cannot know how their data is used, utilised or transferred.

---

336 Harry van Til, Nicolai van Gorp and Katelyn Price, 'Big Data and Competition' (2017) ECORYS Report Paper 36–37 <https://zoek.officielebekendmakingen.nl/blg-813928.pdf>
337 Privacy paradox refers to the situation in which the majority of online service users "care" about their privacy in the online world and ask for more protection but do not act accordingly. Wolfgang Kerber, 'Digital Markets, Data, and Privacy: Competition Law, Consumer Law, and Data Protection' (2016) 11 Journal of Intellectual Property Law and Practice 860–66.
338 Botta and Wiedeman (n 330) 432.
339 European Commission, Data Protection – Report 84 (Special Eurobarometer 431, 2015) <https://ec.europa.eu/commfrontoffice/publicopinion/archives/ebs/ebs_431_en.pdf>
340 Botta and Wiedeman (n 330) 433.

As a behavioural remedy, without any competition intervention in terms of privacy concerns, undertakings in data-driven markets may introduce new methods for their products and services that are less harmful to consumer privacy. For instance, undertakings may offer more transparent business models and privacy policies, such as the DuckDuckGo search engine, which offers a search engine experience without collecting consumer data and still competes with Google.[341] However, the power of data utilisation and the unique characteristics of data-driven markets, such as indirect network effects and ecosystem structure, bring costs to companies like DuckDuckGo. Hence, companies that do not collect and utilise data fall short in offering better quality and more personalised products, ultimately failing in competition.[342] Like other non-price competition parameters, such as innovation or quality, the privacy-competition relation does not seem linear.[343] Although dominant players do not care about privacy protection in highly concentrated markets, it would be hard to make any claims that privacy protection would be much better in competitive markets.

As a result, more use of data in the online world leads to privacy and data protection breaches every day.[344] Although these data protection and privacy breaches affect many consumers individually, competition is also affected. If the data protection violations in data-driven markets are based on Big Data, which is a fundamental source of market power, data violations should become a part of competition assessment eventually. Although consumer protection, data protection and competition laws aim to ensure that consumers' welfare is protected, consumer protection and data privacy are more concerned with individuals' welfare.[345] However, competition law aims to ensure the total welfare of everyone. In other words, data privacy, consumer protection and competition may have similar goals, but their main objectives are distinct. Competition law is the main safeguard against distorted competition in the EU. Also, the legality of an intervention under another legal regime will not prevent any intervention or enforcement of competition law, as CJEU case law has confirmed.[346] In other words, competition law intervention will still be legal, relevant and necessary, even if the abusive conduct occurs in grey zones between data privacy, consumer protection and competition; the competition authorities should intervene in market failures.[347] Moreover, scholars argue that the effects of breaches of privacy and data protection are beyond market competition, and they compromise people's democratic processes and choices.[348]

---

341 Van Til, van Gorp and Price (n 336) 37.
342 ibid.
343 ibid.
344 Ioannis Lianos, 'Competition Law for the Digital Era: A Complex Systems' Perspective' (2019) CLES Research Paper Series 6/2019, 28.
345 Schneider (n 325) 215.
346 Botta and Wiedemann (n 330) 437.
347 ibid.
348 Ariel Ezrachi and Maurice E Stucke, 'The Fight Over Antitrust's Soul' (2018) 9 Journal of European Competition Law and Practice 1; Lianos (n 344) 28; Josef Drexl, 'Economic Efficiency

When there is a competition law breach through data violations, competition authorities should have the power to intervene.[349] As in the *Bundeskartellamt*'s Facebook investigation, authorities must assess the conduct, and if they find abuse that is also a violation of data privacy law or other legal regimes, the violation will give the theory of abuse additional weight.[350] Accordingly, the competition authorities must focus more on Big Data-related issues when dealing with the abusive conduct of dominant undertakings in the new economy. In this sense, even scholars such as Ohlhausen and Okuliar argue that privacy concerns can be better reflected in consumer protection and data privacy laws than in competition law;[351] they express that privacy protection can be considered a parameter of the non-price competition assessment as well.[352] In the EU, the European Commission repeatedly considered privacy-related concerns out of competition law and concluded that data-related privacy issues do not fall within the scope of the EU competition rules.[353]

Nevertheless, privacy as a non-price dimension of competition law should be tested in competition law analysis, just as the *Bundeskartellamt* did in the Facebook investigation. Privacy can be considered a non-price parameter, like innovation and quality. Harbour and Koslov mention that undertakings in data-driven markets adapt their terms of service and additional privacy policies as a reaction to rivals or in response to consumers.[354] This is a piece of evidence that data policies can be part of the competition in the market. Also, if data policies become a part of achieving market power and abusing a dominant position, it becomes a duty for competition authorities to dig deeply into the issue. Therefore, how does privacy play a role in competition, and can it be an objective parameter? Thus, how could a violation of data policy be anti-competitive?

Versus Democracy: On the Potential Role of Competition Policy in Regulating Digital Markets in Times of Post-Truth Politics' in Damien Gerard and Ioannis Lianos (eds), *Competition Policy: Between Equity and Efficiency* (CUP 2017).

349 Maximilian N Volmar and Katharina O Helmdach, 'Protecting Consumers and Their Data Through Competition Law? Rethinking Abuse of Dominance in Light of the Federal Cartel Office's Facebook Investigation' (2018) 14(2) European Competition Journal 203.

350 ibid.

351 Maureen K Ohlhausen and Alexander P Okuliar, 'Competition, Consumer Protection and the Right (Approach) to Privacy' (2015) 80 Antitrust Law Journal 1; Geoffrey A Manne and R Ben Sperry, 'The Problems and Perils of Bootstrapping Privacy and Data into an Antitrust Framework' (20125) 2 CPI Antitrust Chronicle 1; Giuseppe Colangelo and Mariateresa Maggiolino, 'Data Protection in Attention Markets: Protecting Privacy Through Competition?' (2017) 8 Journal of European Competition Law and Practice 363.

352 Ohlhausen and Okuliar (n 351) 156.

353 Case C-238/05 *Asnef-Equifax* [2006] ECLI:EU:C:2006:734, para 63; Case No COMP/M.4731 *Google/DoubleClick* C[2008] 927 final, para 368; Case No COMP/M.7217 *Facebook/WhatsApp* C [2014] 7239 final, para 164; Case No COMP/M.8124 *Microsoft/LinkedIn* C [2016] 8404 final, paras 177-78; Case No COMP/M.7813 *Sanofi/Google/DMI JV* [2016] 1223 final, paras 69-70.

354 Pamela Jones Harbour and Tara Isa Koslov, 'Section 2 in a Web 2.0: An Expanded Vision of Relevant Product Markers' (2010) 76 Antitrust Law Journal 794.

In a situation in which most scholars argue that degradation in privacy is nearly impossible to detect, Samson Esayas argues that the benchmark of "privacy" for measuring competition can be objective and measurable.[355] Evidence of this can be found in the European Commission's assessment of the Microsoft/LinkedIn merger. The Commission considered the possibility of consumer harm where consumers' choice is reduced through promoting LinkedIn on the Windows OS and in Microsoft Office. Therefore, referring to privacy degradation, paragraph 350 of the investigation states:

> These foreclosure effects would lead to the marginalisation of an existing competitor which offers a greater degree of privacy protection to users than LinkedIn. . . . [T]he transaction would also restrict consumer choice in relation to this important parameter of competition when choosing a PSN (professional social network).[356]

In other words, the Commission expressed that a decrease in the level of privacy or loosening of the privacy policies of dominant undertakings can be a result of abusive behaviour, such as promoting LinkedIn on Windows.[357] In this sense, privacy can be used as an assessment tool for competition law purposes.

Since competition law welcomes different benchmarks to assess potential anti-competitive conduct, privacy can also serve as a benchmark for assessing the non-price dimension of competition in a market. If the data collection and processing methods constitute abuse in the online world, just like in the *GDF-Suez* and *Belgian National Lottery* cases, then the data privacy violations and data protection law infringements can also be considered abuses when conduct is not competition on merits. Thus, unfair trading conditions imposed through data privacy policies by dominant undertakings that aim to distort competition, exclusionary or exploitative, should be regarded as Article 102 infringements.

For this very reason, competition law must intervene in the exclusionary and exploitative effects of data privacy breaches when there is a link between market power, abusive behaviour and data violations. Starting from this point of view, the *Bundeskartellamt* ruled Facebook's data privacy policies to be abusive, prohibited the use of terms of service and ordered the termination of the conduct.[358]

---

355 Samson Y Esayas, 'Privacy as a Quality Parameter of Competition: Some Reflections on the Scepticism Surrounding It' in Björn Lundqvist and Michal S Gal (eds), *Competition Law for the Digital Economy* (1st edn, Edward Elgar Publishing 2019) 164.
356 Case No COMP/M.8124 *Microsoft/LinkedIn* C [2016] 8404 final, para 350.
357 Esayas (n 355) 164.
358 B6-22/16, *Facebook Inc., Facebook Ireland Ltd., Facebook Deutschland GmbH, Verbraucherzentrale Bundesverband e.V.* Bundeskartellamt 6th Decision Division (6 February 2019).

Facebook's terms of service were imposing unfair conditions on consumers, and Andreas Mundt wrote:

> Today data are a decisive factor in competition. In the case of Facebook, they are the essential factor for establishing the company's dominant position. On the one hand, there is a service provided to users free of charge. On the other hand, the attractiveness and value of the advertising spaces increase with the amount and detail of user data. It is therefore precisely in the area of data collection and data use where Facebook, as a dominant company, must comply with the rules and laws applicable in Germany and Europe.[359]

The investigation put privacy at the centre of the competition law assessment. Also, privacy has become a parameter to assess the level of competition in a particular data-driven market. These were proper steps toward a new understanding of the competition law assessment, and more will come to competition law in the future. To sum up, privacy considerations should bring data protection and competition laws together and tighten their connection. Therefore, abuse of a dominant position in EU law should be redefined to better reflect the market conditions and capture possible novel abuses when necessary.

5.3.4 Italian Competition Authority's Facebook Investigation

A regulatory and enforcement dilemma exists in Facebook's alleged abuse. Unlike the *Bundeskartellamt*, which found a breach of GWB Section 19 (Article 102 TFEU), the *Autorita' Garante della Concorrenza e del Mercato* (AGCM), the Italian Competition Authority, adopted a decision due to a breach of Italian consumer law rather than competition law in November 2018.[360] The Authority ruled that Facebook violated Articles 21 and 22 of *Codice del Consumo*, the Italian Consumer Code, by misleading consumers about its data collection and processing methods and carrying out aggressive commercial practices to exert undue influence on its consumers by transferring their data between Facebook and other Facebook-owned online services.[361]

Article 21 of the Italian Consumer Code deals with "unfair commercial practices" which provide information to consumers that is false or misleading.[362] Also,

---

359 *Bundeskartellamt*, News, '*Bundeskartellamt* Prohibits Facebook from Combining User Data from Different Sources' (7 February 2019) <https://www.bundeskartellamt.de/SharedDocs/Meldung/EN/Pressemitteilungen/2019/07_02_2019_Facebook.html>
360 Decision of the AGCM adopted on November 29, 2018, in relation to Facebook Inc. and Facebook Ireland Ltd. The (Italian) text of the decision [hereinafter AGCM Decision] and the corresponding press release <https://www.agcm.it/media/comunicati-stampa/2018/12/Uso-dei-dati-degli-utenti-a-fini-commerciali-sanzioni-per-10-milioni-di-euro-a-Facebook>. An English version of the press release <https://en.agcm.it/en/media/press-releases/2018/12/Facebook-fined-10-million-Euros-by-the-ICA-for-unfair-commercial-practices-for-using-its-subscribers%E2%80%99-data-for-commercial-purposes>
361 ibid.
362 Italian Consumer Code, Decreto Legislativo 6 Settembre 2005, n 206 – Codice del consume.

according to Article 22 of the code, commercial practices are considered misleading, when, taking into account all circumstances of the case, as well as the limits of the means of communication used, they omit relevant information that the average consumer needs to make an informed decision, thus inducing or possibly inducing the average consumer to make a commercial decision which they would not otherwise have taken.[363] Article 5(2) of the Unfair Commercial Practices Directive, which the Italian Consumer Code had implemented, also states:

> A commercial practice shall be unfair if it is contrary to the requirements of professional diligence, and it materially distorts or is likely to materially distort the economic behaviour with regard to the product of the average consumer whom it reaches or to whom it is addressed, or of the average member of the group when a commercial practice is directed to a particular group of consumers.[364]

In its decision, the Italian Competition Authority ruled that Facebook's conduct was an aggressive and unfair commercial practice which actually misled consumers about their data collection and privacy.[365] Therefore, the Authority imposed the maximum applicable fine under Italian consumer law: €5 million each for two unfair commercial practices, €10 million in total.[366] The fine seems quite low and possibly ineffective compared to the competition law sanctions and remedies. Although investigations by both the German and Italian Competition Authorities dealt with the same conduct (data collection, transferring and processing methods of Facebook and Facebook-owned online services), the co-existence of two relevant regulatory regimes created a potential future conflict in the EU law. In light of many discussions and disputes over data-related abusive behaviour in the online world regarding competition, consumer and data privacy law, the problem is finding the most accurate and appropriate remedy for data-related abuses. In this sense, thinking of competition law as a whole, including its welfare objectives, remedies for market failures, case law on abuse of dominant position and heavier sanctions and, most importantly, having exclusive competence conferred upon it by the Treaties of the EU, in which the EU alone can legislate and adopt binding competition acts throughout the EU,[367] competition law seems to be an appropriate legal regime to deal with the related market failures and abuses.

---

363 Article 22 of Italian Consumer Code, Decreto Legislativo 6 Settembre 2005, n 206 – Codice del consume.
364 Article 5(2) of the Unfair Commercial Practices Directive.
365 The AGCM Decision.
366 Botta and Wiedemann (n 330) 444; Under Art. 27(9) Codice del Consumo, the AGCM can impose a fine between €5,000 and €5 million.
367 Article 3 of the TFEU.

5.4 Applying Article 102 of the TFEU to Big Data–Related Abuses

In light of the recent abuse cases in Europe and the US, scholars gathered around two camps regarding the abusive behaviour in data-driven markets. One camp argues that competition intervention aimed at fighting the technology giants impedes innovation; thus, it must be avoided. For instance, Daniel Crane writes: "Antitrust law should never seek to destroy dominance by prohibiting dominant firms from innovating to keep up with their customers' changing demands".[368] Comparably, Bork and Sidak, Manne and Rinehart stress that consumer-welfare-enhancing innovation would be impeded if competition intervened in the virtuous cycle of dynamic competition, creating costly errors.[369] In other words, the European Commission and the NCAs should approach issues in data-driven markets in a non-interventionist, more passive way. By doing this, the market can change itself to mitigate problems in the cycle of dynamic competition.

On the other hand, there is an argument for invention in data-driven markets. As analysed previously, data-driven markets have unique characteristics which cannot be reflected by the traditional methods of competition. As a result, a non-interventionist approach will not be successful for a specific reason: the accumulative value of Big Data. Undoubtedly, the dominant technology companies have achieved success thanks to their innovations in data collection, analysis, and processing skills; consumers benefited hugely from these technological advances.[370] However, it is evident that the dominance of technology giants was created through the accumulation and utilisation of Big Data. In a word, Big Data is the main source of their market power. Peter Norvig, the chief scientist of Google, emphasised: "We do not have better algorithms than anyone else. We just have more data".[371]

Therefore, undertakings that have already accumulated vast amounts of data, established network effects and created ecosystems for consumers will continue to rise in the online world. This will bring anti-competitive conduct to the online world as well. However, competition intervention could help prevent abuses and consumer harm in data-driven markets. For instance, when restrictions are placed on the behavioural data collection of undertakings, studies found that the

---

368 Daniel Crane, 'Search Neutrality and Referral Dominance' (2012) 8 (3) Journal of Competition Law & Economics 459–68, 468.
369 Robert H Bork and J Gregory Sidak, 'What Does the Chicago School Teach About Internet Search and the Antitrust Treatment of Google?' (2012) 8 (4) Journal of Competition Law & Economics 663–700, 3; Geoffrey A Manne and William Rinehart, 'The Market Realities That Undermined the FTC's Antitrust Case Against Google' (2013) Harvard Journal of Law & Technology Occasional Paper Series 12.
370 Nathan Newman, 'Search, Antitrust, and the Economics of the Control of User Data' (2014) 31 Yale Journal on Regulation 2, 421.
371 Matt Asay and Tim O'Reilly, '"Whole Web" Is the OS of the Future' *CNET* (18 March 2010) <http://www.cnet.com/news/tim-oreilly-whole-web-is-the-os-of-the-future>

effectiveness of advertising dropped greatly, and the importance of data for online advertising dropped likewise.[372]

As discussed in this chapter, applying Article 102 of the TFEU is problematic in assessing market power and abusive behaviour. The need to move away from the traditional market definition and market power assessment initially addresses abusive behaviour. Online ecosystems and non-horizontal links between adjacent markets in the online world are completely overlooked in the competition law analysis. As a result, many crucial points are missed in merger and abuse of dominant position investigations, starting from the market definition assessment through the enforcement point. Thus, there is an urgent need to implement a more precise assessment method for abuse cases in data-driven markets. At the same time, all challenges related to data processing issues should also be addressed. As seen in abuse through exclusionary and exploitive practices related to data, including access to data issues and data privacy violations, competition law assessment needs to embrace new market characteristics. There could be room for novel abuse types in data-driven markets. Concordantly, the *Bundeskartellamt* investigation is a welcomed step in identifying Big Data—related novel abuses in data-driven markets.

Ultimately, the competition intervention in data-driven markets through Article 102 TFEU might not be enough. Technology giants such as Google, Apple, Facebook, Amazon and Microsoft (GAFAM) have already reached a point where they move into new markets, leverage their data power and easily tip markets. These linked markets create a conglomerate structure and constitute online ecosystems. It is called the "intermediation" power.[373] In online ecosystems, intermediaries that are also creators and owners have pivotal roles as competitors and regulators. To be more precise, due to their vast data power and unbalanced data processing skills, technology giants such as GAFAM have become *de facto* competition regulators in their respective ecosystems. They control every price- and non-price-related transaction, and they impose their own terms on rivals and consumers; they can even adjust how dynamic competition will be in that respective ecosystem and in comprising markets in the ecosystem. In a situation in which a super-dominant undertaking controls everything in a market, healthy competition cannot find a place for itself. The next chapter discusses the newly emerged unwanted regulatory problem in online ecosystems to reveal the need for an intervention in data-driven markets.

---

372 Newman (n 370) citing: Avi Goldfarb and Catherine E Tucker, 'Privacy Regulation and Online Advertising' (2011) 57 Management Science 57.
373 Ioannis Lianos, 'Competition Law for the Digital Era: A Complex Systems' Perspective' (2019) CLES Research Paper Series 6/2019, 125.

6 The Way Forward

6.1 Ways to Approach the Big Data Issue From a Competition Law Perspective

The analysis in this book has revealed a threefold issue for immediate remedial action: the monopolisation problem in which strong platform owners become regulators, the ineffective neoclassical economic tools to assess market power and the identification of novel abusive behaviour in the new economy. The need for reform of these issues is undisputed at this point, yet what should the appropriate approach for these novel issues be?

The identification of the threefold issue enables analysis the opening of a discussion on finding an immediate response for data-driven markets. However, the remedial action could be a regulatory or broader one that delves into competition law theory. Thus, an appropriate approach must be set to resolve current and potential competition law issues in this newly emerged market economy. After summarising the current state and identifying problems needing remedial action, the second step of the analysis should address the approach to be considered and engaged for the addressed problems. Therefore, the analysis that follows is dedicated to justifying potential competition law intervention limits in data-driven markets.

6.1.1 Non-interventionist Approach

The discussion here is more political than the normative competition law analysis throughout the research. Still, it is necessary to determine an approach, either an interventionist or a passive one. For instance, the *laissez-faire* ideology[1] of neoclassical economics suggests that market players should set the level of competition in time, and intervention outside the market would not benefit consumers. In other words, markets will correct themselves in time, and the best approach is not to

---

1 Although *laissez-faire* ideology dates back to 18th century France, John Stuart Mill and Adam Smith developed the understanding, and this led to the creation of modern economics, which advocates that government intervention into markets must be minimal, and authorities should focus on public order and the safety of citizens.

DOI: 10.4324/9781003458791-6

intervene in more or less competitive markets. Academics who argue that markets self-correct also tend to argue that competition law is flexible enough for the application of Article 102 in data-driven markets since it is well-equipped enough.[2]

The application of *laissez-faire* economics (and a consumer welfare approach) has become more evident in EU law due to a more economical approach to the competition policy, especially after the 1980s. However, long before its rise in European law, the progress of consumer welfare can be traced in the US conduct as far as a century ago. First, Harvard and then the Chicago School of competition set the framework for the consumer welfare approach to competition. According to the ideology, competition law specifically concerns consumers and their interests. As Richard Posner indicates, at that time, the Chicago School of competition did not contain a well-rounded philosophy of competition.[3] Instead, it was more of a response to the specific problems encountered in several competition cases.[4]

From a different point of view, Robert Bork, a prominent scholar of the Chicago School, argues that competition law should not determine who controls the wealth – in other words, who should be rich or poor – or deal with expenditures on environmental issues such as pollution.[5] Instead, competition law and policy should focus on ensuring conditions which would be the most favourable to consumers.[6] Thus, competition law should take efficiencies[7] into account and then assess the consumers' welfare, which must be the main concern of competition policy.[8] Since then, the consumer welfare approach has been accepted as the main application of competition law in US antitrust law. Even the court decisions of that era have interpreted the Sherman Act's (1890) real intention, referring to Robert Bork's 1978 work, to prescribe the consumer welfare approach for federal antitrust law.[9]

In the US, strict *laissez-faire* ideas have influenced enforcement in data-driven markets. In the wake of the new economy, many competition proceedings (abusive behaviour cases and mergers investigations) were held before the United States courts and the FTC. Microsoft's[10] abuse of a dominant position case is a good

---

2 Evelin Hlina, 'Dominant Undertakings in the Digital Era: A Call for Evolution of the Competition Policy Towards Article 102 TFEU?' (2016) 9 ICC Global Antitrust Review.
3 Richard A Posner, 'The Chicago School of Antitrust Analysis' (1979) 127 University of Pennsylvania Law Review 925–26.
4 ibid.
5 Robert Bork, *The Antitrust Paradox: A Policy at War with Itself* (1st edn, Basic Books, Free Press 1978) 90–91.
6 ibid.
7 "Efficiencies" here is used in the context of allocative and productive efficiency gains. Except that, terms "consumer welfare" and "efficiency" were used as synonyms by Robert Bork in his book *The Antitrust Paradox* 72–89.
8 Bork (n 5) 405.
9 Case *Reiter v Sonotone Corp.*, 442 U.S. 330 [1979], 343.
10 US Supreme Court *United States v Microsoft Corporation* 253 F.3d 34 (D.C. Circuit 2001).

example of concerns raised regarding possible intervention by competition authorities in the new economy markets.[11] Due to its dynamic and fast-moving character, a passive approach was found to be more appropriate in order not to stifle innovation. Later, in the *Google Search* case, similar ideas were also discussed.[12] The non-interventionist approach relies on the idea that many more start-ups will be ready to challenge incumbent technology giants since innovation is favoured by allowing "self-regulation".[13] However, the passive approach definitely created monopolies or at least high concentrations in data-driven markets, and incumbents became more and more dominant.[14] Moreover, through "killer acquisitions", even a few remaining start-ups and innovations are already being swallowed up or thrown away by incumbent technology giants.

To sum up, it has been well over two decades since the emergence of data-driven markets, and all findings demonstrate that the dominance of incumbents is getting stronger and markets are tipping due to the data power of a few strong dominant undertakings, as new markets are also being created in the online world. Even though the Chicago School of competition has a loud voice on the other side of the Atlantic, the approach to technology giants and data-driven markets is starting to change. On 29 July 2020, the US House of Representatives' antitrust subcommittee held a hearing regarding the anti-competitive behaviour of Big Data user technology giants.[15] Apple's CEO Tim Cook, Google's CEO Sundar Pichai, Facebook's CEO Mark Zuckerberg and Amazon's CEO Jeff Bezos were summoned to the hearing. Democratic members of the House Judiciary subcommittee, including David Cicilline (Chair), Pramilla Jayapal, Val Demings and others, pressured CEOs to reveal how the technology giants channel their data into market power and abuse their powers after "killer acquisitions". Jeff Bezos, Mark Zuckerberg and Sundar Pichai struggled to convince the committee that their business strategies had been for innovation and better products for consumers rather than creating a digital empire to rule the online world.[16] Although Apple's Tim Cook positioned his company differently, there are strong concerns about whether

---

11 Hlina (n 2) 127.
12 European Commission, 'Antitrust: Commission Sends Statement of Objections to Google on Comparison Shopping Service' Press Release of 15 April 2015 (MEMO/15/4781) <http://europa.eu/rapid/press-release_IP-15-4780_en.htm>
13 Nathan Newman, 'Search, Antitrust, and the Economics of the Control of User Data' (2014) 31 Yale Journal on Regulation 2, 454.
14 ibid.
15 Roger McNamee, 'A Historic Antitrust Hearing in Congress Has Put Big Tech on Notice' *The Guardian* (31 July 2020) <https://www.theguardian.com/commentisfree/2020/jul/31/big-tech-house-historic-antitrust-hearing-times-have-changed>
16 Adam Satariano, 'This Is a New Phase: Europe Shifts Tactics to Limit Tech's Power' *New York Times* (30 July 2020) <https://www.nytimes.com/2020/07/30/technology/europe-new-phase-tech-amazon-apple-facebook-google.html>; For the video <https://www.youtube.com/watch?v=PvLtwV7DFwg&list=WL&index=4&ab_channel=Engadget>

Apple is also engaging in abusive behaviour through its App Store in iOS, macOS and Apple Music.

In October 2020, the staff of the Democratic members of the Committee signed a 400-page report on how technology giants abuse their Big Data power, impede competition and stifle innovation.[17] According to the study, technology giants engage in anti-competitive conduct and become "internet gatekeepers" by controlling online markets that are crucial for consumers. By this means, they entrench their market power, pursue start-up acquisitions and eventually monopolise. The study suggests potential regulatory *ex-ante* interventions in data-driven markets by breaking up technology giants into smaller companies. Likewise, Joe Biden, the Democratic president of the US, stresses that he would consider company breakups in the near future.[18] The approaches of US lawmakers and politicians are changing due to the power shift between Republicans and Democrats. Apart from the political movements, the judiciary and authorities also seem concerned regarding data controllers violating antitrust laws and exercising monopolistic powers in the online world. This can be traced in the FTC's newest investigations in data-driven markets against Google, Amazon and Facebook.[19] Thus, even in the US, calls for intervention are getting even more serious than in the past.

Another argument against the competition law intervention in data-driven markets is the data protection and privacy argument discussed in Chapter 5. To nuance it briefly, data violations are found to be a grey zone between data privacy, competition law and consumer protection. Therefore, the increasing use of consumer data and Big Data utilisation will likely cause competition and privacy concerns in the future. As there is an interplay between different areas of law, cooperation is needed while approaching these competition violations. Therefore, the idea of creating a reliable and effective system for data protection, like the new GDPR, to deal with data-related issues and enable innovation and competition is also discussed widely. However, as mentioned before, when a data violation constitutes abusive behaviour related to market power, data protection issues become an internal issue for competition law.[20] Thus, it becomes even more important while addressing potential novel abuse types in the new economy.

The recent *Bundeskartellamt* decision addressing data privacy violations as a competition issue has revealed the potential impact of data power on consumers,

---

17 Five Things to Know About the Big Tech Antitrust Report, *Associated Press* (7 October 2020) <https://apnews.com/article/politics-ac3cce04e38c0bf584cfb9ec04557874>
18 ibid.
19 U.S. Federal Trade Commission, Press Release, 'FTC to Examine Past Acquisitions by Large Technology Companies' (11 February 2020) <https://www.ftc.gov/news-events/press-releases/2020/02/ftc-examine-past-acquisitions-large-technology-companies>; Kari Paul, 'US orders Google, Facebook and others to reveal details of years of acquisitions' *The Guardian* (11 February 2020) <https://www.theguardian.com/technology/2020/feb/11/google-facebook-amazon-us-antitrust-investigations>
20 See Chapter 5.

online markets, and undertakings. Therefore, there is a need for competition authorities to better examine how data is collected and utilised in the online world in terms of competition law.[21] The decision has also revealed the importance of data privacy in the competition law assessment as a potential parameter, so competition law should not be left outside the discussion. In other words, competition and data protection authorities should handle privacy and data protection considerations together. The connection between the lawmakers and enforcers must be strong as the *Bundeskartellamt*'s recent decision successfully identified and addressed the need during the investigation by cooperating with the German data protection institutions.

To sum up, a non-interventionist approach does not seem to be right for competition law issues in the related markets. As can be seen from the recent merger investigations in the EU and the US,[22] the competition authorities were reluctant to intervene in digital ecosystems, and they deduced the idea that competition between technology companies would become more stable. The *laissez-faire* ideas have influenced enforcement, and in many competition proceedings, a passive approach was found appropriate for data-driven markets. As discussed throughout the book, the non-interventionist approach resulted in highly concentrated markets, ultimately monopolising digital ecosystems. More recently, both the EU Commission and the Federal Trade Commission have started post-merger investigations and sector inquiries to identify the problematic approach of competition law and intervene in data-driven markets, and the lack of current regulation in addressing problems in data-driven markets has been revealed. Therefore, academics argue the need to broaden competition law goals for Big Data–related issues.

---

21 Jason Furman, *Unlocking Digital Competition: Report of the Digital Competition Expert Panel* (HM Treasury 2019) 124 <https://www.gov.uk/government/publications/unlocking-digital-competition-report-of-the-digital-competition-expert-panel>
22 Case No COMP/M.4731, Google/DoubleClick C [2008] 927 Final; Case No COMP/M.5727, Microsoft/Yahoo! Search Business C [2010] 1077 Final; Case No COMP/M.6314, Telefónica UK/Vodafone UK/Everything Everywhere/JV C [2012] 6063 Final; Case No COMP/M.6281, Microsoft/Skype C [2011] 7239 Final; Case No COMP/M.7217, Facebook/WhatsApp C [2014] 7239 Final; Case No COMP/M.8124, Microsoft/LinkedIn C [2016] 8404 Final; Case No COMP/M.8228, Facebook/WhatsApp C [2017] 3192 Final; Federal Trade Commission, 'Statement of Federal Trade Commission concerning Google/DoubleClick' FTC File No. 071-0170 <https://www.ftc.gov/system/files/documents/public_statements/418081/071220googledc-commstmt.pdf>; Federal Trade Commission, Dissenting Statement of Commissioner Pamela Jones Harbour, In the matter of Google/DoubleClick F.T.C. File No. 071-0170 (2007) <https://www.ftc.gov/sites/default/files/documents/public_statements/statement-matter-google/doubleclick/071220harbour_0.pdf>

6.1.2 Broadening Competition Law's Goals

As it has many objectives such as market access,[23] market integration[24] and ordo-liberal objectives,[25] the application of the consumer welfare approach in the EU has gained prominence through an economic analysis of the market since consumer welfare is basically measured by economic efficiencies.[26] Jones and Sufrin address the idea that the consumer welfare approach of competition law should stay in the main framework of preventing anti-competitive agreements, abusive conduct and mergers and should not provide mechanisms to promote and enhance competitiveness or other socio-political goals in the first place.[27] Therefore, as the consumer welfare approach has gained prominence in competition law today, analysing how new markets function and why competition policy is ineffective is intrinsically associated with the consumer welfare objective of competition law. As a result,

---

23 Communication from the Commission, Guidance on the Commission's Enforcement Priorities in Applying Article 82 of the EC Treaty to Abusive Exclusionary Conduct by Dominant Undertakings [2009] OJ C45/02, para 6; Case C-6/72 *Europemballage Corporation and Continental Can Company Inc. v Commission of the European Communities* [1973] ECLI:EU:C:1973:22; Case C-85/76 *Hoffman-La Roche & Co. AG v Commission of the European Communities* [1979] ECLI:EU:C:1979:36, para 91; C-62/86 *AKZO Chemie BV v Commission of the European Communities* [1991] ECLI:EU:C:1991:286, para 69.

24 Richard Whish and David Bailey, *Competition Law* (8th edn, OUP 2015) 24; Consolidated Version of the Treaty on European Union art. [3], 2010 O.J. C 83/01; Case T-368/00 *General Motors Nederland BV and Opel Nederland BV v Commission of the European Communities* [2003] ECLI:EU:T:2003:275; Case T-67/01 *JCB Service v Commission of the European Communities* [2004] ECLI:EU:T:2004:3; Case C-53/03 *Synetairismos Farmakopoion Aitolias & Akarnanias (Syfait) and Others v GlaxoSmithKline plc and GlaxoSmithKline AEVE* [2005] ECLI:EU:C:2005:333; Case C-501/06 P *GlaxoSmithKline Services and Others v Commission and Others* [2009] ECLI:EU:C:2009:610.

25 Christian Ahlborn and Carsten Grave, 'Walter Eucken and Ordoliberalism: An Introduction from a Consumer Welfare Perspective' (2006) 2 Competition Policy International 2, 198; Liza Lovdahl Gormsen, 'Article 82 EC: Where Are We Coming from and Where Are We Going to?' (2006) 2 Competition Law Review 2. Ordoliberal objectives are found conflicting with the other objectives of competition law such as consumer welfare by some scholars in the EU: Pinar Akman, 'Searching for the Long-Lost Soul of Article 82EC' (2009) 29 Oxford Journal of Legal Studies 2, 269.

26 Alison Jones and Brenda Sufrin, *EU Competition Law* (5th edn, OUP 2014) 12; Richard Whish and David Bailey, *Competition Law* (8th edn, OUP 2015) 19; Neelie Kroes, European Competition Policy – Delivering Better Markets and Better Choices, SPEECH 05/512 of 15 September 2005 <http://europa.eu/rapid/press-release_SPEECH-05-512_en.htm?locale=en>; Neelie Kroes, Preliminary Thoughts on Policy Review of Article 82, SPEECH 05/537 23 September 2005 <http://europa.eu/rapid/press-release_SPEECH-05-537_en.htm?locale=en>; Communication From The Commission, Guidelines on the applicability of Article 101 of the Treaty on the Functioning of the European Union to horizontal co-operation agreements [2011] OJ C11/1, para 269; European Commission, Guidelines on Vertical Restraints [2010] OJ C130/01, para 7; European Commission, Guidelines on the assessment of horizontal mergers under the Council Regulation on the control of concentrations between undertakings [2004] OJ C31/03, para 8; European Commission, Guidelines on the assessment of non-horizontal mergers under the Council Regulation on the control of concentrations between undertakings [2008] OJ C265/7, para 10.

27 Jones and Sufrin (n 26) 51.

commentators voice alternatives to "mathematical" methods to assess competition, such as consumer choice, fairness and privacy.[28]

In the traditional (economic) competition analysis, the price parameter is the predominant tool to assess the competition. That is the main reason academia argues the ineffectiveness of traditional tools for the type of competition in data-driven markets, as discussed in detail earlier. The criticism here is of the *de facto* hierarchy of the objectives of competition law in which the price-centric assessment for consumers' welfare seems to be a preferential method over privacy, fairness or consumer choice.[29] However, in most data-driven markets, price is zero, and it is impossible to assess consumer surplus, deadweight losses or consumers' willingness to pay through price. Consequently, the demand- or supply-side substitutability analysis becomes ineffective, as well as the relevant product market analysis. To note, price is not non-existent, and consumer information is the actual price in data-driven markets. Monetary price is usually non-existent in the online world apart from premium membership schemes, which are not prerequisites for using these platforms in most circumstances.

Instead of price-centric tools, some commentators propose giving more weight to non-price assessments, arguing that it would provide a better understanding of competition on merits in the new economy. For instance, a privacy assessment based on quality has gained strong grounds after the *Google Search* case[30] and the *Bundeskartellamt*'s Facebook investigation.[31] If privacy can be measured objectively – for instance, the degradation in privacy reflects the quality of the product or service – then there will be no problems regarding privacy being a benchmark and parameter for competition law. In this manner, Samson Esayas

---

28 For more information: Nathan Newman, 'Search, Antitrust, and the Economics of the Control of User Data' (2014) 31 Yale Journal on Regulation 2, 401–54; Frank Pasquale, 'Privacy, Antitrust and Power' (2013) 20 George Mason Law Review 4, 1009–24; Ariel Ezrachi and Maurice Stucke, 'Emerging Antitrust Threats and Enforcement Actions in the Online World' (2017) 13 Competition Law International 2, 10; Giulia Schneider, 'Testing Art 102 TFEU in the Digital Marketplace: Insights from the Bundeskartellamt's Investigation Against Facebook' (2018) 9 Journal of European Competition Law and Practice 4, 219; Christopher Townley, Eric Morrison and Karen Yeung, 'Big Data and Personalised Price Discrimination in EU Competition Law' (2017) 36 Yearbook of European Law 43–45; Ioannis Kokkoris and Ioannis Lianos, *The Reform of EC Competition Law: New Challenges* (Kluwer Law International 2009) 57; Neil Averitt, Robert H Lande and Paul Nihoul, '"Consumer Choice" Is Where We Are All Going – so Let's Go Together' (2011) 2 Concurrences-Revue des droits de la Concurrence 1, 3; Robert H Lande, 'Consumer Choice as the Ultimate Goal of Antitrust' (2001) 62 University of Pittsburgh Law Review 3, 503. For an import of this concept in EU competition law, see Paul Nihoul, Nicholas Charbit and Elisa Ramundo (eds), *Choice – A New Standard for Competition Law Analysis?* (Concurrences 2016).
29 Christopher Townley, Eric Morrison and Karen Yeung, 'Big Data and Personalised Price Discrimination in EU Competition Law' (2017) 36 Yearbook of European Law 45; Giulia Schneider, 'Testing Art. 102 TFEU in the Digital Marketplace: Insights from the Bundeskartellamt's Investigation Against Facebook' (2018) 9 Journal of European Competition Law and Practice 4, 219.
30 Case No COMP/AT.39740, Google Search (Shopping) [2017] 4444 Final.
31 B6-22/16, *Facebook Inc., Facebook Ireland Ltd., Facebook Deutschland GmbH, Verbraucherzentrale Bundesverband e.V.* Bundeskartellamt 6th Decision Division (6 February 2019).

advocates the objective measurability of privacy in data-driven markets for competition law purposes.[32] Also, the European Commission expresses in the Microsoft/ LinkedIn investigation that changes in privacy protection degree can significantly affect the level of competition and restrict consumer choice, which is also a parameter of competition.[33]

Similar to privacy, consumer choice is also found to be an alternative method to assess the level of competition in data-driven markets. Commentators argue that consumer choice can become an objective benchmark, in which competition authorities aim to preserve a specific level of choice of products and services for consumers.[34] As the consumer choice benchmark can provide a wider selection of parameters rather than price, it can become a broader concept than consumer welfare.[35] In this sense, a decrease in consumer choice can indicate consumer harm for competition law purposes. Also, not a decrease in numbers but the manipulation of consumers' choices is also quite possible in data-driven markets. Through the screen of a PC or a smartphone, companies can decide what users see, especially on the targeted and behavioural advertisements, recommendations or search results.[36] In other words, consumer choice is limited to specific content by technology giants, and the choices of consumers can be easily controlled by them for manipulation.

Another recommendation and alternative for the consumer welfare approach is fairness and justice'. Christopher Townley et al. argue that the fairness and justice objectives of the EU competition law found in the Preamble to the TFEU,[37] Article 102 TFEU[38] and Article 3(3) TEU[39] can be used in harmony with the consumer welfare objective.[40] Although there might be conflicts between these objectives, consumer

---

32 Samson Y Esayas, 'Privacy as a Quality Parameter of Competition: Some Reflections on the Scepticism Surrounding It' in Björn Lundqvist and Michal S Gal (eds), *Competition Law for the Digital Economy* (1st edn, Edward Elgar Publishing 2019) 164.
33 Case No COMP/M.8124 *Microsoft/LinkedIn* C [2016] 8404 final, para 350.
34 Ioannis Lianos, 'Competition Law for the Digital Era: A Complex Systems' Perspective' (2019) CLES Research Paper Series 6/2019, 17; Robert H Lande, 'Consumer Choice as the Ultimate Goal of Antitrust' (2001) 62 University of Pittsburgh Law Review *3, 503;* Paul Nihoul, Nicholas Charbit and Elisa Ramundo (eds), *Choice – A New Standard for Competition Law Analysis?* (Concurrences 2016); Neil W Averitt and Robert H Lande, 'Consumer Sovereignty: A Unified Theory of Antitrust and Consumer Protection Law' (1997) 65 Antitrust Law Journal 713, 715; Peter Behrens, 'The Ordoliberal Concept of 'Abuse' of a Dominant Position and its Impact on Article 102 TFEU' (2015) Nihoul/Takahashi, Abuse Regulation in Competition Law, Proceedings of the 10th ASCOLA Conference Tokyo 2015 <https://ssrn.com/abstract=2658045>.
35 Lianos (n 34) 17; Nihoul, Charbit and Ramundo (n 34).
36 Lianos (n 34) 108.
37 Preamble to the TFEU: "[T]hat the removal of existing obstacles calls for concerted action in order to guarantee steady expansion, balanced trade and fair competition".
38 Article 102 TFEU: "[D]irectly or indirectly imposing unfair purchase or selling prices or other unfair trading conditions".
39 Article 3(3) TEU: "It shall combat social exclusion and discrimination, and shall promote social justice and protection".
40 Townley, Morrison and Yeung (n 29) 43–45.

welfare will be the primary focus in applying Article 102 to abuse cases. At the same time, the fairness and justice objectives will play a significant but a secondary role.[41]

To apply these aforementioned objectives, there is no need to abandon the consumer welfare approach. The price analysis might not be sufficient, and consumer surplus and market power might be hard to detect, but properly written and enforced up-to-date tools to assess competition can serve competition law and policy without isolating the consumer welfare objective. In fact, the EU competition law embodies many different objectives. Throughout history, many different political ideas have also affected competition law. Moreover, it is important to point out that the objectives of competition law are constantly changing by the use of different institutional and political ideas, especially in terms of the social goals affecting the interpretation of EU competition law.[42] This is quite important since markets also undergo changes in time, and competition law and policy must reflect market realities. As a result, the interpretation of main principles of competition law such as Article 102 may become diversified through the comments of competition authorities, the decisions of courts, and other political decisions.[43] EU Competition law has been proved to successfully incorporate many different and conflicting objectives such as market integration and consumer welfare.[44]

A novel approach is proposed by some scholars, called New Brandeisians,[45] in the US. This new approach suggests abandoning the consumer welfare approach of competition law and instead focusing on data-driven market structures more to protect markets, the process of competition and smaller competitors from technology giants' abusive behaviour.[46] This new movement's roots go back to Louis Brandeis, justice of the Supreme Court of the United States from 1916 to 1939.[47] Back in the 1890s, Louis Brandeis began to question the "cut-throat competition" and expressed concerns around giant undertakings dominating whole industries back then in the US. In this era, the first competition regulations emerged in the US, such as the Sherman Act of 1890, the Clayton Act of 1914 and the Federal Trade Commission Act of 1914. This era also faced one of the first monopolisation/abusive behaviour cases in history, such as *Northern Securities*,[48] *Standard Oil*[49] and *American Tobacco*,[50] which focused on dismantling giant companies that held control over entire industries and monopolised trade in the US.

---

41 ibid.
42 Lianos (n 34) 3.
43 ibid.
44 Renato Nazzini, *The Foundations of European Union Competition Law* (1st edn, OUP 2011) 27.
45 The movement also called Hipster Antitrust: see the Antitrust Chronicle April 2018 vol 1.
46 Ariel Ezrachi and Maurice Stucke, 'The Fight Over Antitrust's Soul' (2018) 9 Journal of European Competition Law and Practice 1; Ebru Gökçe, 'Competition Issues in the Digital Economy' (2019) UNCTAD Background Note 5; Pinar Akman, 'An Agenda for Competition Law and Policy in the Digital Economy' (2019) Journal of European Competition Law and Practice, Editorial 1, 2.
47 See <https://www.fjc.gov/history/judges/brandeis-louis-dembitz>
48 *Northern Securities Co. v United States*, 193 U.S. 197 (1904).
49 *Standard Oil Co. of New Jersey v United States*, 221 U.S. 1 (1911).
50 *United States v American Tobacco Company*, 221 U.S. 106 (1911).

Louis Brandeis was a proponent of the Madisonian traditions and advocated for intervening in the economic system favouring consumers and democratic contribution of power.[51] In one of his speeches in 1912, he expressed:

> It is less than eighteen months since the decisions in the Standard Oil and Tobacco cases made Americans realize the importance and the urgency of the trust problem . . . A large part of the American people realize today that competition is in no sense in consistent with large-scale production and distribution. . . . We learned long ago that liberty could be preserved only by limiting in some way the freedom of action of individuals; that otherwise liberty would necessarily yield to absolutism; and in the same way we have learned that unless there be regulation of competition, its excesses will lead to the destruction of competition, and monopoly will take its place".[52]

The ideas and philosophy of Louis Brandeis lived until the 1970s, when the Chicago School and the *laissez-faire* ideology gained prominence in competition law.[53] However, lately, an updated anti-monopoly agenda is emerging in the US under the New Brandeis School. In October 2020, the US House Judiciary Committee published a report on an investigation of competition in digital markets regarding the rise and use of market power related to data and the adequacy of existing laws and enforcement in that area.[54] The report comprises many New Brandeisian ideas, such as "reasserting the anti-monopoly goals of competition law and their centrality to ensure democracy".[55] The report also recommends strengthening the Clayton and Sherman Acts by introducing new prohibitions on abuse of dominant position, monopoly leveraging, updating laws on vertical mergers, overriding the current precedent in the case law and many more in order to fight the technology giants: namely, Google, Amazon, Facebook and Apple.[56]

Lina Khan, one of the foremost defenders of the movement, explains the core tenets of the anti-monopoly idea, the New Brandeis School of competition. According to the idea, anti-monopoly is a wide toolbox that consists of antitrust as a tool.[57] Furthermore, anti-monopoly should be regarded as a fundamental philosophy that structures society on a democratic basis.[58] In other words, monopolisation does not

---

51 Lina Khan, 'The New Brandeis Movement: America's Antimonopoly Debate' (2018) 9 Journal of European Competition Law and Practice 3, 131.
52 Louis D Brandeis, 'The Regulation of Competition Versus the Regulation of Monopoly' An Address to the Economic Club of New York on 1 November 1912 <http://louisville.edu/law/library/special-collections/the-louis-d.-brandeis-collection/the-regulation-of-competition-versus-the-regulation-of-monopoly-by-louis-d.-brandeis>
53 Khan (n 51) 131.
54 United States Congress, House of Representatives, Committee on the Judiciary, 'Investigation Of Competition in Digital Markets: Majority Staff Report and Recommendations' (October 2020).
55 ibid 20.
56 ibid 21.
57 Khan (n 51) 131.
58 ibid.

have pure economic outcomes but political ones, which means the concentration of market participants can also lead to political power in time. Therefore, the high-concentration and monopolisation can undermine democratic values in addition to competition in a market. Dominant undertakings can leverage their powers through influence over governments, lobbying, financing, staffing and funding.[59] This is the reason anti-monopoly is wider than antitrust. However, this also does not mean that big is bad in every scenario.[60] There may be monopolies that are valuable and contribute to society and consumers more specifically. Overall, the anti-monopoly idea focuses on market structures and competitive processes more than the consumer welfare approach.[61] In the anti-monopoly idea, outcomes do not have higher importance just as market structures.

The findings of New Brandeisians are actually quite similar to the findings of this book: that the high-concentration, indirect network externalities and accumulation of Big Data in data-driven markets lead to the rise of "internet gatekeepers". Therefore, in an age when people access entertainment, shopping, news and many other important services online, a decrease in competition can lead to wider consequences than in the past.[62] For instance, traditional product or service monopolies may lead to poorer quality products and higher prices. However, online monopolies – the data-opolies – can affect not only consumers' wallets but also their privacy, well-being and even democracy.[63] Therefore, according to the New Brandeis School, competition policy needs to move forward to embrace wider problems regarding consumers and markets.

Lina Khan argues that the consumer welfare approach has failed to detect and deter anti-competitive behaviour; thus, it must be replaced by an approach more oriented around the market structures and the 'process' of competition than consumer welfare.[64] In this approach, undertakings and market structures must be assessed for exclusionary and discriminatory conduct by focusing on entry barriers, cross-leverage market advantages, competitive bottlenecks and intermediary powers.[65] In this sense, a proper analysis of the economics of data-driven markets can identify most of the anti-competitive benefits related to Big Data utilisation. However, additional tools are needed. For instance, new regulatory principles are needed in order to tackle anti-competitive behaviour, such as banning vertical integration for specific markets and undertakings, applying the essential facilities doctrine to Big Data-–rich undertakings or limiting the ability of dominant online intermediaries to abuse their data power by imposing neutrality.[66]

---

59 ibid.
60 ibid 132.
61 ibid.
62 Ariel Ezrachi and Maurice Stucke, 'The Fight Over Antitrust's Soul' (2018) 9 Journal of European Competition Law and Practice 1, 1.
63 ibid.
64 Lina Khan, 'Amazon's Antitrust Paradox' (2016) 126 Yale Law Journal 3, 803.
65 ibid.
66 ibid.

However, there is no need to leave the consumer welfare approach in favour of something else or broaden the scope of the goals of competition by incorporating fairness and justice as the primary objectives since it already contains these objectives as well as many others. The approach of the New Brandeis movement is not superior to the *laissez-faire* approach and does not seem feasible at all. The main claim of the movement and Lina Khan is to interpret social and political ideas into competition law in order to "fight" with big tech companies. Thus, banning vertical integration in such markets to limit the ability of technology giants does not have a rightful place in competition law theory. If this approach had been utilised in Facebook/WhatsApp or Google/DoubleClick, it would have had serious consequences regarding innovation and growth in data-driven markets. Limiting integration through regulation would have consequences on innovation, and unlawful barriers would be imposed on companies such as Google and Facebook. Therefore, protecting competition by crippling technology giants through socio-political intentions and fear of big tech companies is not the right way of intervention by competition authorities. In order to create appropriate rules and tools for the application of competition law, authorities and courts should not adjudicate through political theories, and the *raison d'etre* of intervention should be the "healthy competition" by promoting innovation and growth, as discussed in Chapter 4. Therefore, the last resort for broadening competition law's objectives is to create a sector-specific regulation for the Big Data sector and data-driven markets.

6.1.3 Sector-Specific Regulation

In 2019, the European Commission adopted a new regulation called the Platform to Business Regulation, aiming to promote fairness and transparency in the online world.[67] In this sense, all online platforms are obliged not to discriminate against other businesses inside an ecosystem, irrespective of their market power.[68] However, this regulation does not offer anything substantial for immediate concerns. As a result, on 15 December 2020, the European Commission published a set of proposals for the regulation of data-rich undertakings, data-driven markets and the use of Big Data. As part of the wider Digital Single Market Strategy and the P2B Regulation,[69] which aimed to promote transparency for online intermediation services, the European Commission revealed the Digital Services Act[70] (DSA) and

---

67 Regulation (EU) 2019/1150 of the European Parliament and of the Council of 20 June 2019 on promoting fairness and transparency for business users of online intermediation services (Text with EEA relevance) PE/56/2019/REV/1 OJ L 186, 11.7.2019 (P2B Regulation).
68 On 13 February 2019, the European Parliament, the Council of the European Union and the European Commission reached a political deal on a Proposal for an EU Regulation on promoting fairness and transparency for business users of online intermediation services (April 2018) <https://ec.europa.eu/digital-single-market/en/news/regulation-promoting-fairness-and-transparency-business-users-online-intermediation-services>
69 The P2B Regulation.
70 Regulation (EU) 2022/2065 of the European Parliament and of the Council of 19 October 2022 on a Single Market For Digital Services and amending Directive 2000/31/EC (Digital Services Act) (Text with EEA relevance) OJ L 277.

Digital Markets Act[71] (DMA) package for the EU. According to the Commission, both regulations have two main goals: creating a safe online space where all fundamental rights of consumers are protected and creating a level playing field for competitors in order to foster competitiveness and innovation.[72] The new Brandeisian ideas can also be found in the foundation of these regulations as Thierry Breton, the Commissioner for the Internal Market, expressed that:

> Many online platforms have come to play a central role in the lives of our citizens and businesses, *and even our society and democracy at large*. . . .With harmonised rules, ex-ante obligations, better oversight, speedy enforcement, and deterrent sanctions, we will ensure that anyone offering and using digital services in Europe benefits from security, trust, innovation and business opportunities.[73]

This package is the biggest reconsideration of the digital world in the EU since the eCommerce Directive[74] back in 2000 and the first comprehensive analysis of digital markets from a competition law perspective. Although the main focus will be on the DMA for the issues addressed in this research, the DSA is worth mentioning since it addresses the data protection standards and how online undertakings can operate in the EU. In addition to the existing GDPR, the DSA brings additional rules for the removal of illegal online content; new obligations for data-rich undertakings, including online advertising and the use of algorithms for the recommendation of content to users; new rules on traceability of business of users in order to tackle with illegal content, products and services; and additional measures to protect users and their information available on the platforms.[75] Therefore, the DSA brings EU-wide obligations for the protection of users' fundamental rights in the online world.[76] By this means, the new regulation plans to rebalance the rights and responsibilities of online intermediaries, public authorities and consumers based on human rights, democracy, the rule of law and other fundamental European values.[77]

---

71 Regulation (EU) 2022/1925 of the European Parliament and of the Council of 14 September 2022 on contestable and fair markets in the digital sector and amending Directives (EU) 2019/1937 and (EU) 2020/1828 (Digital Markets Act) OJ L 265.
72 Shaping Europe's Digital Future, 'The Digital Services Act Package' <https://ec.europa.eu/digital-single-market/en/digital-services-act-package>
73 European Commission, Press Release, 'Europe Fit for the Digital Age: Commission Proposes New Rules for Digital Platforms' (Brussels, 15 December 2020) <https://ec.europa.eu/commission/presscorner/detail/en/ip_20_2347> (emphasis added).
74 Directive 2000/31/EC of the European Parliament and of the Council of 8 June 2000 on certain legal aspects of information society services, in particular electronic commerce, in the Internal Market ('Directive on electronic commerce') OJ L 178, 17 July 2000.
75 European Commission, Press Release, 'Europe fit for the Digital Age: Commission Proposes New Rules for Digital Platforms' (Brussels, 15 December 2020) <https://ec.europa.eu/commission/presscorner/detail/en/ip_20_2347>
76 ibid.
77 ibid.

On the other hand, the second *ex-ante* regulation, DMA,[78] introduces new rules for "specific" undertakings operating in the online world. The proposal identifies intermediary platforms like GAFAM as the "internet gatekeepers" between business users and end users, thus imposing special responsibilities and bans. Article 2 of the regulation lists online search engines, social networks, online marketplaces, communication services, application stores, operating systems, video-sharing platforms, online advertising services and cloud computing services as the "core platform services" to which the regulation will apply.[79] In addition, not every core or intermediary platform is under scrutiny. According to Article 3(1) of the DMA, platform services are considered gatekeepers if their services have a significant impact on the internal market, operate as important gateways for business users to reach end users and enjoy an entrenched and durable position in their operations or likely will in the near future.[80] These are the qualitative thresholds for the applicability of the DMA for data-driven markets.

Therefore, the regulation also brings certain additional quantitative thresholds. Having a significant impact on the internal market, the Commission expresses, means at least €7.5 billion for annual turnover or €75 billion for market capitalisation.[81] For being a gateway, the Commission requires at least 45 million monthly active end users in the EU and more than 10.000 yearly active business users on a given platform/intermediation service.[82] On top of that, the third requirement, entrenched and durable position, is presumed to be existent if the company meets these thresholds for three consecutive financial years.[83] Undertakings must notify the European Commission if they meet these criteria and comply with the DMA's obligations laid down in Articles 5 and 6.

There are many do and do not type of obligations, which include data merging and utilisation bans, not blocking users from uninstalling software or apps, providing undertakings necessary information for advertising purposes (both to publishers and advertisers), allowing their business users to promote their offers and conclude their contracts within platforms and many others.[84] For the enforcement of the regulation, the European Commission has the power to impose penalties and extensive investigative powers for platforms. When identified "gatekeepers" do not comply with the DMA, the Commission then may impose fines on a gatekeeper not exceeding 10% of its total annual turnover[85] or periodic penalty payments not exceeding 5% of its average daily turnover for a period of time.[86]

---

78 Regulation (EU) 2022/1925 of the European Parliament and of the Council of 14 September 2022 on contestable and fair markets in the digital sector and amending Directives (EU) 2019/1937 and (EU) 2020/1828 (Digital Markets Act) OJ L 265, 12 October 2022.
79 Article 2 of the DMA.
80 Article 3(1) of the DMA.
81 Article 3(2) of the DMA.
82 ibid.
83 ibid.
84 Article 5 and 6 of the DMA.
85 Article 30 of the DMA.
86 Article 31 of the DMA.

This new regulation seems problematic in several ways. First, by regulating and enforcing this type of *ex-ante* regulation, the Commission avoids dealing with problems in the applicability of EU competition law to data-driven markets. There are specific problems that are identified by this research in the market power assessment tools for abuses or merger control. However, instead of fitting competition law for data-driven markets, the DMA aims to create a framework in order to capture big fish and penalise them. By this means, the relevance and importance of competition law assessment are being vanished, and a static regulation takes the place of competition in highly innovative and dynamic online markets. The problem with the regulation is its quantitative and qualitative thresholds. All thresholds are static, which may reflect the market structures of today. However, intervention in data-driven markets must be future-proof in order not to impede competition in a decade or two. In this sense, it can be assumed that the DMA is not future-proof.

The second is the problem of the far-reaching consequences of obligations listed in Articles 5 to 8 of the DMA.[87] Damien Geradin touches on important concerns such as installation of third-party app stores to mobile operating systems or prohibiting the utilisation of non-public data from business users in an online market and many others.[88] A thorough impact analysis must be engaged before enforcing such obligations. However, the impact assessment was engaged for the only current situation of data-driven markets. The Commission stresses that the regulation will increase the contestability of the digital sector, which helps the smaller rivals of gatekeepers (GAFAM) in the sector by blocking technology giants' unfair practices.[89] According to the study, the regulation contributes to new platforms that provide higher-quality products at competitive prices through innovation.[90] The Commission overlooks that these online platforms did not come into existence by the hand of God or nature. Thus, there are no barriers to the emergence of new platforms at all. The way the Commission assesses these online platforms is like technology giants "secured" and then "abused" these ecosystems that were found to exist before Big Data or the internet. This is a mistake. Technology giants such as Amazon or Google "created" their platforms. There is no evidence that new platforms "will emerge" if such obligations are imposed on Google and others.

Also, Geradin underlines that there could be far-reaching obligations regarding data portability and interoperability.[91] In Chapter 5, it was identified that the application of the essential facilities doctrine, mandatory data sharing or similar obligations might have serious consequences on data privacy or the functioning of data-driven markets. The success of super-dominant tech companies lies in the ability to derive value from huge datasets in order to develop better, higher-quality

---

87 Damen Geradin, 'The EU Digital Markets Act in 10 Points' *The Platform Law Blog* (16 December 2020) <https://theplatformlaw.blog/2020/12/16/the-eu-digital-markets-act-in-10-points/>
88 ibid.
89 European Commission, Proposal for a Regulation of The European Parliament and of The Council on contestable and fair markets in the digital sector (Digital Markets Act) COM/2020/842 final 11.
90 ibid.
91 Geradin (n 87).

products and services. Data itself is not useful for companies. Thus, data sharing would not be an effective remedy for data-related competition issues. Instead, the valued data should be under the radar of competition authorities and the essential facilities doctrine. However, in this case, it would be impossible to assess data objectively by looking at the sheer volume of data held by undertakings or which datasets could be relevant to become an essential facility. The main reason behind the ample competitive advantage between undertakings is the difference between data and pieces of information extracted to become relevant for higher quality services and products.

In addition, imposing mandatory data-sharing methods would create problems regarding consumers' privacy since the shared data would end up in the hands of new entrant third parties without consent in data-driven markets. Also, applying the essential facilities doctrine would disincentivise technology companies from collecting data and ultimately hinder innovation in data collection, processing and analytics methods. For instance, if data interoperability becomes a competition law remedy, end users will be able to access all their information on a platform – say, Facebook – from another app, like Google+. In the end, companies will obtain and utilise this third-party data which cannot be otherwise obtained in adjacent markets. Data-sharing remedies contain serious potential consumer harm and can become tools for novel anti-competitive behaviour in the age of algorithms. In brief, the DMA is not a future-proof regulation for dynamic data-driven markets and does not seem to be the appropriate method to intervene in online ecosystems. Therefore, the appropriate approach should be to optimise the current regulatory framework of the EU competition law.

6.1.4 Optimising the Current Legal Framework

A non-interventionist approach or the new anti-monopoly agenda of Lina Khan, which ostracises the consumer welfare objective of EU competition law, might not be the relevant agenda for immediate remedial action for data-driven markets in Europe. Also, the EU's new regulation, the DMA, seems far from ideal in terms of competition law assessment. Intervention by regulatory means should be kept at a minimum for the fast-evolving markets of the new economy.[92] However, another option which is also an active one can be easily conceivable. Without the need to rewrite the core principles of EU competition law or a completely new regulation that leaves competition aside and forces static rules in data-driven markets, such as the DMA, new tests can be applied for a better and more relevant assessment of the competition in data-driven markets. In this approach, enforcers (courts and competition authorities) can encourage and ensure more competition in the online world while not distorting innovation and the dynamic structure of these markets.

---

92 Evelin Hlina, 'Dominant Undertakings in the Digital Era: A Call for Evolution of the Competition Policy Towards Article 102 TFEU?' (2016) 9 ICC Global Antitrust Review 131.

Although the ideal way for EU competition law is to identify emergent challenges through case law one by one and create a solid precedent for data violations or self-preferencing as abuse or market power assessment and relevant market definitions, this seems impossible for the time being. However, sector-specific regulation and new rules for dynamic markets are not desirable. This period, the wake of the Big Data age, must be seen as a transition period for commercial life and economic activities. Many more innovations are about to come alive; thus, there should not be a hard law that will need additional regulatory measures to stay valid in the near future. Therefore, a soft law must assist this period while markets are still evolving by new technological developments on the data front, such as the Internet of Things and more advanced algorithms fitted with deep-self learning mechanisms. Otherwise, none of the criteria set in the regulations of the EU will be relevant to identify the 'real' power of undertakings that utilise consumer data. As Article 288 of the TFEU establishes, the EU can exercise its competence on competition law (in the internal market) by adopting a soft law as well.[93] Although this kind of EU measure will not have a binding legal force on competition authorities or courts, soft law is a decent alternative for data-driven markets since it opposes hard law and is not too heavy handed.[94] In this sense, a guideline on applying Article 102 to data-driven markets, including new assessment methods filled with reconfigured terminology, will help competition enforcers adopt a singular approach and contribute to creating a decent precedent by generating a European response to data-driven markets ultimately.

There are some examples of proposed non-binding soft laws in Europe. For instance, for the UK competition policy, the Furman Report (2019) introduces data mobility and data openness in addition to a code of conduct for online platforms based on a set of core principles.[95] On the one hand, the proposed code of conduct aims to identify specific undertakings that have a strategic status to reveal the real power of these platforms. Consequently, the special principles are targeted towards undertakings to safeguard competition and prevent consumer harm and anti-competitive behaviour.[96] The Furman Report exemplifies such behaviour that is considered unwanted. For instance, self-preferencing (intermediaries giving an unfair advantage to their products) or exclusionary behaviour (intermediaries which exclude rival products in their platforms) are mentioned in the report.[97] Although the code of conduct is intended to govern anti-competitive conduct to some extent, complementing data mobility and data openness tools for competition assessment might not be as effective as intended.

The Furman Report proposes applying a "sandbox" mechanism to create widely available open data for data-driven markets. The idea comes from Transport for

---

93 Article 288 of the TFEU.
94 Alina Kaczorowska-Ireland, *European Union Law* (4th edn, Routledge 2016) 151–52.
95 Furman Report (n 21) 59.
96 ibid 60.
97 ibid 61.

London's (TfL) provision of free, available data regarding public transport.[98] In 2009, the TfL released all available real-time data with third parties (and rivals) such as Citymapper, which also offers "journey planner" services.[99] It seems to be a successful experiment. However, the same concerns are applied to the essential facilities doctrine and data openness. The Furman Report argues that access to Big Data is a key barrier to entry in data-driven markets, and the accumulation of Big Data entrenches the dominance of some platform owners. The report sees that "access to data" become "essential in some situations and expresses the need for intervention if its benefits outweigh the costs".[100] Although it is argued to be a pro-competitive tool, the negatives and potential damage to innovation and market structures are far-reaching, as explained earlier. Although it can be regulated as a "soft law", it may become far more interventionist and detrimental for the businesses operating in data-driven markets. Therefore, it is not feasible to create an "open data" structure for markets in which all data float between all market participants.

As an alternative, a guideline on the market power assessment and application of Article 102 TFEU to data-driven markets can be the initial move. In this soft law, optimising the current regulatory framework should be the top priority for data-driven markets. In this sense, the application of appropriate tools and notions of competition law should be revisited without trying to reshape markets through interventions like the Digital Markets Act. Since data-driven markets have unique characteristics such as the multi-sidedness and indirect network externalities linked to multi-sidedness, "free" products or ecosystems which are not relevant for many other traditional markets for the purposes of competition law, revisiting the competition law notions such as "dominance" and "abusive behaviour" seems to be important for the enforcement of competition law *ex-post*. As Akman underlines, the new business operation in data-driven markets intrinsically challenges the traditional competition law tools such as the market definition or market power assessment.[101] Moreover, the new business strategies of online undertakings also challenge the existing types of abusive behaviour.[102] According to Akman, the main challenge is finding the most appropriate way to apply the competition rules to data-driven markets while addressing the least developed aspects of the competition law assessment for the new economy.[103]

Therefore, the need for an intervention is undeniable. However, as an alternative to the DMA, a code of conduct type of intervention or data openness mechanisms for technology giants, a guideline on the market power assessment and application of Article 102 TFEU to data-driven markets seems to be a plausible action that will

---

98 ibid 75.
99 ibid.
100 ibid 76.
101 Pinar Akman, 'An Agenda for Competition Law and Policy in the Digital Economy' (2019) Journal of European Competition Law and Practice, Editorial 1, 1.
102 ibid.
103 ibid.

initially support case law in order to create more efficient competition enforcement in data-driven markets without impeding their innovative character. Since there are many diverse types of data-driven markets in which innovation cycles are quite short and structurally too complicated for a static set of rules, market failures must be addressed without undermining innovation and economic growth in the digital sector. Thus, the next step should be to determine benchmarks for a guideline-type regulatory intervention in data-driven markets.

6.2 Benchmarks for Intervention

6.2.1 Necessity

Regulating data-driven markets through the Digital Services Act and Digital Markets Act as led by the EU Commission or through a New Brandeisian–led regulatory and enforcement move as outlined by the Subcommittee on Antitrust and Committee on the Judiciary in the US are quite arguable in terms of necessity. As can be seen from the regulation proposal and the report, the targets are Google, Amazon, Facebook and Apple specifically. Thus, both papers suggest creating checklists and other legal frameworks that capture and put these undertakings on a blacklist to control and penalise their conduct and break their corporate structures apart. Therefore, the question is: Is there a real need for sector-specific regulation (EU law) for data-driven markets? It must be identified before drawing a roadmap.

An *ex-ante*, sector-specific regulation means policymakers do not trust and rely on competition law instruments to regulate and enforce data-driven markets. To be more exact, lawmakers somehow control and impose specific and static market structures for competition assessment and enforcement. However, these static market structures will feel artificial and obsolete sooner due to the dynamic nature of data-driven markets. In other words, bypassing the implementation of improved competition tools and instead imposing a static checklist could backlash and become detrimental for all participants in dynamic markets, including businesses and consumers alike. These checklists will apply to every situation in which Google, Amazon or Facebook is a part, even when there are no competition problems due to the nature of the DMA or the code of conduct. There, applying the same rules to every situation would not be the desired outcome from a competition law perspective. It may be feasible only when political reasons overwhelm the competition concerns.

In addition, all methods in the Digital Markets Act to combat the anticompetitive behaviour of the "internet gatekeepers" can be addressed and enforced with the current competition law and policy, if necessary legal improvements are undertaken properly. As seen from the European Commission's and NCA's competition investigations in the EU, such as the *Bundeskartellamt*'s Facebook investigation, current competition tools are not completely useless. For Google, Amazon and Facebook, there have been relatively successful investigations which were at least able to address the concerns about "self-preferencing", "abuse through data privacy violations", and the "dual role of internet intermediaries"

204 The Way Forward

through an assessment of the accumulation of data, network externalities, quality assessment and possible conglomerate effects. These concerns are real and apply to the dominant undertakings of data-driven markets. However, the definition of market power and dominance needs a re-evaluation for competition law purposes through a legal test.

In simple and clear terms, drafting a regulation and enforcing it as a part of EU law mean leaving all competition parameters aside. In a regulated data-driven sector, the effects of data on the economies of scale and scope, indirect network externalities or Big Data collection and utilisation will not be assessed properly since they lose their importance for the enforcement of competition law. Instead, different benchmarks in the DMA, such as certain annual turnovers or monthly active users, will be assessed.[104] Also, a need for a regulation discloses that there would be no need for investigation on market definitions and market power on a case-by-case basis. To be more precise, the new regulation method attempts to eliminate the ineffectiveness of the product market definition and market shares. However, instead of completely putting the current competition tools aside in data-driven markets, the necessary improvements for the competition tools, such as a new market definition or a new definition of dominance, can be exercised by the Commission for assessment and enforcement purposes. As a side note, case law is and has been the most important part of EU Competition law, which contributed to the evolution of competition law, not in the EU but also in the world; thus, it should not be alienated from competition law's lawmaking process.

Therefore, a guideline on the market power assessment and application of Article 102 TFEU to data-driven markets seem to be the most convenient and appropriate way to approach concerns, at least for now. It actually seems to be the only viable option for dynamic and constantly evolving data-driven markets without impeding competition or leaving the goals of competition law. In this sense, new and updated legal tests should apply by the competition authorities and courts in the EU under the guidance of the European Commission.[105]

6.2.2 Proportionality

If there is going to be a regulatory action – either a regulation, a directive or a guideline – the second benchmark should be proportionality. The proportionality principle is essential in order to ensure the pro-competitiveness of the intervention. In the absence of proportionality, the benefits of action may not outweigh the detrimental effects, especially in dynamic industries like data-driven markets. Therefore, the application of new legal tests must be determined precisely.

A framework must be drawn when it comes to the applicability of new tests. At this point, it is crucial to differentiate online sectors from each other. Not

---

104 Article 3 of the DMA.
105 See Chapter 6.3.

every digitalised market is the same. As mentioned in Chapter 3, there are specific data-driven markets in which the accumulation of data and other unique characteristics are in the foreground. Thus, remedial regulatory actions need to address issues in these specific markets. For instance, there are some markets in which data has a primary role, such as search engines, social networking, online advertising, mobile application markets and e-commerce platforms. In these markets, Big Data and data utilisation are the main sources of market power, along with the network externalities. All problems identified in this book, such as intermediation power, Big Data power and novel abusive behaviour, are linked to data-driven markets. Therefore, necessary actions must take place in and for these markets.

On the other hand, there are other digitalised, data-driven markets in which data has no prominent role. In other words, Big Data is also collected, utilised and used in these markets but only has a secondary role in competition and the functioning of the markets. These markets can be exemplified by the online supermarket and cooked food delivery sector (Deliveroo, Uber Eats, Tesco online and others), online taxi booking systems (Uber, Cabubble), or online hotel booking sector (Booking.com, Trivago, Expedia). Although network effects are quite strong in these markets, there are direct network effects more specifically. In these vertical search markets, the indirect network externalities belong to Google (mainly) and its smaller rivals via the online advertising sector. Secondly, although Big Data may also be important for these sectors, consumer data only has a secondary role there. Thus, any data necessary for the functioning of the markets, such as information about taxi drivers, hotels or restaurants, can easily be catalogued by providers on request. In this case, information asymmetry will not be an issue.

Consequently, any remedial action must be proportional and aim to address issues in the former group of data-driven markets since the competition problems are unique to these bigger platforms. In the downstream, specialised and vertical markets, such as the vertical search engines, the competition is fierce, and entry is rather easy. The only concern would be the technology giants trying to swallow up or integrate these markets into their ecosystems. However, this issue belongs to the regulatory-intermediation powers of technology giants and their possible abusive conduct. In other words, regulatory actions should address the concerns arising from "online ecosystems". Therefore, regulatory actions should prioritise addressing the Big Data–related concerns and aim to address the Big Data–related power properly in this regard.

6.2.3 Fostering Innovation

The other benchmark for intervention should be "innovation". As the characteristics of data-driven markets reveal, innovation is an important aspect of developing higher-quality products and a predominant characteristic of online competition. Due to the emergence of data-driven markets, most incumbents and new entrants experience fierce competition on the innovation level nowadays. Undoubtedly, innovation is the main pillar of competition assessment in data-driven markets since innovation is considered the main engine of growth.[106] In this sense, competition authorities and enforcers must sustain an innovation-friendly market environment through competition law enforcement.[107] In promoting innovation, the role of the competitive process is widely accepted.[108] Thus, competition regulation and enforcement must carefully address innovation and innovative incentives in each case or investigation for mergers or abuse of a dominant position.

The digital sector is growing swiftly. Accordingly, many companies are also growing in this sector, like a new universe with galaxies expanding inside. Apple hit a $1 trillion market capitalisation in September 2018.[109] The trend was followed by Amazon, Microsoft and Google (Alphabet) in 2018, 2019 and 2020, respectively.[110] However, all these numbers are irrelevant to the assessment and application of competition law. Competition law should not be a tool to destroy or break the powers of some specific companies. Big does not mean bad. It is irrelevant to competition law how big a sector or any business can be. Competition law must ensure that innovation is not impeded by any anti-competitive means or regulation to achieve important goals such as ensuring healthy competition (competitive process) and consumer (also total) welfare.

Without question, innovation in the digital world requires a serious upfront investment.[111] Moreover, it is often for uncertain rewards. Often, it is quite hard for new entrants to race incumbents on the investment and research and development fronts. Technology giants are amongst the biggest companies engaged in research and development. According to the PwC 2018 Global Innovation 1000 study,[112] Amazon and Google (Alphabet) are the two biggest companies globally that spend money on research and development. Apple and Microsoft are in the top 10, and Facebook is in the top 15. Numbers show that GAFAM spent 70.5 billion dollars on research and development between 2012 and 2018. As a matter of course, these numbers on investments and innovation deliver many benefits for consumers and society.[113]

---

106 Ioannis Lianos, 'Competition Law for the Digital Era: A Complex Systems' Perspective' (2019) CLES Research Paper Series 6/2019, 17.
107 ibid 18.
108 ibid.
109 Rob Davies, 'Apple Becomes World's First Trillion-Dollar Company' *The Guardian* (2 August 2018) <https://www.theguardian.com/technology/2018/aug/02/apple-becomes-worlds-first-trillion-dollar-company>
110 Lydia DePillis, 'Amazon Is Now Worth $1,000,000,000,000' *CNN Business* (4 September 2018) <https://money.cnn.com/2018/09/04/technology/amazon-1-trillion/index.html>; Sergei Klebnikov, 'Google Parent Alphabet Passes $1 Trillion in Market Value' *Forbes* (13 January 2020) <https://www.forbes.com/sites/sergeiklebnikov/2020/01/13/google-parent-alphabet-set-to-hit-1-trillion-in-market-value/?sh=7fd27bb54dcf>
111 Lianos (n 106) 18.
112 PwC 2018 Global Innovation 1000 study: Values are R&D Expense of public companies during the last fiscal year, as of June 30, 2018.
113 Furman Report (n 21) 20.

As the situation reveals, innovation by the technology giants is huge. Therefore, while tackling anti-competitive behaviour, preserving innovation becomes much more important. After all, all this spending contributes to further technological developments and life-changing innovations in favour of consumers and society. In this sense, a pro-competitive tool is needed in order to sustain an innovation-friendly market environment while addressing anti-competitive conduct. The sector-specific regulations that aim to fight and break technology giants would have serious risks impeding competition in data-driven markets by ultimately limiting innovation and investments. Therefore, for any intervention, it is necessary to promote competition while also fostering innovation.

In the age of Big Data, data-driven markets and algorithms are identifiers of a transition period. As Yuval Noah Harari underlines in his book *21 Lessons for the 21st Century*, the age of Big Data is defined as a start of a new age.[114] In his opinion, as there are two major revolutions throughout human history – the cognitive revolution and the agricultural revolution – the scientific revolution and data on the forefront have the power to create their history.[115] In this regard, a huge revolution in law should be expected since most modern laws are based on the concepts of agricultural revolution (property, land, crime related to land and others). The new laws based on data might even undermine the core principles of today's modern law. Therefore, creating a competition law resisting the data revolution, the changing world, market structures and, most importantly, innovation would not be fruitful for consumers, businesses or society.

6.3 New Legal Tests to Apply

The benchmarks are set. The next step is to provide remedies for a possible EU soft law for the application of competition law to data-driven markets. As the discussion earlier revealed, there is a threefold issue related to Big Data in terms of competition law and policy: the monopolisation problem, in which strong platform owners become regulators; the ineffective neoclassical economic tools to assess market power; and the identification of novel abusive behaviour in the new economy.

In this section, identified problems will not be addressed together since one size does not fit all, and an independent understanding of each is necessary for the appropriate prescription.[116] In other words, although all problems related to Big Data and data utilisation, the findings regarding the structures of data-driven markets, regulatory gaps and inadequate tools have made it necessary for a toolkit approach rather than a single approach as the remedy. Therefore, the basis of a guideline on the market power assessment and application of Article 102 TFEU

---

114 Yuval Noah Harari, *21 Lessons for the 21st Century* (1st edn, Random House 2018).
115 ibid.
116 Pinar Akman, 'Competition Policy in a Globalized, Digitalized Economy' White Paper Series (World Economic Forum 2019) 4 <https://www.weforum.org/whitepapers/competition-policy-in-a-globalized-digitalized-economy>

to data-driven markets should appear after this final analysis. In this part, all three findings are enunciated individually to ensure clarity.

6.3.1 Intermediation-Regulatory Powers

In the third chapter, the characteristics of data-driven markets and the role of innovation in these markets are dealt with extensively. As a result, the relationship between competition law challenges and market characteristics such as indirect network externalities and multi-sided nature is established. Then, in light of the tendencies of online platforms, the monopolisation problem is mentioned. The monopolisation and high-concentration problems are sourced by the accumulation of Big Data and data-driven acquisitions in the online world. Nicolas Petit puts forward the term *moligopolists* for platform owners such as Google, Facebook, Amazon, Microsoft and Apple.[117] By this means, he tries to explain vertical and horizontal competition. The well-known technology giants have established superdominant positions in specific markets and compete in third markets with each other. It is called the "three-dimensional competition".[118] However, As Ioannis Lianos suggests, it is still unclear what constitutes a potential or existing competitor in the data-driven industry since undertakings in the online world tend to outstretch market segments (vertical, horizontal or conglomerate), where competitive pressure is not present.[119] As mentioned in section 3.2.3, undertakings innovate to escape competition, and by this means, they shape competition for the market.

In addition to the "escape competition", the accumulation of data and indirect network externalities lead to winner-takes-all competition in the new economy.[120] As a result, specific undertakings gain unprecedented market power in their respective markets by having control over an online platform where high concentration is present. Eventually, horizontal competition weakens significantly in these highly concentrated markets since even the second and third biggest players may not be able to offer a competitive product or service, as identified in the Microsoft/Yahoo merger investigation.[121] At the same time, the platform owners also dominate a wider value chain (main market and adjacent markets) by linking them through the creation of online ecosystems, which also weakens vertical competition.[122]

The main platforms of online ecosystems generally form a competitive bottleneck.[123] They accumulate significant profits by aggressively signing users to their various online services and locking them into the ecosystem while restricting

---

117 Nicholas Petit, 'Technology Giants, the Moligopoly Hypothesis and Holistic Competition: A Primer' (2016) SSRN <https://ssrn.com/abstract=2856502>
118 See Chapter 3.
119 Lianos (n 106) 57.
120 ibid.
121 ibid; Case No COMP/M.5727, Microsoft/Yahoo! Search Business C [2010] 1077 Final.
122 Lianos (n 106) 57.
123 Mark Armstrong and Julian Wright, 'Two-Sided Markets, Competitive Bottlenecks and Exclusive Contracts' (2007) 32(2) Economic Theory 353–80.

intra-platform competition. The competition inside online ecosystems is too weak since platform owners compete with smaller rivals in their ecosystems. At this point, the importance of being an intermediary becomes visible, and the "intermediation power" emerges. In many online platforms, platform owners act like regulators by setting up rules for consumers and their rivals, designing the market for themselves and even setting the level of competition they desire.[124] The rule-setting role could occur in different ways.[125] For instance, search engine platforms can regulate how search results are shown to consumers, such as organic results and paid results. Moreover, the coding of online algorithms used to generate search results can be adjusted accordingly. Another regulatory role example would be the conduct of e-commerce platforms. An e-commerce platform can set rules regarding access to products/sellers, the way offers are presented, data collection and sharing, grading and feedback systems, return policies, delivery services, search result algorithms in the marketplace and many others in order to "design" a marketplace. In that way, they also set the rules of competition for that marketplace.

When the platform owner/intermediary gains regulatory powers as exemplified here, special responsibilities and a higher degree of responsibility should be applicable.[126] As being a dominant undertaking is not seen as anti-competitive *per se* and may not require special attention by authorities in traditional markets, the situation in the new economy is obviously dissimilar. Due to the nature of "three-dimensional" competition, in which some players create a marketplace for buyers and sellers and become a buyer and a seller, abusive behaviour and market power can hardly be identified by competition officials. As mentioned in the EU Commission report, special principles can be utilised in data-driven markets to resolve issues regarding data accumulation and indirect network externalities.[127] If the platform is driven by indirect network externalities and the accumulation of data which results in information asymmetries between rivals, the intermediary role of some players becomes quite important. In this case, the platform owner should be regarded as the regulator of the platform since owners cannot be expected to abandon control of the ecosystem/marketplace.

However, platform owners must have obligations to ensure access for their competitors (third-party sellers), create a level playing field for them, not discriminate, not impose dissimilar terms for the participants and not engage in abusive behaviour.[128] Although this may seem to be an overreaction, regulators must be reasonable and fair and display non-discriminatory conduct.[129] If the intermediaries have

---

124 Jacques Crémer, Yves-Alexandre de Montjoye and Heike Schweitzer, *Competition Policy for the Digital Era: Final Report* (Publications Office of the European Union 2019) 60.
125 ibid.
126 Björn Lundqvist, 'Regulating Competition in the Digital Economy with a Special Focus on Platforms' in Björn Lundqvist and Michal Gal (eds), *Competition Law for the Digital Economy* (Edward Elgar Publishing 2019) 28.
127 Crémer Report (n 124) 69–70.
128 Lundqvist (n 126) 28.
129 ibid.

regulatory powers, these ideas must be established. The commentary also argues that these special obligations should be well applied to non-dominant intermediaries.[130] The reason is that the regulatory power may exist in platforms where strong network effects are current when the intermediaries are not dominant: in other words, when the market shares are below 40%.[131] However, this will lead to erroneous judgments. If there is no dominance established in terms of market shares, this does not mean there is no dominance. Rather, it means that market share analysis does not apply to data-driven platforms, and a change in how the competition law defines dominance is needed for the new economy markets. Thus, a new definition of market power and dominance should be made for EU competition law.[132]

Instead of creating special obligations for technology giants through regulation, like the DMA, the bottleneck market power should be addressed properly for competition law purposes in the online world. Through their data capabilities and *de facto* regulatory powers, some technology giants exercise their market power to exclude competitors rather than to control prices.[133] Krattenmaker et al. make a distinction between the "power to control price" and the "power to exclude competitors".[134] According to the authors, proposed exclusionary market power is achieved by denying inputs to its rivals to raise their costs, causing them to restrain their output.[135] Thus, market power or dominance becomes identifiable without price indicators. According to Lianos, this can lead to a different approach from the neoclassical analysis of market power, which focuses on the "power to control price".[136] In data-driven markets, the exclusionary market power concept can estimate dominance by identifying exclusionary conduct first and then determining a level of market power.[137] In the concept of "exclusionary market power", indirect network externalities, the dual role of platform owners and controlling a bottleneck in the online world all become highly relevant and may become parameters for exclusionary market power assessment.[138]

When a business controls a strategic bottleneck, gateway or intermediary role, competition law needs to leave analysis based on relevant product market definition and market shares to address dominance adequately. The legal concept of relevant markets bears legal and practical problems in estimating dominance.[139]

---

130 Crémer Report (n 124) 70; Lianos (n 106) 126.
131 Crémer Report (n 124) 70.
132 See Chapter 6.5.
133 Thomas G Krattenmaker, Robert H Lande and Steven C Salop, 'Monopoly Power and Market Power in Antitrust Law' (1987) 76 The Georgetown Law Journal 241, 248.
134 ibid 248.
135 ibid 249–53.
136 Lianos (n 106) 124.
137 ibid.
138 Henry Farrell and Abraham L Newman, 'Weaponized Interdependence: How Global Economic Networks Shape State Coercion' (2019) 44 International Security 1, 42, 46.
139 Jan Krämer and Michael Wohlfarth, 'Market Power, Regulatory Convergence, and the Role of Data in Digital Markets' (2108) 42(2) Telecommunications Policy 154–71; Jan Krämer and Daniel Schnurr, 'Competition Policy in Platform and Data-Driven Markets: Long-term Efficiency and

The Way Forward 211

Therefore, the competition authorities and courts should develop and adopt a test based on these attributes to address dominance adequately.[140] In data-driven markets, companies that are not in a dominant position according to the traditional assessment methods can be dominant and exercise huge market power. As a result, a new market power definition should be identified for competition law assessment and enforcement in data-driven markets.

Therefore, two new cumulative tests must be exercised to identify the market power of undertakings operating in the online world. These specific market power analysis parameters are the "intermediation power" and the "data utilisation" tests. Therefore, as explained earlier, the intermediation power test would identify undertakings active on one or more linked segments of an online ecosystem that can connect businesses to end users, such as online advertising, or for networking purposes, leading to controlling of platforms and online ecosystems. In place of a neoclassical mechanism to identify market power, competition authorities and courts should apply these tests to better identify market power by reflecting the unique characteristics of data-driven markets in a correct way. Although these cumulative tests aim to capture the "new" dominance and replace the current economic market power analysis, it should not become a hard law. Instead, the authorities should be encouraged to exercise these new tests in competition issues in data-driven markets.

As discussed, the intermediation power test can identify the exclusionary market power of undertakings operating in the online world. However, the intermediary and regulatory capabilities would not be enough alone for the identification of market power. Therefore, the data utilisation test must also be exercised for abuse of dominant position cases and relevant merger investigations since all data-driven mergers have conglomerate structures today in addition to the intermediation power test.

6.3.2 Big Data as a Source of Market Power

In data-driven markets, establishing dominance by identifying a relevant product market for determining market shares is almost impossible. Even if it is not, product markets are not relevant, as seen and explained in the Facebook/WhatsApp merger. In other words, the current regulatory framework is out of date.[141] Moreover, self-regulation in the online world is not working since some market participants actually regulate data-driven markets. Without an intervention, technology giants gain more market power by extracting more data from consumers and entrenching their

---

Exploitative Conducts' 'Contribution to the Call: Shaping Competition Policy in the Era of Digitization' (2018) 4 <https://ec.europa.eu/competition/information/digitisation_2018/contributions/daniel_schnurr_jan_kraemer.pdf>***
140 Furman (n 21) 81.
141 Ebru Gökçe, 'Competition Issues in the Digital Economy' (2019) UNCTAD Background Note 12.

212 *The Way Forward*

positions.[142] Therefore, in order to address problems in the R&D mergers – killer acquisitions – and abusive behaviour, an additional parameter of the exclusionary market power assessment should be added for a new dominance definition.

As the neoclassical competition law tools are not fit for digital business models,[143] the link between market power and Big Data must be established for the competition law analysis. In addition to intermediary powers, the personal data collected by undertakings also becomes a major source of market power in the digital sector. That is why these digital markets are now characterised as "data-driven markets". Personal data holds strategic significance as an input for many online services.[144] As discussed previously, data collection and utilisation were integrated into the competition law analysis to some extent in recent merger decisions and abuse of dominant position cases. It is clear today that data is highly relevant for competition in the online world and not a mediocre, non-rivalrous or ubiquitous input for businesses, as argued before.[145] Although the collected personal data – Big Data – is a valuable asset and a value creation mechanism for online businesses, it is not a relevant market itself.[146]

Regarding value creation mechanisms, large technology giants that utilise data for various purposes form conglomerate structures in the online world.[147] Through the conglomerate links, technology giants can exploit their data advantage through the cross-market collection and utilisation of data.[148] This exploitation risk is particularly dangerous for the "access to data" types of remedies, such as applying the

---

142 Gökçe (n 141) 12; House of Lords, 'Select Committee on Communications Regulating in a digital world' 2nd Report of Session 2017-19 HL Paper 299 (9 March 2019) <https://publications.parliament.uk/pa/ld201719/ldselect/ldcomuni/299/29902.htm>

143 Pinar Akman, 'Competition Policy in a Globalized, Digitalized Economy' White Paper Series (World Economic Forum 2019) 4; Ioannis Lianos (n 106) 116.

144 See Chapter 2; Inge Graef, 'Data as Essential Facility: Competition and Innovation on Online Platforms' (PhD Thesis, KU Leuven Faculty of Law 2016); David Evans, 'Attention Rivalry Among Online Platforms' (2013) 9 Journal of Competition Law and Economics 31, 36.

145 Daniel Sokol and Roisin Comerford, 'Antitrust and Regulating Big Data' (2016) 23 George Mason Law Review 5 1129; Andres Lerner, 'The Role of Big Data in Online Platform Competition' (2014) SSRN Working Paper; Darren S Tucker and Hill B Wellford, 'Big Mistakes Regarding Big Data' (2014) 14 Antitrust Source 1.

146 Inge Graef, 'Market Definition and Market Power in Data: The Case of Online Platforms' (2015) 38 World Competition 4; Jan Kupcik and Stanislav Mikes, 'Discussion on Big Data, Online Advertising and Competition Policy' (2018) 39 European Competition Law Review 9, 393–402, 396.

147 Ben Holles de Peyer, 'EU Merger Control and Big Data' (2017) 13 Journal of Competition Law and Economics 4, 767–90, 775; Furman (n 21); Heike Schweitzer, Justus Haucap, Wolfgang Kerber and Robert Welker, 'Modernising the Law on Abuse of Market Power: Report for the Federal Ministry for Economic Affairs and Energy (Germany)' (2018) <https://papers.ssrn.com/sol3/papers.cfm?abstract_id=3250742>; Inge Graef, 'Rethinking the Essential Facilities Doctrine for the EU Digital Economy' (2019) 53(1) Revue juridique Thémis de l'Université de Montréal; Massimiliano Kadar and Mateusz Bogdan, ' "Big Data" and EU Merger Control – A Case Review' (2017) 8 Journal of European Competition Law and Practice 8 486; Case No COMP/M.9660, Google/Fitbit [2020] Prior Notification of a Concentration OJ 2020/C 210/09.

148 Schweitzer Report (n 147) 4.

essential facilities doctrine[149] or obligations listed in the Digital Markets Act of the EU.[150] As Crémer et al. argue, the mandatory access to data type of obligations can feed technology companies and their conglomerate strategies for anti-competitive means.[151] On some occasions, combining third-party data coming through obligations with their data may entrench dominant positions. As in the example given earlier, Facebook can receive Google's search data if they create a new search engine and exploit data access obligations targeted to Google. Possible expansions and conglomerate risks are quite high in access to data remedies of Article 102.

Consequently, data becomes a problematical issue for two reasons: a valuable asset and a value creation mechanism that brings conglomerate links. For both merger control (to deal with conglomerate structures) and abusive behaviour (to deal with data analytics capability) decisions, the authorities and courts must include the data-related theories of harm in their analysis. Although there were discussions on data and conglomerate effects on market power analysis in recent decisions, a reliable test should be introduced. Therefore, a solution that addresses both aspects is needed. A "data utilisation" test that takes the place of the neoclassical economic tools gathered around price analysis must be undertaken as data possession and data capabilities of undertakings become specifically important when they also have "intermediary/regulatory" roles, which initially lead to information asymmetry in data-driven markets.

The information asymmetry gives a competitive edge to some undertakings. In this sense, data utilisation is the middle ring of a bigger value chain of "data collection – data combining and analytics – better services and targeted advertisements – more consumers through network effects – more data utilisation – the creation of ecosystems – tipping markets – and finally, monopolisation". Thereby the new test takes shape: Undertakings that have extensive capabilities on collected or acquired data through algorithms for the conglomerate and vertical means are on the radar of dominance. In addition to applying the intermediation power test, determining cross-market data utilisation capabilities that create information asymmetry for rivals should be considered "dominance".

Therefore, the competition authorities and courts must monitor and examine the 4Vs of data in light of a company's conduct and how actually these data strategies of bigger players affect the business strategies of smaller rivals. In this sense, the *volume* and *variety* of data must be monitored in order to reveal the value created by businesses, such as targeted advertisements and tailored services.[152] However, another issue comes to mind: How can legal authorities assess data and data analytics? Various algorithms and deep learning systems are far from legal experts' reach scientifically.

---

149 Graef (n 146) 33–72.
150 Articles 5 to 8 of the DMA.
151 Crémer Report (n 124) 108.
152 Jan Kupcik and Stanislav Mikes, 'Discussion on Big Data, Online Advertising and Competition Policy' (2018) 39 European Competition Law Review 9, 393–402, 396.

214   The Way Forward

The only solution to this problem would be the inclusion of Big Data management and data science in the competition law assessment. As economics plays a huge role in competition analysis and always has, data science becomes particularly important for competition law assessments in the near future. Competition authorities, governments and other regulatory and enforcement bodies are at an enormous disadvantage compared to the technology giants regarding data utilisation.[153] This disadvantage creates a situation in which lawmakers and enforcers come under the influence of the technology giants while trying to establish rules or decisions for data-driven markets. In order to ensure stability regarding data-related decision making, more input from data scientists and market participants is expected. In order to avoid suboptimal decisions or regulations, decision-makers must improve their expertise in data analytics and the Big Data area.[154] Also, enforcers might need to mimic data analytic methods and capabilities of data-driven businesses by developing tools to monitor data activities and even markets as a whole.

To sum up, the assessment of Big Data capabilities or data possession will serve as a better test for the market power assessment in the online world. Without data, no business can reach a point at which it dictates its rules to other participants or gain ground in adjacent markets. Big Data is a new magical tool for undertakings, and "data power" strongly implies "market power". Even without a deeper and further understanding of Big Data in the absence of data science applied as part of the proposed parameter of competition law – namely, the data utilisation test, a pure analysis of the possession of data analysing the sheer volume and variety that companies have – will be much more relevant for assessing the market power of undertakings in the online world compared to the traditional market share analysis.[155]

Additionally, a data utilisation test will also contribute to the wider goals of competition law in the EU. The well-identified capabilities on data will have implications for the online advertisement market and consumers' privacy and provide more transparency for competition and the market itself. Competition law can address privacy-related concerns such as data collection, data violations or data merging more accurately if the data utilisation test takes place in the investigations. The data utilisation test is a competitive effects test rather than a static market definition test based on the price and output effects of an undertaking's strategy for a specific product and its substitutes within a relevant geographical area.

6.3.3 Novel Abusive Behaviour Related to Big Data

Data-related problems do not pertain to the market power assessment and definition of dominance. The problems also occur in the identification of abuses and the enforcement of obligations and penalties. In data-driven markets, the identification of anti-competitive conduct poses risks since courts and authorities can

---

153   Akman (n 143) 16.
154   ibid 14.
155   Kupcik and Mikes (n 152) 396.

give erroneous conclusions on whether the conduct of an undertaking is abusive.[156] As Chapter 5 revealed, there are two main problems at the moment in terms of identifying abusive behaviour. First is the leveraging market power: specifically, defensive leveraging in the form of self-preferencing or self-favouring. The second is the abuse through data violations. Although access to data and the possible mandatory data-sharing remedies are discussed extensively, the findings show that Big Data should not be regarded as an essential facility. Instead, it can be said that it is a core component and a valuable asset for businesses in data-driven markets. Nevertheless, not being an essential facility does not imply that there cannot be novel abusive behaviour related to data accumulation and access to data.

Although the EU competition law rules and guidelines identify specific abusive behaviour, such as exclusive dealing, tying-bundling, predation, refusal to supply or margin squeeze,[157] abuse of dominant position types is not limited to these exclusively. The wording of Article 102 TFEU allows a wider analysis and helps the law keep up with the changing market structures and business strategies.[158] Therefore, technological developments may shape new markets, and new types of abusive behaviour can emerge subsequently.[159] Engaging in data-related, quite possibly novel abuses with existing abusive behaviour is also a mistake. As Pinar Akman argues, Google's abusive behaviour (in the *Google Shopping* case) does not fit any established categories of Article 102 TFEU cases of abuse: refusal to deal, discrimination or tying.[160] Akman's positive and normative assessment of the abuse of Google demonstrates difficulties with fitting Google's abuse into the existing framework of this specific abusive behaviour.[161] Many other commentators also followed similar steps to identify Google's abuse.[162]

Although the law aims to create a guideline for both undertakings and enforcers in order to protect market participants and provide legal certainty and predictability, this does not mean that novel abusive behaviour will never be conducted by dominant undertakings, especially in the new economy. Moreover, the established abuse of dominant types results from a developing competition law through decades, and the NCAs, the European Commission, national courts and the CJEU had quite important roles in identifying abusive behaviour throughout the history

---

156 Geoffrey A Manne and Joshua D Wright, 'Google and the Limits of Antitrust: The Case Against the Antitrust Case Against Google' (2011) 34 Harvard Journal of Law and Public Policy 171, 181.
157 *European Commission*, Communication from the European Commission, Guidance on the Commission's enforcement priorities in applying Article 82 of the EC Treaty to abusive exclusionary conduct by dominant undertakings (Text with EEA relevance) [2009] OJ C45/9.
158 Magali Eben, 'Fining Google: A Missed Opportunity for Legal Certainty?' (2018)14 European Competition Journal 5.
159 ibid.
160 Pinar Akman, 'The Theory of Abuse in Google Search: A Positive and Normative Assessment Under EU Competition Law' (2017) 2 Journal of Law, Technology and Policy 301, 307–50.
161 ibid 355.
162 Benjamin Edelman, 'Does Google Leverage Market Power Through Tying and Bundling?' (2015) 11 Journal of Competition Law and Economics 2, 365; Bo Vesterdorf, 'Theories of Self-Preferencing and Duty to Deal – Two Sides of the Same Coin?' (2015) 1 Competition Law and Policy Debate 4.

216 The Way Forward

of the EU. In other words, typing of abusive behaviour is a result of abuses and precedent, and abuses are not a result of or limited to typing of them. Therefore, the competition authorities and enforcers have a vital role in the new economy in identifying novel abuses, especially related to Big Data. As can be seen in the *Google Shopping* decision of the Commission[163] and the *Facebook* decision of the *Bundeskartellamt*,[164] new types of abuses are present, and the role of the lawmakers is to contribute to the creation of established precedent, thus developing guidance for the NCAs in the identification of abuses in data-driven markets.

The ineffective market definitions made the application of article 102 TFEU harder for data-related abuses. Nevertheless, the Commission found that Google gives more favourable positioning and display to its own services and products, in addition to favouring its own comparison shopping services while discriminating against competing comparison shopping services.[165] As the remedy, the Commission stated: "Google treats competing comparison shopping services no less favourably than its own comparison shopping service within its general search results pages",[166] and any measure taken by Google must "subject Google's own comparison shopping service to the same underlying processes and methods for the positioning and display in Google's general search results pages as those used for competing comparison shopping services".[167] However, the Commission also stated:

[I]t is not novel to find that conduct consisting in the use of a dominant position on one market to extend that dominant position to one or more adjacent markets can constitute an abuse (leveraging). Such a form of conduct constitutes a well-established, independent form of abuse.[168]

Although the Commission put the abuse as a form of leveraging market power, which is true, it also avoided contradicting the established law that self-preferencing is not an abuse of a dominant position situation, *per se*. The reason is that Article 102 TFEU does not prohibit dominant undertakings from favouring their own products. There is an exception, however. According to the essential facilities doctrine, undertakings have a special responsibility not to engage with defensive leveraging such as self-preferencing.[169] Since data should not be regarded as an

---

163 Case C-252/21 – Meta Platforms vs. Bundeskartellamt [2022] ECLI:EU:C:2022:704; Case No COMP/AT.39740, Google Search (Shopping) [2017] 4444 Final.
164 Case T-612/17 – *Google and Alphabet v Commission (Google Shopping)* [2021] ECLI:EU:T:2021: 763; B6-22/16, *Facebook Inc., Facebook Ireland Ltd., Facebook Deutschland GmbH, Verbraucherzentrale Bundesverband e.V.* Bundeskartellamt 6th Decision Division (6 February 2019).
165 Case No COMP/AT.39740, Google Search (Shopping) [2017] 4444 Final 76–197.
166 ibid para 699.
167 ibid para 700.
168 ibid para 649.
169 See Chapter 5.2.2.

essential facility, the second exception should be for the platform owners that are intermediaries in online ecosystems. As explained earlier, in a thorough analysis conducting new tests of the intermediation power and data utilisation, the dominant platform owners such as Google can be identified without errors. In this sense, the definition of dominance will also be changed, and consequently, novel abuses such as self-referencing can be addressed as anti-competitive *per se*. Decision makers and regulators must refer to and build on the undertakings of this abuse type in the future. That being said, further investigations of Google, Apple and Amazon and the already-given decisions hopefully set a precedent for dual role/intermediary abuses and market power related to data in data-driven markets, which ultimately opens the way for identifying novel abuse types correctly.

Similarly, the report of the United States House Judiciary Subcommittee on Antitrust, Commercial and Administrative Law also identified the conduct of favouritism and self-preferencing as anti-competitive.[170] The findings show that the dominant platform owners are the only viable paths to specific markets; thus, the favouritism of their own products and services has led to a discriminatory effect: the ability to pick winners and losers (business users) in that platform.[171] In addition to Google's conduct in the search engine market, the study expresses that

> [O]ver the course of the investigation, numerous third parties also told the Subcommittee that self-preferencing and discriminatory treatment by the dominant platforms forced businesses to lay off employees and divert resources away from developing new products. . . . [S]ome of the harmful business practices of the platforms discouraged investors from supporting their business and made it challenging to grow and sustain a business even with highly popular products. Without the opportunity to compete fairly, businesses and entrepreneurs are dissuaded from investing and, over the long term, innovation suffers.[172]

Facebook's data-violating abusive behaviour is the second novel abuse already addressed by a competition authority. The decision of the *Bundeskartellamt* introduces quite a novel approach to identifying abusive behaviour. The German Competition Authority took a different conception instead of a traditional analysis and considered the collected data as the source of its market power.[173] Thus, in this case, the origin of the alleged abuse would be Facebook's unlawful utilisation of

---

170 United States Congress, House of Representatives, Committee on the Judiciary, 'Investigation of Competition in Digital Markets: Majority Staff Report and Recommendations' (October 2020) 383.
171 ibid.
172 ibid.
173 *Bundeskartellamt*, News, '*Bundeskartellamt* Initiates Proceeding Against Facebook on Suspicion of Having Abused Its Market Power by Infringing Data Protection Rules' (2 March 2016) <https://www.bundeskartellamt.de/SharedDocs/Meldung/EN/Pressemitteilungen/2016/02_03_2016_Facebook.html>

data.[174] Instead of focusing on the existing case law and established rules of anti-competitive conduct, the *Bundeskartellamt* focused its investigation on data collection and added data privacy violations into consideration. The novel approach interpreted the data protection provisions as a part of market power and abuse assessments while cooperating with the German data protection authority.[175] It is a landmark decision for the years to come.

The most important point regarding the alleged abuse was the link between abusive behaviour and data privacy violation. Although there has been an extensive discussion on the interaction between data privacy, consumer protection and competition laws regarding the data issue,[176] the decision identified data violations as a way to abuse Facebook's dominance. The link between abusive behaviour and data violation is an indication that data privacy issues can be a part of competition law in data-driven markets. Interestingly enough, the data privacy violations of data-rich undertakings have implications regarding data privacy and are relevant to competition law. Therefore, with these kinds of abusive behaviour, allegations regarding the irrelevance of competition law cannot be argued. In this sense, privacy law cannot be used as a shield against competition law assessment and enforcement. To sum up, competition authorities must be careful in identifying novel abuse types related to Big Data. As in the example of *Bundeskartellamt*, authorities must intervene if privacy is used as a tool for anti-competitive conduct.

To sum up, the approach of *Bundeskartellamt* clearly demonstrates how competition law assessment should evolve for the changing market structures in the new economy. Focusing on the dual role of platforms and their intermediation power and data power will bring a better understanding of the competition in data-driven markets. Applying newly proposed tests to market power assessment and abuse of dominant position will open up new analyses, such as *Bundeskartellamt*'s, in

---

174 Giulia Schneider, 'Testing Art. 102 TFEU in the Digital Marketplace: Insights from the Bundeskartellamt's Investigation Against Facebook' (2018) 9 Journal of European Competition Law and Practice 4, 217.
175 Bundeskartellamt, News, 'Bundeskartellamt Prohibits Facebook from Combining User Data from Different Sources' (7 February 2019) <https://www.bundeskartellamt.de/SharedDocs/Meldung/EN/Pressemitteilungen/2019/07_02_2019_Facebook.html>
176 Maureen K Ohlhausen and Alexander P Okuliar, 'Competition, Consumer Protection and the Right (Approach) to Privacy' (2015) 80 Antitrust Law Journal 1; Marco Botta and Klaus Wiedemann, 'The Interaction of EU Competition, Consumer, and Data Protection Law in the Digital Economy: The Regulatory Dilemma in the Facebook Odyssey' (2019) 64(3) The Antitrust Bulletin 428–46; Lisa Kimmel and Janis Kestenbaum, 'What's Up with WhatsApp? A Transatlantic View on Privacy and Merger Enforcement in Digital Markets' (2014) 29 Antitrust 48; Geoffrey A Manne and Joshua D Wright, 'Google and the Limits of Antitrust: The Case Against the Antitrust Case Against Google' (2011) 34 Harvard Journal of Law and Public Policy 171, 212; Daniel Sokol and Roisin Comerford, 'Does Antitrust Have a Role to Play in Regulating Big Data?' in Roger D Blair and Daniel Sokol, *The Cambridge Handbook of Antitrust, Intellectual Property and High Tech* (CUP 2017) 271, 277; Damien Geradin and Monika Kuschewsky, 'Data Protection in the Context of Competition Law Investigations: An Overview of the Challenges' (2014) 37 World Competition 69; Francisco Costa-Cabral and Orla Lynske 'Family Ties: The Intersection Between Data Protection and Competition EU Law' (2017) 54 Common Market Law Review 11, 17.

identifying novel abuse types that are now a reality for the new economy. The decision also marks another crucial point: when necessary, strong cooperation with other regulatory bodies is highly needed to identify novel abuses. As the prime example, this is how competition authorities should shift their analysis methods for abuses and market power in the age of Big Data. Such analysis will contribute to the creation of a strong precedent for novel abuses.

6.3.4 Application

Therefore, the final step is to demonstrate how these new tests can be applied to abusive behaviour cases and merger investigations in the EU and how these recent decisions could have applied competition law to data-driven markets differently. Therefore, these tests are applied to the Google/DoubleClick acquisition on a theoretical basis since it was the most important decision which has led to erroneous precedent in the EU regarding merger investigations and also to the *Google Shopping* abuse case, which is the only landmark abusive behaviour case discussed thoroughly by academia in the recent past.

As identified in Chapter 4, the Google/DoubleClick merger was cleared by the European Commission. The Commission ruled that Google and DoubleClick were not competitors since the Commission segmented online advertising into separate markets in order to define a relevant market.[177] Thus, Google was found to be dominant in the ad intermediary segment of the online advertising sector, whereas Yahoo and Microsoft were found to be rivals.[178] However, DoubleClick was found to be dominant in the display ad servicing segment of the online advertising sector, where aQuantive/Atlas, Real Media/OpenAdStream and ADTECH/AOL were found to be the rivals.[179] The idea of defining a relevant product market by narrowing the online advertising market was clearly a problematic ruling. After the acquisition of DoubleClick, as an intermediary that was the dominant player in ad intermediation globally, Google has gained super dominance in the online advertising sector worldwide by creating a value chain and an ecosystem through technological experience and access to huge datasets and availability and relevance of user data.[180]

Additionally, the European Commission overlooked the possible foreclosure effects of data merging between Google and DoubleClick.[181] It was ruled that Google could not use DoubleClick's datasets to foreclose the market. On the contrary, such data merging would not have detrimental effects on the competition in the online advertising sector due to rivals' data utilisation techniques. According to the ruling, rivals of Google, such as Yahoo! and Microsoft, offer search engine

177 Case No COMP/M.4731 *Google/DoubleClick* C[2008] 927 final, paras 74–81.
178 ibid para 92.
179 ibid para 113.
180 French Competition Authority, Opinion 18-A-03 on data processing in the online advertising sector (6 March 2018) paras 218, 240.
181 Case No. COMP/M.4731 *Google/DoubleClick* C[2008] 927 final, paras 356–66.

services, ad services and ad intermediation. As a result, it was ruled that potential data merging between Google and DoubleClick would not affect competition in the online advertising sector due to the available data of rivals.[182]

In the absence of intermediation power and data utilisation tests, it was almost impossible to identify the non-horizontal relationship and the value chain created by the Big Data utilisation. As mentioned in Chapter 4, Google operates on both ad intermediation and ad-serving services in the online advertising sector.[183] Moreover, although rivals of Google, such as Microsoft and Yahoo!, offer ad-serving services through search engines, they were never as active in the ad intermediation segment as Google was. Through its intermediary role, Google has created a value chain by utilising data and algorithm-based methods to derive value from data collected by its online ad services' display and search advertising segments.[184] In the end, Google effectively used valued data throughout its whole ecosystem, gained ample competitive advantage by generating information from all available data and used it for all its services and products. Without the intermediation power and data utilisation tests, it cannot be expected for the competition authorities to identify the "real" market power of undertakings by narrowing down markets to simple product/geographic markets.

Thus, the intermediation power and data utilisation tests should have been cumulatively applied to the Google/DoubleClick merger investigation. As discussed earlier, the intermediation power test would identify the position of an undertaking in a market. Suppose an undertaking is found to be active in one or more segments of an ecosystem, such as online advertising in the Google/DoubleClick investigation, and has a unique role compared to its rivals to connect its them to end users while also having control of the online platform or ecosystem, such as Google in the online advertising sector. In that case, the intermediation power can be identified. Instead of the neoclassical mechanism to identify market power, the relevant market analysis and the possible intermediation power must be identified in data-driven markets. By doing this, wider effects in a sector can be adequately identified. In this sense, the application of intermediation power will enable competition authorities to identify the market power of dominant undertakings since the analysis in this test reflects the unique characteristics such as the dynamic, data-driven, multi-sided and ecosystem nature of data-driven markets by identifying all of them in order to find the possible intermediary role.

However, the intermediation power test alone will not enable the identification of market power. An intermediary which does not collect, store or utilise data but provides services just like its rivals on its own platform might not have market power in the absence of a market share test. For instance, in theory, if Google did not collect data from search queries like the DuckDuckGo search engine, the Double-Click merger would not have any foreclosure effects due to the data accumulation

---

182 ibid paras 364–65.
183 French Competition Authority (n 180) para 144.
184 ibid para 145.

and utilisation. Therefore, the second test should be included in the competition law analysis: the data utilisation test. As Big Data plays a huge, irreplaceable role in business strategies and commercial transactions, data science should become a part of competition law analysis just like economics did in the past. Data science will become an internal part of competition law. However, none of the competition authorities or other regulatory bodies are aware of data science, and they are at a huge disadvantage compared to big tech companies.[185] Thus, due to information asymmetry and the lack of data science knowledge, competition authorities have difficulties assessing the market power of undertakings. In many instances, authorities came under the influence of big tech companies since they notified authorities that they would not merge/utilise data after the proposed merger.[186] Therefore, decision-making processes lost accuracy in addressing market power.

As identified in Chapter 4, Big Data is a source of market power; thus, having data power is a strong implication of having a market power. As a result, the data utilisation test, which assesses Big Data capabilities and the data possession of undertakings, will be a better fit for competition law analysis. In order to achieve a proper data utilisation test, input and expertise from data scientists are expected for decision-making processes in competition law. Moreover, decision makers need to improve their knowledge of Big Data, data analytics and the related area.[187] The data utilisation test should be exercised as a theoretical method where data possession, control over access to data, analytics and data utilisation capabilities of technology companies are monitored for a time period. In order to achieve this goal, data monitoring tools must be used by competition authorities, and the authorities must simulate data analytics methods of tech giants. Even in the absence of a deeper understanding of data science applied in competition law, the aid of monitoring tools and huge data possession of undertakings in terms of volume, variety, and velocity would contribute to the market power analysis. If these tests were applied, the data utilisation capabilities, data possession and data merging availability of Google would have been interpreted differently in Google/DoubleClick.

Additionally, an idea similar to the data utilisation test can be found in the draft act on the Digitalisation of German Competition law and the report of the study by Schweitzer et al.[188] According to the German study, control over access to data and its importance for competition assessment makes it necessary for competition authorities to integrate data access dimension into the analysis, thus

---

185 Akman (n 143) 16.
186 Case No COMP/M.4731 *Google/DoubleClick* C [2008] 927 final; Case No COMP/M.7217 *Facebook/WhatsApp* C [2014] 7239 final.
187 Akman (n 143) 14.
188 Bundesministerium für Wirtschaft und Energie, 'Modernisierung der Missbrauchsaufsicht für marktmächtige Unternehmen' (4 September 2018) <https://www.bmwi.de/Redaktion/DE/Publikationen/Wirtschaft/modernisierung-der-missbrauchsaufsicht-fuer-marktmaechtige-unternehmen.html> (hereinafter *Modernisierung* Study). Schweitzer Report summary <https://www.bmwi.de/Redaktion/DE/Downloads/Studien/modernisierung-der-missbrauchsaufsicht-fuer-marktmaechtige-unternehmen-zusammenfassung-englisch.html>

re-conceptualising the understanding of market power. Accordingly, the German Ministry of Economics and Energy recently studied a case on data possession and utilisation.[189] The study indicates that controlling a vast amount of data becomes increasingly important for the market power assessment in finding dominance.[190] Moreover, the study reveals that data can provide both superior (horizontal) market power and relational (vertical and conglomerate) market power.[191] The implication from the analysis would be that the data possession, control over access to data, and data utilisation capabilities should become criteria for the market power assessment instead of the price-output and market share analysis in both abuse of dominant position cases and merger investigations.

Also, the intermediation power and data utilisation tests will be applied theoretically to the *Google Search (Shopping)* case. Similar to the market power assessment in the Google/DoubleClick investigation, the Commission has narrowed down markets in the *Google Search (Shopping)* case to identify a relevant product market and has ruled that the online comparison shopping service and the online search advertising service were separate markets in which Google operates distinctly.[192] The decision stresses that there is limited substitutability between comparison shopping and online advertising services.[193] However, as discussed in Chapter 5, the traditional method to assess market power is not accurate. Online (search) advertising and online comparison shopping are in the same ecosystem as Google; thus, they should be regarded as one market from consumers' and advertisers' perspectives.[194] If the intermediary power test had been undertaken, the intermediary role of Google in online comparison shopping services would have been revealed. Google is the dominant undertaking in the online advertising market, and through this business (Google Search), it has become an intermediary in online comparison shopping services. However, this service is exclusively available through the Google Search engine, which is as widespread as the internet itself and the most used service. Thus, comparison shopping and online advertising services are also integral to the search engine. In other words, Google has a dual role. The tech giant has a rivalry with the other comparison shopping and online advertising services inside its ecosystem, where it acts as a regulator and an intermediary. Inherently, Google can exercise "exclusionary abuse" due to its dual role, and the "intermediation power" test enables it to identify *de facto* regulatory capabilities and the company's market power in the online advertising sector.

---

189 The *Modernisierung* Study.
190 Ioannis Lianos, 'Competition Law for the Digital Era: A Complex Systems' Perspective' (2019) CLES Research Paper Series 6/2019, 116, taken from The *Modernisierung* Study.
191 ibid.
192 Case No COMP/AT.39740, *Google Search (Shopping)* C[2017] 4444 Final, para 193.
193 ibid paras 196–97.
194 Detailed analysis can be find in Chapter 5.4.2; Sébastien Broos and Jorge Marcos Ramos, 'Google, Google Shopping and Amazon: The Importance of Competing Business Models and Two-Sided Intermediaries in Defining Relevant Markets' (2017) 62(2) The Antitrust Bulletin 11.

However, the data utilisation test should also be exercised together with the intermediation power test. The identification of an intermediary role alone would not be enough for the indication of true market power. As discussed earlier, the Big Data capabilities and data possession of Google must also be identified since this is how the company abuses its dominant position through data utilisation. Moreover, the data utilisation test will also contribute to the wider objectives of EU competition law by addressing consumers' data usage, privacy and transparency. If this test is utilised, it can be possible for the competition law enforcers to identify and address any privacy-related concerns regarding data collection, data violations or data merging. As mentioned before, since the data utilisation test is a competitive effects test rather than a static market definition test, the other relevant consumer-centred concerns, such as privacy, can also be addressed accurately within competition law and policy.

In addition to the application of the aforementioned legal tests, the approach to abusive behaviour should also evolve. As the prime example, the approach of *Bundeskartellamt* is a demonstration of how competition should be assessed and abusive behaviour should be addressed. Big Data power, intermediation power, multi-sidedness and the dual role of online platforms must be addressed to better understand and apply competition rules to data-related competition law issues. Legal tests such as intermediation power and data utilisation tests will provide accurate data for the market power assessment and ultimately for the identification of novel abusive behaviour as novel abuse types will be common in the new economy. The Facebook decision of *Bundeskartellamt* must be regarded as a landmark case in this sense.

6.4 Concluding Remarks

The problems stemming from data collection and utilisation, network effects, data as a source of market power and online market structures are utterly new. Thus, the current competition tools are ineffective against the problems mentioned. Therefore, different methods to approach these challenges are discussed in this chapter as the first step. The first discussion was about the effectiveness of a non-interventionist approach. It is followed by the approach of broadening competition law's goals. The analysis then introduced new *ex-ante* mechanisms, a sector-specific regulation for data-driven markets. Lastly, optimising and improving the current legal framework is discussed. As the analysis has revealed that the competition law rules do not need to be reset, the most appropriate remedy is to update the competition law tools for the new era to increase the effectiveness of competition law assessment and enforcement for the problems unique to data-driven markets.

The remedies must be necessary, proportional, and pro-competitive. Thus, the best approach would be to make reforms on specific competition tools in the form of soft law. For instance, a guideline on the market power assessment and application of Article 102 TFEU to data-driven markets for competition authorities and courts will support and harmonise the decisions in the EU. Regarding the soft law mechanisms, the main aim should be to keep competition working efficiently through

224 The Way Forward

case law and investigations in the EU. The new assessment methods proposed in this guideline will eventually support the case law in creating efficient competition enforcement in data-driven markets without impeding the innovative character of the new economy. There is a new series of investigations against Apple (App Store), Google, Facebook and Amazon (self-preferencing). There will be landmark decisions for EU law which will hopefully contribute to creating a solid precedent.

In conclusion, the book proposed two new tests to apply in data-driven markets in the form of soft law: the intermediation power and data utilisation tests. Both tests aim to determine the true market power of undertakings by evaluating the multi-sided market structures, the dual roles of undertakings, data collection and utilisation capabilities, which indicate market power appropriately. Moreover, the application of Article 102 TFEU in data-driven markets must be more responsive since there are new types of abusive behaviour in data-driven markets. The authorities and courts should not limit their assessments around specific abuse types or align an abuse to an established abuse.

7 Epilogue

This book discusses the application of competition law to Big Data–related issues in the digital economy. In the analysis, the application of current tools and the method of applying these rules are found to be problematic in many ways. Therefore, a few points are addressed through a step-by-step approach to engage in systematic analysis. At first, major findings related to Big Data are identified as follows: the rapid monopolisation problem in data-driven markets, issues in assessing market power of undertakings in abuse cases and merger investigations, and the identification of abusive behaviour in online ecosystems.

After that, the problematic application of competition law rules in assessing market power and abusive behaviour are discussed. The book's main finding is that Big Data is a source of market power due to indirect network externalities and the accumulation of data. It is identified by this study that undertakings in the online world accumulate and acquire data to gain market power and create global value chains through data utilisation. Ultimately, high concentration occurs, and the creation of digital platforms (online ecosystems) leads to abusive practices. As a result of the analysis conducted in Chapters 3 to 5, the assessment of market power through relevant market definitions and market share analysis is found to be problematic. Moreover, abuse through leveraging market power is identified as a major problem in data-driven markets. Also, this book determines that novel abuse behaviour, such as violation of data privacy or abuse through access to data, is common in data-driven markets.

All these points lead to filling the gap by providing an adequate solution for the competition law analysis. Although it is argued that Big Data is a source of market power today, a roadmap for short-term action is proposed in the absence of established case law. For the action to be taken, soft law is found to fit the purposes of competition law instead of the new Digital Markets Act. Since the failures arise from the ineffective tools used to address market power and abusive behaviour, an intervention seemed to be necessary in the area of law regarding the assessment of market power rather than an *ex-ante* regulation. Therefore, this research evaluated the weaknesses and strengths of EU competition law, its effectiveness and its assessment tools applied to competition issues in digital markets. Thus, a critical assessment of how the European competition authorities should react to the Big

DOI: 10.4324/9781003458791-7

Data issue and newly emerging data-driven markets is conducted. As a result, the need for reform is finally identified in Chapter 6.

Without intervention, it would not be possible for competition authorities to assess market power, detect abusive behaviour, or identify consumer harm. In line with the idea of necessary intervention, recommendations for remedies to mitigate the current and future conflicts concerning the effectiveness of the competition law regulation are made. Thus, this study proposes new legal tests for the market power assessment in the data-driven sector as the immediate response. The remedy consists of two new legal tests to be applied cumulatively and on a case-by-case basis in data-driven markets in the form of soft law: the intermediation power and data utilisation tests. These new legal tests should be applied to data-related abuses/merger control assessment instead of an *ex-ante* sector-specific regulation.

Competition law must abandon the analysis based on product market definitions in issues related to the online world since the legal concept of relevant markets bears problems in the data-driven sector. Instead, the intermediation power test can be developed and adopted. The intermediation power test brings the exclusionary market power concept to competition law analysis. This test aims to detect undertakings active on one or more linked segments of an online ecosystem that can connect businesses to end-users, such as online advertising or networking purposes, and then aims to identify the 'market position' of undertakings by evaluating the multi-sided structures of platforms, the dual role of platform owners and their capabilities. In a scenario in which a business has control over a strategic bottleneck, gateway or dual role, the intermediation power test becomes relevant. In the concept of exclusionary market power, indirect network externalities and the dual role of platform owners are the parameters for market power assessment. In this sense, the test first identifies the market position and possible exclusionary conduct and then determines a level of market power to identify dominance in place of a neoclassical mechanism to identify market power.

Although the intermediation power test can identify the exclusionary market power of undertakings in the online world, the intermediary and regulatory capabilities would not be enough to determine market power. The data utilisation test must also be exercised cumulatively. Undertakings create a Big Data value chain and gain a competitive advantage due to the information asymmetry provided by the value chain. Data utilisation is the most important part of the value chain of data collection, data analytics, data utilisation, better services, network effects, more data, more data utilisation, lock-in effects, creation of ecosystems, tipping markets and finally, monopolisation. Thus, the data utilisation test aims to identify the capabilities of undertakings regarding the utilisation of collected or acquired data through algorithms for the conglomerate and vertical means. In addition to identifying the dual role and the intermediary powers of undertakings, the determination of cross-market data utilisation capabilities that create information asymmetry should be a part of the new dominance analysis. Identification of the data possession and the assessment of Big Data capabilities seems inevitable for the competition law issues in data-driven markets. Without Big Data, no one business can obtain *de facto* regulatory powers in the free market economy and reach a point at which it dictates its own rules to other participants or gains grounds in adjacent markets. Big Data is a magical tool for undertakings, and Big Data power strongly implies market power.

In total, the intermediation power and data utilisation tests aim to identify the market power of technology giants by evaluating the multi-sided market structures, the dual roles of these undertakings, data collection and utilisation capabilities. Competition authorities and courts should apply these tests to better identify market power by reflecting the unique characteristics of data-driven markets instead of the current tools. Although these cumulative tests aim to detect dominance and replace the current market power analysis, they should not become hard law. Instead, the authorities should be encouraged to exercise these new tests to competition issues in cases and investigations. The data-driven sector is under constant change, and this is a transition period in the age of Big Data. In a decade or two, there could be a completely different online world having completely novel characteristics. Therefore, the best approach would be to reform specific competition tools in the form of soft law. In this sense, the main aim should be to keep competition working efficiently through case law and investigations in the EU. The new assessment methods will eventually support the case law in creating efficient competition enforcement in data-driven markets without impeding the innovative character of the new economy. Gradually, case law can be established. There is currently a new series of investigations against Apple (App Store), Google, Facebook and Amazon, and the application of proposed tests would hopefully contribute to creating a solid precedent.

In conclusion, it is advised that the dynamics of new economy markets are considerably different from the traditional ones; thus, unique characteristics must be reflected in competition law assessment in the EU. By this means, competition authorities need to extend the competition law assessment beyond the traditional tools and specific abusive behaviour types. Although it is a transition period and the soft law is the most appropriate approach as the immediate response, long-term action must also be conducted. However, data-driven markets are truly global, and undertakings active in the sector deliver spread technology and new business methods all over the globe, establishing new links and creating one big community. Consequently, when a problem occurs, the problem is also on a global scale. Thus, a long-term roadmap should also be studied in the near future for a harmonised and coherent application of competition law rules to the data-driven sector on a global scale. In other words, cross-border cooperation between national and regional competition authorities is needed in the future. In other words, the exchange of experiences, increased harmonisation and even common rules for data-driven competition will benefit consumers and healthy competition the most. In this sense, the proposed new legal tests would even contribute to this approach, and they can become part of a wider action by the European Commission, NCAs in the EU and other competition authorities and officials around the world for stronger and more effective competition enforcement.

Bibliography

Primary Sources

Cases

B6-22/16, *Facebook Inc., Facebook Ireland Ltd., Facebook Deutschland GmbH, Verbraucherzentrale Bundesverband e.V*. Bundeskartellamt 6th Decision Division [6 February 2019]

Belgian Competition Authority, Beslissing nr. BMA-2015-P/K-27-AUD [van 22 September 2015], Zaken nr. MEDE-P/K-13/0012 en CONC-P/K-13/0013

Case C-6/72 *Europemballage Corporation and Continental Can Company Inc. v Commission of the European Communities* [1973] ECLI:EU:C:1973:22

Cases C-6 and 7/73 *Istituto Chemioterapico Italiano and Commercial Solvents v Commission* [1974] ECLI:EU:C:1974:18

Case C-27/76 *United Brands Company and United Brands Continentaal BV v Commission of the European Communities* [1978] ECLI:EU:C:1978:22

Case C-85/76 *Hoffman-La Roche & Co. AG v Commission of the European Communities* [1979] ECLI:EU:C:1979:36

Case C-311/84 *CBEM v CLT & IPB (Télémarketing)* [1985] ECLI:EU:C:1985:394

Case C-53/87 *Renault v Maxicar* [1988] ECLI:EU:C:1988:472

Case C-238/87 *Volvo v Eric Veng* [1988] ECLI:EU:C:1988:477

Case C-62/86 *AKZO Chemie BV v Commission of the European Communities* [1991] ECLI:EU:C:1991:286

Case T-30/89 *Hilti AG v Commission of the European Communities* [1991] ECLI:EU:T:1991:70

Case C-241/91 P (Joined Cases C-241/91 P, C-242/91 P) *Radio Telefis Eireann (RTE) and Independent Television Publications Ltd (ITP) v Commission of the European Communities (Magill)* [1995] ECLI:EU:C: 1995:98

Case C-333/94 P *Tetra Pak International SA v Commission of the European Communities* [1996] ECLI:EU:C:1996:436

Case C-7/97 *Oscar Bronner GmbH & Co. KG v Mediaprint Zeitungs – und Zeitschriftenverlag GmbH & Co. KG and Others* [1998] ECLI:EU:C:1998:569

Case T-219/99 *British Airways v Commission* [2003] ECLI:EU:T:2003:343

Case T-368/00 *General Motors Nederland BV and Opel Nederland BV v Commission of the European Communities* [2003] ECLI:EU:T:2003:275

Case C-418/01 *IMS Health GmbH & Co. OHG v NDC Health GmbH & Co. KG.* [2004] ECLI:EU:C: 2004:257

Bibliography 229

Case T-67/01 *JCB Service v Commission of the European Communities* [2004] ECLI:EU:T:2004:3
Case C-53/03 *Synetairismos Farmakopoion Aitolias & Akarnanias (Syfait) and Others v GlaxoSmithKline plc and GlaxoSmithKline AEVE* [2005] ECLI:EU:C:2005:333
Case C-238/05 *Asnef-Equifax Servicios de Información sobre Solvencia y Crédito, SL v Asociación de Usuarios de Servicios Bancarios* [2006] ECLI:EU:C: 2006:734
Case T-201/4 *Microsoft Corp. v Commission of the European Communities* [2007] ECLI:EU:T:2007:289
Case C-501/06 P *GlaxoSmithKline Services and Others v Commission and Others* [2009] ECLI:EU:C:2009:610
Case C-32/11 *Allianz Hungaria Biztosito and Others v Gazdasági Versenyhivatal* [2013] ECLI:EU:C: 2013:160
Case T-79/12 *Cisco Systems, Inc. and Messagenet SpA v European Commission* [2013] ECLI:EU:T:2013:635
Case C-131/12 *Google Spain SL and Google Inc. v Agencia Española de Protección de Datos (AEPD) and Mario Costeja González* [2014] ECLI:EU:C:2014:317
Case C-74/14 *Eturas UAB and Others v Lietuvos Respublikos konkurencijos taryba* [2016] ECLI:EU:C: 2016:42
Case VI-Kart 1/19 (V) *Facebook/Bundeskartellamt*, The Decision of the Higher Regional Court of Düsseldorf [26 August 2019]
Case T-612/17 *Google and Alphabet v Commission (Google Shopping)* [2021] ECLI:EU:T:2021:763
Case C-252/21 *Meta Platforms vs Bundeskartellamt* [2022] ECLI:EU:C:2022:704
Case *Northern Securities Co. v United States*, 193 U.S. 197 [1904]
Case *Standard Oil Co. of New Jersey v United States*, 221 U.S. 1 [1911]
Case *United States v American Tobacco Company*, 221 U.S. 106 [1911]
Case *Reiter v Sonotone Corp.*, 442 US 330 [1979]
Case *United States v Microsoft Corporation*, 253 F.3d 34 [D.C. Cir. 2001].
Case *United States v Apple* 791 F. 3d 290, 332 (2d circuit) [2015]
French Competition Authority, Decision No: 14-D-06 Cegedim [8 July 2014]
French Competition Authority, Decision No. 14-MC-02 (GDF-Suez Decision) [9 September 2014]
UK Office of Fair Trade, *Google/Waze* ME/6167/13

European Commission Decisions

Case COMP/C-3/37.792 Microsoft, Commission Decision of 24 March 2004 Relating to a Proceeding Under Article 82 of the EC Treaty Against Microsoft Corporation C [2004] 900 final
Case COMP/C-3/39.530 Microsoft, Commission Decision of 16 December 2009 Relating to a Proceeding Under Article 102 of the Treaty on the Functioning of the European Union and Article 54 of the EEA Agreement
Case No COMP/AT.39530-Microsoft (Tying), Commission Decision of 6 March 2013 Addressed to Microsoft Corporation Relating to a Proceeding on the Imposition of a Fine Pursuant to Article 23(2)(c) of Council Regulation (EC) No 1/2003
Case No COMP/AT.40099, Google Android [2018] Commission Decision of 18 July 2018, C(2018) 4761 final
Case No COMP/AT.39740, Google Search (Shopping) [2017] 4444 Final, Commission Decision of 27 June 2017 Relating to Proceedings Under Article 102 of the Treaty on the Functioning of the European Union

230   Bibliography

Case No COMP/AT.40411 Google AdSense [2019] Commission Decision of 20 March 2019 Relating to a Proceeding Under Article 102 of the Treaty on the Functioning of the European Union and Article 54 of the EEA Agreement, C(2019) 2173

Case No COMP/M.4731, Google/DoubleClick C [2008] 927 Final, Commission Decision of 11/03/2008 Declaring a Concentration to Be Compatible with the Common Market and the Functioning of the EEA Agreement

Case No COMP/M.5727, Microsoft/Yahoo! Search Business C [2010] 1077 Final, Commission Decision of 18 February 2010 Declaring a Concentration to Be Compatible with the Common Market According to Council Regulation (EC) No 139/2004

Case No COMP/M.6314, Telefónica UK/Vodafone UK/Everything Everywhere/JV C [2012] 6063 Final, Commission Decision of 4 September 2012 Declaring a Concentration to Be Compatible with the Internal Market and the Functioning of the EEA Agreement

Case No COMP/M.6281, Microsoft/Skype C [2011] 7239 Final, Commission Decision Pursuant to Article 6(1)(b) of Council Regulation No 139/2004

Case No COMP/M.7217, Facebook/WhatsApp C [2014] 7239 Final, Commission Decision Pursuant to Article 6(1)(b) of Council Regulation No 139/2004

Case No COMP/M.8124, Microsoft/LinkedIn C [2016] 8404 Final, Commission Decision Pursuant to Article 6(1)(b) in Conjunction with Article 6(2) of Council Regulation No 139/2004 and Article 57 of the Agreement on the European Economic Area

Case No COMP/M.8228, Facebook/WhatsApp C [2017] 3192 Final, Imposing Fines Under Article 14(1) of Council Regulation (EC) No. 139/2004 for the Supply by an Undertaking of Incorrect or Misleading Information

Case No COMP/M.7813 Sanofi/Google/DMI JV [2016] 1223 final

Case No COMP/M.9660, Google/Fitbit [2020] Prior Notification of a Concentration OJ 2020/C 210/09

Case No COMP/SA.38373 Commission Decision of 30.8.2016 on State Aid (2014/C) (ex 2014/NN) (ex 2014/CP) Implemented by Ireland to Apple Brussels, 30.8.2016 C (2016) 5605 final

Statutes and Statutory Instruments

Act Against Restraints of Competition (Competition Act – GWB) (Germany)

Clayton Antitrust Act of 1914 (US)

Consolidated Version of the Treaty on European Union [2010] OJ C 83/01

Consolidated Version of the Treaty on the Functioning of the European Union [2008], OJ C 115/47

Council Regulation (EC) No. 1/2003 of 16 December 2002 on the Implementation of the Rules on Competition Laid Down in Articles 81 and 82 of the Treaty (Text with EEA Relevance) [4 January 2003], OJ L 1

Council Regulation (EC) No. 4064/89 on the Control of Concentrations [1989], OJ L 395/1, corrected version in 1990 OJ L 257/13

Directive 2000/31/EC of the European Parliament and of the Council of 8 June 2000 on Certain Legal Aspects of Information Society Services, in Particular Electronic Commerce, in the Internal Market ('Directive on Electronic Commerce') [17 July 2000], OJ L 178

Directive 2005/29/EC of the European Parliament and of the Council of 11 May 2005 Concerning Unfair Business-to-Consumer Commercial Practices in the Internal Market and Amending Council Directive 84/450/EEC, Directives 97/7/EC, 98/27/EC and 2002/65/EC of the European Parliament and of the Council and Regulation (EC) No 2006/2004 of the European Parliament and of the Council ('the Unfair Commercial Practices Directive') (Text with EEA Relevance) [2005] OJ L 149

EU, General Data Protection Regulation (GDPR), Entry into Force 25 May 2018

European Commission, Communication from the European Commission, Guidance on the Commission's Enforcement Priorities in Applying Article 82 of the EC Treaty to Abusive Exclusionary Conduct by Dominant Undertakings (Text with EEA Relevance) [2009], OJ C45/9

European Commission, Proposal for a Regulation of the European Parliament and of the Council on Promoting Fairness and Transparency for Business Users of Online Intermediation Services, Brussels [26 April 2018], COM(2018) 238 final

Federal Trade Commission Act of 1914 (US)

Italian Consumer Code, Decreto Legislativo [6 Settembre 2005], n. 206 – Codice del Consume

Regulation (EU) 2016/679 of the European Parliament and of the Council of 27 April 2016 on the Protection of Natural Persons with Regard to the Processing of Personal Data and on the Free Movement of Such Data, and Repealing Directive 95/46/EC (General Data Protection Regulation) (Text with EEA Relevance) OJ L 119

Regulation (EU) 2019/1150 of the European Parliament and of the Council of 20 June 2019 on Promoting Fairness and Transparency for Business Users of Online Intermediation Services (Text with EEA Relevance) PE/56/2019/REV/1 [11 July 2019], OJ L 186 (P2B Regulation)

Regulation (EU) 2022/1925 of the European Parliament and of the Council of 14 September 2022 on Contestable and Fair Markets in the Digital Sector and Amending Directives (EU) 2019/1937 and (EU) 2020/1828 (Digital Markets Act) OJ L 265

Regulation (EU) 2022/2065 of the European Parliament and of the Council of 19 October 2022 on a Single Market For Digital Services and Amending Directive 2000/31/EC (Digital Services Act) (Text with EEA Relevance) OJ L 277

Sherman Antitrust Act of 1890 (US)

Treaty on European Union (Maastricht Text) [29 July 1992], OJ C 191/1

Other EU Sources

European Commission, Notice on the Definition of Relevant Market for the Purposes of Community Competition Law (Text with EEA Relevance) [1997] OJ C 372/5; Draft Revised Version, Notice on the Definition of Relevant Market for the Purposes of Union Competition Law [8 November 2022]

European Commission, Guideline on Vertical Restraints [2000] OJ C291/01

European Commission, Guidelines on the Assessment of Horizontal Mergers Under the Council Regulation on the Control of Concentrations Between Undertakings [2004] OJ C31/03

European Commission, Guidelines on the Assessment of Non-Horizontal Mergers Under the Council Regulation on the Control of Concentrations Between Undertakings [2008] OJ C265/7

European Commission, Guidance on the Commission's Enforcement Priorities in Applying Article 82 of the EC Treaty to Abusive Exclusionary Conduct by Dominant Undertakings [2009] OJ C45/02

European Commission, Guidelines on Vertical Restraints [2010] OJ C130/01

European Commission, Guidelines on the Applicability of Article 101 of the Treaty on the Functioning of the European Union to Horizontal Co-Operation Agreements [2011] OJ C11/1

French Competition Authority, Decision No. 14-MC-02 (GDF-Suez Decision) [9 September 2014]

Bibliography

Secondary Sources

Books

Areeda P and Hovenkamp H, *Antitrust Law: An Analysis of Antitrust Principles and Their Application* (2nd edn, Wolter Kluwer International 2002)
Bork R, *The Antitrust Paradox: A Policy at War with Itself* (1st edn, Basic Books, Free Press 1978) (2nd edn, Basic Books 1993)
Ezrachi A and Stucke M, *Virtual Competition: The Promise and Perils of the Algorithm-Driven Economy* (1st edn, Harvard UP 2016)
Friedman M, 'The Methodology of Positive Economics' in *Essays in Positive Economics* (Chicago UP 1966)
Graef I, *EU Competition Law, Data Protection and Online Platforms: Data as Essential Facility* (1st edn, Kluwer Law International 2016)
———, 'Data as Essential Facility: Competition and Innovation on Online Platforms' (PhD Thesis, KU Leuven Faculty of Law 2016)
Harari Y, *21 Lessons for the 21st Century* (1st edn, Random House 2018)
Hoffman S, *Regulation of Cloud Services Under US and EU Antitrust, Competition and Privacy Laws* (Peter Lang 2016)
Jones A and Sufrin B, *EU Competition Law* (5th edn, OUP 2014)
Kaczorowska-Ireland A, *European Union Law* (4th edn, Routledge 2016)
Kokkoris I and Lianos I, *The Reform of EC Competition Law: New Challenges* (Kluwer Law International 2009)
Mayor-Schonberger V and Cukier K, *Big Data: A Revolution That Will Transform How We Live, Work and Think* (1st edn, John Murray Publishers 2013)
Nazzini R, *The Foundations of European Union Competition Law* (1st edn, OUP 2011)
Nihoul P, Charbit N and Ramundo E (eds.), *Choice – A New Standard for Competition Law Analysis?* (Concurrences 2016)
Parker G, Van Alstyne M and Choudary S, *Platform Revolution: How Networked Markets Are Transforming the Economy – and How to Make Them Work for You* (W. W. Norton & Company 2016)
Pasquale F, *The Black Box Society: The Secret Algorithms That Control Money and Information* (1st edn, Harvard UP 2015)
Patel K and Schweitzer H, The Historical Foundations of EU Competition Law (1st edn, OUP 2013)
Posner R, *Antitrust Law* (2nd edn, Chicago UP 2001)
———, *Economic Analysis of Law* (7th edn, Wolters Kluwer 2007)
Stucke M and Grunes A, *Big Data and Competition Policy* (1st edn, OUP 2016)
Tirole J, *The Theory of Industrial Organisation* (1st edn, MIT Press 1988)
Weatherill S, *Cases & Materials on EU Law* (6th edn, OUP 2003)
Whish R and Bailey D, *Competition Law* (8th edn, OUP 2015)

Contribution to Edited Books

Bania K, 'The European Commission's Decision in Google Search: Exploring Old and New Frontiers of Competition Enforcement in the Digital Economy' in Björn Lundqvist and Michal S Gal (eds), *Competition Law for the Digital Economy* (1st edn, Edward Elgar Publishing 2019)

Burri M, 'Understanding the Implications of Big Data and Big Data Analytics for Competition Law: An Attempt for a Primer' in Klaus Mathias and Avishalom Tor (eds), *New Developments in Competition Behavioural Law and Economics* (1st edn, Springer 2018)

Drexl J, 'Economic Efficiency Versus Democracy: On the Potential Role of Competition Policy in Regulating Digital Markets in Times of Post-Truth Politics' in Damien Gerard and Ioannis Lianos (eds), *Competition Policy: Between Equity and Efficiency* (CUP 2017)

Esayas S, 'Privacy as a Quality Parameter of Competition: Some Reflections on the Scepticism Surrounding It' in Björn Lundqvist and Michal S Gal (eds), *Competition Law for the Digital Economy* (1st edn, Edward Elgar Publishing 2019)

Evans D and Schmalensee R, 'Some Economic Aspects of Antitrust Analysis in Dynamically Competitive Industries' in Adam B Jaffe, Josh Lerner and Scott Stern (eds), *Innovation Policy and the Economy*, vol 2 (1st edn, MIT Press 2002)

—— and Schmalensee R, 'The Antitrust Analysis of Multi-Sided Platform Businesses' in Roger Blair and Daniel Sokol (eds), *Oxford Handbook on International Antitrust Economics* (OUP 2013)

Gürkaynak G, Aktüre B and Coşkunoğlu S, 'Challenges of the Digital Age: The Relevant Product Market Definition in Online and Offline Sales' in Gönenç Gürkaynak (ed), *The Second Academic Gift Book of ELIG Gürkaynak Attorneys-at-Law on Selected Contemporary Competition Law Matters* (Legal Yayincilik 2019)

Gürkaynak G, Uçar A and Buharali Z, 'Data-Related Abuses in Competition Law' in Nicolas Charbit and Sonia Ahmad (eds), *Frédéric Jenny Liber Amicorum, Standing Up for Convergence and Relevance in Antitrust* (Concurrences 2019)

Hagiu A and Yoffie D, 'Network Effects' in Mie Augier and David Teece (eds), *The Palgrave Encyclopedia of Strategic Management* (Palgrave Macmillan 2018)

Lundqvist B, 'Regulating Competition in the Digital Economy with a Special Focus on Platforms' in Björn Lundqvist and Michal S Gal (eds), *Competition Law for the Digital Economy* (1st edn, Edward Elgar Publishing 2019)

Marshall A, 'The Present Position of Economics' (1885), reprinted in AC Pigou (ed), *Memorials of Alfred Marshall* (Macmillan & Co. 1925)

Schmidt H, 'Taming the Shrew: Is There a Need for a New Market Power Definition for the Digital Economy?' in Björn Lundqvist and Michal S Gal (eds), *Competition Law for the Digital Economy* (1st edn, Edward Elgar Publishing 2019)

Sokol D and Comerford R, 'Does Antitrust Have a Role to Play in Regulating Big Data?' in Roger D Blair and Daniel D Sokol (eds), *Cambridge Handbook of Antitrust, Intellectual Property and High Technology* (CUP 2017)

Vanberg V, 'Consumer Welfare, Total Welfare and Economic Freedom: On the Normative Foundations of Competition Policy' in Josef Drexl, Wolfgang Kerber and Rupprecht Podszun (eds), *Competition Policy and the Economic Approach* (1st edn, Edward Elgar Publishing 2011)

Journal Articles

Ahlborn C, Evans D and Padilla J, 'Competition Policy in the New Economy: Is European Competition Law up to the Challenge?' (2001) 22 European Competition Law Review 5

Ahlborn C and Grave C, 'Walter Eucken and Ordoliberalism: An Introduction from a Consumer Welfare Perspective' (2006) 2 Competition Policy International 2

Akman P, 'Searching for the Long-Lost Soul of Article 82EC' (2009) 29 Oxford Journal of Legal Studies 2

——, 'A Preliminary Assessment of the European Commission's Google Search Decision' (2017) 3 CPI Antitrust Chronicle 7

——, 'The Theory of Abuse in Google Search: A Positive and Normative Assessment Under EU Competition Law' (2017) 2 Journal of Law, Technology and Policy 301

——, 'An Agenda for Competition Law and Policy in the Digital Economy' (2019) Journal of European Competition Law and Practice, Editorial 1

Armstrong M, 'Competition in Two-sided Markets' (2006) 37 The RAND Journal of Economics 3, 668–91

—— and Wright J, 'Two-Sided Markets, Competitive Bottlenecks and Exclusive Contracts' (2007) 32 Economic Theory 2, 353–80

Auer D and Petit N, 'Two-Sided Markets and the Challenge of Turning Economic Theory into Antitrust Policy' (2015) 60 Antitrust Bulletin 4

Averitt N and Lande R, 'Consumer Sovereignty: A Unified Theory of Antitrust and Consumer Protection Law' (1997) 65 Antitrust Law Journal 713

——, Lande R and Nihoul P, ' "Consumer Choice" Is Where We Are All Going – so Let's Go Together' (2011) 2 Concurrences-Revue des droits de la concurrence 1

Baker J, 'Taking the Error Out of "Error Cost" Analysis (2015) 80 Antitrust Law Journal 1, 1–38

Baxter W, 'The Definition and Measurement of Market Power in Industries Characterized by Rapidly Developing and Changing Technologies' (1984–1985) 53 Antitrust Law Journal 717

Biancotti C and Ciocca P, 'Opening Internet Monopolies to Competition with Data Sharing Mandates' (2019) Policy Brief 19-3, Peterson Institute for International Economics

Binns R and Bietti E, 'Dissolving Privacy, One Merger at a Time: Competition, Data, and Third Party Tracking' (2020) 36 Computer Law and Security Review

Bork R and Sidak G, 'What Does the Chicago School Teach About Internet Search and the Antitrust Treatment of Google?' (2012) 8 Journal of Competition Law and Economics 4

Botta M and Wiedemann K, 'The Interaction of EU Competition, Consumer, and Data Protection Law in the Digital Economy: The Regulatory Dilemma in the Facebook Odyssey' (2019) 64 The Antitrust Bulletin 3

Broos S and Ramos J, 'Google, Google Shopping and Amazon: The Importance of Competing Business Models and Two-Sided Intermediaries in Defining Relevant Markets' (2017) 62 The Antitrust Bulletin 2

Caillaud B and Jullien B, 'Chicken and Egg: Competition Among Intermediation Service Providers' (2003) 34 The RAND Journal of Economics 2, 309–28

Capobianco A and Nyeso A, 'Challenges for Competition Law Enforcement and Policy in the Digital Economy' (2018) 9 Journal of European Competition Law and Practice 1, 19–27

Carlton D, 'A General Analysis of Exclusionary Conduct and Refusal to Deal: Why Aspen and Kodak Are Misguided' (2001) 68 Antitrust Law Journal 3

Colangelo G and Maggiolino M, 'Big Data as Misleading Facilities' (2017) 13 European Competition Journal 2–3

——Colangelo G, 'Data Protection in Attention Markets: Protecting Privacy Through Competition?' (2017) 8 Journal of European Competition Law and Practice 363

Cole M, 'Does the EU Commission Really Hate the US? Understanding the Google Decision Through Competition Theory' (2019) 44 European Law Review 4

Corden W, 'The Maximisation of Profit by a Newspaper' (1953) 20 The Review of Economic Studies 3

Costa-Cabral F and Lynske O, 'Family Ties: The Intersection Between Data Protection and Competition EU Law' (2017) 54 Common Market Law Review 11

Cowen T, 'Big Data as a Competition Issue: Should the EU Commission's Approach Be More Careful' (2016) 4 European Networks Law and Regulation Quarterly 14
Crane D, 'Search Neutrality as an Antitrust Principle' (2012) 19 George Mason Law Review 1199
———, 'Search Neutrality and Referral Dominance' (2012) 8 Journal of Competition Law & Economics 3
Davilla M, 'Is Big Data a Different Kind of Animal? The Treatment of Big Data Under the EU Competition Rules' (2017) 8 Journal of European Competition Law and Practice 6
De Mauro A, Greco M and Grimaldi M, 'A Formal Definition of Big Data Based on Its Essential Features' (2016) 65 Library Review 3, 122–35
Director A and Levi E, 'Law and the Future: Trade Regulation' (1956) 51 Northwestern University Law Review 281
Easterbrook F, 'The Limits of Antitrust' (1984) 63 Texas Law Review 1
Eben M, 'Fining Google: A Missed Opportunity for Legal Certainty?' (2018) 14 European Competition Journal
———, 'Market Definition and Free Online Services: The Prospect of Personal Data as Price' (2018) 14(2) I/S: A Journal of Law and Policy for the Information Society 227
Edelman B, 'Does Google Leverage Market Power Through Tying and Bundling?' (2015) 11 Journal of Competition Law and Economics 2
Ellison J and others, 'A New Frontier for Privacy and Competition' Slaughter and May Report (March 2018)
Engels B, 'Data Portability Among Online Platforms' (2016) 5 Internet Policy Review 2
Evans D, 'The Antitrust Economics of Multi-Sided Platform Markets' (2003) 20 Yale Journal on Regulation 2
———, 'Some Empirical Aspects of Multi-Sided Platform Industries (2003) 2 Review of Network Economics 3
———, 'Antitrust Issues Raised by the Emerging Global Internet Economy' (2008) 102 Northwestern University Law Review
———, 'The Online Advertising Industry: Economics, Evolution, and Privacy' (2009) 23 Journal of Economic Perspectives 3
———, 'The Antitrust Economics of Free' (2011) Competition Policy International 71
———, 'Attention Rivalry Among Online Platforms' (2013) 9 Journal of Competition Law and Economics 2
——— and Noel M, 'The Analysis of Mergers that Involve Multisided Platform Businesses' (2008) 4 Journal of Competition Law and Economics 3
Evans D and Schmalensee R, 'The Industrial Organization of Markets with Two-Sided Platforms' (2007) 3 Competition Policy International
Ezrachi A and Stucke M, 'Emerging Antitrust Threats and Enforcement Actions in the Online World' (2017) 13 Competition Law International 2
———, 'The Fight Over Antitrust's Soul' (2018) 9 Journal of European Competition Law and Practice 1
Farrell H and Newman A, 'Weaponized Interdependence: How Global Economic Networks Shape State Coercion' (2019) 44 International Security 1, 42
Ferro M, 'Ceci n'est pas un marché: Gratuity and Competition Law' (2015) Concurrences 10
Filistrucchi L, 'A SSNIP Test for Two-Sided Markets: The Case of Media' (2008) 34 NET Institute Working Papers
———, Geradin D and Van Damme E, 'Identifying Two-sided Markets' (2012) TILEC Discussion Paper No. 2012-008

Filistrucchi L and others, 'Market Definition in Two-Sided Markets: Theory and Practice' (2014) 10 Journal of Competition Law and Economics 2

Gal M and Rubinfeld D, 'The Hidden Costs of Free Goods: Implication for Antitrust Enforcement' (2016) 80 Antitrust Law Journal 521

Gebicka A and Heinemann A, 'Social Media & Competition Law' (2014) 37 World Competition 2, 149–72

Geradin D, 'Limiting the Scope of Article 82 of the EC Treaty: What Can the EU Learn from the U.S. Supreme Court's Judgment in Trinko in the Wake of Microsoft, IMS, and Deutsche Telekom' (2004) 41 Common Market Law Review

—— and Katsifis D, 'An EU Competition Law Analysis of Online Display Advertising in the Programmatic Age' (2018) 15 European Competition Journal 55–96

Geradin D and Kuschewsky M, 'Competition Law and Personal Data: Preliminary Thoughts on a Complex Issue' (2013) 2 Concurrences

Goldfarb A and Tucker C, 'Privacy Regulation and Online Advertising' (2011) 57 Management Science

—— and Tucker C, 'Substitution Between Offline and Online Advertising Markets' (2011) 7 Journal of Competition Law and Economics 37

Gormsen L, 'Article 82 EC: Where Are We Coming from and Where Are We Going to?' (2006) 2 Competition Law Review 2

Graef I, 'Market Definition and Market Power in Data: The Case of Online Platforms' (2015) 38 World Competition 4

——, 'Rethinking the Essential Facilities Doctrine for the EU Digital Economy' (2019) 53(1) Revue juridique Thémis de l'Université de Montréal 33–72

——, Wahyuningtyas S and Vackle P, 'Assessing Data Access Issues in Online Platforms' (2015) 39(5) Telecommunications Policy 375–87

Graef I, Verschakele J and Valcke P, 'Putting the Right to Data Portability into a Competition Law Perspective' [2013] The Journal of the Higher School of Economics, Annual Review 53–63

Gürkaynak G, Inanılır Ö, Diniz S and Yasar A, 'Multi-Sided Markets and the Challenge of Incorporating Multi-Sided Considerations into Competition Law Analysis [2017] Journal of Antitrust Enforcement 5

Hagiu A and Wright J, 'Multi-Sided Platforms' (2015) 43 International Journal of Industrial Organization 5

Harbour P and Koslov T, 'Section 2 in a Web 2.0: An Expanded Vision of Relevant Product Markers' (2010) 76 Antirust Law Journal

Haucap J, 'Competition and Competition Policy in a Data-Driven Economy' (2019) 54 Intereconomics 201–8

Hesse R, 'Two-Sided Platform Markets and the Application of the Traditional Antitrust Analytical Framework' (2007) 3 Competition Policy International

—— and Soven J, 'Defining Relevant Product Markets in Electronic Payment Network Antitrust Cases' (2006) 73 Antitrust Law Journal 709

Hlina E, 'Dominant Undertakings in the Digital Era: A Call for Evolution of the Competition Policy Towards Article 102 TFEU?' (2016) 9 ICC Global Antitrust Review

Holles de Peyer B, 'EU Merger Control and Big Data' (2017) 13(4) Journal of Competition Law and Economics 767–90

Hoofnagle C and Whittington J, 'Free: Accounting for the Costs of the Internet's Most Popular Price' (2014) 61 UCLA Law Review 606, 608–26

Höppner T, 'Defining Markets for Multi-Sided Platforms: The Case of Search Engines' (2015) 38 World Competition 3, 349–66

Hylton K, 'Digital Platforms and Antitrust Law' (2019) Boston University School of Law, Law and Economics Research Paper No. 19-8

Jacobides M, Cennamo C and Gawer A, 'Towards a Theory of Ecosystems' (2018) 39 Strategic Management Journal

Jacquemin A, 'Theories of Industrial Organisation and Competition Policy: What Are the Links?' (2000) European Commission Forward Studies Unit, Working Paper

Janka S and Uhsler S, 'Antitrust 4.0 – The Rise of Artificial Intelligence and Emerging Challenges to Antitrust Law' (2018) 39 European Competition Law Review 3

Kadar M and Bogdan M, '"Big Data" and EU Merger Control – A Case Review' (2017) 8 Journal of European Competition Law and Practice 8

Kathuria V and Globocnik J, 'Exclusionary Conduct in Data-Driven Markets: Limitations of Data Sharing Remedy' (2019) Max Planck Institute for Innovation and Competition Research Paper No. 19-4

Kerber W, 'Digital Markets, Data, and Privacy: Competition Law, Consumer Law, and Data Protection' (2016) 11 Journal of Intellectual Property Law and Practice

Khan L, 'Amazon's Antitrust Paradox' (2016) 126 Yale Law Journal 3

——, 'The New Brandeis Movement: America's Antimonopoly Debate' (2018) 9 Journal of European Competition Law and Practice 3

Kimmel L and Kestenbaum J, 'What's Up with WhatsApp? A Transatlantic View on Privacy and Merger Enforcement in Digital Markets' (2014) 29 Antitrust 48

Kokkoris I, 'The Google Saga: Episode I' (2018) 14(2–3) European Competition Journal 462–90

Krämer J and Wohlfarth M, 'Market Power, Regulatory Convergence, and the Role of Data in Digital Markets' (2108) 42 Telecommunications Policy 2, 154–71

Krattenmaker T, Lande R, and Salop S, 'Monopoly Power and Market Power in Antitrust Law' (1987) 76 The Georgetown Law Journal 241

Kupcik J and Mikes S, 'Discussion on Big Data, Online Advertising and Competition Policy' (2018) 39 European Competition Law Review 9, 393–402

Lande R, 'Consumer Choice as the Ultimate Goal of Antitrust' (2001) 62 University of Pittsburgh Law Review 3

Landes W and Posner R, 'Market Power in Antitrust Cases' (1980) 94 Harvard Law Review 937

Lao M, 'Search, Essential Facilities, and the Antitrust Duty to Deal' (2013) 11 Northwestern Journal of Technology and Intellectual Property 275

Lasserre B and Mundt A, 'Competition Law and Big Data: The Enforcers' View' (2017) 4 Italian Antitrust Review

Lianos I, 'Some Reflections on the Question of the Goals of EU Competition Law' (2013) CLES Working Paper Series 3 January

——, 'Competition Law for the Digital Era: A Complex Systems' Perspective' (2019) CLES Research Paper Series 6/2019

—— and Motchenkova E, 'Market Dominance and Search Quality in the Search Engine Market (2012) 9(2) Journal of Competition Law and Economics 419–55

Lind R, Muysert P and Walker M, 'Innovation and Competition Policy, Part I, Conceptual Issues: Report Prepared for the Office of Fair Trading by Charles River Associates' (2002) Discussion Paper 3

Lopatka J and Page H, 'Devising a Microsoft Remedy that Serves Consumers' (2001) 9(3) George Mason Law Review 691–726

Lucchini S and others, 'Online Digital Services and Competition Law: Why Competition Authorities Should be More Concerned About Portability Rather Than About Privacy' (2018) 9 Journal of European Competition Law and Practice 9

Lugard P and Roach L, 'The Era of "Big Data" and EU/U.S. Divergence for Refusals to Deal' (2017) 31(2) Antitrust

Mandrescu D, 'Applying EU Competition Law to Online Platforms: The Road Ahead – Part 1' (2017) 38(8) European Competition Law Review 353–65

———, 'Applying EU Competition Law to Online Platforms: The Road Ahead – Part 2' (2017) 38(9) European Competition Law Review 410–22

Mankhe R, 'Big Data as a Barrier to Entry' (2015) 2 Competition Policy International Antitrust Chronicle

Manne G and Rinehart W, 'The Market Realities that Undermined the FTC's Antitrust Case Against Google' (2013) Harvard Journal of Law and Technology Occasional Paper Series 12

Manne G and Sperry B, 'The Problems and Perils of Bootstrapping Privacy and Data into an Antitrust Framework' (20125) 2 CPI Antitrust Chronicle 1

Manne G and Wright J, 'Google and the Limits of Antitrust: The Case Against the Antitrust Case Against Google' (2011) 34 Harvard Journal of Law and Public Policy

Mays L, 'The Consequences of Search Bias: How Application of the Essential Facilities Doctrine Remedies Google's Unrestricted Monopoly on Search in the United States and Europe' (2015) 83(2) The George Washington Law Review 721–60

Mehra S, 'Antitrust and the Robo-Seller: Competition in Time of Algorithms' (2015) 100 Minnesota Law Review 1323

Meriani M, 'Digital Platforms and the Spectrum of Data Protection Competition Law Analyses' (2017) 38 European Competition Law Review 2

Modrall J, 'Antitrust Risks and Big Data' [2017] Norton Rose Fulbright Competition World 14

Moore J, 'Predators and Prey: A New Ecology of Competition' (1993) 71 Harvard Business Review 3

Nazzini R, 'Google and the (Ever-Stretching) Boundaries of Article 102' (2015) 6 Journal of European Competition Law and Practice 5

———, 'Online Platforms and Antitrust: Where Do We Go from Here?' (2018) 5 Italian Antitrust Review

Newman J, 'Antitrust in Zero-Price Markets Foundations' (2015) 164 University of Pennsylvania Law Review

———, 'Antitrust in Zero-Price Markets: Applications' (2016) 94 Washington University Law Review 1

Newman N, 'The Costs of Lost Privacy: Consumer Harm and Rising Economic Inequality in the Age of Google (2014) 40 William Mitchell Law Review 849

———, 'Search, Antitrust, and the Economics of the Control of User Data' (2014) 31 Yale Journal on Regulation 2

Ohlhausen M and Okuliar A, 'Competition, Consumer Protection and the Right (Approach) to Privacy' (2015) 80(1) Antitrust Law Journal 121

Page W, 'Mandatory Contracting Remedies in the American and European Microsoft Cases' (2008) 75 Antitrust Law Journal

——— and Childers S, 'Measuring Compliance with Compulsory Licensing Remedies in the American Microsoft Case' (2009) 76 Antitrust Law Journal

Pasquale F, 'Privacy, Antitrust and Power' (2013) 20 George Mason Law Review 4

Patterson M, 'Google and Search-Engine Market Power' [2013] Harvard Journal of Law and Technology 1

Posner R, 'The Chicago School of Antitrust Analysis' (1979) 127 University of Pennsylvania Law Review 925

Ratliff J and Rubinfeld D, 'Is There a Market for Organic Search Engine Results and Can Their Manipulation Give Rise to Antitrust Liability?' (2014) 10 Journal of Competition Law and Economics 1–25
—— and Rubinfeld D., 'Online Advertising: Defining Relevant Markets' (2010) 6 Journal of Competition Law and Economics 3
Reddaway W, 'The Economics of Newspapers' (1963) 73 The Economic Journal 290
Robertson V, 'The Relevant Market in Competition Law: A Legal Concept' (2019) 7 Journal of Antitrust Enforcement 158–76
Rochet JC and Tirole J, 'Cooperation Among Competitors: Some Economics of Payment Card Associations' (2002) 33(4) The RAND Journal of Economics 549–70
—— and Tirole J, 'An Economic Analysis of the Determination of Interchange Fees in Payment Card Systems' (2003) 2 Review of Network Economics 2
—— and Tirole J, 'Platform Competition in Two-Sided Markets' (2003) 1(4) Journal of the European Economic Association 990–1029
—— and Tirole J, 'Two-Sided Markets: A Progress Report' (2006) 37(3) The RAND Journal of Economics 645–67
Rubinfeld D and Gal M, 'Access Barriers to Big Data' (2017) 59 Arizona Law Review 339
Russo F and Stasi M, 'Defining the Relevant Market in the Sharing Economy' (2016) 5 Internet Policy Review 2
Rysman M, 'The Economics of Two-Sided Markets' (2009) 23(3) Journal of Economic Perspectives
Schepp N and Wambach A, 'On Big Data and Its Relevance for Market Power Assessment' (2016) 7(2) Journal of European Competition Law and Practice 120–24
Schneider G, 'Testing Art. 102 TFEU in the Digital Marketplace: Insights from the Bundeskartellamt's Investigation Against Facebook' (2018) 9 Journal of European Competition Law and Practice 4
Shapiro C, 'Exclusivity in Network Industries' (1999) 7 George Mason Law Review 673
Shelanski H, 'Information, Innovation, and Competition Policy for the Internet' (2013) 161 University of Pennsylvania Law Review 6
Sidak G and Lipsky A, 'Essential Facilities' (1999) 51(5) Stanford Law Review 1187–249
Sivinski G, Okuliar A and Kjolbye L, 'Is Big Data a Big Deal? A Competition Law Approach to Big Data' (2017) 13(2–3) European Competition Journal
Sokol D and Comerford R, 'Antitrust and Regulating Big Data' (2016) 23(5) George Mason Law Review 1129
Spulber D, 'Unlocking Technology: Antitrust and Innovation' (2008) 4(4) Journal of Competition Law & Economics
Stakheyeva H and Toksoy F, 'Merger Control in the Big Data World: To Be or Not to Be Revisited?' (2017) 38(6) European Competition Law Review 265–71
Stucke M, 'Should We Be Concerned About Data-Opolies?' (2018) 2 Georgetown Law Technology Review 275
—— and Ezrachi A, 'When Competition Fails to Optimize Quality: A Look at Search Engines' (2016) 18 Yale Journal of Law and Technology 70
Stylianou K, 'Exclusion in Digital Markets' (2018) 24(2) Michigan Telecommunications and Technology Law Review
Swire P and Lagos Y, 'Why the Right to Data Portability Likely Reduces Consumer Welfare: Antitrust and Privacy Critique' (2013) 72(2) Maryland Law Review
Tamke M, 'Big Data and Competition Law' (2017) 15(4) Zeitschrift für Wettbewerbsrecht

Teece D, 'Next-Generation Competition: New Concepts for Understanding How Innovation Shapes Competition and Policy in the Digital Economy' (2012) 9 Journal of Law, Economics and Policy

Thépot F, 'Market Power in Online Search and Social Networking: A Matter of Two-sided Markets' (2013) 36(2) World Competition

Townley C, Morrison E and Yeung K, 'Big Data and Personalised Price Discrimination in EU Competition Law' (2017) 36 Yearbook of European Law

Tucker D and Wellford H, 'Big Mistakes Regarding Big Data' (2014) 14 The Antitrust Source

Vanberg A and Unver M, 'The Right to Data Portability in the GDPR and EU Competition Law: Odd Couple or Dynamic Duo?' (2017) 8(1) European Journal of Law and Technology

Vesterdorf B, 'Theories of Self-Preferencing and Duty to Deal – Two Sides of the Same Coin' (2015) 1 Competition Law and Policy Debate

Volmar M and Helmdach K, 'Protecting Consumers and Their Data Through Competition Law? Rethinking Abuse of Dominance in Light of the Federal Cartel Office's Facebook Investigation' (2018) 14(2) European Competition Journal

Wagner-von Papp F, 'Should Google's Secret Sauce Be Organic?' (2015) 16(2) Melbourne Journal of International Law

Waller S and Sag M, 'Promoting Innovation' (2015) 100 Iowa Law Review 2223–47

Whittington J and Hoofnagle C, 'Unpacking Privacy's Price' (2012) 90 North Carolina Law Review 1327

Wismer S, Bongard C and Rasek A, 'Multi-Sided Market Economics in Competition Law Enforcement' (2017) 8(4) Journal of European Competition Law and Practice

Wright J, 'One-Sided Logic in Two-sided Markets' (2004) 3(1) Review of Network Economics

Yuen S, 'Exporting Trust with Data: Audited Self-Regulation as a Solution to Cross-Border Data Transfer Protection Concerns in the Offshore Outsourcing Industry' (2007) 9 Columbia Science and Technology Law Review 41

Online Articles

Akman P, 'Competition Policy in a Globalized, Digitalized Economy' White Paper Series (World Economic Forum 2019) <https://www.weforum.org/whitepapers/competition-policy-in-a-globalized-digitalized-economy>

Almunia J, Vice President of the European Commission Responsible for Competition Policy, 'Competition in the Online World: LSE Public Lecture, London' (11 November 2013) <https://ec.europa.eu/commission/presscorner/detail/en/SPEECH_13_905>

Argentesi E and others, 'Ex-Post Assessment of Merger Control Decisions in Digital Markets' LEAR Final Report (2019) <https://www.learlab.com/publication/ex-post-assessment-of-merger-control-decisions-in-digital-markets/>

Balto D and Lane M, 'Monopolizing Water in a Tsunami: Finding Sensible Antitrust Rules for Big Data' (2016) SSRN <https://ssrn.com/abstract=2753249 or http://dx.doi.org/10.2139/ssrn.2753249>

Behrens P, 'The Ordoliberal Concept of "Abuse" of a Dominant Position and Its Impact on Article 102 TFEU' (Nihoul/Takahashi, Abuse Regulation in Competition Law, Proceedings of the 10th ASCOLA Conference, Tokyo, 2015) <https://ssrn.com/abstract=2658045>

Brown B, Chui M and Manyika J, 'Are You Ready for the Era of Big Data' *McKinsey Quarterly* (2011) <https://www.mckinsey.com/business-functions/strategy-and-corporate-finance/our-insights/are-you-ready-for-the-era-of-big-data>

―――― and others, *Big Data: The Next Frontier for Innovation, Competition, and Productivity* (McKinsey Global Institute, 2011) <https://www.mckinsey.com/business-functions/digital-mckinsey/our-insights/big-data-the-next-frontier-for-innovation>

Evans D, 'Two-Sided Market Definition' (2009) ABA Section of Antitrust Law, Market Definition in Antitrust: Theory and Case Studies <https://papers.ssrn.com/sol3/papers.cfm?abstract_id=1396751>

――――, 'The Economics of Attention Markets' (2017) Global Economics Group; University College London <https://papers.ssrn.com/sol3/papers.cfm?abstract_id=3044858>

―――― and Noel M, 'Analyzing Market Definition and Power in Multi-Sided Platform Markets' (2005) SSRN <https://ssrn.com/abstract=835504>

Geradin D, 'The EU Digital Markets Act in 10 Points' (*The Platform Law Blog*, 16 December 2020) <https://theplatformlaw.blog/2020/12/16/the-eu-digital-markets-act-in-10-points/>

Gökçe E, 'Competition Issues in the Digital Economy' (2019) UNCTAD Background Note, <https://unctad.org/system/files/official-document/ciclpd54_en.pdf>

Grullon G, Larkin Y and Michaely R, 'Are U.S. Industries Becoming More Concentrated?' (2017) SSRN <https://ssrn.com/abstract=2612047 or http://dx.doi.org/10.2139/ssrn.2612047>

Heinz S, 'Bundeskartellamt Ends Abuse Probe After Amazon Agrees to Changing Business Terms for Dealers' (*Kluwer Competition Law Blog*, 30 July 2019) <http://competitionlawblog.kluwercompetitionlaw.com/2019/07/30/bundeskartellamt-ends-abuse-probe-after-amazon-agrees-to-changing-business-terms-for-dealers/?doing_wp_cron=1590500147.1006309986114501953125>

Höppner T and Westerhoff P, 'The EU's Competition Investigation into Amazon Marketplace' (*Kluwer Competition Law Blog*, 30 November 2018) <http://competitionlawblog.kluwercompetitionlaw.com/2018/11/30/the-eus-competition-investigation-into-amazon-marketplace/?doing_wp_cron=1591716526.0472819805145263671875>

Kersting C and Dworschak S, 'Does Google Hold a Dominant Market Position? – Addressing the (Minor) Significance of High Online User Shares' (2014) 16 Ifo Schnelldienst 7 SSRN <https://ssrn.com/abstract=2495300>

Krämer J and Schnurr D, 'Competition Policy in Platform and Data-Driven Markets: Long-Term Efficiency and Exploitative Conducts, Contribution to the Call: Shaping Competition Policy in the Era of Digitization' (2018) <https://ec.europa.eu/competition/information/digitisation_2018/contributions/daniel_schnurr_jan_kraemer.pdf>

Lambrecht A and Tucker C, 'Can Big Data Protect a Firm from Competition?' (2015) SSRN Paper <https://ssrn.com/abstract=2705530 or http://dx.doi.org/10.2139/ssrn.2705530>

Lerner A, 'The Role of Big Data in Online Platform Competition' (2014) SSRN Working Paper <https://ssrn.com/abstract=2482780 or http://dx.doi.org/10.2139/ssrn.2482780>

Mager T and Neideck P, 'European Union: Data-related Abuse of Dominance' (2018) Global Competition Review <https://globalcompetitionreview.com/insight/e-commerce-competition-enforcement-guide/1177726/european-union-%E2%80%93-data-related-abuse-of-dominance>

Maurer H and others, *Report on Dangers and Opportunities Posed by Large Search Engines, Particularly Google 16* (Institute for Information Systems and Computer Media, Graz University of Technology 2007) <http://citeseerx.ist.psu.edu/viewdoc/download?doi=10.1.1.94.5633&rep=rep1&type=pdf>

McAfee A and Brynjolfsson E, 'Big Data: The Management Revolution' (2012) 90 Harvard Business Review 10 <https://hbr.org/2012/10/big-data-the-management-revolution>

Miller A, 'The Dawn of the Big Data Monopolists' (2016) <https://ssrn.com/abstract=2911567>

242 Bibliography

Muret P, 'Introducing the Google Analytics 360 Suite: An Enterprise-Class Solution for a Multi-Screen World' (15 March 2016) <https://www.blog.google/products/marketingplatform/360/introducing-google-analytics-360-suite>

Petit N, 'Theories of Self-Preferencing Under Article 102TFEU: A Reply to Bo Vesterdorf' (2015) SSRN Electronic Journal <https://plu.mx/ssrn/a/?ssrn_id=2592253>

──, 'Technology Giants, the Moligopoly Hypothesis and Holistic Competition: A Primer' (2016) SSRN <https://ssrn.com/abstract=2856502>

Prescott A, 'Bibliographic Records as Humanities Big Data' [2013] IEEE International Conference on Big Data 57 <https://doi.org/10.1109/BigData.2013.6691670>

Prüfer J and Schottmüller C, 'Competing with Big Data' (2017) Tilburg Law School Research Paper No. 06/2017, TILEC Discussion Paper No. 2017-006, Center Discussion Paper 2017–007, SSRN <https://ssrn.com/abstract=2918726>

Renda A, 'Searching for Harm or Harming Search? A Look at the European Commission's Antitrust Investigation Against Google' (2015) CEPS Special Report No. 118 <http://aei.pitt.edu/67571/>

Rochet JC and Tirole J, 'Defining Two-Sided Markets' (2004) <https://web.mit.edu/14.271/www/rochet_tirole.pdf>

Strowel A and Vergote W, 'Responses to the Public Consultation on the Regulatory Environment for Platforms, Online Intermediaries, Data and Cloud Computing and the Collaborative Economy' (2016) <http://ec.europa.eu/information_society/newsroom/image/document/2016-7/uclouvain_et_universit_saint_louis_14044.pd>

Stucke M and Grunes P, 'No Mistake About It: The Important Role of Antitrust in the Era of Big Data' (2015) The Antitrust Source April, University of Tennessee Legal Studies Research Paper No. 269, SSRN <https://ssrn.com/abstract=2600051>

────── and Grunes P, 'Debunking the Myths Over Big Data and Antitrust' (2015) Competition Policy International Antitrust Chronicle, University of Tennessee Legal Studies Research Paper No. 276, SSRN <https://ssrn.com/abstract=2612562>

────── and Grunes P, 'Data-Opolies' (2017) Concurrences No. 2, University of Tennessee Legal Studies Research Paper No. 316, SSRN <https://ssrn.com/abstract=2927018>

Veljanovski C, 'Network Effects and Multi-Sided Markets' (2007) 7 <https://papers.ssrn.com/sol3/papers.cfm?abstract_id=1003447&download=yes>

Vezzoso S, 'Competition Policy in a World of Big Data' in F Xavier Olleros and Majlinda Zhegu (eds), *Research Handbook on Digital Transformations* (Edward Elgar 2016) SSRN <https://ssrn.com/abstract=2717497>

Reports from Official Authorities

Autorité de la Concurrence, French Competition Authority, Opinion 18-A-03 on Data Processing in the Online Advertising Sector (6 March 2018) <https://www.autoritedelaconcurrence.fr/sites/default/files/integral_texts/2019-10/avis18a03_en_.pdf>

Bourreau M, de Steel A and Graef I, 'Big Data and Competition Policy: Market Power, Personalised Pricing and Advertising' [2017] Centre on Regulation in Europe Project Report

Bundeskartellamt, 'Competition Restraints in Online Sales After Coty and Asics – What's Next?' (2018) Series of Papers on Competition and Consumer Protection in the Digital Economy <https://www.bundeskartellamt.de/SharedDocs/Publikation/EN/Schriftenreihe_Digitales_IV.pdf?__blob=publicationFile&v=2>

Bibliography 243

Bundeskartellamt and *Autorité de la Concurrence*, Competition Law and Data (2016) <https://www.bundeskartellamt.de/SharedDocs/Publikation/DE/Berichte/Big%20 Data%20Papier.html;jsessionid=FCE1A15B6F85CD160925E13F58EE7524.1_cid378? nn=3600108>

Bundesministerium für Wirtschaft und Energie, Modernisierung der Missbrauchsaufsicht für marktmächtige Unternehmen (4 September 2018) (The *Modernisierung* Study) <https://www.bmwi.de/Redaktion/DE/Publikationen/Wirtschaft/modernisierung-der-missbrauchsaufsicht-fuer-marktmaechtige-unternehmen.html>

Case Summary B6-22/16, Facebook, Exploitative Business Terms Pursuant to Section 19(1) GWB for Inadequate Data Processing (15 February 2019) <https://www.bundeskartellamt.de/SharedDocs/Entscheidung/EN/Fallberichte/Missbrauchsaufsicht/2019/B6-22-16.html>

Competition and Markets Authority, 'The Commercial Use of Consumer Data Report on the CMA's Call for Information' (2015) <https://www.gov.uk/cma-cases/commercial-use-of-consumer-data>

Competition and Markets Authority, 'A New Pro-Competition Regime for Digital Markets: Advice of the Digital Markets Taskforce' (December 2020) <https://assets.publishing.service.gov.uk/media/5fce7567e90e07562f98286c/Digital_Taskforce_-_Advice.pdf>

Crémer J, de Montjoye Y and Schweitzer H, *Competition Policy for the Digital Era: Final Report* (Publications Office of the European Union 2019) <http://ec.europa.eu/competition/information/digitisation_2018/report_en.html>

Data Brokers: A Call for Transparency and Accountability, a Report of the Federal Trade Commission (May 2014) <https://www.ftc.gov/reports/data-brokers-call-transparency-accountability-report-federal-trade-commission-may-2014>

European Commission, 'Why We Need a Digital Single Market, Factsheets on Digital Single Market' (6 May 2015) <https://ec.europa.eu/commission/publications/why-we-need-digital-single-market_en>

———, 'Consultation on Evaluation of Procedural and Jurisdictional Aspects of EU Merger Control' (2016) <http://ec.europa.eu/competition/consultations/2016_merger_control/index_en.html>

———, 'Data Protection – Report 84 (Special Eurobarometer 431, 2015)' <https://ec.europa.eu/commfrontoffice/publicopinion/archives/ebs/ebs_431_en.pdf>

European Data Protection Supervisor, 'Report of EDPS Workshop on Privacy, Consumers, Competition and Big Data' (2014) <https://edps.europa.eu/data-protection/our-work/publications/reports/report-edps-workshop-privacy-consumers-competition-and_en>

Federal Trade Commission, 'Dissenting Statement of Commissioner Pamela Jones Harbour, in the Matter of Google/DoubleClick' F.T.C. File No. 071-0170 (2007) <https://www.ftc.gov/sites/default/files/documents/public_statements/statement-matter-google/doubleclick/071220harbour_0.pdf>

———, 'Concurring and Dissenting Statement of Commissioner J. Thomas Rosch Regarding Google's Search Practices, in the Matter of Google Inc.' FTC File No. 111-0163 (2012) <https://www.ftc.gov/sites/default/files/documents/public_statements/concurring-and-dissenting-statement-commissioner-j.thomas-rosch-regarding-googles-search-practices/130103googlesearchstmt.pdf>

———, 'Statement of Federal Trade Commission concerning Google/DoubleClick' FTC File No. 071-0170 <https://www.ftc.gov/system/files/documents/public_statements/418081/071220googledc-commstmt.pdf>

Bibliography

Furman J, *Unlocking Digital Competition: Report of the Digital Competition Expert Panel* (HM Treasury, 2019) <https://www.gov.uk/government/publications/unlocking-digital-competition-report-of-the-digital-competition-expert-panel>

German Monopolies Commission (*Monopolkommission*), 'Competition Policy: The Challenge of Digital Markets' (2015) Special Report No 68

House of Lords, 'Select Committee on Communications Regulating in a Digital World' 2nd Report of Session 2017-19 HL Paper 299 (9 March 2019) <https://publications.parliament.uk/pa/ld201719/ldselect/ldcomuni/299/29902.htm>

OECD, *Exploring the Economics of Personal Data: A Survey of Methodologies for Measuring Monetary Value*, OECD Digital Economy Papers, No. 220 (OECD Publishing 2013) <https://www.oecd-ilibrary.org/science-and-technology/exploring-the-economics-of-personal-data_5k486qtxldmq-en>

———, *Policy Roundtable: The Role and Measurement of Quality in Competition Analysis* (OECD Quality Report October 2013) <http://www.oecd.org/competition/Quality-in-competition-analysis-2013.pdf>

———, *Data-Driven Innovation, Big Data for Growth and Well-Being* (OECD Publishing 2015)

———, Thiemann A and Gonzaga P, 'Big Data: Bringing Competition Policy to the Digital Era' [2016] DAF/COMP (2016)14

Opinion of *Autorité de la Concurrence* on the Exploitation of Data in the Internet Advertising Sector, No: 18-A-03 English Version (6 March 2018) <http://www.autoritedelaconcurrence.fr/doc/avis18a03_en_.pdf>

Preliminary Opinion of the European Data Protection Supervisor, 'Privacy and Competitiveness in the Age of Big Data: The Interplay Between Data Protection, Competition Law and Consumer Protection in the Digital Economy' (March 2014) <https://edps.europa.eu/sites/edp/files/publication/14-03-26_competitition_law_big_data_en.pdf>

Schweitzer H and others, 'Modernising the Law on Abuse of Market Power: Report for the Federal Ministry for Economic Affairs and Energy (Germany)' (2018) <https://papers.ssrn.com/sol3/papers.cfm?abstract_id=3250742>

Turner V and Reyna A, 'Market Definition in EU Competition Law Enforcement: Need for An Update' BEUC's Response to the Public Consultation (2020) <https://www.beuc.eu/publications/beuc-x-2020-092_beuc_response_public_consultation_on_market_definition.pdf>

United States Congress, House of Representatives, Committee on the Judiciary, 'Investigation of Competition in Digital Markets: Majority Staff Report and Recommendations' (October 2020)

Van Gorp N and Batura O, 'Challenges for Competition Policy in a Digitalised Economy', A Study for the ECON Committee, Directorate General for Internal Policies, European Parliament, July 2015, IP/A/ECON/2014-12 PE 542.235

Van Til H, Van Gorp N and Price K, 'Big Data and Competition' (2017) ECORYS Report Paper <https://zoek.officielebekendmakingen.nl/blg-813928.pdf>

Speeches

Almunia J, 'Competition and Personal Data Protection' SPEECH 12/860 of 26 November 2012 <https://ec.europa.eu/commission/presscorner/detail/en/SPEECH_12_860>

———, 'Competition and Privacy in Markets of Data' Speech at Privacy Platform Event: Competition and Privacy in Markets of Data, Brussels, 26 November 2012 <http://europa.eu/rapid/press-releaseSPEECH-12-860_en.htm>

Brandeis L, 'The Regulation of Competition Versus the Regulation of Monopoly', An Address to the Economic Club of New York on 1 November 1912<http://louisville.edu/law/library/special-collections/the-louis-d.-brandeis-collection/the-regulation-of-competition-versus-the-regulation-of-monopoly-by-louis-d.-brandeis>

Delrahim M, 'Good Times, Trust Will Take Us Far: Competition Enforcement and the Relationship Between Washington and Brussels' SPEECH in Brussels, 21 February 2018 <https://www.justice.gov/opa/speech/assistant-attorney-general-makan-delrahim-delivers-remarks-college-europe-brussels>

Franken A, 'How Privacy Has Become an Antitrust Issue' Speech at the American Bar Association Section of Antitrust Law Spring Meeting Dinner, 29 March 2012 <https://www.huffpost.com/entry/how-privacy-has-become-an_b_1392580>

Kroes N, 'European Competition Policy – Delivering Better Markets and Better Choices' SPEECH 05/512 of 15 September 2005, http://europa.eu/rapid/press-release_SPEECH-05-512_en.htm?locale=en.#

———, 'Preliminary Thoughts on Policy Review of Article 82' SPEECH 05/537, 23 September 2005, http://europa.eu/rapid/press-release_SPEECH-05-537_en.htm?locale=en

Monti M, 'The Future for Competition Policy in the European Union' SPEECH 01/340 of 9 July 2001, http://europa.eu/rapid/press-release_SPEECH-01-340_en.htm?locale=en

Schmidt E, '(Testimony), Executive Chairman, Google Inc. Before the Senate Committee on the Judiciary Subcommittee on Antitrust, Competition Policy, and Consumer Rights, 112th Congress' (21 September 2011)

Vestager M, 'Competition in A Big Data World' DLD 16, Munich, 17 January 2016

———, 'Big Data and Competition EDPS-BEUC Conference on Big Data', Brussels, 29 September 2016 "Check Against Delivery"

Press Releases

Belgian Competition Authority, Press Release, 'The Belgian Competition Authority Imposes a Fine of 1.190.000 EUR on the National Lottery for Having Abused Its Dominant Position When Launching Its Sports Betting Product Scooore! N°15/2015' (23 September 2015) <https://www.belgiancompetition.be/en/about-us/actualities/press-release-nr-15-2015>

Bundeskartellamt, News, '*Bundeskartellamt* Initiates Proceeding Against Facebook on Suspicion of Having Abused Its Market Power by Infringing Data Protection Rules' (2 March 2016) <https://www.bundeskartellamt.de/SharedDocs/Meldung/EN/Pressemitteilungen/2016/02_03_2016_Facebook.html>

———, 'Review of 2018' (20 December 2018) <https://www.bundeskartellamt.de/SharedDocs/Meldung/EN/Pressemitteilungen/2018/20_12_2018_Jahresrueckblick.html>

———, '*Bundeskartellamt* Initiates Abuse Proceeding Against Amazon' (29 November 2018) <https://www.bundeskartellamt.de/SharedDocs/Meldung/EN/Pressemitteilungen/2018/29_11_2018_Verfahrenseinleitung_Amazon.html>

———, '*Bundeskartellamt* Prohibits Facebook from Combining User Data from Different Sources (7 February 2019) <https://www.bundeskartellamt.de/SharedDocs/Meldung/EN/Pressemitteilungen/2019/07_02_2019_Facebook.html>

———, '*Bundeskartellamt* Obtains Far-Reaching Improvements in the Terms of Business for Sellers on Amazon's Online Marketplaces' (17 July 2019) <https://www.bundeskartellamt.de/SharedDocs/Meldung/EN/Pressemitteilungen/2019/17_07_2019_Amazon.html;jsessionid=98F173CFCF40CBB4E3AA149FF088832E.1_cid362>

Bibliography

Bundeskartellamt, Press Release, 'Preliminary Assessment in Facebook Proceeding: Facebook's Collection and Use of Data from Third-Party Sources Is Abusive' (19 December 2017) <https://www.bundeskartellamt.de/SharedDocs/Meldung/EN/Pressemitteilungen/2017/19_12_2017_Facebook.html>

——, '*Bundeskartellamt* Launches Sector Inquiry into Market Conditions in Online Advertising Sector' (1 February 2018) <https://www.bundeskartellamt.de/SharedDocs/Meldung/EN/Pressemitteilungen/2018/01_02_2018_SU_Online_Werbung.html>

Bundeskartellamt, B2-88/18, 'Case Summary from 17 July 2019: Amazon Amends Its Terms of Business Worldwide for Sellers on Its Marketplaces – Bundeskartellamt Closes Abuse Proceedings' (17 July 2019) <https://www.bundeskartellamt.de/SharedDocs/Entscheidung/EN/Fallberichte/Missbrauchsaufsicht/2019/B2-88-18.html;jsessionid=6F46AFC4DECD4268BD11E5D792299FD1.1_cid362?nn=3600108>

Bundeskartellamt, Publications, 'Preliminary Opinion on the Investigation of Facebook – Background on the Facebook Proceeding' (19 December 2017) <https://www.bundeskartellamt.de/SharedDocs/Publikation/EN/Diskussions_Hintergrundpapiere/2017/Hintergrundpapier_Facebook.pdf?__blob=publicationFile&v=6>

Competition and Markets Authority, Press Release, 'CMA to Investigate Google's Privacy Sandbox Browser Changes' (8 January 2021) <https://www.gov.uk/government/news/cma-to-investigate-google-s-privacy-sandbox-browser-changes>

European Commission, Press Release, 'Antitrust: Commission Obtains from Google Comparable Display of Specialised Search Rivals' (Brussels, 5 February 2014) <https://ec.europa.eu/commission/presscorner/detail/en/IP_14_116>

European Commission, Press Release, 'Antitrust: Commission Sends Statement of Objections to Google on Comparison Shopping Service; Opens Separate Formal Investigation on Android' (Brussels, 15 April 2015) <https://ec.europa.eu/commission/presscorner/detail/en/IP_15_4780>

——, 'Mergers: Commission Fines Facebook €110 Million for Providing Misleading Information About WhatsApp Takeover' (Brussels, 18 May 2017) <http://europa.eu/rapid/press-release_IP-17-1369_en.htm>

——, 'Antitrust: Commission Fines Google €2.42 Billion for Abusing Dominance as Search Engine by Giving Illegal Advantage to Own Comparison Shopping Services' (Brussels, 27 June 2017) <https://ec.europa.eu/commission/presscorner/detail/en/IP_17_1784>

——, 'Antitrust: Commission Fines Google €1.49 Billion for Abusive Practices in Online Advertising' (Brussels, 20 March 2019) <https://ec.europa.eu/commission/presscorner/detail/en/IP_19_1770>

——, 'Antitrust: Commission Opens Investigation into Possible Anti-Competitive Conduct of Amazon' (Brussels, 17 July 2019) <https://ec.europa.eu/commission/presscorner/detail/en/IP_19_4291>

——, 'Antitrust: Commission Opens Investigations into Apple's App Store Rules' (Brussels, 16 June 2020) <https://ec.europa.eu/commission/presscorner/detail/en/ip_20_1073>

——, 'Merger: Commission Opens In-Depth Investigation into the Proposed Acquisition of Fitbit by Google' (Brussels, 4 August 2020) <https://ec.europa.eu/commission/presscorner/detail/en/ip_20_1446>

——, 'Europe Fit for the Digital Age: Commission Proposes New Rules for Digital Platforms' (Brussels, 15 December 2020) <https://ec.europa.eu/commission/presscorner/detail/en/ip_20_2347>

——, 'Competition: Commission Seeks Feedback on Draft Revised Market Definition Notice' (Brussels, 8 November 2022) <https://ec.europa.eu/commission/presscorner/detail/en/ip_22_6528>

Google, Press Release, 'Google Builds World's Largest Advertising and Search Monetization Program' (4 March 2003) <http://www.google.com/press/pressrel/advertising.html>

Italian Competition Authority, Press Release, 'Facebook Fined 10 Million Euros by the ICA for Unfair Commercial Practices for Using Its Subscribers' Data for Commercial Purposes' (7 December 2018) <http://en.agcm.it/en/media/press-releases/2018/12/Facebook-fined-10-million-Euros-by-the-ICA-for-unfair-commercial-practices-for-using-its-subscribers%E2%80%99-data-for-commercial-purposes>

Press Release CJEU No 158/22 Luxembourg, 20 September 2022 Advocate General's Opinion C-252/21 | Meta Platforms and Others (General Terms of Use of a Social Network)

US Federal Trade Commission, Press Release, 'FTC to Examine Past Acquisitions by Large Technology Companies' (11 February 2020) <https://www.ftc.gov/news-events/press-releases/2020/02/ftc-examine-past-acquisitions-large-technology-companies>

Newspaper Articles

Abkowitz A, 'The Internet Tightens: Popular Chinese WeChat App to Become Official ID' *The Wall Street Journal* (31 December 2017) <https://www.wsj.com/articles/internet-tightens-popular-chinese-wechat-app-to-become-official-id-1514541980>

Albanesius C, 'More Americans Go to Facebook Than MySpace' *The PC Mag* (16 June 2009) <https://www.pcmag.com/article2/0,2817,2348822,00.asp>

Amatriain X, '10 Lessons Learned from Building Machine Learning Systems' (2014) *MLconf* 2014 San Francisco <https://mlconf.com/sessions/10-lessons-learned-from-building-real-life-large-s/>

Asay M and O'Reilly T, '"Whole Web" Is the OS of the Future' *CNET* (18 March 2010) <http://www.cnet.com/news/tim-oreilly-whole-web-is-the-os-of-the-future>

Balakrishnan A, 'Here's How Billions of People Use Google Products' *CNBC* (18 May 2017) <https://www.cnbc.com/2017/05/18/google-user-numbers-youtube-android-drive-photos.html>

Bernal N and Titcomb J, 'EU Opens Formal Competition Investigation into Amazon Over Use of Merchant Data' *The Telegraph* (San Francisco, 16 July 2019) <https://www.telegraph.co.uk/technology/2019/07/16/eu-open-formal-competition-investigation-amazon-within-days/>

Canales K, 'WhatsApp Is Delaying a New Policy Change After Critics Claimed the Update Would Have Turned Over' *BusinessInsider* (15 January 2021) <https://www.businessinsider.com/whatsapp-privacy-policy-delay-three-months-2021-1?r=US&IR=T#:~:text=WhatsApp%20is%20delaying%20its%20privacy,company%20blog%20post%20published%20-Friday.&text=WhatsApp%20also%20said%20no%20one's,scheduled%20to%20go%20into%20effect>

Constine J, 'WhatsApp's First Half of 2014 Revenue Was $15M, Net Loss Of $232.5M Was Mostly Issuing Stock' *Techcrunch* (29 October 2014) <https://techcrunch.com/2014/10/28/whatsapp-revenue/>

Cukier M, 'Data, Data Everywhere' *The Economist* (London, 25 February 2010) <https://www.economist.com/special-report/2010/02/25/data-data-everywhere>

Davies R, 'Apple Becomes World's First Trillion-Dollar Company' *The Guardian* (2 August 2018) <https://www.theguardian.com/technology/2018/aug/02/apple-becomes-worlds-first-trillion-dollar-company>

DePillis L, 'Amazon Is Now Worth $1,000,000,000,000' *CNN Business* (4 September 2018) <https://money.cnn.com/2018/09/04/technology/amazon-1-trillion/index.html>

Bibliography

Ek D, 'A Level Playing Field, Consumers and Innovators Win on a Level Playing Field' *Newsroom Spotify* (13 March 2019) <https://newsroom.spotify.com/2019-03-13/consumers-and-innovators-win-on-a-level-playing-field/>

Five Things to Know About the Big Tech Antitrust Report, *Associated Press* (7 October 2020) <https://apnews.com/article/politics-ac3cce04e38c0bf584cfb9ec04557874>

Guniganti P, 'Google Shopping Remedies Have Had Effect, Vestager Says' *Global Competition Review* (18 June 2018) <https://globalcompetitionreview.com/google-shopping-remedies-have-had-effect-vestager-says>

Haselton T, 'Microsoft Recommends Switching to iPhone or Android as It Prepares to Kill Off Windows Phones' *CNBC* (18 January 2019) <https://www.cnbc.com/2019/01/18/microsoft-ending-windows-10-mobile-says-switch-to-iphone-or-android.html>

Isaac M and Wakabayashi D, 'Russian Influence Reached 126 Million Through Facebook Alone' *The New York Times* (30 October 2017) <https://www.nytimes.com/2017/10/30/technology/facebook-google-russia.html>

Klebnikov S, 'Google Parent Alphabet Passes $1 Trillion in Market Value' *Forbes* (13 January 2020) <https://www.forbes.com/sites/sergeiklebnikov/2020/01/13/google-parent-alphabet-set-to-hit-1-trillion-in-market-value/?sh=7fd27bb54dcf>

Kotapalli S, 'First-Party Data for Enriched, Responsible Marketing' *Use Insider* (29 September 2020) <https://useinsider.com/first-party-data-strategy/>

McNamee R, 'A Historic Antitrust Hearing in Congress Has Put Big Tech on Notice' *The Guardian* (31 July 2020) <https://www.theguardian.com/commentisfree/2020/jul/31/big-tech-house-historic-antitrust-hearing-times-have-changed>

Metz C, 'We Probe the Google Antitrust Probe: Vigorously' *Register* (1 December 2010) <http://www.theregister.co.uk/2010/12/01/google_eu_investigation_comment>

Nelson D, 'Microsoft, LinkedIn Should Heed Vestager's Warning About "Unique" Data' *MLex Market Insight* (9 September 2016) <https://mlexmarketinsight.com/insights-center/editors-picks/mergers/europe/microsoft-linkedin-should-heed-vestagers-warning-about-unique-data>

Paul K, 'US Orders Google, Facebook and Others to Reveal Details of Years of Acquisitions' *The Guardian* (11 February 2020) <https://www.theguardian.com/technology/2020/feb/11/google-facebook-amazon-us-antitrust-investigations>

Russia Complains About Facebook and Google Election Ads, *BBC News* (9 September 2019) <https://www.bbc.co.uk/news/technology-49634688>

Satariano A, 'This Is a New Phase: Europe Shifts Tactics to Limit Tech's Power' *New York Times* (30 July 2020) <https://www.nytimes.com/2020/07/30/technology/europe-new-phase-tech-amazon-apple-facebook-google.html>

Schlimpert D, 'Victory for Facebook as Düsseldorf Court Suspends the Bundeskartellamt's Decision' *CMS Law Now* (30 August 2019) <https://www.cms-lawnow.com/ealerts/2019/08/victory-for-facebook-as-duesseldorf-court-suspends-the-bundeskartellamts-decision?cc_lang=en>

Scott M, 'WhatsApp, the Internet Messenger, to Become Free Digital Economy' *The New York Times* (18 January 2016) <https://bits.blogs.nytimes.com/2016/01/18/whatsapp-the-internet-messenger-to-become-free/?_r=0>

University of Warwick, 'Adaptive "Nowcasting" Key to Accurate Flu Data Trends Using Google Search Terms' *Science Daily* (30 October 2014) www.sciencedaily.com/releases/2014/10/141030114853.htm

'The World's Most Valuable Resource Is No Longer Oil, but Data – The Data Economy Demands a New Approach to Antitrust Rules' *The Economist* (6 May 2017) <https://www.economist.com/leaders/2017/05/06/the-worlds-most-valuable-resource-is-no-longer-oil-but-data>

Bibliography 249

What Is Facebook's Revenue Breakdown? *Nasdaq.com* (28 March 2019) <https://www.nasdaq.com/articles/what-facebooks-revenue-breakdown-2019-03-28-0>

White A and Lacqua F, 'Facebook Probe Is in Antitrust, Privacy Gray Zone, EU Says' *Bloomberg Tech* (14 September 2016) <https://www.bloomberg.com/news/articles/2016-09-14/facebook-probe-in-antitrust-and-privacy-gray-zone-vestager-says>

Other Online Sources

Adobe, Global Digital Advertising Report Adobe Digital Index Q4 2014, 12–14 <https://offers.adobe.com/en/na/marketing/landings/_64058_q414_digital_advertising_report.html>

Google, Targeting Your Ads <https://support.google.com/google-ads/answer/1704368?hl=en>

Marketing Charts, 'MySpace Got 76% of US Social Network Traffic in 07, Facebook's Grew 51%' (18 January 2008) <https://www.marketingcharts.com/demographics-and-audiences/youth-and-gen-x-3075>

Schuh J, 'Building a More Private Web: A Path Towards Making Third Party Cookies Obsolete' *Chromium Blog* (14 January 2020) <https://blog.chromium.org/2020/01/building-more-private-web-path-towards.html>

Search Engine Market Share Europe (2019) <https://gs.statcounter.com/search-engine-market-share/all/europe/2019>

Shearer M, '3rd-Party Is Dead: How to Improve Your First-Party Data Strategy' *Claravine* (29 January 2020) <https://www.claravine.com/2020/01/29/first-party-data-strategy/>

What Are My Ad Preferences and How Can I Adjust Them on Facebook <https://en-gb.facebook.com/help/247395082112892?helpref=uf_permalink>

Index

21 Lessons for the 21st Century (Harari) 207

abusive behaviour in data-driven markets; *see also individual headings*: Article 102, TFEU applications to 183–84; through access to data 146–69; through data privacy 169–82; through leveraging market power 126–46

abusive behaviour through access to data 146–69; data portability as remedy for 165–69; essential facilities doctrine, applicability of 152–60; overview of 146–47; refusal to/discriminatory access 147–51; sharing mandates as remedy for 160–65

abusive behaviour through data privacy 169–82, 203; Article 102, TFEU privacy policies 177–81; *Bundeskartellamt* Facebook investigation of 170, 171–77; Italian Competition Authority Facebook investigation of 181–82; novel abuse status of 169–70; overview of 169

abusive behaviour through leveraging market power 126–46; "frenemy" situation in multi-sided markets 141–46; Google and theory of harms 133–41; overview of 126–28; self-preferencing and 128–33

acquisitions: data-driven 65–73; of nascent rivals 66–7; third-party data and 13

Adobe 98

ADTECH/AOL 83

advertising-media model 43–5

affiliation 48

Ahlborn, C. 114

Airbnb 148

Akman, P. 24, 134, 143–44, 149, 157, 202, 215

Alexa 142

algorithms 4–5, 11, 15, 34, 40, 42, 57, 81, 100–101, 139, 169, 201, 207, 209, 213–14

Alibaba 39, 43

Almunia, J. 33, 166

AltaVista 4, 40, 140

Amazon 4, 10, 38, 39, 187; anti-competitive conduct cases 29; competition in data-driven markets 61; hybrid platform investigation of 130–33; monopolisation and 21; online advertising model 43

amazon.com 38

Android 23, 62, 120, 138; anti-competitive conduct cases 30

Android open-source project (AOSP) 138

anti-competitive behaviour 3; in data-driven markets 29–34; evolution of ecosystems and 5; leveraging data advantage as 31; refusal to supply/provide access to data as 31–2; tying example of 30–1

anti-competitive strategies 1

AOL 40

Apple 21, 28, 39, 62, 187–88; anti-competitive conduct cases 29; competition in data-driven markets 61; data-driven acquisitions 67–8; ecosystem 119, 120; frenemy abuse 142

Apple/Shazam merger 117

Index

application programming interfaces (APIs) 32
aQuantive/Atlas 83
Article 102, TFEU 24, 26, 127, 150, 170–71, 192–93, 202–3, 204, 207–8, 215, 216, 223; abusive conduct list 134; applying, to abusive conduct 150; applying, to Big Data related abuses 183–84; applying, to relevant market 77; *Bundeskartellamt* Facebook investigation and 32–3; competition tools and market share assessment 28–9; data protection rules violations and 72; mandatory data sharing as remedy 160–65; privacy policies under 177–81
assessment of market power 26–9; competition tools and 28–9; microeconomic theory approach to 27; overview of 26–7; SSNIP test and 28; undertakings operations/roles and 28
assessment tests for data-related market power 109–24; Big Data role in 114–18; dynamic competition model and 110–11; multi-sided markets and 121–24; new economy, innovative character of 111–14; online ecosystems, creation of 118–21; overview of 109
assessment tools, data-related market power 99–108; market shares and 105–8; overview of 99–100; substitutability and 102–5; zero-price problem 100–101
attention markets 44, 45
Auer, D. 103
Autorita' Garante della Concorrenza e del Mercato (AGCM) 181–82
Autorité de la Concurrence 151; essential facilities doctrine and 152–60; on privacy concerns 163–64

Balto, D. A. 24, 152
Batura, O. 110, 112
Belgian Competition Authority 31; data sharing mandates and 161
Belgian National Lottery case 31, 161–62, 180
Bezos, J. 187
Biden, J. 188

Big Data: accumulation, data-driven markets and 54–8; characteristics of 9–11; competition law and 3, 16, 20; competitive significance of 15–21; definition of 8–9; effects 5; essential facilities doctrine and 158–60; market power and 2–3; monetisation of free products and 20; ordinary data *vs.* 9; regulatory problems derived from 25–6; role in data-driven economy 2–6; role in market power assessment 114–18; value chain, creation of 11–15, 26; value of 10–11; variety of 10; velocity of 9–10; volume of 9
Big Data-related infringement cases in data-driven markets 94–9
Big Data value chain, creation of 11–15
Bing 22, 23, 24, 52–3, 55, 140, 152
BlackBerry 62, 120
Bogdan, M. 70
booking.com 95
Bork, R. H. 24, 136, 140, 157–58, 183, 186
Botta, M. 177
Brandeis, L. 193–94
Breton, T. 197
British Airways v Commission 58
Broos, S. 98, 123–24
Bundeskartellamt (German Competition Authority) 32, 94, 218–19; Amazon marketplace abusive behavior investigation 130–33; on discriminatory access 151; essential facilities doctrine and 152–60; Facebook abusive behavior investigation 170, 171–77; on privacy concerns 163–64, 188–89

Carlton, D. 150
Cegedim case 151
CERRE report on Big Data 14
Chicago School of competition 136, 150, 186–87, 194
Cicilline, D. 187
Citymapper 202
CJEU *see* Court of Justice (CJEU)
Clayton Act of 1914 193
click-and-query data 20
cloud computing 14
Colangelo, G. 158
Comerford, R. 19, 20, 152–53
Commercial Solvents 153–54

252   Index

Commission *see* European Commission
comparison shopping/online advertising market discussions 96–8
competition 1; advantages of Big Data for 15–21
competition law; *see also* competition law intervention in data-driven markets: anti-competitive conduct 29–34; Big Data and 3, 16, 20; data acquisitions and 17–18; data and 2; data-driven businesses and 16–17; definition of Big Data for 8–9; personal data collection and 16; snowball effect and 17
competition law intervention in data-driven markets 185–224; application of new tests, described 219–23; benchmarks for 203–7; Big Data as market power source and 211–14; broadening goals for 190–96; current legal framework, optimising 200–203; innovation and 205–7; intermediation-regulatory powers and 208–11; necessity and 203–4; new legal test applications for 207–23; non-interventionist approach 185–89; novel abusive power and 214–19; overview of 185; proportionality and 204–5; sector-specific regulation 196–200
competition law's goals, broadening 190–96; alternatives to mathematical assessment methods 191; consumer choice and 192; fairness and justice approach 192–93; New Brandeisians approach 193–96; price *vs.* non-price assessments 191–92
Competition Policy for the Digital Era (European Commission report) 109
conglomerate effects of data-driven acquisitions 68–73; of start-up by technology giant 68–9
conglomerate mergers 66
consumer welfare approach 5, 21, 183, 195; competition policy and 72, 115–16; Delrahim on 33; EU application of 190–93; *laissez-faire* economics and 186; maximising 24–25; New Brandeis movement and 194–96; US application of 193
Cook, T. 187–88
cookies 12
Cordon, W. M. 45

Cortana 142
Court of Justice (CJEU) 76; *Bronner* case 154; *Cisco v Commission* 107; *IMS Health GmbH & Co. OHG v NDC Health GmbH & Co. KG* 154, 155; on market shares and dominant positions 105–6; *Microsoft Corp. v Commission of the European Communities* 154, 155; product functionality test and 77–8
Cowen, T. 159
Crane, D. 24, 183
Crémer, J. 71, 100, 109, 127–28, 213
cross-site tracking 13–14
Cukier, K. 2, 15

data: analytics 14, 15; brokers 14; click-and-query 20; competition law and 2; first-party 12; 4Vs of 213; freshness of 10; importance of 1; location/geographical, of consumers 11; related abuses 5–6; storage 14; third-party 12–13; tools to collect/analyse 2; used for behavioural advertising 118; utility of 9, 15; value of 2
data collection and mining 1; from social networks 11; sources for 15
data-driven acquisitions 17–18, 65–73; concerns related to 65–6; conglomerate effects of 68–73; data privacy and 72–3; global value chains and 66–8; turnover-based thresholds in 70–71
data-driven markets/economy; *see also* competition law intervention in data-driven markets; data-related market power: abusive behaviour in (*see* abusive behaviour in data-driven markets); anti-competitive conduct and 29–34; barriers to entry in 12–13, 21–2; Big Data accumulation and 54–8; Big Data role in 2–6; competition issues with 1; data-opoly in 24–5, 61–4; described 37–8; digitalised markets and 34, 38–9; indirect network externalities of 49–54; information as currency in 101; introduction to 1–6; issues in 21–34; market characteristics of 45–58; market power assessments in 6–7, 26–29; monopolisation in 21–6, 58–64; multi-sided nature

of 45–9; newly emerged markets 39–42; new technologies 1, 4; non-interventionist approach to 35; online advertising as market 43–5; technology giants and 3–4; transformation process 1; undertakings in 4
data fusion 10
data interoperability 168–69
data moving 92–4
data-opoly 24–5; concerns over 61–4
data portability 165–69; criticism of 167–68; *vs.* data interoperability 168–69; defined 165; EDPS and 166; GDPR and 165–68; support of 166–67
data privacy, data-driven acquisitions and 72–3
data processing (analytics) 1
data-related market power assessment: Big Data and assessment of 114–18; data moving and 92–4; dynamic competition and assessment of 110–11; functionality test and 90–2; market definition 75–8; market segmentation and 80–3; market segment overlap and 94–9; market shares and 105–8; multi-sided markets and 121–24; new economy, innovative character of 111–14; new tests for 109–24; non-horizontal effects and 83–90; online ecosystems and 118–21; relevant product market, identification of 78–80; substitutability and 102–5; tools, ineffective 99–108; zero-price problem 100–101
datasets, uniqueness of 12
data sharing mandates 160–65; GDPR and 164–65; irrelevance of 163; privacy concerns over 163–64
data storage 1
data utilisation 211, 213
Delrahim, M. 33
demand-side economies of scale 22
demand-supply side substitutability assessment 75, 78
De Mauro, A. 9
Demings, V. 187
Department of Justice (DOJ), United States 24; Antitrust Division 33; comparisons to EU laws 33
digitalisation 1–2

digitalised markets 38–9; defined 38; evolving into data-driven markets 34; types of 37–8
Digital Markets Act (DMA) 197, 198, 199, 203
Digital Services Act (DSA) 196, 197
Digital Single Market Strategy 196
discriminatory access cases 147–51
dominance: monopolisation and 58–9; tipping effects and 55
dominant position concept 75
DuckDuckGo 178
Dworschak, S. 108
dynamic competition model 110–11

eBay 38, 39, 43
eCommerce Directive 197
ECON Committee 30
economy: dynamic nature of new 110–11; innovative character of new 111–14
ECORYS report 177
ecosystem(s) 5; creation of online 118–21; Google 22–4; value chain in 12
EDPS *see* European Data Protection Supervisor (EDPS)
Engels, B. 166–67
Esayas, S. 180, 191–92
essential facilities doctrine 31–2; applicability of 152–60; *Commercial Solvents* case 153–54
Euris 151
European Commission 19; ad network/exchange definitions 48–9; Amazon marketplace abusive behavior investigation by 130–33; combined datasets and 13; comparison shopping/online advertising market discussions 96–8; data moving potential and 92–4; data-sharing mandate 160–65; defining relevant markets based on functionality 113–14; on Enforcement Priorities 28; Facebook/WhatsApp merger 53, 69–70, 72, 86–7, 90–2; General Data Protection Regulation 88; Google/DoubleClick investigation/merger 13, 53–4, 69, 80–3; Google/Fitbit investigation 89–90; *Google Search (Shopping)* decision 77, 100–101, 102, 160, 163; as interventionist against unilateral conduct 6; on manufacturer savings with Big Data 16–17; market

definition and 75; Microsoft/
   LinkedIn decision 87–9, 180;
   Microsoft/Skype decision 54,
   86, 87, 106; Microsoft/Yahoo!
   investigation 85–6; multi-sided
   platforms and 52–4; "Notice on
   the Definition of Relevant Market"
   77; online advertising and 80–3;
   relevant geographical market
   definition 78; vertical/general
   (horizontal) search engines and
   95–6
European Data Protection Supervisor
   (EDPS) 166
European Parliament's Directorate-General
   for Internal Policies 26
European Union (EU) legislation 7;
   comparisons to US laws 33
Evans, D. 44, 47, 101, 106, 107, 111, 112
ex-ante merger control measures 70, 72
Ezrachi, A. 51–2, 141

Facebook 4, 19, 28, 39, 41, 57, 59, 148, 187;
   advertisements 11; anti-competitive
   conduct cases 29; *Bundeskartellamt*
   investigation of 32, 170, 171–77;
   competition in data-driven
   markets 61; ecosystem 119–20;
   monopolisation and 21; network
   effects and 22; online advertising
   model 43; revenue sources of 41–2;
   terms of service as unfair 181;
   WhatsApp acquisition by 24–5,
   69–70, 72, 86–7, 90–2, 152
Facebook Messenger 61, 120
Federal Trade Commission (FTC) 24, 69,
   143, 169; Google/DoubleClick data
   combination findings 84, 117–18;
   online advertising and 82
Federal Trade Commission Act of 1914 193
Filistrucchi, L. 103, 121, 122
first-party data 12
Foundem (Infederation Ltd.) 95, 136, 139
Franken, A. 116
freemium goods 100
free-to-use services online 65
French Competition Authority 81–2; data
   sharing mandates and 161–62
"frenemy" situation in multi-sided markets
   141–46
frequently bought together products
   service 20
Friedman, M. 76

Friendster 41
functionality test 90–2
Furman Report 61, 148, 201–2

Gal, M. S. 10
GDF-Suez case 161–62, 180
GDPR *see* General Data Protection
   Regulation (GDPR), 2016
Gebicka, A. 104–5
General Data Protection Regulation
   (GDPR), 2016 88; data portability
   regulations 165–68; privacy for
   data sharing 164–65
Geradin, D. 82, 199
German Competition Act (ARC) 70–1
German Competition Authority *see*
   Bundeskartellamt (German
   Competition Authority)
global value chains, data-driven
   acquisitions and 66–8
Globocnik, J. 156, 163
Gmail 22
Google 4–5, 6, 10, 19, 28, 39, 187; ad,
   location, and map services 11;
   anti-competitive conduct cases/
   fines 24, 29, 30; competition in
   data-driven markets 61; cross-site
   tracking and 13–14; data-driven
   acquisitions 67–8; ecosystem 22–4,
   119–20; Fitbit acquisition 68, 89–90;
   frenemy abuse 142–43; learning-
   by-doing/trial-and-error method
   40, 41; monopolisation and 21–4;
   network effects and 22–3; objective
   of 40; online advertising model 43;
   Premium Placement clause 146;
   search engine service 40–1, 62; self-
   preferencing and 128–30; and theory
   of harms 133–41; third-party cookies
   and 13–14
Google Ad 43–4
Google AdSense case 30, 83, 94, 137,
   145–46, 161
Google Assistant 142
Google/DoubleClick 219–20; data privacy
   concerns 169; investigation 13,
   53–4, 117–18; merger 48–9,
   68, 69; non-horizontal effects in
   segments of online advertising
   sector 83–5; online advertising and
   80–3
Google Drive 22
Google Play Store 138–39

Google+ 22, 23, 41
Google Search 22, 23, 156
Google/Waze merger 54–5
Graef, I. 43, 113
Grunes, A. 10, 16, 17, 51, 55
Gundotra, V. 23
Gürkaynak, G. 47, 48

Hagiu, A. 48
Hangouts 61
Harari, Y. N. 207
Harbour, P. J. 84, 117, 118, 149–50, 169, 179
Heinemann, A. 104–5
Helmdach, K. 32–3, 170
Hlina, E. 33–4
Hoofnagle, C. J. 57
Höppner, T. 123, 124, 132
Horizontal Merger Guidelines 65
horizontal mergers 65
horizontal search engines, described 95
hypothetical monopolist test (HMT) 75, 102

iMessage 61
IMS Health GmbH & Co. OHG v NDC Health GmbH & Co. KG 32, 154, 155
indirect network externalities of data-driven markets 49–54
Infederation Ltd. (Foundem) 95, 136, 139
information as currency in data-driven markets 101
innovation as benchmark 205–7
Instagram 32, 41, 120
Intel 6
interaction 48
intermediation power 184, 211
intermediation-regulatory powers 208–11
Internal Market 197
Internet Explorer 142
internet gatekeepers 195
internet intermediaries, dual role of 203–4
Internet of Services 115
Internet of Things (IoT) 10, 115–16, 126
intervention as core feature of data-driven markets 35
Italian Competition Authority Facebook investigation of abusive behaviour 181–82

Jacquemin, A. 27, 110
Jayapal, P. 187
Jones, A. 190

Index 255

Kadar, M. 70
Kathuria, V. 156, 163
Katsifis, D. 82
Kersting, C. 108
Khan, L. 194–96, 200
Kokkoris, I. 111, 135, 156
Koslov, T. I. 118, 179
Krattenmaker, T. G. 210
Kroes, N. 33

Lagos, Y. 167
laissez-faire competition 24, 73, 185–6, 189, 194, 196
Lambrecht, A. 153
Lane, M. 152
legal test applications for competition law intervention 207–23; application of, described 219–23; Big Data as market power source and 211–14; intermediation-regulatory powers and 208–11; novel abusive power and 214–19; overview of 207–8
Lerner, A. V. 11–12, 20, 152–53
leveraging: data advantage 31; defensive 127; market power 126–46; offensive 127
Lianos, I. 1, 111–12, 117, 121, 208, 210
LinkedIn 41
lock-in (consumer) effects 22
Lugard, P. 156

M (personal assistant) 142
Maggiolino, M. 158
mandatory data sharing 160–65; GDPR and 164–65; irrelevance of 163; privacy concerns over 163–64
Mandrescu, D. 29, 106
Manne, G. A. 24, 183
market definitions 75–8
market power; *see also* data-related market power: abusive behaviour through leveraging 126–46; Article 102 TFEU and 26; assessment of 26–9; Big Data as source of 2–3; collected personal data as source of 15–16; in data-driven markets 6–7
market segmentation: overlaps in 94–9; relevant product market and 80–3
market shares, digital ecosystems and 105–8
Marshall, A. 76
Maurer, H. 60
Mayor-Schonberger, V. 2

256   *Index*

McAfee 9
medical nowcasting 10
mergers, third-party data and 13
Metz, C. 60
Microsoft 6, 22, 24, 52–3, 62, 83;
 anti-competitive conduct cases/fines 29–30; competition in data-driven markets 61; frenemy abuse 142; LinkedIn merger non-horizontal effects 87–9; Skype merger non-horizontal effects 86–7; tying example 30–1; Windows Mobile 120; Yahoo! merger non-horizontal effects 85–6
Microsoft Corp. v Commission of the European Communities 32, 154, 155
moligopolists 60–1, 74, 208
monopolisation/abusive behaviour cases, early historic 193
monopolisation in data-driven markets 21–6, 58–64; data-opoly concerns 61–4; dominance in market and 58–9; as harmful to consumers 25; moligopolists and 60–1; network effects and 22–3; overview of 58
Monopolkommission (Monopolies Commission of Germany) 96, 157
Monti, M. 33
Moore, J. 119
multi-homing practices 152
multi-sided markets: data-driven markets as 45–9; "frenemy" situation in 141–46; market power assessment and 121–24
Mundt, A. 131, 170, 181
Myspace 28, 41, 59

National Competition Authorities 19
near monopolies 74
necessity as benchmark 203–4
Netflix 148
Netscape 142
network effects 22–3
New Brandeisians approach 193–96
newly emerged markets 39–42; described 39; search engine market 39–41; social network market 41–42
Newman, J. 101, 102
Newman, N. 136
New York Times 63
non-horizontal effects in segments of online advertising sector 83–90

Non-Horizontal Merger Guidelines 66
non-interventionist approach: to competition law intervention 185–89; to data-driven markets 35; to dynamic markets 2
Norvig, P. 10–11, 183
novel abusive power 214–19
nowcasting 4; medical 10

Oculus 42
OECD 17
Ohlhausen, M. K. 179
Okuliar, A. P. 179
One Key 151
one-sided platforms 46–7
online advertising 43–5
online businesses, click-and-query data and 20
online ecosystems, creation of 118–21
online platforms/intermediaries as data-driven market 37–8
Opera 142
ordinary data *vs.* Big Data 9
Oscar Bronner GmbH & Co. KG v Mediaprint Zeitungs-und Zeitschriftenverlag GmbH & Co. KG and Others 32

Parker, G. 62–3
Pasquale, F. 139
Patterson, M. 108
PayPal 38
personal assistants 142
personalised services 20, 23
Petit, N. 60–1, 103, 104, 208
Pichai, S. 187
Platform to Business Regulation 196
political elections, Big Data and interference with 63–4
Posner, R. 186
predictability, anti-competitive conduct and 169
Prescott, A. 10
privacy degradation 179–80
privacy paradox 177
product, defined 76
proportionality as benchmark 204–5
Prüfer, J. 55, 56
P2B Regulation 196
PwC 2018 Global Innovation 1000 study 206

Ramos, J. M. 98, 123–24
Rantos, A. 173
Ratliff, J. D. 123

R&D mergers 65; *see also* data-driven acquisitions
Real Media/Open AdStream 83
recommended products personalised service 20
Reddaway, B. 45–6
refusal to access cases 147–51
relevant market: concept of 75; defining, on product/geographical dimensions 76–7; definitions of 78–80; dimensions of 76–7; identification of 75–6
relevant product market, identification of 78–99; data moving and 92–4; functionality test and 90–2; market segmentation and 80–3; market segment overlap and 94–9; non-horizontal effects and 83–90; relevant market definition and 78–9
ResearchGate 41
reverted market share-based analysis 108
Rinehart, W. 183
Roach, L. 156
Rochet, J-C. 46–7
Rosch, T. 143
Rosoff, M. 23
Rubinfeld, D. L. 10, 123

Samsung 62
Schmalensee, R. 47, 106, 107, 111, 112
Schottmüller, C. 55, 56
Schweitzer, H. 221
Science Daily 10
search engine market 39–41; user groups 50
search engines 5, 23; Höppner and three sides of 123
sector-specific competition law regulation 196–200
segmentation for ad intermediation/ad servicing markets 82–3
self-preferencing 127–33, 143, 203
Sherman Act (1890) 186, 193
Sidak, J. G. 24, 136, 140, 157–58, 183
Signal 120
single-monopoly-profit theorem 136
single-user data profile 136
Siri 142
Skype 61
small but significant and non-transitory increase in price (SSNIP) test 28, 75, 102–5
Snapchat 120, 148, 153
snowball effect 17, 54
social network market 41–42

social networks, data collection from 11
Sokol, D. D. 19, 20, 152–53
Spotify 145
SSNDQ (small but significant nontransitory decline in quality) test 105
SSNIP *see* small but significant and non-transitory increase in price (SSNIP) test
Stucke, M. 10, 16, 17, 51–2, 55, 141
substitutability, data-related market power and 102–5
Sufrin, B. 190
super-dominance 58–9, 63
super online platforms 2
Swire, P. 167, 169

technological development 1; for data collection and analytics 2; decision-making processes and 1–2; transactions and 1–2
Teece, D. 119
Telegram 120
Tencent Holdings 63
TFEU *see* Article 102, TFEU
theory of harms 133–41
third-party data 12–14
three-dimensional competition 208
Tinder 41, 148, 153
tipping effect 54, 55
Tirole, J. 46–7
Townley, C. 192
transaction platforms 38–9
transparency 2
Transport for London (TfL) provision 202
Tucker, C. E. 152, 153
Tucker, D. S. 22
turnover-based thresholds in data-driven acquisitions 70–71
Twitter 41
two-sided platforms 45–7
tying 30–1

Uber 148
undertakings 16, 18, 20; assessing market power of 26–29; Big Data and 11–15, 55–57, 115–16; data-driven 65–73; data importance in 1; data-rich 4, 17, 126–28; ecosystem controlling 135–37; indirect network effects and 49–54; monopolisation and 58–64; relevant market and 75–78; technology and 3

usage externalities, multi-sided markets and 122
US DOJ *see* Department of Justice (DOJ), United States

value chain, creation of Big Data 11–15, 26
value of Big Data 10–11
Vanberg, A. D. 167
Van Gorp, N. 110, 112
variety of Big Data 10
velocity of Big Data 4, 9–10
vertical/general (horizontal) search engine discussions 95–6
vertical mergers 65–6
vertical search engines, described 95
Vestager, M. 1, 33, 69, 89, 130, 131, 137, 138, 145, 170
Viber 120
Volmar, M. 32–3, 170
volume of Big Data 9

Walmart 9, 10
web-based platforms 39
website cookies 12
WeChat 63
Wellford, H. B. 22
WhatsApp 24–5, 32, 42, 69–70, 90–2, 120, 152
Whittington, J. 57
Wiedemann, K. 177
Windows Mobile 120
Wright, J. 48
Wright, J. D. 24

Yahoo! 4, 11, 40, 52, 59, 83, 140
Yelp 142
YouTube 22, 23

zero-price problem, data-related market power and 100–101
Zoja 154
Zuckerberg, M. 187

Printed in the United States
by Baker & Taylor Publisher Services